2D Artwork

and

3D Modeling

for

Game

Artists

David Franson

PREMIER PRESS

Premier
p
Press

An accompanying CD is enclosed inside this book

Publisher: Stacy L. Hiquet

Marketing Manager: Heather Hurley

Acquisitions Editor: Emi Smith

Series Editor: André LaMothe

Project Editor: Estelle Manticas

Technical Reviewer: Lorenzo Phillips

Copy Editor: Kate Welsh

Interior Layout: Marian Hartsough

Cover Designer: Mike Tanamachi

Indexer: Sharon Shock

Proofreader: Sandy Doell

ISBN: 1-931841-33-0

Library of Congress Catalog Card Number: 2001097576

Printed in the United States of America

03 04 05 06 07 BH 10 9 8 7 6 5 4 3 2 1

Premier Press, a division of Course Technology
2645 Erie Avenue, Suite 41
Cincinnati, Ohio 452081

This book is dedicated to my mother, Shirlee,
and my father, William.
They've been the most profound
and supportive people in my life.

I love you both!

Acknowledgments

There were so many people involved with this book, I don't know where to start. But here goes: The first and foremost thanks goes to André LaMothe. His influential presence got me into the game industry. I actually flew out to California to attend the Game Developer's Conference looking to have him sign my copy of his *Tricks of the Game Programming Gurus*, but in seeking him out I instead found the editors at Premier Press, who enticed me to become an author. André is the Series Editor for Premier, a leader in the game industry, and a true genius. Thanks, André.

Thanks to Emi Smith, my acquisitions editor, who is one of the driving forces at Premier and is a friend at the same time. To Kate Welsh, my copy editor and the English master who made my text beautiful. Next goes to Estelle Manticas, my Project Editor: thank you for your patience, for being a friend, and for being the sister I've never had. Without you I'd be lazy and deadlines wouldn't have been met! To Marian Hartsough, the layout designer—how exactly did you do it, putting up with me while laying out over a thousand of my images? To Lorenzo Phillips, my technical editor, a knowledgeable and kind person, thank you so much.

To Lars Ricaldi, for doing the sketches in my book—you truly have an artistic talent. Now let's meet at the next GDC for cryin' out loud! Oh yeah—does this also mean I have to send you a signed copy of my book??

Thanks to the Caligari Corporation; these people influenced me to get deep into the 3D modeling industry. Particular thanks got to Roman Ormandy for developing such a lovely product, to Bibiana Gasparik, and to Norm Fortier, for tech-supporting me to the end.

On the other side of the globe in New Zealand, thank you Right Hemisphere, and Mary Alice Krayecki (hey, cup of coffee at the GDC '03, remember?). Your software is totally unreal; job *so* well done!

Next, thanks go out to Adobe—to Gwyn Weisberg, and to all of the people there for your unbelievable software. I think the whole world agrees!

Finally to Discreet, specifically Liz Tan and Peter Nguyen: thank you so much for your help in allowing me to incorporate 3D Studio Max into my book. I can't believe how prompt and courteous you were!

About the Author

DAVID FRANSON has been a professional in the field of networking, programming, and 2D and 3D computer graphics since 1990. In 2000, he resigned his position as Information Technologies Director at one of the largest entertainment law firms in New York City to pursue a full-time career in game development. Between being distracted by flying remotely controlled airplanes and studying tae kwon do, artistry for games has become the new passion in David's life.

Contents at a Glance

Contents

CHAPTER 3
MODELING THE RF-9 PLASMA
GUN WITH TRUESPACE 6 25

CHAPTER 4
MODELING THE SLOGRE
CHARACTER WITH TRUESPACE 6 65

Part Two
Unwrapping the UVs with DeepUV.... 95

CHAPTER 5
U-V MAPPING THE RF-9 PLASMA
GUN WITH DEEPUV 97

CHAPTER 6
U-V MAPPING THE SLOGRE
WITH DEEPUV 149

Part Three
Unwrapping the UVs with DeepUV . . . 183

CHAPTER 7
GAME TEXTURING 185

CHAPTER 8
INORGANIC TEXTURE TUTORIALS
WITH PHOTOSHOP 193

CHAPTER 9
ADVANCED TEXTURING EXAMPLES . . . 353

CHAPTER 10
ORGANIC TEXTURE TUTORIALS
WITH PHOTOSHOP · · · · · · · · · · · · 395

CHAPTER 11
SKINNING THE RF-9 PLASMA
GUN WITH DEEP PAINT 3D
AND PHOTOSHOP · · · · · · · · · · · · · · 429

Chapter 14
Making the Slogre
Game-Ready with 3D Studio
Max and Character Studio 535

LETTER FROM THE SERIES EDITOR

If you just picked this book up and are trying to decide whether it's cool, then let me tell you: it's beyond cool. In fact, there are words I would like to use to describe it that are illegal in most states, so I will refrain.

2D Artwork and 3D Modeling for Game Artists is the first book to really bridge the gap between art and game design. Most books about game art are written by non-technical artists, or by non-engine programmers. We were lucky to find David, as he is a gifted artist and modeler *and* can program as well. I guarantee that there's nothing like this book. You're going to be blown away by the sheer amount of amazing material and graphics in this book. What's more, this book includes step-by-step annotated explanations of every single operation you will need to create 2D art and 3D models for your games.

The book starts out with a very cool historical review of game art; after that, it begins to show you how to storyboard an idea, something simple: a plasma gun. Then, step-by-step, every single detail of the design, art, and modeling of this weapon is detailed. When you're done with that, David takes you deeper and deeper into every single aspect of 2D art and 3D modeling for games. The book is simply insane! Look at the Table of Contents right now—it's just too good to be true: advanced texturing, skinning, bones, character animation, advanced texture preparation, putting everything together to create complete game ready assets with 3D Studio Max, and then dropping them into the Torque Engine to see them run.

I am primarily a technical person, but I'm also an artist; I can draw, 3D model, do sound, design, and write. But when you see someone with David's talent then you realize who the real artist is! This book really rocks, and it can only improve your skill set. Nowhere but in *2D Artwork and 3D Modeling for Game Artists* will you find such a complete treatise on 2D artwork and 3D modeling for games or interactive media.

Sincerely,

André LaMothe
Series Editor,
Premier Game Development Series

Introduction

Welcome to the wonderful world of graphic artistry and design for video games! If you're like me, you've taken a keen interest in learning how to create all of those cool graphics you've been seeing while perched behind your personal computer, Playstation, Nintendo, or Sega. Well, that's what this book is all about.

For the most part, the digital gaming art world encompasses a few primary categories: 2D texture and background creation, 3D modeling and animation, and level design. We'll be diving deep into the first two, then adding our hard-earned work to a live video game. Level design, however, is subject for another book entirely (don't tempt me)! My intention with this book is to rev up your engine and get you saturated with many of the how-to's of game artwork—with hopes that with your natural creativity I'll see your work in a hot game title in the future.

As a fairly creative person myself, I find it easy to quickly absorb artistic ideas that get me going with tons of unique creations. I don't want this book to be anywhere near boring; rather, as you dig into each section I want you to feel that I'm giving you some totally cool ideas. But before you lay down a single pixel in your blank, eagerly awaiting image, you'll need a heads-up on the required hardware and software you'll need to have, and what you should be familiar with in order to accomplish many of the tasks in this book. On that note, read on, and I'll make sure not to conceal any secrets!

What You Need to Know

This book assumes one of the following:

- You're an aspiring video game artist with no graphical talent whatsoever.
- You have an aptitude for graphics and want to explore the field of video game design.
- You have been creating computer graphics for a while but need direction when it comes to applying your talent in video games.

Either way, I hope that at the very least you have a solid knowledge of the Microsoft Windows 95, 98, Me, XP, or NT/NT2000 operating system environment. This book requires lots of Ctrl+clicking, Alt+clicking, dragging-and-dropping, and whatnot, along with critical file saves and retrievals, dialog box interaction, all the intermediate functions of general Windows operation. If your Windows skills are a little rusty, please pick up a refresher course to help keep up.

I'm going to assume, however, that you don't know much at all about the programs discussed in this book. Even so, I won't spend too much time teaching you each program in its entirety. Instead, I'll cover procedures and examples that will be helpful to you when it comes to game design. Besides, I believe the best way to learn is by doing. Don't think you'll be wallowing around in easy soup all of the time, however; as each section progresses, I'll demonstrate more and more complex techniques. That way, even if you are already familiar with the program being discussed, you might be able to pick up some tricks, tips, or techniques that are new to you.

> **TIP**
> There are trueSpace and Photoshop tutorials located on this book's CD-ROM that will help to introduce you to these programs. I'll cover modeling and texturing using these two powerful tools, so I highly recommend that you check those out if you're new to them.

What You Need to Have

First and foremost, you must have a computer (d'oh!), an IBM-compatible running Windows 95 or (preferably) better. For graphics development with 3D Studio Max, which we'll use in Part IV, "Preparing Assets for Games with 3D Studio Max," it's better to run NT2000 or higher for stability and its OpenGL environment. I usually do my work and play games on Windows 98, however.

As far as the machine itself, of course I'd love to see you driving the Lamborghini of all computers, but most game artists (like me) usually don't have that kind of budget. Nowadays computers are so darn good that for under $1,000 you can get a Pentium 4, 2+ GHz with 512MB RAM, a 128MB video card, and 60GB hard disk space. For what you'll be doing, that's *ample.* Consider this: For development, I have a PIV-1.7GHz with a GeForce 3 card and 512MB of RAMBUS memory. This system does what I want, but will slide off the deep end as the bigger and better software comes out.

Besides having a computer, you may find it comes in handy to have a graphics tablet when creating textures for your game environment. Mine's a Wacom 6×8 that you can pick up for something like $250. Textures are a vital part of game art-work—the detailed images that are applied to walls, floors, and other 3D objects that give them the illusion of realism—and a graphics tablet makes hand-painting them much easier, since it's much more like working with pen and paper.

Also, a digital camera is invaluable; if you're going to texture or model anything, by all means go outside and take snapshots of the real thing. This will help you keep things looking realistic and acceptable. In fact, many textures in games are compos-ites—that is, images derived from a photograph combined with artistic effects that you apply.

When it comes to games and graphics, use this list when prioritizing what your sys-tem should have, in order of importance:

1. **Video card with 3D acceleration.** This is probably the most important feature of a computer when playing games or making graphics and animations. Your card should have a high-end processor and as much memory as you can afford—games store their textures and graphics in this lightning-fast mem-ory, and without it your system will appear slow. My card has 128MB, and the graphics are smooth and good (for now). If you invest in a brand-name card like a 3DLabs Wildcat or a card with a GeForce3+ chip onboard, you're set. Also pay attention to the processing ability of the card's graphics processing unit (GPU)—if the card has a fill rate of over a billion pixels per second and/or a processing rate over 30-million triangles per second, you'll tear your graphics up!

2. **Pentium III central processing unit (CPU) or better.** Much of the newer 3D software and games can barely run on anything less than a PIII; I can barely even run 3D Studio Max 4 on my old P-II. Again, it comes down to what you can afford (and how much time you want to wait when rendering), but keep in mind that even if you have the baddest video card around, it won't make a hill of beans of a difference if your CPU is slow. You have to strike a balance: If your video card is fast and your CPU is slow, the computer will lag because the video card is waiting for the CPU to chew away on the data. Conversely, if you've got a hot P-4 2GHz CPU and a lousy video card, things will appear very fast but you won't have nearly the resolution and/or color information you'd like.

3. **Computer memory.** I think we've reached a bit of a plateau in the memory business; the average system seems to have around 256 MB and does fine. I'd

recommend that you have at least 512MB, however, because when you start doing renderings and animations, you'll find that memory speeds things up. Programs like trueSpace and 3D Studio Max are extremely math and graphics intensive; to aid in their processing, they use as much RAM as is available to store temporary data. Besides, memory has become fairly cheap.

4. **Monitor.** After all, you're a graphics person, and you need to see what you're doing, right? Personally, I hate having to constantly scroll all over the place to see my work. The larger the monitor, the easier it is for you to see everything. You should have, at minimum, a 17-inch screen; fortunately, monitor sizes are continuing to go up and the prices down. I have an (now I'm going to brag) NEC 21-inch monitor; once you've worked with that for a while, you want to cry any time you try to work on something smaller. I can see from here to the moon with this thing. I've also installed a second video card in my system and hooked up a smaller 15-inch screen to that. If you're running Windows 98/Me/Xp/NT2000, you can tell Windows to split up the desktop across *both* screens, so you can see your work on one screen and have another window open on the other screen. Kind of neat, huh? This really helps me when I'm modeling, since I can put all my pilot windows on the smaller screen.

5. **Hard drive.** Most computers purchased after 1998 have at least 10GB of disk space. If your hard drive is low on disk space, this will be a problem. Programs like Photoshop, which you'll use extensively, cache out tons of temporary data on the drive while you work; without free space, the program will slow to a halt, sometimes freezing your system. Make sure that your system has a good 5GB free disk space after all your programs are installed, especially since graphic images and animations pile up quick. Hard drives are so cheap nowadays anyway that it almost hurts—for $100, you can pick up a 40GB drive, more than enough to contain all the programs you'll need with plenty of space left over. If you want some serious drive power, however, consider purchasing an Ultra160 SCSI card and drive combination—these two components (most commonly purchased from Adaptec) make your data tranfers between your hard drive and the rest of your system absolutely rock at 160MB per second.

6. **CD-ROM.** Obviously you need this to load up your software and play games, but speed isn't so much an issue anymore. A good thing to have is a writable or re-writeable CD-ROM (CDW or CDRW, respectively)—as you collect pictures, textures, and animations, it's good to offload them to CD instead of letting them linger on your hard drive, eating up space. Also, this is an inexpensive way to back up your data from time to time.

7. **Tape backup unit.** I can't tell you how important it is to back up your data! As an artist, you'll spend hours and hours creating and animating, sometimes just one object or scene. If your data isn't backed up daily and your hard drive crashes, you risk losing your work, and, as a result, throwing your good computer out a second-story window. Backup units are somewhat cheap, and I think spending $150 to save countless hours of work is worth it. You can use your CD-writer to back up the data effectively, but the advantage of the tape unit is that the storage space is typically 10 to 20 times more than that of a writable CD. I have a two-week library system, 10 tapes in all, in which I rotate the backup sets. This way, if I need to restore work I've deleted or lost, I can go back as far as two weeks ago and retrieve the data.

8. **Input devices.** Having a tablet, camera, scanner, or any other device that will allow you to capture and process images is always helpful, but not necessary. They do, however, make your life easier and more productive, and at the same time help you make your work more original.

9. **Software.** The last, and most obvious thing you'll need to have, are the programs required to perform your game art creations. This book primarily teaches the use of trueSpace, an excellent 3D modeling program with a powerful NURBS (non-uniform rational b-spline) interface for creating highly realistic organic models; DeepUV, for unwrapping and manipulating texture coordinates on 3D models; Photoshop, one of the most powerful 2D art and imaging programs in the world, which we'll use for the creation of textures; and 3D Studio Max, one of the most widely used modeling and animations programs in the gaming industry. All of these programs are included on this book's CD-ROM as demo versions.

Well, I hope this helps a little. Remember, this is all about money and what you can afford. I happen to be a computer professional as well, so over the years I've amassed quite a bit of equipment (in fact, I can't even see my desks anymore). I don't expect you to have a $15,000 system, but if you consider my list and prioritize, you should be good to go—you can always add on or upgrade later on.

How This Book Is Organized

This is a fairly large book because there's so much material to cover and so many cool tutorials. That said, I couldn't possibly fit every technique the gaming industry uses in 10 books, let alone one. I've tried to arrange things so you can get your feet wet and gain some experience, with the hopes that you'll set off in your own direction.

I've broken the book into five parts. The first part, "3D Modeling with trueSpace," starts everything off by developing concept sketch art, then using Caligari trueSpace to generate 3D game models based on the sketches. trueSpace is, in my opinion, quite possibly the best modeling program I've ever used due to its intuitive development interface.

Part II, "Unwrapping the UV's with DeepUV," we'll transfer our freshly created models to DeepUV, a specialized program dedicated to preparing models for proper texture alignment.

Part III, "Texturing with Photoshop and Deep Paint 3D", I'll show you how to generate a broad spectrum of textures that may be applied to anything from game levels, background art, 3D models, and then some. Deep Paint 3D will be our middle man and helper tool in conjunction with Photoshop to create the skin textures for our models from Part I.

Part IV, "Preparing Assets for Games with 3D Studio MAX," we'll import our textured models into one of the most powerful and important modeling and animation programs, 3D Studio, and prepare them for video games.

Part V, "Bringing It All Together: Level Design," you'll take all of your hard-earned texturing, modeling, and animation work and place it into a live gaming environment. This book includes a demo of the Torque game engine, into which I'll show you how to place everything you've created and see it all in action in a beautiful 3D game world.

What's on the CD-ROM?

I've compiled so much stuff for you to look at, it almost pains me to think about it all. Aside from the hundreds of free textures and models, the Programs section contains demo versions of all the software you'll need and then some. If you don't already own trueSpace 6, DeepUV 1, Photoshop 7, or 3D Studio Max 5, you can use these demos to get through most of the book; they do, however, have a few drawbacks. Demos usually have a built-in feature that limits you in some way, perhaps preventing you from saving your work, or causing the demo to "expire" after 30 days. If you find yourself keenly interested in game development, I highly recommend that you flat-out purchase the programs you need. Photoshop and trueSpace are relatively inexpensive at around $600 each (I say relatively, as it relates to most other graphics programs with muscle); the full version of Max, on the other hand, weighs in near a whopping $3,500. It is, however, a titanium sword in your belt if you've got it.

I've also included Realm Wars, which is a 3D FPS (first person shooter) game and demo of Garage Game's Torque Engine, which you'll need for seeing your work in action. Also, you must have DirectX, downloadable from http://www.microsoft.com/directx , installed in order to play the 3D games and to use the 3D software.

Unfortunately, this book had to be printed in black and white (can you imagine if it was in color? It'd be $1200 a copy!), so you won't be able to get a decent sense of what the color graphics really look like just by reading. For this reason, all the sample graphics and figures from each chapter are stored in separate directories on the CD-ROM. I encourage you to view all the images on the CD as you follow along.

One Final Note . . .

The digital gaming world is an unbearably exciting place to be, because it keeps our minds alive and active and stimulates human creativity. As the ancient Greek philosopher Protagoras said, "Man is the measure of all things." Therefore, I believe that as you read, learn, and do, you'll be propelled on your own track, using your new-found wisdom and creativity to sow the seeds of your own success. Enjoy!

CHAPTER I

THE HISTORY OF GAME GRAPHICS

In this chapter I will cover

- A brief compilation of the history of games and thier graphical content
- The progress of gaming technology and the impact it had on the quality of games
- How arcade-style games dissolved in the eyes of the personal computer
- The competition between game consoles and the personal computer
- The revolution of 3D games and their progress due to better computing technology
- The future of the gaming industry

I've been playing video games since I got my first Coleco in 1977. Although the wondrous days of *Pong* and *Tank Battle* are long gone, they were the roots of modern-day gaming. Back then, seeing simple black and white squares of pixels moving around on your television screen—at your command—was truly phenomenal. We had no idea that things could get much better than that. The electronics industry, however, having seen the excitement in our eyes as we clutched our game paddles for hours on end, foresaw an extreme future for video gaming, and out popped the video game console.

Companies like Mattel, producing the Intellivision (*sigh*), and Atari, with its model 2600, were among the first to introduce awesome interactive game consoles—small computers that were specifically designed for game play. These devices were constructed to accept program cartridges that contained code written in a specific language that ultimately encapsulated a unique game engine with graphic design of the game programmer's choice.

Up until around 1981, games were usually programmed and designed in a matter of months, usually by only one or two people! Nowadays a top-selling game usually requires a team of 20 or more, at least a couple of years, and millions of dollars to produce. The graphic content alone is typically generated by a half dozen game artists—people like yourself.

The Birth of the Computer Game Artist

In the early 1980s, the game industry was booming. The affordable home consoles and new computer systems such as Tandy, Commodore, and Apple that were capable of running games were good, but nothing beat the stand-up video games at arcades. I must've spent 80 percent of my allowance at the arcade every week! The graphics and sounds on those machines were incredible. Midway, Bally, Namco, Atari and Konami were among dozens of electronics manufacturers racing furiously to pump out new and improved arcade games.

There was nothing boring about the arcade. With a new game released almost every month, the graphics became more robust, with some in the mid-1980s, such as *Tron* and *I Robot*, being among the first to simulate 3D graphics using vector-based rendering techniques. Although these games lacked texture, they gave people the first view of what video games were to become in the years ahead.

Around 1982, game design was becoming so complicated it needed to be segregated into several fields. Gone were the days that a two-man programming team could create a game. If you were an independent game developer who wanted to make it in the big leagues, you needed one or two programmers, one or several graphic artists, and a sound expert. Programmers were the ones who made the games possible; in many instances it was (and still is) the programmer who could take a game with simple graphics and make it one of the hottest sellers in history. (*PacMan*, anyone?) Even so, in many respects, the artists were the most important people in the group. From a sales standpoint, the game had to

TIP

If you want to indulge yourself with nearly all of the arcade games from the 1980s, and have a Pentium-level personal computer, check out http://www.classicgaming.com. This site can provide you with special emulating software that, when loaded on your PC, will "emulate" the hardware of the old arcade machines. Then, it's only a matter of downloading any one of the hundreds of ROM files (ROM stands for *read-only memory*, the original unaltered game file that was loaded into the arcade machine), placing it into the ROM directory of the emulator, and firing it up. You won't be getting a remake of the game—it's the real McCoy. These ROM files are also available for download at this site.

be prodigiously visual or it wouldn't produce; a typical game required hundreds and hundreds of sprites (that is, drawings of a single character in various positions), quality background art, and eye-catching special effects.

Thanks to these advancements in games, not to mention the advent of such gaming platforms as Sega, Nintendo, and the Intel x86-based personal computer, general graphic-design and illustration professionals saw more and more openings in the game industry to create game products that had outstanding consumer potential; as a result, many graphic artists dropped their jobs to take on game design.

The Arcade Moves Back Home

By 1985, Sega of America was introducing its 8-bit Sega Master System game console to the world, alongside Nintendo's NES (Nintendo Entertainment System). These consoles ported games found in arcades directly to the player's home, with the only drawback being the resolution difference between the arcade's screen and your television's. But here was the upswing: for a low, low price (which, no doubt, involved you mowing 20 or 30 lawns), you no longer had to waste your parents' money on arcade games! Great games like *Phantasy Star*, *Super Mario Brothers*, and *Final Fantasy* kept kids in the abode.

Nintendo was the forerunner through the late 1980s, suppressing Sega. Most programmers and artists worked for Nintendo due to the company squelching 90 percent of the home entertainment market; in 1989, however, Sega revamped its equipment to produce the Sega Genesis system, running games at 16-bit speeds. This system was by far more exciting; the graphics, sounds, and general game play catapulted over the NES.

With this new console, Sega's checkmate move on the game market was with the top seller *Sonic Hedgehog*. Utilizing fast-paced parallax scrolling (layered images whose background moves slower than the foreground, giving the illusion of depth) and flattened 3D imagery (3D models rendered as 2D sprite animations), Sega reopened its doors to success. *Sonic Hedgehog* truly captured state-of-the-art arcade-style graphics that would become the forerunner of games in production for other console systems.

I've spoken briefly about the history of console systems and the excitement of home-video game play, without recognizing the brilliance of the Sega Dreamcast, Nintendo64, or Sony Playstation. The modeling and texturing tutorials in this book

About Bit-Processing Speeds

Frequently you'll hear about 8-, 16-, 32-, 64-, and 128-bit this that and the other. Although people use these terms with abandon, not everybody knows that they mean! Here's the skinny: Computers are based on binary, where all numbers are a power of two. The CPU (*central processing unit*) of the console or personal computer is designed by engineers to process programming instruction sets (for example, game code) using these numbers as the length, in terms of bits per instruction, of game code that it cranks through every cycle.

So as you play a game, if the machine you're playing on is, say, 64-bit, then every computer cycle (each time the data is pumped through the system per second) the CPU will process an instruction 64 bits in length. This may seem a bit (no pun intended) confusing, but it just means the higher the bit number, the faster the machine; and the faster the machine, the more complex graphics, sound, and general game code it can handle. You'll also see these bit capabilities applied to other things like sound and video cards. See Appendix B, "A 2D Graphics Primer," for more information on bitwise graphics.

can also be applied to these systems. Although this book encompasses a wide range of graphics techniques, it will focus mainly on a unique gaming device that seemed somewhat tentative in light of the gaming arena at one point in time. . . .

The Personal Computer Blossoms

So far we're up to the late 1980s and early 1990s, but my discussion hasn't been much about the personal computer, largely due to the fact that, for the most part, home computers weren't considered by many to be a popular gaming mechanism in the 1980s. The personal computer wasn't dedicated to playing games, and therefore lacked the game-specific CPU and video-processing power that console systems had. We used computers back then for more general things like word processing, spreadsheets, business, and communications. Yes, there were some games, but for the most part, they stunk.

My first computer was this great Tandy CoCo (*Color Computer*) my folks bought me in 1983, on which I learned how to program in BASIC and made some pretty cool programs that displayed interesting polygon-filled graphics. My second, well, was some 80286 I think I bought in 1988 at Montgomery Ward for a gazillion dollars. It was my first true personal computer capable of running Windows 3.1—a revolutionary platform that I believe shook the computer world and charged up consumers to investing in their own computers.

By 1989, I'd learned a great deal about computers and set off to actually build my own 486 from scratch. I put together a 486SX-25 with 4MB of RAM and an 80MB hard drive (can you believe that?? 80MB!!). This thing was hot—everything I ran on it was lightning. At one point I think I saw blue smoke coming out of the back! Anyway, as I recall, this was sort of a turning point—we now had computers with enough memory, fast enough processors, and decent swappable video cards to run appealing video games.

The first noticeable shareware games (I was always into shareware—free games with limited levels that sucked you into buying the rest of the game) that I played on my 486 were games like *Crystal Caves* and *Commander Keen*, (you can still download these games from Apogee; go to http://www.apogee1.com/downloads.html. If your computer is a Pentium or better, you might need a pre-Pentium emulator to play in MS-DOS mode).

By now many programmers and artists were shifting their attentions to the personal-computer gaming market. They saw the potential for making zillions by developing games for this platform; computers were becoming more and more flexible and multi-faceted, without being labeled as $2000 video-game consoles. Computers were also moving away from EGA (*extended graphics array*) video cards and moving toward VGA (*video graphics array*) and Super VGA cards, opening the doors for revolutionary 3D games. These cards in the early 1990s had 256-color capabilities, more than enough to present high-color and a typical 640×480 resolution.

The Gaming Revolution

Most of the world delighted in playing games that appeared to be 3D, but not many people expected to be able to actually walk around in a virtual 3D world. id Software, however, did. Most of the games that had 3D geometry in the early 1990s merely presented a flattened 3D image illusion on-screen. What people believed to be 3D images were 2D sprites jumping and spinning in all sorts of different poses.

Soon after id released *Commander Keen*, the company worked feverishly on creating the first 3D MS-DOS game for the personal computer. John Carmack, co-founder and lead programmer of id; Adrian, his brother and lead artist; and the rest of the id Software team shocked the world in 1992 with the release of *Wolfenstein 3D*. This game not only had a great plot, but while playing the game you could literally walk around walls, objects, and people! *Very* unheard of. The only problem back then was that the objects you walked around kept facing you, unlike the modern 3D games we play nowadays. (I forgive 'em, don't you?)

Wolfenstein captured the world. The game play was awesome, the textures on walls were decent; it was only a matter of time before new and improved computers and video hardware came out that would rocket the 3D industry.

Shortly thereafter, Apogee released *Blake Stone*, another great 3D game, but id came right back in 1993 with *DOOM*. If you had the newest hardware, man, this game was hot. The graphics were less pixilated; images were sharper, there were great texture-mapped floors and ceilings, things were gory, the player had awesome weapons, you name it. id was on top of the world, and just kept building on its own technology to crank out the next head-bashing game in 1994: *DOOM II*.

The Graphics Revolution

By the mid 1990s, personal-computer gaming was hotter than ever. Of course, so were (and still are) console systems, with products like Nintendo64 and Sega Saturn selling like crazy, but computers were becoming so abundant that almost every household had one—making the market for personal-computer games unstoppable. More and more people demanded super-hot titles, which in turn fueled the need for better and more suitable video cards to handle these games.

More important than the need for the great hardware was the programming barricade—developing a 3D video game from scratch would take years, buying a game engine (the actual million or so lines of code developed over the years by other gaming companies) typically cost $30,000. Plus, writing software that enabled games to support a 3D environment was tedious and time consuming anyway; even if you could, your game had to cater to the 100 or so different video cards that people had in their computers or it wouldn't work. So can you guess who came up with the solution to all of this?

Microsoft, upon releasing its 32-bit operating system Windows 95, acquired rights to and began development of a special SDK (*Software Development Kit*) called DirectX in 1995. DirectX was to be the programmers' solution for importing 3D objects, textures, and animations into a game engine and creating a realistic 3D world; in addition, DirectX enabled programmers to alter their game worlds so that objects no longer faced you as you walked around them. The first few versions of DirectX were quite horrific, but near 1996 things started to pan out. DirectX became the focus of both 2D and 3D programming, with nearly all 3D games utilizing this SDK. Artists could create outstanding textures and models, develop levels, and hand it all to the programmers. The programmers could then take all the artist's stuff and use DirectX to manipulate, rotate, light, and special-effect it all.

So again id Software sprang out (expectedly) with another shocker—*Quake*. This 1996 release was truly magnificent. id had the upper hand because of its quintessential game-programming experience over the years, and in 1997 pumped out *Quake II* (by the way, if you haven't played this game . . . man, where have you been?). I can honestly say that this game was one of my all-time favorites. At that exact time I bought this ridiculous Diamond FireGL 4000 video card, which I needed for 3D modeling (ridiculous because it pinched me for $1,500), and with the OpenGL support in both my card and the game, my jaw dropped. The textures in the game were far beyond phenomenal. Encapsulating real-time lighting effects, explosions flew brilliantly off the screen, bullet holes and blood decaled the walls and floors, you name it.

So with the ever-increasing DirectX technology, the whole world was turning out 3D first-person shooters, 3D third-person RPG (*role-playing game*) perspectives, you name it. Even 2D parallax scrolling games used DirectX, such as Team 17's *Worms Armageddon*. DirectX was the ultimate game-development tool—not just a programmers' graphics tool, it incorporated multimedia, sound, and the ability for network and Internet play.

By this time, the gaming industry was so intense that it needed to be broken down into a hierarchical structure. There was too much to handle, and artwork needed to fly minute-by-minute to achieve deadline performance. A typical game-development company might have a graphics team that looked like this:

- Creative Director
- Art Director
- Lead Artist
- Artist(s)
- Lead Animator
- Animator(s)
- Lead Level Designer
- Level Designer(s)

With a graphics team like that, along with four or five programmers and sound people, a company could make a game that would hit the top 10.

In the wake of *Quake* (I'm a poet and didn't know it!) other great games came about, in particular one from Eidos: *Tomb Raider*. But it wasn't just the 3D games taking the stage; after all, not everyone likes the first-person shoot 'em up stuff. Microsoft put out that fire with *Age of Empires*, a perspective strategy (which I'll cover later on), leading the way for a slew of other perspectives, strategies, and RPGs such as Blizzard's *Diablo*.

Third-Stage Booster

After *Tomb Raider*, along comes Valve, a subsidiary of Sierra, to blow the gaming market away. Utilizing id's *Quake* engine, the Valve team summoned up its forces and in 1998 spat out the number one–selling game, *Half-Life*. This game truly set me on fire. It wasn't just a game, but more like watching a five-star science-fiction movie—a 30-hour movie at that. From just the introduction, where the main character Freeman takes a ride into the Black Mesa facility, I was stunned. These people created such a believable atmosphere that throughout the course of the game, I'd just stop, walk up to walls, doors, objects, whatever, and just gaze at the texture or design. In some instances I thought Valve must have had architects working with them to achieve realistic interior building designs! I had been working with models and animations for a while, but from that point on I set out to learn how to create the graphics I saw in that game.

I can honestly say that if it weren't for *Half-Life*, I don't think I'd be writing this book. My mind is open to all types of games, but as you can see, a 3D first-person shooter is my favorite. *Half-Life* was such a phenomenon and success that Valve couldn't possibly stop there—over the next four years, Valve exhausted all possible perspectives on this game, releasing *Opposing Force*, a view from the military's standpoint, and *Counter-Strike*, probably the most popular Internet game ever. I've sat up many nights whacking people (and getting whacked!) from all over the world in this game; eventually I had to

NOTE

One of the great things about many 3D games like *Quake* and *Half-Life* is the fact that the programmers left their games open-ended. In conjunction with a level-editing program like World Craft, you can take *Half-Life* and build your own 3D game world using all of its models, textures, sprites, and animations, as well as your own. The models and textures demonstrated throughout this book may be used for games like these.

give it up for a while because one day, while I was out shopping, I closed my eyes for a few seconds and could see the game play! I felt like a digital junkie.

The New Millennium

As of this writing, midway through 2002 (and about the time of the release of *Blue Shift*, the fourth version of *Half-Life*, developed by Gearbox Software), a few other notable games were published that need mentioning here. First and foremost, I want to mention EA Games' *Undying*, a really cool and gory creep show, with incredible textures—lots of rotting wood, moldy window panes, torn-up carpet, crumbling bricks, organic slime, you name it. Legend Entertainment's *Unreal Tournament*, a killer Internet arena player, totally rocks—particularly the weapons and textures. And once again, id ricochets with *Return to Castle Wolfenstein* to take the lead again in the 3D-shooter industry.

The Future of Computer Games

I'm not forgetting the game consoles or their power. The latest systems such as Sony's Playstation II, Nintendo's Gamecube, and Microsoft's XBox are running 128-bit technologies with mind-boggling graphics and speed, but are still hindered by the television set. I know that'll change soon, but because computers have matured, I've leaned more toward developing games on this platform rather than consoles because the graphics resolutions are way too cool. Don't get me wrong—I believe the future of computers (and games) rests heavily on gaming consoles. The architecture of the console can produce graphic and game-play speeds that sail high over the personal computer, and one day we might see a new generation of computer that no is longer based on 8088 technology. Rather, there might be a merge of console and computer into one unit that has RISC (*Reduced Instruction Set Computing*) technology, which makes consoles like the Gamecube so fast.

So what do I believe to be the future of digital games? Obviously we're heading directly toward pure photorealism. I don't think the next decade will show us *Matrix*-style worlds, but if you look at some of the CGI movies released recently, like *Final Fantasy*, just imagine that that *wasn't* a movie, but a game on your computer screen. If it can be produced on a computer, all we need is the hardware to support it in order to move around in that world in real time—and the hardware to let us do that is literally right around the corner. Just be patient, my young Jedi. . . .

PART ONE

3D Modeling with TrueSpace

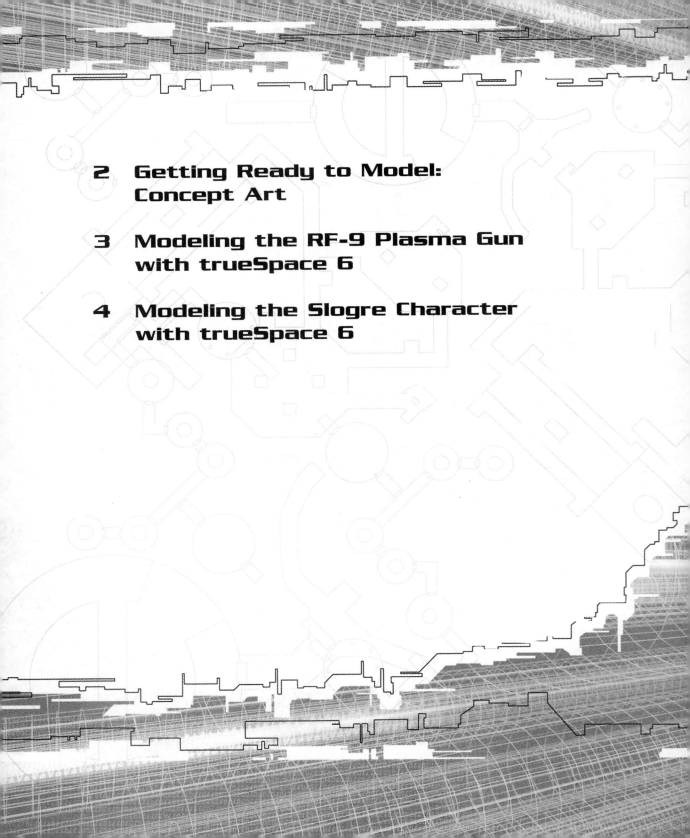

CHAPTER 2

GETTING READY TO MODEL: CONCEPT ART

Before any game content is created, be it character models, textures, or even game levels, it is vital that a working game scenario be laid down. That is, your development team must construct a game plan with a generalized theme or synopsis, and detail the profile and anatomy of one or several lead characters. The working game scenario would also include a general game objective or mission, presenting the game's environment and opening the doors for the creative process.

Once this groundwork is in place, the next step toward generating the game content is to engage one or several sketch artists to generate concept art. Typically, sketch artists can crank out character and model sketches with lightning speed (that is, in a matter of minutes); these individuals are usually very creative, and flood the development team with ideas. That is what this chapter is all about: seeing the birth of game content through the eyes of a sketch artist.

In this chapter I will cover

- Sketch art and its importance when generating game models
- The game-content (asset) creation process
- Tools used in this process
- Generating ideas and concept art for a character and weapon models
- The components for these models and how they will affect the model's complexity

Importance of Sketch Art

Before I got into gaming on a professional basis, I frequently created models and animations onscreen, without trying to get the ideas down on paper. I'd concoct something in my mind, and improvise as I went along. Wrong! I can't tell you what a difference it makes when you're modeling something based on either pictures or sketches, and not on a whim. The reasoning behind this sketch-art stuff is that *all* financed game-development teams are on a tight time schedule to finish a game project; there's usually *no* time during work hours to goof around, experiment, and create your own stuff. (Of course, creating at home for extra points is another story altogether!) As a team member and modeler, you'll typically be handed sketch art of characters or models needing to be created, and off you'll go using just the sketches as reference.

The Asset Process

Having a few freshly developed pages of sketch art in your possession is no doubt enough to make you want to beam over to your workstation and start cranking out some sweet 3D models. However, there's quite a bit more you ought to know before you create a single polygon onscreen—such as the type or style of 3D mesh you'll create, the texture that will be wrapped around it, and so forth. Such specifications are assets that flow together in the creative process, and you should be aware of what they are and how they are closely linked to one another.

Literally speaking, an *asset* is any entity belonging to an individual or group that is of any value. Likewise, in gaming, nearly every component that comprises a video game may be considered an asset—models, textures, sounds, maps, and even code are usually categorized into asset structures.

A *compound asset* is typically a collection of two or more asset entities to make a whole. An example of a compound asset is a character model, which typically consists of a mesh, a texture skin, and an animation (or set of animations) all wrapped up in a nice game-ready package. Figure 2.1 illustrates the workflow for creating a compound asset such as a character model.

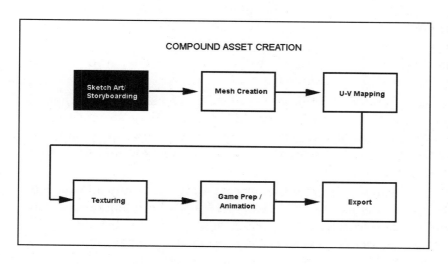

Figure 2.1 *The workflow for creating a compound asset.*

As you can see, things are fairly straightforward here, and the first cell represents this chapter and your starting point. Here's a quick explanation of what's what:

- **Sketch art/storyboarding**. This is the beginning of the creation process and the basis for this chapter. All ideas or plans to create anything should be in this form so everyone has a clear overview of what to expect.

- **Mesh creation**. This is the 3D (or 2D, in some cases) model created in any one of dozens of modeling programs on the market. The most common modeling programs used are trueSpace (I'll be showing you how to model with that), 3D Studio Max, Maya, Lightwave, and MilkShape3D.

- **U-V mapping**. Before textures can be applied to a mesh, the U-V coordinates (also called *texture coordinates*) must be spread out flat and aligned properly onto a texture map so the texture artist can do his or her job more easily. In this book, I'll show you how to use DeepUV to unwrap and align the U-Vs of your mesh objects. In addition, programs such as trueSpace and 3D Studio Max can also perform this function as well.

> **NOTE**
>
> A common misconception about modeling programs is that higher-end programs yield better models. Mesh objects, however, are generally low resolution with high-detail skins; higher-end 3D programs are usually labeled as such due to their outstanding animation, rendering, and production abilities, *not* their modeling abilities.

- **Texturing**. This is the process of creating textures onto a U-V–mapped canvas (or skin, if it applies to 3D models). Alternatively, this term refers to the creation of texture frames for use in level design. Either way, I'll show you both types of texturing techniques using Photoshop, with assistance from a 3D texturing program called Deep Paint 3D.

- **Animation**. This step is for a compound asset such as a character or other model requiring motion. Typically, during this phase, a bone structure is introduced into the mesh of a model, and the bones themselves are animated, deforming the mesh surrounding them. I'll show you how to do this (and more) using 3D Studio Max.

- **Final export**. This is the last step in the process. In it, you dump all your hard work into the game engine of your choice. It is usually here that certain considerations must be made, such as into what game engine the 3D object you've created will be placed. Exporting is game-engine specific, and requires unique steps depending on the engine in question.

The Making of Two Compound Assets

Suppose you're an artist on a game development team that is making a 3D game based on some futuristic world on another planet. (How original!) Not surprisingly, this planet is fairly hostile, and there's an active battle going on between the Trevalan (the good guys) and the Engandea (the foes). In the game, the Trevalan have front-line war characters, called *slogres*, that are huge and aggressive, have minimal intelligence, and basically go into battle to mop the floor with the enemy. These slogres are capable of holding and firing a specialized weapon, called the *RF-9 plasma gun*, which, when handled properly, can disintegrate anything within 50 meters.

As an artist, your goal is to create the slogre and the plasma gun (discussed in this chapter), skin them, animate them, and export them for the team's game engine. As mentioned previously, the first step is to brainstorm, developing ideas about what traits the character and weapon will possess, and then to come up with some sketches of them.

In My Mind's Eye: The Slogre

For the slogre character, I envisioned a huge, lumbering beast that possesses unbelievable muscle mass, and who stands about four meters (13 feet) tall. It is, needless to say, very intimidating to all who try to defy it. Of course, because the slogre is from another planet, not to mention being from the future, it needed be unique in comparison to any animals you're used to.

That said, as in *Star Wars*, *Star Trek*, and just about any other science-fiction world you can imagine, the physiques and personalities of many sci-fi characters derive from objects or ideas that exist in *this* world. Take the sloth, for example. They're very weird-looking animals that inhabit South America. Having four-inch long nails for grasping branches, not to mention disproportionate arms, they are excellent tree climbers—though they move so slowly they may as well be traveling backward. In addition, they appear to be fairly numb upstairs.

As it happens, ancestors of the modern South American sloth thrived thousands of years ago—before the last Ice Age—and were much larger than their modern cousins. Indeed, back then, they were closer in size to bears. These ancient sloths served as a great launching point for the slogre I wanted to create.

Of course, simply copying nature and creating a creature identical to the extinct sloth won't cut the mustard here. That's why I decided to modify the extinct sloth a bit. I figured that if the character were to have such great muscle mass, it might be slumped over from the weight, and could even have a big fat belly, much like that of the ogre in *Dungeons and Dragons*. For you who aren't D&D fans, an *ogre* is a fictional, Quasimodo-like character that somewhat fits the profile I'm describing: huge muscles, not too bright, lumbering around, ugly, carrying a ridiculously huge weapon, and generally being totally unpleasant.

There. I established a base for my character—part sloth, part ogre (hence the name "slogre"). The slogre is, for the most part, bipedal—that is, it can walk on two legs. It has two eyes, but they are monocular, so it sees from the sides of its head the way a bird or an iguana does; it has no depth perception, however, making it good only for up-close combat. The slogre has very long arms that reach to the ground, so it can support itself when resting, and can place one hand on the ground when walking (like a primate) or when firing a weapon. Finally, it has long, vicious claws for turning unfortunate enemies to mincemeat that got too close. In keeping with these characteristics, I came up with a (very) quick first sketch, shown in Figure 2.2.

Figure 2.2
The first draft of the slogre concept.

Notice that in my sketch, I gave the slogre inverted fangs (like an ogre), and a harness with backpack for carrying munitions, and cuffs on the wrists, reminiscent of those worn by slaves—indicating that the slogre has been domesticated by some other being, or perhaps that the slogre becomes slave-like when detained. At least now I have something to work with—my sketch, and my photos of both modern and extinct sloths—and something to give to—you guessed it—a real sketch artist!

In my case, I'm fortunate to work with an artist who possesses much stronger sketching skills than I: Lars Ricaldi. Lars and I split up the artwork at Samu Games, but he is the beef when it comes to sketch art. Most of the complex models I need to create come from his dusty, charcoal-laden fingers. I gave Lars my sketch and photos, and soon thereafter, he handed me the sketch shown in Figure 2.3.

Not too shabby, eh? Of course, there were a few minor things I wanted changed before I began modeling. For example, I felt the slogre's hands should contain four fingers rather than five, and that he should wear wrist bands and a harness made of leather. Within a ridiculously short period of time, Lars produced a second sketch, shown in Figure 2.4.

Figure 2.3
Lars' first draft of the Slogre concept (courtesy Lars Ricaldi).

Figure 2.4
The revised slogre sketch, as per our conversation (courtesy Lars Ricaldi).

This is a great, workable character, very overpowering, and very alien. I asked Lars to give me a few more sketches so we could model this character with ease; Figure 2.5 features the sketches Lars drew in response.

You can see now how helpful it is to have a decent concept sketch of the model you'll be creating. (Try making the mesh from *my* sketch!) Once you've hammered down the concept sketch of the slogre, it's time to work on the second object: the RF-9 plasma gun.

The RF-9 Plasma Gun

I figured that since the slogre is huge, nasty, and somewhat shallow, he'd need a weapon that's easy to use but packs a punch—something that is very big with a wide muzzle, and perhaps a huge, idiot-proof trigger. I also wanted the weapon to have that dusty *Road Warrior* look. After I sent my ideas to Lars, he sent me the sketches in Figure 2.6.

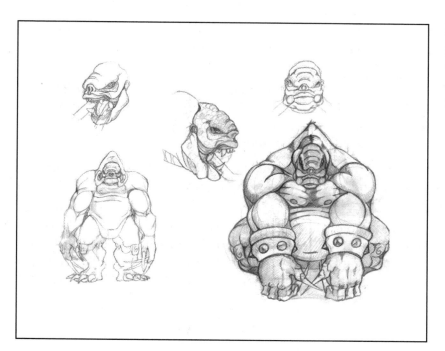

Figure 2.5
Other perspective views of the slogre (courtesy Lars Ricaldi).

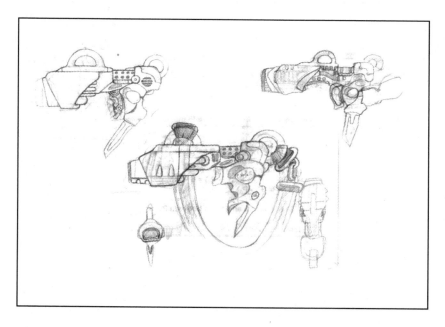

Figure 2.6
Lars' suggestions for the slogre's main weapon.

These sketches were great! I loved the idea of the big steel hoops for a harness. I asked if he'd make the gun longer, so it would retain more of that "hose" look on the outside; the finished gun is shown in Figure 2.7.

My last beg-and-plea to Lars was to give the two models some texture and get the slogre in a firing pose, holding the plasma gun. Once again, he came through; Figures 2.8 and 2.9 feature some images that will complete your picture. For a full-color shot, see the color-plate section in the middle of the book.

These sketches will make your lives much easier as you model the slogre and his weapon. Lars' artistic talent and the perspective he used in his sketches

allow you to envision these objects as 3D models. This envisioning process is not quite over, however; you need to decide what textures your model will use. Indeed, skinning is usually the keystone, and can make or break a model. In fact, until computers allow games to have extraordinarily high-resolution models, you'll create your objects with just the essential detail meshes, and trick the player by wrapping highly detailed textures around them.

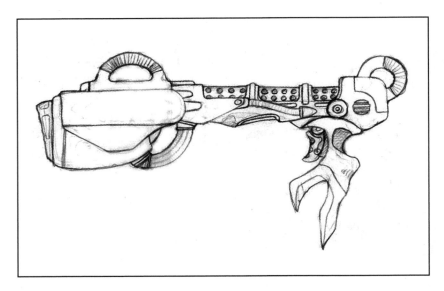

Figure 2.7
The final draft of the plasma gun.

Figure 2.8
The slogre in action
(courtesy Lars
Ricaldi).

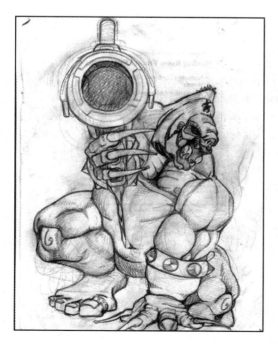

Figure 2.9
*Another money shot
of the slogre in action*
(courtesy Lars
Ricaldi).

The Final Objective

Having the two object models in mind, I want you to pause a minute and think about why I chose them. The RF-9 plasma gun is a great start. Although it's no ordinary object, it's not too difficult to model, and for now will have no moving parts. This is my favorite type of object to model and texture, because it's generally quick to develop and has what I would consider an easy texture skin. Beveled, futuristic metal is fun and looks really cool, so I think you'll enjoy it—in fact, that will be your first modeling project to get your feet wet.

The slogre model, on the other hand, will be by far the most complex. The slogre will consist of only one skin mesh, but will have an internal skeletal structure (known in 3D Studio Max as a *biped object*) that will be used to drive the mesh deformation. That is, as the bones in the biped object move around, the vertices in the mesh will follow. On top of that, you'll be weighting the mesh (adjusting the behavior of the mesh around the bones) and skinning. Lastly, dummy nodes must be placed all over the slogre to signify locations for the character to mount weapons, backpacks, point-of-view cameras, and the like. The model itself, being organic, will also be the most time consuming, so we'll save that for last.

Summary

Developing a complex 3D game model is definitely a time-consuming process that must be well-planned in order for your model to be successful and presentable in a gaming environment. The development can be broken down into several basic steps, beginning with an initial concept sketch to provoke modeling ideas (which leads to creating the model itself in a 3D modeling program), followed by U-V mapping, texturing, possibly applying a bones system to deform the mesh, and finally outputting to a game engine of choice.

Lars provided some great sketches that you can use as you create the models and textures for this game. Of course, you don't have to stick like glues to the sketches (although it should be close); feel free, by all means, to make up your own models as you go. The techniques I'll show you—from modeling, to U-Ving, to skinning and animation—will still apply.

The next step in the development process is creating the actual object meshes, and in this part of the book, I've broken down the creation of the plasma gun and slogre mesh objects into their own chapters (Chapters 3 and 4, respectively). Using the modeling techniques I will describe, you should be able to make just about anything!

CHAPTER 3

MODELING THE RF-9 PLASMA GUN WITH TRUESPACE 9

In the previous chapter, where I introduced you to the logical structure of creating game assets, I envisioned and generated (with the help of my sketch art colleague, Lars) a draft of a cool weapon that I'll now show you how to create in 3D. In this chapter you will

- Set up the trueSpace 6 environment in preparation for game modeling.
- Logically plan out the modeling attributes for the RF-9 plasma gun.
- Build the RF-9 step-by-step using primitives and point-editing techniques.
- Optimize the RF-9 mesh and check for errors.
- Export the model.

An Overview

You've fleshed out the concept for the RF-9 plasma gun and generated some detailed sketches. The next step is mesh creation, as indicated by the workflow depicted in Figure 3.1.

To give you a quick review, Figure 3.2 shows the RF-9 plasma gun sketch that you'll be using to model the plasma gun; you probably remember from Chapter 2, "Getting Ready to Model: Concept Art," that this sketch was generated by me and my colleague Lars Ricaldi.

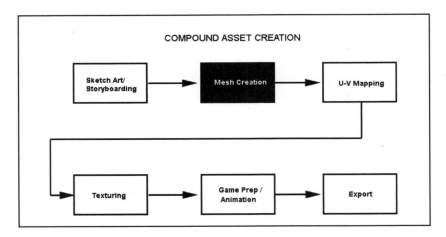

Figure 3.1
The next step in compound-asset development: mesh creation.

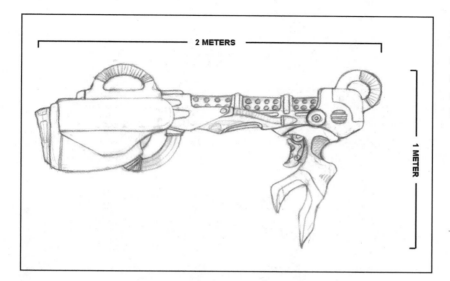

Figure 3.2
The RF-9 you'll be modeling in this chapter (sketch courtesy Lars Ricaldi).

NOTE

The sections that follow explain how to modify the trueSpace 6 environment for modeling, as well as other items you should consider before you begin. If you're already familiar with trueSpace and want to jump right into the modeling, go ahead and skip to the section titled "Modeling the RF-9."

When you're finished, you should end up with something like the mesh shown in Figure 3.3.

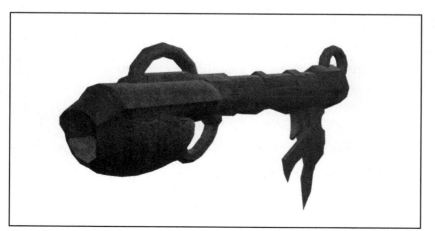

Figure 3.3
The completed plasma-gun mesh.

Setting Up the trueSpace 6 Environment

In case you have not yet installed any version of trueSpace on your computer, I've provided a demo of trueSpace 6 on the CD-ROM that accompanies this book. Install it as you would any other program, and then copy the file **G-LoK.tsc** (as well as **truespace.key** and **keylist.txt** if you want to adhere to my keyboard short-cuts) from the CD-ROM to the \trueSpace6\ folder of your program's installation directory.

After the **G-LoK.tsc** file is copied, it's time to load this custom modeling configuration. To do so, click on the Configuration Library button, right-click in the library's blank space, and choose Import. Then browse to **G-LoK.tsc** file and click OK. You should end up with a configuration that looks like the one shown in Figure 3.4. G-LoK, by the way, is my game artist 'handle', so if you ever see art with my "GLK" logo, you know it's yours truly.

> **NOTE**
>
> **G-LoK.tsc** is an interface-configuration file that will set up your modeling environment my way, displaying three orthogonal views (Left, Front, and Top) as well as a background Perspective view. Over the years I've found that this is a fairly optimal way to model, but by all means, you should arrange the environment to your liking.

The next few sections explain other settings that help with your modeling environment.

Changing the World and Object Units

Generally speaking, one meter in the trueSpace modeling environment equals one meter in the world of the video game you're creating. (It's a good idea to use the metric system because most game engines are based on it.) To ensure that your modeling environment is set to use the metric system, do the following:

1. Right-click the Object button (with the white arrow) to open the Object Info panel (see Figure 3.5).

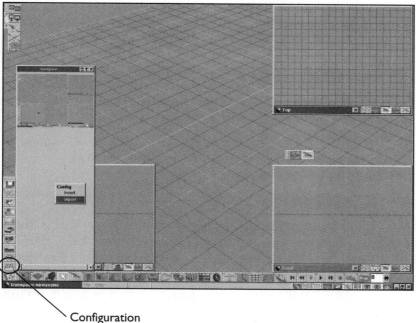

Figure 3.4
*Changing the modeling-interface configuration by importing the **G-LoK.tsc** file.*

Configuration
Library button

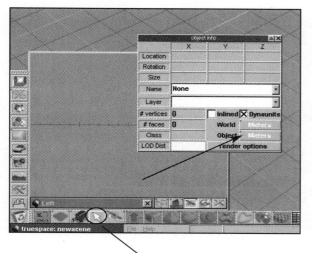

Figure 3.5 *Setting the modeling units in the Object Info panel.*

The Object button

2. Click the red triangle in the upper-right corner of Object Info panel to expand it.

3. Set the World field to Meters.

4. Set the Object field to Meters.

TIP

Rather than closing the Object Info panel, it's a good idea to move it over to the corner of the screen; that way, you can reference your polygon count as you model.

Setting the Dynamic Rendering Mode

trueSpace (and most other modeling programs) allows you to apply various settings to the video mode of your modeling environment, such as wireframe, solid, transparent, and so on. I find it easiest to create mesh objects in Transparent Wireframe mode, which means your models are see-through, and that both the edges and vertices of the model are displayed at the same time. To switch to this mode, do the following:

1. Click on the Display Options button in the bottom-right portion of the screen (see Figure 3.6).

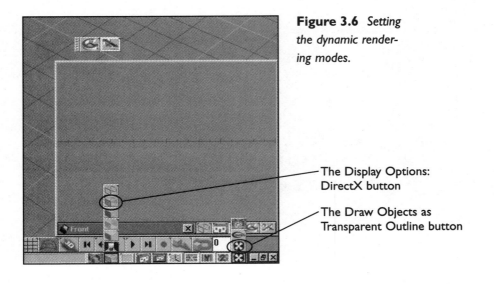

Figure 3.6 *Setting the dynamic rendering modes.*

The Display Options: DirectX button

The Draw Objects as Transparent Outline button

2. Select either DirectX or OpenGL mode. (One mode might outperform the other depending on your video card, so check your video-card manufacturer's documentation for more information.)

3. Select the Draw Objects tool, and press and hold down your mouse button. Then, choose the Draw Objects as Transparent Outline button.

> **NOTE**
> The rendering options described here will apply only to the active window. To activate a window, left-click on it.

Texture Resolution

If you apply bitmaps to any object in your dynamically rendered world, you'll need to crank up the dynamic texture resolution—otherwise, your textures will appear pixelated. Do this by right-clicking the Draw Objects tool (or by clicking File, Display Options), and setting the Txt Res option to 512×512.

Keeping the Point Edit Tools Handy

Much of the modeling you'll be doing is based on point editing—that is, building or modifying your objects at the vertex (point) and face level. I like to keep the Point Edit tools right next to the Eye Rotate and Eye Move tools, at the middle-right of the screen, to make them easily accessible. To make a copy of these tools, press and hold the Ctrl key as you drag the Point Edit tools to the desired area (see Figure 3.7). If you click once on the tool's anchor bar (just to its left), it will expand the tool list and anchor it to that area.

> **NOTE**
> The Point Edit tools will be visible only when an object is present and you're in Point Edit mode (obtained simply by right-clicking on a mesh object).

Modeling Considerations

If you saw the movie *Final Fantasy*, you were probably struck by the incredible detail of the characters, weapons, environments, and so on. That photorealistic detail was the product of the extraordinarily high polygon meshes used to make the models used in the film; indeed, a typical character model's face alone had well over

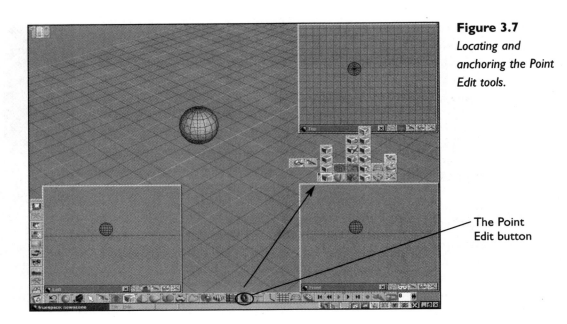

Figure 3.7
Locating and anchoring the Point Edit tools.

The Point
Edit button

50,000 polygons. Sadly, however, if you were to use such high polygon meshes for your game, the player's computer would come to a screeching halt trying to render all of the detail. In fact, what you saw in *Final Fantasy* was the result of countless hours of post-production rendering on very powerful computers (most likely in a rendering array, with dozens of computers linked together, sharing the rendering process).

Models for games are different from models for production, such as cover art, television, and movies. That's because games have dynamic rendering environments; that is, as a player moves around in 3D space, all 3D mesh objects are rendered to screen at least 30 times per second. That means the player's computer's CPU and graphics processors must constantly transform the game world and render it at the same time—which in turn limits the number of polygons your models may contain. Models with high levels of polygonal detail may look better, but will be so slow to render on a player's computer as to make them unusable.

Put simply, models for games must be created to accommodate the average computing power of home computers on the market. These days, that equates to designing your models to work with computers in the Pentium IV and V range, at about 2.5 to 3.0 GHz. That means rather than creating character models with 50,000–100,000 polygons, as seen in the film *Final Fantasy*, you'll need to create character models with polygons in the neighborhood of 2,000 to 5,000, and weapons possessing only 500–2,000 polygons. This need for a low polygon (poly) count will deeply affect the way you model; with every step you take to shape your object, you'll work to minimize the count.

In addition to considering poly count, you'll also want to think about texture mapping as you model. By making nice seams in your models in hidden areas, you'll make the process of unwrapping the U-V texture coordinates much easier. For details on unwrapping U-Vs, see Part II, "Unwrapping U-Vs with DeepUV."

TIP

One way to avoid high poly counts is to apply textures to low-poly-count models for a similar effect. For instance, the RF-9 has a hose-like item running the length of the action, but modeling a hose would require hundreds of polygons. Instead, you can use a simple curved cylinder, and later apply a texture map that features an image of the bumps in a hose to that area. If you can fake something with a 2D map, then it might not be necessary to have high poly counts for certain areas.

Modeling the RF-9

Creating a model of the RF-9 plasma gun will be quick and fairly simple; for overall good looks, you'll rely more on texturing the weapon than creating a highly detailed mesh. Modeling the RF-9 is, in this case, essentially a seven-step process:

1. Plan the model's dimensions and poly count, and build reference plane.
2. Build the muzzle.
3. Build the barrel.
4. Build the grip.
5. Build the hoops and hose.
6. Optimize and triangulate.
7. Export the model for texturing.

In the sections that follow, I'll show you how to use trueSpace, which features one of the best modeling interfaces on Earth, to model the RF-9 plasma gun using the steps outlined here. Of course, you can use any modeling program you wish, including 3D Studio Max (a demo of which is included on the CD-ROM); the modeling techniques I'll show you can be ported to other programs. It's up to you to know how those programs and their tools work, however.

NOTE

In the event you need a primer on using trueSpace, I've included on this book's CD-ROM a tutorial covering trueSpace 4. I focused the tutorial on trueSpace 4, rather than trueSpace 6, because version 4 is clean and considerably less complicated than version 6, but uses the same basic modeling environment. Once you have a handle on using version 4, it's less likely you'll be confused and overwhelmed by the plethora of advanced modeling tools in version 6.

Step 1: Planning the Model's Dimensions and Poly Count, and Creating a Reference Plane

Before you start dropping objects all over your scene, it's a good idea to plan your model and set up your environment so that you can avoid the most frustrating mistake that modelers make *all the time*: getting halfway finished with your model and having to scrap it all or backtrack because you didn't plan ahead. Following are a few things to consider.

The RF-9: Pea Shooter or @$$-Kicker?

I mentioned in Chapter 2 that the slogre stands at about four meters (13 feet) tall. Given that the slogre is more than twice the size of an average human male, the RF-9 can be big and heavy, despite the fact that, as illustrated in the sketches you saw in Chapter 2, the slogre carries it in one hand. I figure a beast that possesses the size and strength of a slogre can handle a weapon that's roughly two meters in length—half of his height—with the height from the gun's strap hoop to the bottom of the handle being about one meter (refer to Figure 3.2). Knowing the dimensions of the weapon will sure come in handy as you proceed with creating the model!

Target Polygon Count

Until your computer hardware lets you make objects suitable for *The Matrix*, you'll have to devise a target polygon count for your model. To give you a framework to

Levels of Detail

When you build a game, you'll typically need several versions of the same weapon model, each with different levels of detail (LOD). One, which will have very high resolution, will be seen only by the player as he holds his own weapon (because the player will be able to see the model up close, a higher level of detail is required); one or several less-detailed versions will feature a lower polygon count, and will be seen being held by other players. These polygon counts may also vary with distance. For information on creating LODs, see Part IV, "Preparing Assets for Games with 3D Studio Max."

work from, 3D FPS games from the late 1990s had weapons that hovered around 300 polygons, while more recent games feature weapons in the 700-polygon range. Keeping with this linear growth, you can safely target your weapon's poly count to be around 1000. That's pretty good detail, allowing you to include more 3D and less texture. Of course, with good texturing, an expert modeler can keep the poly count well below that, but for the sake of expediency, let's not worry about that just yet.

NOTE

There aren't really any rules to modeling; some techniques, such as point editing, are more efficient, producing fewer polygons. Other techniques, such as Boolean operations with primitives and NURBS, accelerate the process. Of course, accelerating the modeling process may require you to clean up any unnecessary polygons at the end. See Chapter 4 for details on advanced modeling with NURBS (non-uniform rational b-spline) objects.

The Reference Plane

Unless you're making models on-the-fly, which will happen occasionally, you'll need to reference a sketch or picture as you model. You can do this in one of several ways, such as taping a hard copy to the edge of your monitor, flipping back and forth between trueSpace and another program that houses the image, or—my personal preference—creating a *reference plane* (a 2D plane you create in trueSpace that has the actual sketch painted on it).

To set up a reference plane, do the following:

1. Add a plane primitive to the scene (the primitives are found among the libraries at the bottom-left of the screen). If you're not familiar with performing simple object operations in trueSpace, such as adding and manipulating primitives, please review the trueSpace 4 tutorial located on this book's CD-ROM.

2. Right-click the Object tool (the white arrow at the bottom of the screen) to open the Object Info screen.

3. Scale the primitive to two meters by one meter by entering the dimensions in the Object Info screen. You'll see a Size field in this screen; just enter these values for X and Y (length and width, respectively).

4. Enable the Grid Snap tool. This is the icon with a blue colored grid located at the bottom of the screen.

5. Using the Object Rotate tool (X on your keyboard), rotate the plane 90 degrees so it runs the length of the RF-9. This operation is best done in an orthogonal view, such as Left, and right-clicking and dragging until the plane is rotated so it stands upright in your scene.

6. Use the Move tool (Z on your keyboard) to move the plane up so the bottom is flush with the scene's reference grid.

7. Use the Material Editor in conjunction with the Paint Face tool to paint the face of the plane with the image in the file **RF-9 Plasma Gun.jpg**, located in the Chapter 3 Data section on the CD-ROM (see Figure 3.8).

Because the default perspective space of trueSpace is huge, you'll need to use the Eye Move tool to reposition your view as I have in Figure 3.8. Notice that the grid's units are one meter square; your plane should be proportionate to it. (If you're a little confused up to this point, just load the **step1.scn** file on the CD-ROM.)

TIP

I've saved the individual modeling steps as trueSpace .scn files in the Chapter 3 Data section on the CD-ROM in case you get confused.

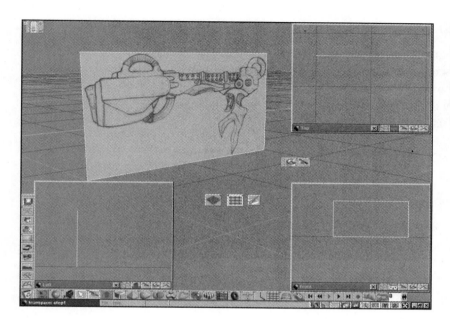

Figure 3.8 *Painting the face of a properly scaled and rotated reference plane with the RF-9 Plasma Gun.jpg image.*

Step 2: Build the Muzzle

Now that you've determined the model's dimensions and established a poly count, it's time to start building the model. The part of the RF-9 plasma gun that's easiest to model is the muzzle. Notice how the muzzle is really just a large, egg-shaped sphere primitive with two adjoined cylinders on the top sides. This is the resonating chamber, where the charged energy pellet enters a plasma-injection chamber and gets superheated in a fraction of a millisecond, before annihilating a nearby targeted object.

> **NOTE**
>
> The modeling techniques I use for the rest of this chapter can be applied by anyone using trueSpace version 4.0 and later. In the next chapter, however, when you model the slogre and other objects, you'll use some of the new tools included with trueSpace 6.

To build the muzzle, do the following:

1. Add a 12-segmented sphere primitive to the scene. You can set the segments manually by right-clicking any of the primitives, or you can use the Magic Ring. (I don't use the Magic Ring, and have disabled it in the Preferences dialog box.)

2. Rotate the sphere 90 degrees.

3. Using the Scale tool (C on your keyboard), scale, elongate, and move the sphere so it matches the one in the reference plane (see Figure 3.9). Again, this is best done using the orthogonal views (such as Left, Front, and Top) to help with the scaling and positioning.

4. Right-click the sphere to enter Point Edit mode.

5. Right-click the Select Using Rectangle tool and enable the Backside option. The Backside option will allow you to make selections on your model that include polygons nearest your point of view and those hidden behind it, or on the model's backside.

6. With the Select Using Rectangle tool, select the first four segments of the sphere as shown in Figure 3.10. This selection operation is best done in an orthogonal window; I did it in Front view.

TIP

To open the basic Primitives panel, press 6. If you use trueSpace version 5.x or higher, you can also open the Primitives panel by clicking on the Primitives Library button, located in the vertical toolbar in the bottom-left portion of the screen. This contains a more extensive and helpful list of primitives.

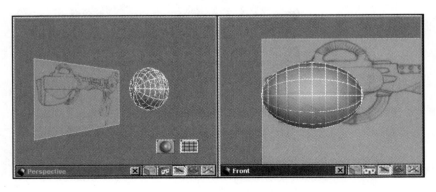

Figure 3.9

Add a 12-segment sphere primitive, rotate it 90 degrees, and elongate it to match the sketch.

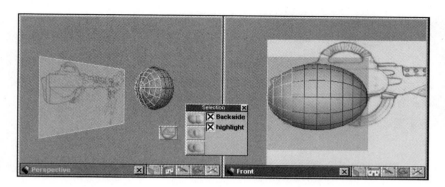

Figure 3.10 *Use the Select Using Rectangle tool to select the first four segments of the sphere.*

7. Click the Erase Vertices tool, located within the Point Edit tools, to delete the selection from the sphere, as shown in Figure 3.11. (From now on, when I want you to remove something, I'll simply say "Select, and delete." That's your cue to repeat this step.)

TIP

If you're having trouble finding the various tools mentioned throughout this chapter, check out trueSpace tutorial on the CD-ROM that accompanies this book.

8. Press Ctrl+C to make a copy of the sliced sphere. In trueSpace 6, your cursor will change to an arrow with a plus sign beneath it—just left-click once in the scene to add the copy, and immediately right-click to exit the copy mode.

9. Scale and position the copy as shown in Figure 3.12; it should line up with the reference plane's sketch.

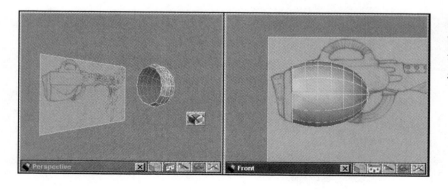

Figure 3.11 *Use the Erase Vertices tool to delete the selection.*

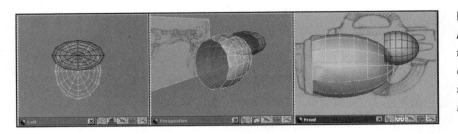

Figure 3.12
Make a copy of the existing sphere object, and then scale and position it as shown.

10. Right-click the copy to enter Point Edit mode.

11. Select and delete the first two segments of the new copy, as shown in Figure 3.13.

12. Using the Point Edit: Faces tool, select the front face of the copied sphere.

13. Use the Sweep tool to extrude the object; extend the extrusion until it's even with the lower sphere by dragging it to the left in an orthogonal view (see Figure 3.14). It will help to lock the X axis for this operation to keep it straight.

14. Use the Object Union tool to join both sphere objects together. If both objects' faces were aligned evenly before the union, you should get one solid object with only one front face (see Figure 3.15).

15. Select the front face of the muzzle; you'll extrude this to form the muzzle's flare (see Figure 3.16).

Figure 3.13
Select the first two segments of the top sphere object and delete them.

Figure 3.14 *Sweep the front face of the sphere and continue the extrusion until it matches the face of the lower sphere.*

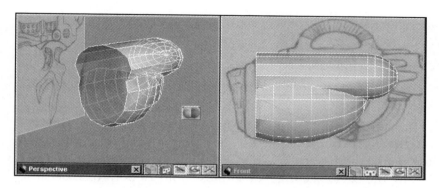

Figure 3.15 *Use the Object Union tool to fuse both sphere objects together.*

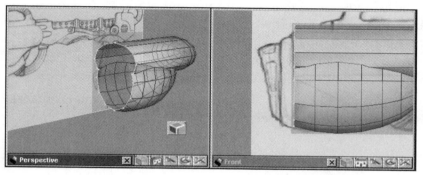

Figure 3.16 *Select the front face of the muzzle.*

16. Use the Sweep tool to extrude the face of the muzzle.

17. Move and scale the extrusion in an orthogonal view so that it matches the reference plane sketch, as shown in Figure 3.17. (Remember to use the Point Edit: Move, Rotate, and Scale tools to do this, and not the Object Move, Rotate, and Scale tools. These tools are located in the Point Edit tools that pop up when in Point Edit mode.)

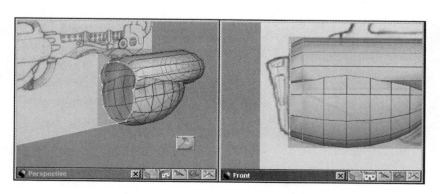

Figure 3.17 *Sweep the front face of the muzzle, then move and scale the extrusion to match the sketch.*

18. Sweep the face again, and then move, rotate, and scale the new extrusion to match the sketch (see Figure 3.18).

19. The top six edges of the muzzle's end must be tapered down slightly. Use the Point Edit: Edges tool to select them, and scale and/or move them down a bit, as shown in Figure 3.19.

20. To hollow out the muzzle, you could use the Object Subtract tool to subtract a cylinder from the inside of the muzzle—but doing so wastes polygons, because by subtracting a cylinder the hollowed result is in the shape of a cylinder, including the back face that constitutes about 10 polygons. Because players generally won't be peering deep into the end of the RF-9, you can get away with subtracting a cone primitive instead—this will save you those 10 polygons since a cone is shaped to a single vertexed tip. To do so, add, rotate, scale, and position an eight-sided cone primitive to the scene, and position it as shown in Figure 3.20.

21. Select the muzzle object, click on the Object Subtraction tool, and then click the cone to hollow everything out (see Figure 3.21).

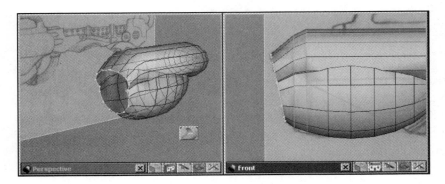

Figure 3.18
Sweep the face again and move, rotate, and scale it to match the sketch.

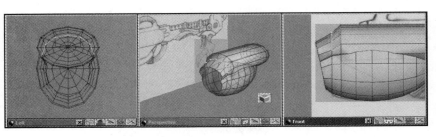

Figure 3.19
Select the top six edges near the muzzle's end and scale/move them down.

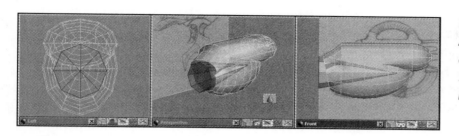

Figure 3.20
Add an eight-sided cone primitive. Scale and position it as shown.

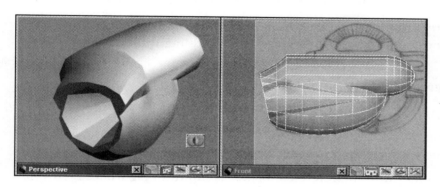

Figure 3.21
Use the Object Subtraction tool to remove the cone from the muzzle.

Voilá! A muzzle! Obviously, you could do a lot more to make it more closely resemble the sketch, but I want to keep things simple for now. Interestingly, however, the twenty or so steps it took to create the muzzle constitute more than 80 percent of the modeling operations required to create most objects; that means you're well on your way to creating niftier, more complicated models.

CAUTION

Occasionally, when performing Boolean operations such as Object Union and Object Subtraction, trueSpace will encounter an error because the objects are positioned in such a way that the operation is not doable. If this happens, reposition the target object slightly and try again. You may also need to slightly adjust the Identity value in the tool's Options panel for things to work smoothly. This value is what trueSpace uses to determine what vertices between the two objects should be included or subtracted from the resulting Boolean operation.

Step 3: Build the Barrel

The barrel is the acceleration chamber for the charged energy pellet. See the circular device at the back of the chamber, just above the grip and trigger? That's the removable pellet clip, holding up to 100 rounds of static energy pulse modules that, when activated by the trigger, bolt forward and begin expanding along the length of the barrel. Once a static energy pulse module hits the resonating chamber (muzzle), it gets superheated with plasma, and all hell breaks loose.

Modeling the barrel requires a simple cylinder primitive that has a bunch of Boolean subtractions applied to it, with a bit of point editing to finish it off. Here goes:

1. Add an eight-sided cylinder to the scene.

2. Using the Grid Snap tool, rotate the cylinder 90 degrees.

3. Scale the cylinder along the long axis using an orthogonal window, and squash it a bit vertically so it has more of an oval shape.

4. Align the cylinder with the reference plane, as shown in Figure 3.22. (If you prefer, you can build the cylinder away from the muzzle and join the two later.)

5. The underside of the barrel has some sharp angled lines to it; to eliminate them, you can use a cube (or any other object) to subtract from an existing object, a procedure called *drilling*. Add a cube primitive to the scene, and scale and position it where you want to hack away from the barrel.

6. Select the barrel, click the Object Subtraction tool, then click the cube to subtract it (Figure 3.23). Continue drilling additional angles and dents in the barrel, but stop at the middle where the barrel curves; you'll use a cylinder primitive for that.

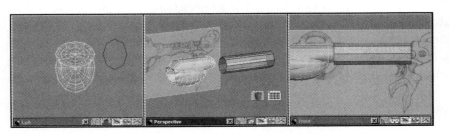

Figure 3.22

Add an eight-sided cylinder, rotate it 90 degrees, and scale it to match the sketch.

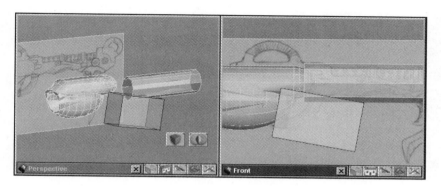

Figure 3.23 *Use cube primitives in conjunction with the Object Subtraction tool to chisel away at the barrel.*

7. Repeat steps 5 and 6 using a 10-sided cylinder as a drill to carve out an arc-shaped area under the barrel, as shown in Figure 3.24.

8. Select the back face of the barrel and use the Sweep tool to extrude it.

9. Reposition the face in relation to the sketch using the Point Edit: Move tool (see Figure 3.25).

TIP

When performing multiple object subtractions using the same object as a drill, it helps to click the Keep Drill option in the tool's Options panel. That way, the drilling object does its job but remains in the scene.

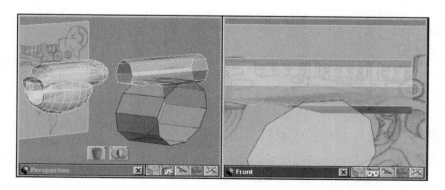

Figure 3.24 *Use a 10-sided cylinder to carve an arc in the bottom of the barrel.*

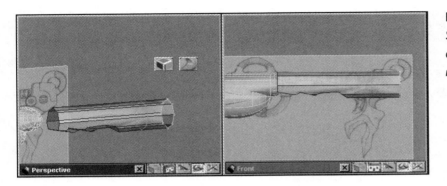

Figure 3.25
*Sweep the back face
of the barrel to
match the sketch.*

10. To bevel the top-rear of the bar-
    rel, begin by selecting the top two
    faces toward the back. To do so,
    use the Point Edit: Faces tool, and
    press and hold down Ctrl key as
    you click each face to select it
    (see Figure 3.26).

11. With the two faces selected, click
    the Bevel tool.

TIP

**Locking the X or Y axes (bottom-
right corner of the screen) when
extruding faces or performing other
point-edit operations will keep your
movements aligned with the orthogonal views.**

12. Click and drag slightly anywhere in the scene to adjust the bevel as I have
    done in Figure 3.27.

13. To carve out the notches in the top of the barrel, begin by adding, scaling,
    and positioning a cube primitive as shown in Figure 3.28. Align it so it
    matches the sketch.

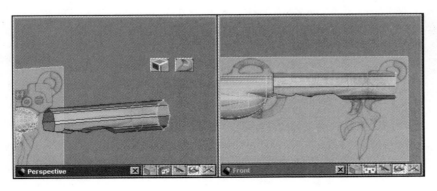

Figure 3.26
*Select the top two
faces at the rear of
the barrel.*

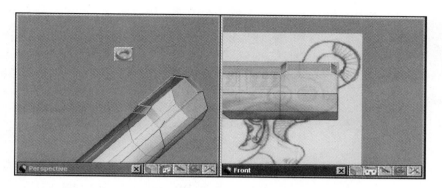

Figure 3.27
*Bevel the faces using
the Bevel tool.*

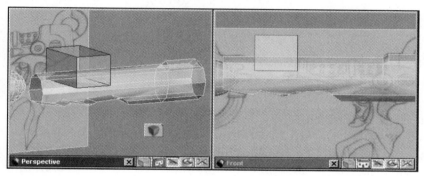

Figure 3.28 *Add a
cube primitive and
position it as shown.*

14. Use the cube primitive to drill out a notch in the barrel. Repeat to create the other two notches, as shown in Figure 3.29.

15. Add a 10-sided cylinder primitive to the scene, and scale and position it as shown in Figure 3.30. When you're satisfied with the position (make sure you view it from Front, Top, and Left orthogonal views), use the Object Union tool to weld it into place.

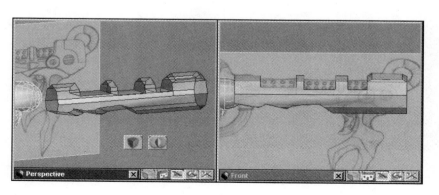

Figure 3.29 *Use
the cube to drill
notches in the barrel.*

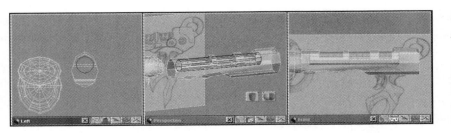

Figure 3.30 *Add, scale, and position a 10-sided cylinder primitive to the barrel. Use the Object Union tool to weld it in place.*

This completes the barrel. Don't worry about the holes along the cooling jacket in the sketch; we're going to fake those with some slick texturing later on in Part III, "Texturing with Photoshop and Deep Paint 3D." You can now position the entire barrel unit behind the muzzle and Object Union the whole thing together.

Step 4: Build the Grip

Because the slogre's hand is huge, and features 10-inch-long nails for slashing enemies, his dexterity is hindered, which is why the grip and trigger are oversized and simplified. For added mayhem, the end of the grip features a twin blade that our lovely behemoth can use to impale the heads of unfortunate saps that get too close. Here's how to build the grip:

1. Add a 10-sided cylinder primitive to the scene.

2. Position, scale, and squash the cylinder laterally so it takes on the shape of the grip in the reference plane (see Figure 3.31). Don't worry about the blades for now; we'll extrude them separately later on.

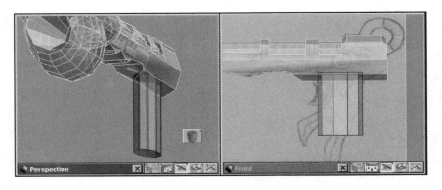

Figure 3.31 *Add a 10-sided cylinder to the scene, scale it, and position it in relation to the sketch.*

2. Aside from the trigger, you can carve out the front and back of the grip with spheres. To begin, add two 12-segmented sphere primitives to the scene—these will be your drills for the front and back of the grip.

3. Position, scale, and rotate the spheres, using the sketch as a reference.

4. Use the Object Subtraction tool to drill the grip with the spheres (see Figure 3.32).

5. Using a cube primitive, slice the bottom of the grip at an angle (use the reference plane as a guide). This is where the blades will be placed. (See Figure 3.33.)

6. Select the angled face at the bottom of the grip.

7. Using the Sweep tool, extrude the angled face outward.

8. Scale and rotate the resulting face so it's a bit tapered, as shown in Figure 3.34.

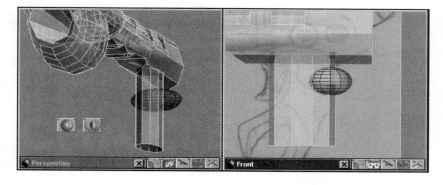

Figure 3.32 *Use 12-segmented sphere primitives to carve arcs in the front and back of the grip as per the reference plane.*

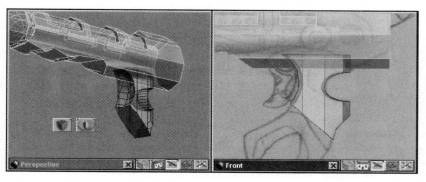

Figure 3.33 *Use a cube primitive to drill an angle in the bottom of the grip.*

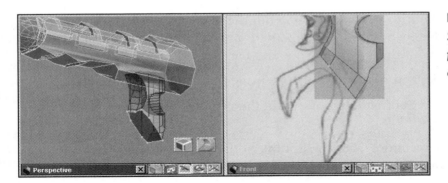

Figure 3.34
*Sweep the bottom
face of the grip out,
and taper it.*

9. Now for the blades. To create them, you'll split the bottom face of the grip, and then extrude each face individually to form the twin blades. To begin, use the Add Edges tool in the Point Editing group to create an edge between the two vertices, as shown in Figure 3.35.

> **NOTE**
>
> This technique is a manual way to create a *subdivision surface*; you can also create subdivision surfaces with other tools (such as the Quad Divide tools) if you need to add more detail and/or smoothing.

10. Now that the bottom has two faces, use the Point Edit: Faces tool to select the top face.

11. Using the Sweep tool, extrude the selected face.

12. Position and scale the extruded face so that it thins out like a metal blade (see the sketch in the reference plane), as shown in Figure 3.36.

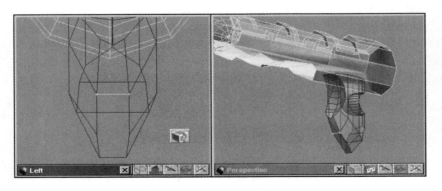

Figure 3.35 *Divide
the bottom face of
the grip using the
Add Edges tool.*

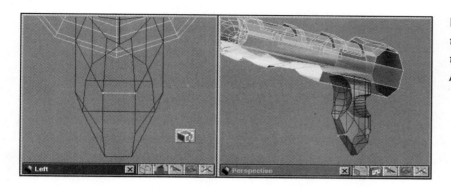

Figure 3.35 *Divide the bottom face of the grip using the Add Edges tool.*

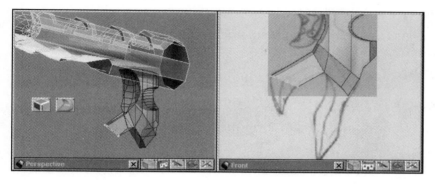

Figure 3.36 *Extrude the beginning of the top blade, tapering it a bit.*

13. Sweep the face once more, angling it downward via the sketch. Taper it even more so it resembles a sharpening blade.

14. Use the Tip tool to draw the blade to a fine point (see Figure 3.37).

15. Repeat the extrusion and tip process for the lower blade, as shown in Figure 3.38.

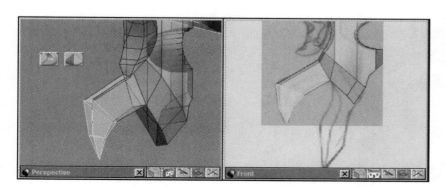

Figure 3.37 *Finish the blade with a sweep and tip.*

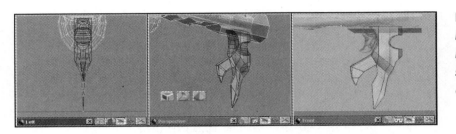

Figure 3.38
Finish the lower blade using the same techniques as for its cousin.

16. Using the orthogonal views, align the grip to the barrel.

17. Using the Object Union tool, meld the grip and barrel together.

18. Now for the trigger; start by adding a six-sided cylinder primitive to the scene.

19. Scale and position the trigger as shown in the reference plane.

20. Select the front-most edge of the trigger with the Point Edit: Edges tool.

21. Move the edge inward so it starts to form the curved trigger (see Figure 3.39).

22. Position the base of the trigger at an angle into the body of the barrel object, and use Object Union tool to fuse them together.

23. Select the bottom face of the trigger.

24. Sweep the selected face down, angling and tapering it a bit to conform somewhat to the shape in the sketch (see Figure 3.40).

25. Sweep, rotate, and taper (scale) the trigger once more. The grip and trigger assembly should now be complete and resemble the one shown in Figure 3.41.

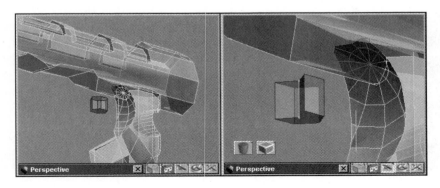

Figure 3.39
Add a six-sided cylinder primitive for the trigger. Push in the front edge.

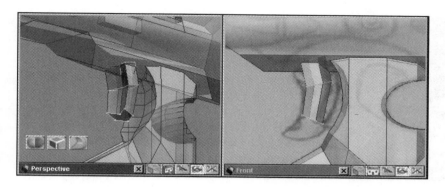

Figure 3.40 *Join the base of the trigger to the barrel, and sweep the bottom face of the trigger down.*

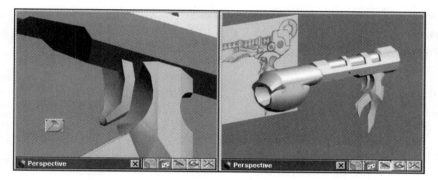

Figure 3.41 *Sweep and taper the trigger end once more to complete it.*

Step 5: Build the Hoops and Hose

Now it's time to add those donut-like appendages that give the RF-9 its futuristic, Mad Max look. The top two hoops are meant for big, thick leather straps or a harness, while the hose beneath the gun vents power toward the muzzle's resonating chamber at the exact moment the energy pellet enters it. Here's what to do:

1. Let's begin with the top front hoop. Add a 12-sided torus primitive (the donut shape) to the scene.

2. Rotate the torus 90 degrees, and scale/position it to match the sketch.

3. Right-click the torus primitive in the Primitives panel to access the torus's Options panel, then adjust the inner radius of the torus to about 0.65 or so. (See Figure 3.42.)

4. Using the Rectangular Selection tool, select the bottom-half of the torus.

5. Delete the selection using the Erase Vertices tool.

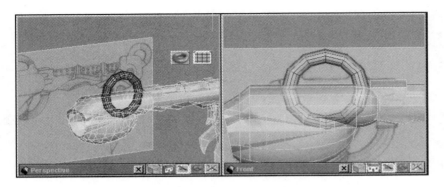

Figure 3.42 *Add a 12-sided torus primitive, and scale and rotate it to match the sketch.*

6. Add a rounded-cylinder primitive to the scene, as shown in Figure 3.43. This will be the base of the hoop. .

7. Using the Object Union tool, fuse the rounded cylinder to the body of the gun.

> **NOTE**
>
> For trueSpace 4 users, this primitive isn't an option. Try joining two sphere primitives to the end of a cylinder primitive to achieve this shape.

8. Again using the Object Union tool, fuse the torus to the rounded cylinder. You should end up with a gun that looks something like the one in Figure 3.44. If not, try moving the objects slightly and repeat the union operations.

9. Before adding the hoop at the rear, bevel the back face of the barrel as shown in Figure 3.45. (A bevel is simply a face that is extruded but shrinks in size.) To do so, use the Point Edit: Faces tool to select the face, and click the Bevel tool. Click and drag to adjust the bevel in accordance with the sketch.

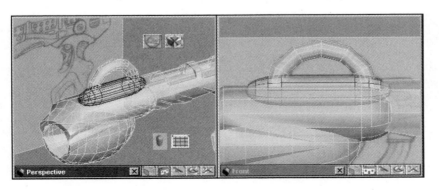

Figure 3.43 *Cut off the bottom-half of the torus, and add a rounded cylinder primitive as the hoop's base.*

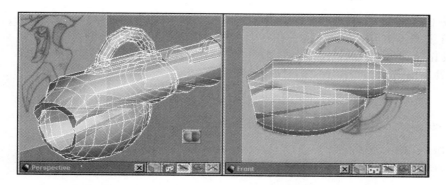

Figure 3.44
Object Union the cylinder and torus to the gun's body.

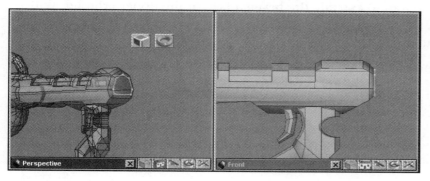

Figure 3.45 *Bevel the rear of the barrel in preparation for the back hoop.*

10. Add a 12-segmented torus primitive for the back hoop.

11. Using the torus's Options panel, adjust the inner radius of the torus to about 0.55 or so. Rotate, scale, and position this over to the back hoop, aligning it with the reference plane.

12. When satisfied, Object Union the torus into place (see Figure 3.46).

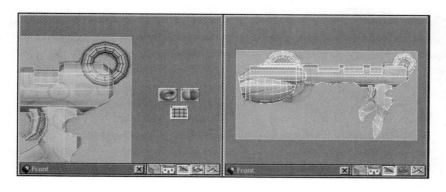

Figure 3.46 *Add a 12-segmented torus primitive for the back hoop and fuse it to the gun.*

13. Now for the last item: the feeder hose underneath the RF-9. I'd like to add caps to start and end the hose for a more authentic look, then sweep the hose manually so it looks more saggy. To create the caps, begin by adding two six-sided cylinder primitives to the scene.

14. Scale, rotate, and position the cylinders as shown in Figure 3.47.

15. Use the Object Union tool to weld the cylinders into place.

16. Select and bevel the exposed face of the top cylinder. This taper will begin the hose (see Figure 3.48).

17. Use the Sweep tool to extrude the beveled face of the upper cylinder. With every sweep, rotate and position the face so it moves toward the other cylinder (see Figure 3.49).

18. When the end of the hose is close to the bottom cylinder, it's time to join the two. Because they are technically the same object (due to the Union operation you did just before), you can't just use the Object Union tool to fuse

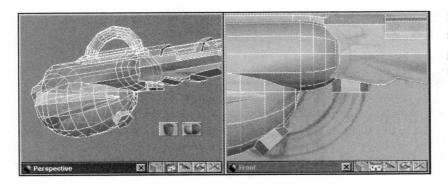

Figure 3.47 *Add two six-sided cylinder primitives and weld them into place.*

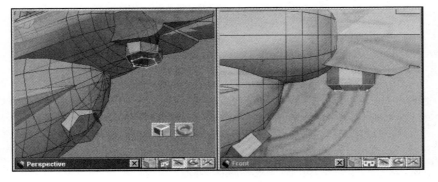

Figure 3.48 *Select and bevel the face of the top cylinder.*

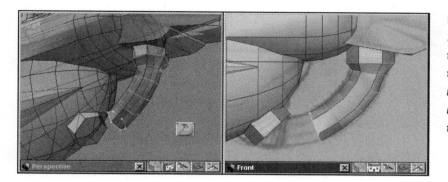

Figure 3.49
Sweep the face of the cylinder several times to make the hose. Make sure it moves over toward the other cylinder.

them. Instead, you'll have to use the Add Edges tool to link vertices from the hose to the cylinder (see Figure 3.50). This tool is also located within the Point Edit tools. When this tool is active, simply clicking on a vertex from the end of the hose, then a vertex on the cylinder nearest it will join the two with an edge.

NOTE

Once an edge is created, trueSpace may or may not install a face that defines a closed boundary. If you don't see a shaded area come to life after you add an edge, you may need to use the Add Face tool to add the face manually. To do so, click the Add Face tool then click the questionable area to add a face. Usually if a hole exists in your model the Add Face tool will highlight the area when you move your mouse cursor over a hole.

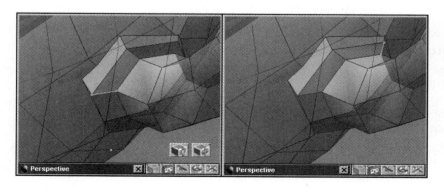

Figure 3.50 *Join the hose to the lower cylinder by linking the two with the Add Edges tool. Use the Add Faces tool if necessary to close up the model.*

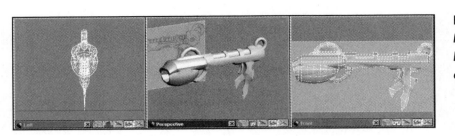

Figure 3.51
Finished with the basic construction of the RF-9.

Alrighty then! You're finished with the basic construction of the RF-9, and it's looking good (see Figure 3.51).

Step 6: Optimize and Triangulate

Although you've finished the basic construction of the RF-9, there are a few things you need to handle before you can consider this model complete. First, the polygon count is almost twice the target; you can tell by right-clicking on the Object tool, which reveals stats on the vertici and face counts of the model. Mine has a little over 700 faces—a lot, considering that at bare minimum, each face requires two triangles (polygons), and sometimes more depending on the shape of the face.

If you determine that your model's polygon count is high, you can reduce it by cleaning up all the unnecessary faces, edges, and whatnot that are a negative side effect of Boolean object modeling. You see, welding all those fancy primitive objects to make a model is quick and dirty, but leaves a trail of excess polygons.

To begin, it helps to paint the model with a basic, bright color, and set the wireframe to a contrasting color. To do so, use the Paint Object tool in the Material Editor panel to paint the model with a color such as a bright green, as I have done in Figure 3.52. To change the wireframe color, switch to Point Edit mode, choose File, Display Options, and change the Edit color.

Next, so that you can clearly see the wireframe of your solid object without seeing the non-visible wireframe of the opposite sides of the model, set the render mode to Draw Objects as Solid Outline (the second tool from the left, on the bottommost toolbar on your screen).

Using the Object Rotate tool (X on your keyboard), move around the object and search for areas with a bunch of vertices clumped together. One such area is the side of the muzzle, as shown in Figure 3.53. Notice that there are several faces that

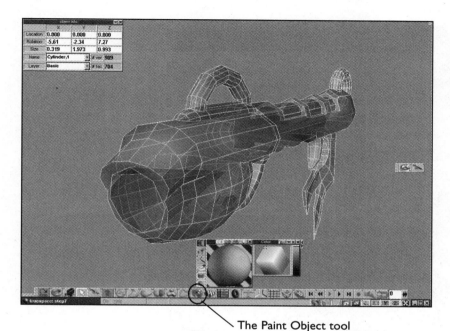

The Paint Object tool

are just slivers of detail—totally unnecessary, as they do not contribute any significant detail to our model. To eliminate excess vertices, right-click the model to enter Point Edit mode, choose the Point Edit: Vertices tool, hold down the Ctrl key, and click the individual vertices you want to combine into one. Once they're highlighted, click the Weld Vertices tool. Alternatively, use the Point Edit: Edges tool to select the edge between two very close vertices, and click the Weld Vertices tool. Either way, you should end up with a clean area, as shown in Figure 3.54.

After you've reduced polygon counts in the obvious areas, switch to plain wireframe mode and zoom really close into areas of high mesh concentration, or into parts where one primitive object was united with another. In Figure 3.55, I've zoomed to a typical area that has an obnoxious number of stray vertices and insignificant edges. These aren't errors, mind you, but details that no player could possibly discern in a game. As before, select the excess vertices that are close to each other, and click the Weld Vertices tool to unite them.

Lastly, while in Draw Objects as Solid mode, spin your model around and see if you can spot any holes. They'll show up only in solid mode, and will display an open

Too much detail here

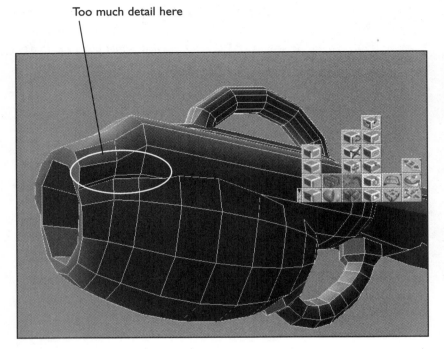

Figure 3.53 *Small, insignificant faces that only add to the polygon count of the model.*

Ah, much better.

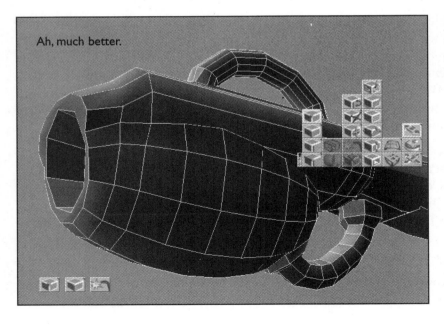

Figure 3.54 *Get rid of the unnecessary faces by welding vertices together.*

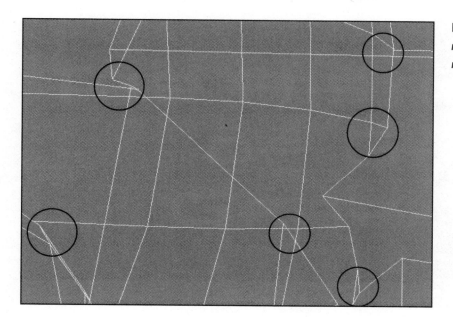

Figure 3.55 *More minute details that need welding.*

face through which you can see into your hollow model. As shown in Figure 3.56, I found a hole where we joined the hose to the resonating chamber. To fix this problem, use the Add Edges tool to link vertices across the hole, and/or use the Add Face tool.

Once you've performed these steps, you should at least be close to the target poly count. If you want to see my results, open the step6.scn file on the CD-ROM (see Figure 3.57).

NOTE

For every superfluous face you eliminate, you reduce the polygon count of the model by at least two. If this is a significant model for your game, it would be wise to spend an hour or two optimizing your model in this manner; get rid of details people won't see, and reduce the poly count to a reasonable number.

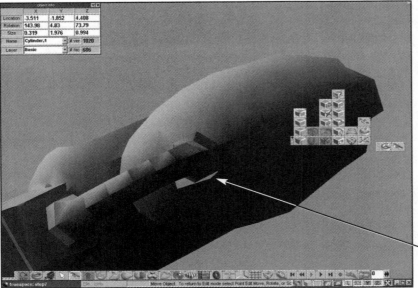

Open face

Figure 3.56 *Check your model for holes while in Draw Objects as Solid mode.*

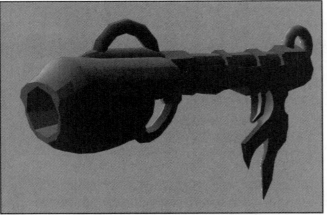

Figure 3.57
The cleaned-up RF-9 plasma gun.

Apply the Triangulation

When you export the model for 3D Studio Max, all faces get *triangulated*, meaning all vertices are interconnected at the rudimentary level, so that the entire model is made up of three–sided polygons. This triangulation dictates the final polygon count. (Mine came to over 1,800 polygons before I cleaned it up!) What you see during the process of modeling are ordinary faces—a polite way of trueSpace hiding edges to make your model easier to manipulate. Triangulation is the last phase, which reverts the mesh into its raw polygon form.

First save your scene, then click the Triangulate tool, located among the Quad Divide tools. Your mesh should suddenly appear a bit entangled, but this is only the result of the faces being divided into their constituent triangles. Checking the polygon count of your model one final time now will show you the grand total your game engine will be dealing with.

> **CAUTION**
>
> The triangulation operation, which you perform by clicking the Triangulate Object tool, is NOT undoable. You should save your model before performing this operation.

Export the Model

At this point, your mesh object should be clean, tidy, and complete. The next logical step is to prepare it for texturing by unfolding the U-V texture coordinates and laying them out flat so the texturing process happens in two dimensions. There are a number of ways to unwrap U-Vs. The way I do it is popular, fun, and easy: I use 3D Studio Max in conjunction with Right Hemisphere's DeepUV.

Before you can use these programs, you must first export your model to a file format that they can understand. trueSpace 6 has a number of formats available from which you may choose; the best format for our needs is STL. Short for *stereolithography*, this format is used in the modeling industry for machines designed to carve an actual, physical model based on your 3D mesh. The STL format is raw and straightforward, presenting just the mesh object and the faces it contains. As an added bonus, 3D Studio Max has a nice STL import feature that checks the model for duplicate vertices, holes, and other possible errors, and fixes them. In addition, once you've imported your model into Max, you can run an STL Check modifier that will analyze your mesh for any other errors. This way, you can assure your game engine that the model you're preparing is nice and clean and won't cause a system crash!

Exporting the RF-9 to STL is easy: Just click File, Save As, Object, and choose .STL from the Save As Type list at the bottom of the dialog box. Then just give it a name and click Save.

If you're ready to proceed with UV unwrapping at this point, skip to Part II, "Unwrapping the U-Vs with DeepUV." There, I show you how to briefly intercept the RF-9 model with 3D Studio Max, and work with DeepUV to unfold the texture coordinates in preparation for texturing the model. It's really fun and interesting, and I think you'll get a kick out of it.

Summary

In this chapter, I showed you how to set up the trueSpace 6 environment in preparation for modeling the RF-9 plasma gun weapon. More than just building at a whim, game models such as this need to be carefully planned out, including determining dimensions and polygon counts, before building it in a 3D world. Finishing up models with optimization techniques are a vital process as well. All in all, because of these steps your end results and overall modeling operations are smooth, predictable, and work well in a game engine.

CHAPTER 4

Modeling the Slogre Character with trueSpace 6

This chapter continues with the modeling techniques and environmental setups as described in Chapter 3, "Modeling the RF-9 Plasma Gun with trueSpace 6." Figure 4.1 shows your place in the compound-asset creation workflow.

In this chapter you will

NOTE

If you're new to modeling with trueSpace, or have skipped straight to this chapter, you will find it beneficial to first read the first few sections of Chapter 3 for information on how to set up your modeling environment and become familiar with the basic interface of trueSpace 6. There is also a trueSpace 4 tutorial located on the CD-ROM, which may be of help as well—much of the functionality from that version has found its way to version 6.

- Logically plan out the modeling attributes for the slogre.
- Build the slogre step-by-step using NURBS and point-editing techniques.
- Analyze and develop proper joint details on the model to allow for smooth animations.
- Optimize the slogre mesh and check for errors.
- Export the model in preparation for texturing.

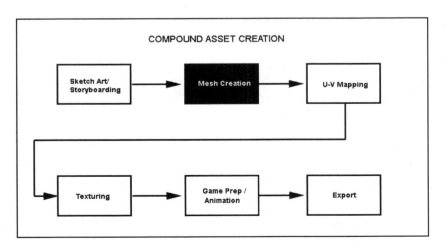

Figure 4.1 *The next step in compound-asset development: mesh creation.*

To give you a quick preview, Figures 4.2 and 4.3 show the slogre sketches that you'll be working from to create the slogre character, as devised by me and my sketch-artist friend and colleague, Lars Ricaldi. The first image indicates the approximate height of this character; when squatting, he still lumbers about at a two-meter height.

Figure 4.2 *The slogre you'll be modeling in this chapter* (sketch courtesy Lars Ricaldi).

Figure 4.3 *Another money shot* (sketch courtesy Lars Ricaldi).

Figure 4.4 *The completed slogre mesh.*

Once you're finished, you should end up with something like the mesh shown in Figure 4.4.

Modeling Pre-Considerations

As I mentioned in the last chapter, a decent character model for personal computers with Pentium-IV processors will average 2,000 polygons; with the advent of computers with higher processing capabilities, these numbers will only go up. id Software's *Doom III* is said to have characters with polygon counts of 5,000 or more—offering spectacular smoothness to the mesh and adding detail that you previously had to fake in texturing.

Because I'd like to see this book extend its use to the middle of the first decade of the 21st century, I'd like to target a *Doom III*–like game for the slogre model, without going overboard for those computers not capable of handling huge polygon counts. Seeing how character models at the turn of the century contained an average of just below 1,000 polys, I'd like to shoot for 3,000 for the slogre.

The modeling techniques you'll employ for this character will be a combination of NURBS modeling (unbelievably impressive and exciting, but extremely taxing on polygon counts) and point-edit modeling. I want to hybrid the model in this manner to show you that you can do this any number of ways—some being better than others—with the end result being a model that comes out decent. Besides, NURBS modeling is the future of video-game characters; no doubt in the very near future you'll be able to create your models completely with NURBS, retaining their spline parameters without converting to a welded-shut polygonal mesh. The future game engines will import your NURBS objects and allow for dynamic B-spline deformations during game play.

Modeling the Slogre

As mentioned previously, I'll show you how to model this character using trueSpace 6, the demo of which is on the CD-ROM. Once installed, you should get a default modeling interface that looks something like the one in Figure 4.5.

For our purposes, I have narrowed down this interface, grouped most of the tools needed for this chapter into one small toolbar, and arranged windows so they appear much as they do in other popular modeling programs' interfaces. I highly recommend that you make your setup the same as mine—just click the Configuration Library icon in the vertical toolbar at the bottom-left corner of the interface to load the configuration file **G-LoK TS6.tsc** on the CD-ROM (see Figure 4.6). This file is different from the file I had you load in the last chapter.

My custom modeling interface loaded, with the essential tools present.

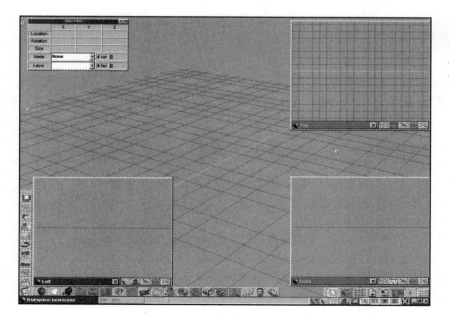

Figure 4.5 *The default modeling interface of trueSpace 6.*

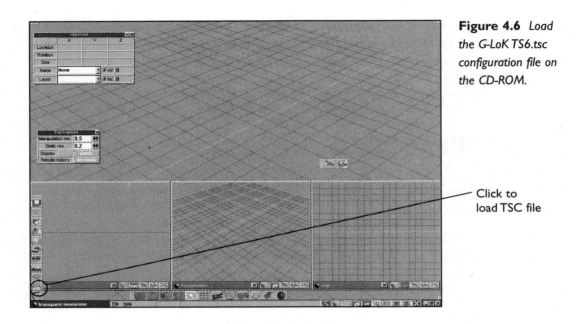

Figure 4.6 *Load the G-LoK TS6.tsc configuration file on the CD-ROM.*

Click to load TSC file

NOTE

In the **NURBS** tools group are Patch Edit icons that let you select what type of **NURBS** element you want to manipulate. In each figure in this section, I've included a small icon representation of the tool used to perform the operation discussed.

Step 1: Build the Body

To build the slogre's body, start by adding a NURBS sphere to the scene; you'll use this single object to create the entire body—and quite literally in record time. To do so, right-click on the NURBS Sphere icon (located in the toolbar at the bottom of the screen) to open its Options panel, and change the latitude to 6 and the longitude to 8. Your cursor will change to an arrow with a yellow primitive icon attached; just left-click once in the middle of the screen to create the sphere (see Figure 4.7). Multiple left-clicks will add more spheres, so just right-click to exit the creation mode.

In Figure 4.7, the Object Info panel displays the current number of faces present in the sphere—over 900! That's because NURBS are very high-density meshes that

3D Controls

The default configuration of trueSpace 6 has 3D controls active; these help you move, rotate, scale, and perform other modeling operations on your objects. I, however, think they clutter my workspace, so throughout this tutorial I have them turned off, except when building the foot using the Draw Panel tool (which requires that 3D controls be turned on). Turn these on and off by clicking File, Preferences, and unchecking the 3D Controls item.

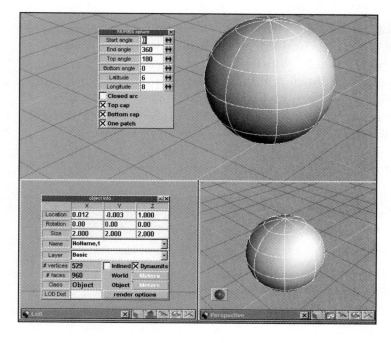

Figure 4.7
Add a NURBS sphere to the scene.

give a beautifully smooth end result. You can change the resolution of the NURBS objects simply by right-clicking on the Convert NURBS Patch to Polyhedron tool to bring up the Patch Options panel, and adjusting the Static Res number. Also, you can right-click the sphere to enter the NURBS modeling/deformation mode. In Figure 4.8, I have the resolution set to 0.3, which will leave the body of the slogre model with about 1100 polygons. The Manipulation Res variable will change the

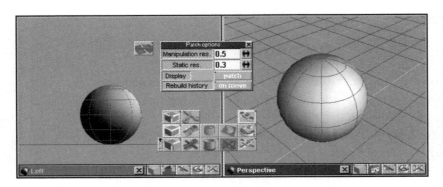

Figure 4.8 *Right-click the sphere to enter the NURBS modeling mode; right-click the Convert NURBS Patch to Polyhedron tool to adjust the resolution of the object.*

density of the displayed polygons as you model; just decrease this if you notice that modeling is slow and choppy.

When you right-click the sphere, another panel opens, containing a small group of NURBS modeling tools. Drag it by its control handle to move it out of the way, while at the same time keeping it handy. Notice that when you pass your cursor over the sphere (assuming you've right-clicked it and entered the modeling mode), the curves and vertices of the object become highlighted. The curves are called *NURBS isocurves,* and are simply pliable spline curves that intersect to form NURBS patches. A *patch* is sort of like one of the leather pentagons and hexagons that make up a soccer ball—as you manipulate the isocurves or vertices along them, the patches deform and hence you change the shape of your object.

Now that you're oriented, let's get to work on the slogre's body (remember to use the slogre sketches at the beginning of this chapter as a reference):

1. Start forming the belly of the slogre by rotating the sphere in a Left orthogonal view so the top is tilted forward slightly.

2. Select a vertical isocurve of the sphere, and drag it slightly downward. (Use the Move, Rotate, and Scale tools located in the NURBS tool group that popped up when you right-clicked on the sphere to move this curve.) Figure 4.9 shows my results.

NOTE

Modeling with **NURBS** may seem a little crazy at first, but in no time you'll be smooth and quick with it.

TIP

If you don't know how to use the basic object-manipulation functions of trueSpace, read the trueSpace tutorials on the **CD-ROM.**

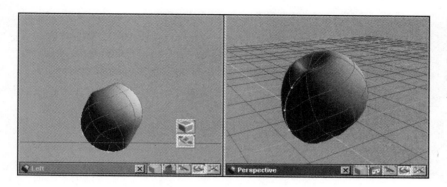

Figure 4.9 *Click and drag a vertical curve to begin forming the belly of the slogre.*

3. Activate the Patch Edit: Points tool to click on the vertex at the bottom of the sphere, and move it away slightly to form the tail (see Figure 4.10).

4. Use the Eye Rotate tool to rotate around to the back of the sphere. While holding down the Ctrl key, click two of the upper points of the sphere and scale them outward, forming the back and shoulders of the beast (see Figure 4.11).

5. Pinch in the sides at the same time by Ctrl+clicking a point on each side of the sphere and scaling them inward (see Figure 4.12).

TIP

Use the orthogonal views (Left, Front, Top, and so on) when modeling with NURBS to help align your modeling actions. Modeling in the Perspective view can cause confusion, particularly if you have 3D Controls turned off.

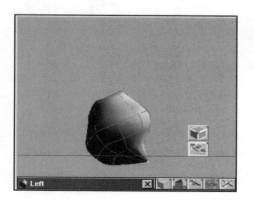

Figure 4.10 *Form the tail of the slogre by dragging the bottom vertex away.*

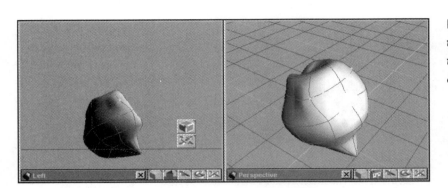

Figure 4.11 *Scale two points at the top to form the shoulders and back.*

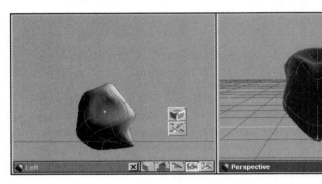

Figure 4.12 *Push in the sides of the sphere to give the body more definition.*

6. The top of the slogre character is adorned with a hump. Create this by dragging a single point upwards, as I did in Figure 4.13. Note that if you right-click this point, Control Vertex handles will appear, allowing you to further adjust the spline curve at this point.

NOTE

Working uniformly like this is important to symmetrical modeling; in this example, however, it's not critical because at the end you'll just be copying half of the slogre and pasting it to the other half.

7. This character has a bizarre, elongated head that protrudes from the hump. Start forming this by dragging the single end point of the sphere as I have done in Figure 4.14.

8. To continue creating the head, you need to increase the resolution of the sphere by increasing the amount of isocurves at the end. To do so, first click on the last curve at the end to highlight it, click the Refine Patch tool, and

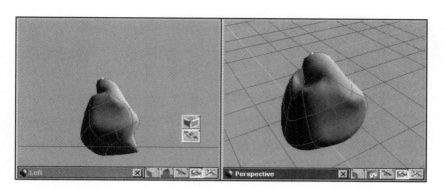

Figure 4.13 *Drag a single point at top to form the hump.*

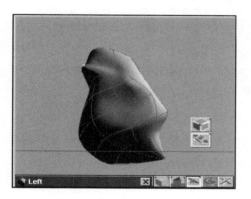

Figure 4.14 *Start forming the head by dragging the top end point of the sphere.*

click and drag along the length of the body (you'll see an orange curve, as shown in Figure 4.15). When you reach the spot where want to place the curve, release the mouse button. You can continue to add curves by left-clicking; for now, however, just right-click to deselect this tool.

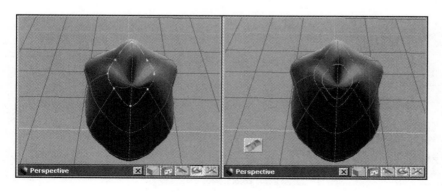

Figure 4.15 *Create a new isocurve on the head using the Refine Patch tool.*

> **TIP**
>
> If you're having trouble switching back and forth between operating on a single point or entire curve, just click the Object tool (white arrow), then right-click the **NURBS** object to re-enter the edit mode. Then just select the Patch Edit tool of choice to continue modeling.

9. Pinch in two points on either side of the newly created isocurve to further define the head. To do so, Ctrl+click one on each side, then scale them slightly (see Figure 4.16).

10. To increase the hump's definition, making it more pronounced, right-click one of the top points of the hump to bring up the control handles, and click and drag the handles to change the sharpness at that point (see Figure 4.17).

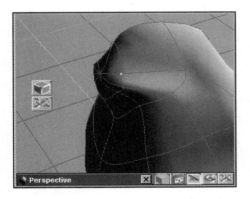

Figure 4.16
Pinch the head a bit to further define it.

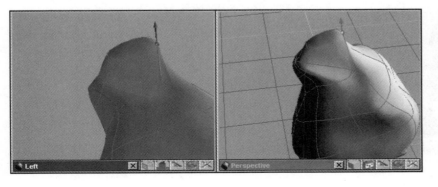

Figure 4.17
Sharpen the hump by adjusting the control handles of a point on top.

11. To extend the head even further, Ctrl+click both the last isocurve and the end point of the head and drag to stretch it. The results are shown in Figure 4.18 (I also rotated and scaled that last curve a bit).

12. Continue refining the head using the Refine Patch tool to create new curves, and move/rotate/scale them, as well as the end point, as I have done in Figure 4.19.

13. Once you're satisfied with the head, continue making small curve and point adjustments around the body in the same manner until the body is how you want it to be (see Figure 4.20). You don't have to go nuts adding isocurves; only a few make the body very smooth.

14. When finished, exit editing mode by clicking the Object tool.

15. Save this piece by clicking File, Save As, Object, and name it **body.cob**. (You'll need to recall it at the end so you can attach the other pieces.)

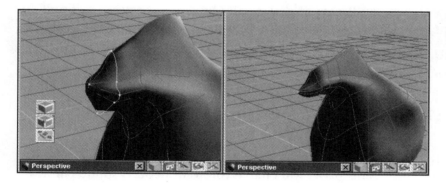

Figure 4.18 *Pull the end of the head out further.*

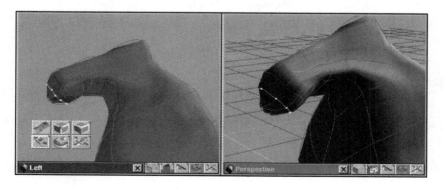

Figure 4.19 *Add and adjust more isocurves to continue refining the head.*

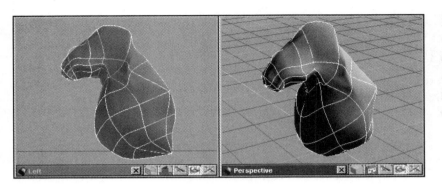

Figure 4.20

Continue manipulating the rest of the body's curves and points to reach the shape you desire.

Step 2: Build the Leg

You'll build this next piece using the Draw Panel tool to explore some other NURBS modeling techniques that trueSpace has to offer. Draw Panel enables you to draw a simple spline curve and then extrude it—only in this case, the extrusion becomes a NURBS object. You'll start by making the basic foot pattern, and pull the entire leg right out of it!

1. To use the Draw Panel tool, you must turn on 3D Controls in the Preferences panel. To do so, choose File, Preferences, and select the 3D Controls option in the dialog box that appears (see Figure 4.21).

2. Click on the Draw Panel tool, located in the toolbar at the bottom of the screen.

3. To add a panel to the screen, click and drag in the main Perspective view as I have in Figure 4.22. This panel will enable you to draw a 2D spline curve and extrude it. Notice that when you add the panel, an entire suite of tools pops up as well; these offer a multitude of ways in which you can draw curves on the panel.

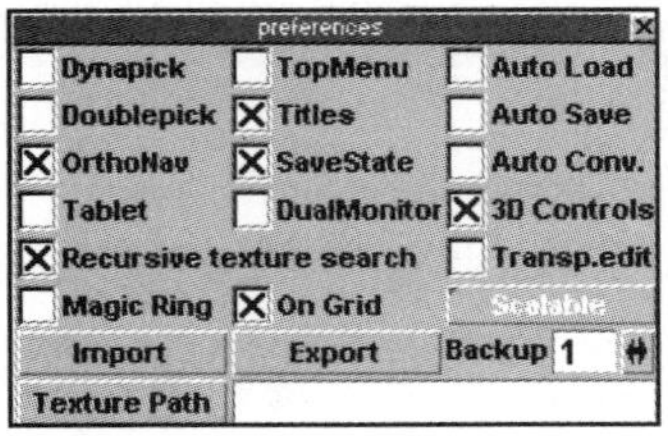

Figure 4.21

Enable the 3D Controls option for this next exercise.

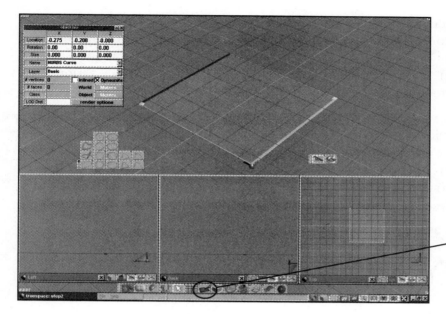

Figure 4.22 *Click on the Draw Panel tool and add a panel to the scene.*

The Draw Panel tool

4. Choose the Add Curve tool and create a foot-shaped pattern, as shown in Figure 4.23; when you reach the start point of the curve, right-click to close the shape. (The shape of the foot doesn't have to be perfect; you'll adjust it in the next step.)

NOTE

You can switch to a top orthogonal view above the panel by clicking one of the panel's corner points.

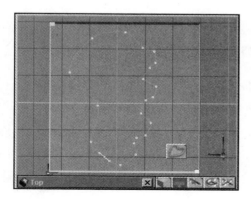

Figure 4.23 *Add a foot-shaped pattern to the panel using the Add Curve tool. Use the slogre sketch as a reference.*

5. Once the general shape has been created, click on any of the curve points to display its control handles, and use these handles to adjust the shape of the curve at that point—as well as to drag those points to new locations (see Figure 4.24). You can also add and delete points using any of the various vertex-edit tools that accompany this operation.

6. When you're satisfied with your shape, right-click anywhere outside the panel to exit, or click the Object tool. Another small set of tools appears; these enable you to extrude your shape. Click the Extrude tool to display a double-ended control handle, perpendicular to the face of your shape, and then click and drag on the endpoint of one handle to extrude the base of the foot slightly as I have done in Figure 4.25.

7. When the base of your foot is created, right-click to exit extrusion mode. The object you just created is now a modifiable NURBS object, just like the slogre's body you created earlier. The only difference here is that both ends are open and faceless (don't worry about that for now; you'll cap the bottom

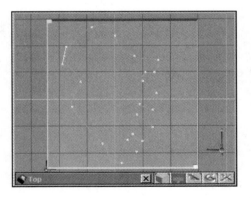

Figure 4.24 *Adjust the shape of the foot using the control handles of the points.*

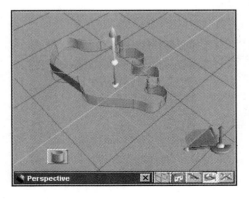

Figure 4.25 *Use the Extrude tool to sweep the face of the foot into 3D.*

later). To begin shaping the foot, use the Refine Patch tool to add an isocurve as you did with the slogre's body. In Figure 4.26, I created a couple new curves and scaled them to form the foot.

8. For each time you want to extrude your shape vertically, remember to first create an isocurve, and then pull the last curve upward. When the general shape of the foot is done, use the Delete Row of Points tool (opposite the Refine Patch tool) to remove unnecessary curves. Remember, the more curves you have, the higher the number of polygons in the resultant model. Figure 4.27 shows my slogre foot after I killed several superfluous curves.

9. When you're satisfied with the foot, right-click the last, top curve to edit the points along the edge. Move these points into a circular ankle shape. Then, continue adding isocurves and extruding the ankle portion of the leg (see Figure 4.28).

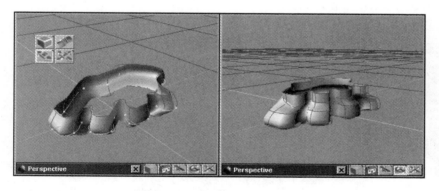

Figure 4.26 *Add new isocurves to the foot object and move and scale them to shape it.*

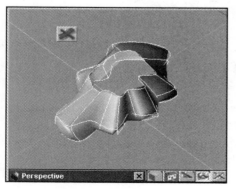

Figure 4.27
Remove unnecessary curves using the Delete Row of Points tool.

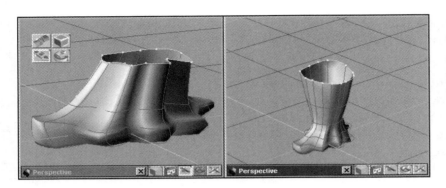

Figure 4.28 *Move the points at the top into a circular shape for the leg, and continue extruding.*

10. Continue extruding the rest of the leg, forming a calf muscle and thigh by scaling and shifting the isocurves at those locations. If the points from the foot made indentations along the leg at any point, simply select the individual points and reposition them. The NURBS properties of the object make things sweet and smooth (see Figure 4.29).

11. When you're finished extruding the leg and are satisfied, save this object as **leg.cob** so you can retrieve it later.

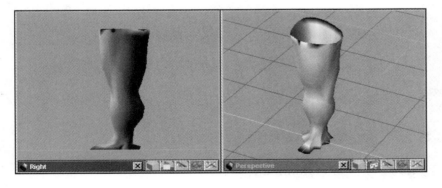

Figure 4.29 *Continue pulling out the rest of the leg, making adjustments to form the calf and thigh.*

Step 3: Build the Arm

You could create the arm just as you did the leg, but the arm is a lot more complicated—especially around the hand. For this operation, then, it's best to use plain old point editing to build and sweep the arm. This doesn't mean a whole lot as far as the resulting model is concerned; in fact, the polygon count will be much lower. The arm will suffer in its organic-ness, however, because point editing has nothing on NURBS objects when it comes to creating realistic organic shapes. When you bring the model into 3D Studio Max and smooth it out, however, you really won't be able to tell the difference. I think the most noticeable difference between point-edit modeling and NURBS modeling is the speed. In the time it will take to model this one arm, I could finish the body and leg portions twice over!

1. Let's start with the wrist area of the slogre. If you refer to the slogre sketch, you'll notice that he's wearing slave-like bands with sharp, pointed studs. Create a band by adding a 10-sided cylinder primitive to the scene and scaling it down to size, as shown in Figure 4.30. (The cylinder primitive is also located in the toolbar at the bottom of the screen.)

2. To create the pointed studs, first right-click the cylinder to enter point-edit mode. (This is the same as NURBS mode, but without the NURBS isocurve functionality.)

3. Using the Point Edit: Faces tool, click on a face to select it, and pull it quickly to a tip using the Tip tool. Repeat this process for every other face (see Figure 4.31).

4. The tips of the spikes are too long—use the Point Edit: Vertices tool to select each tip's point while you hold down the Ctrl key. When all points are selected, scale them down to size (see Figure 4.32).

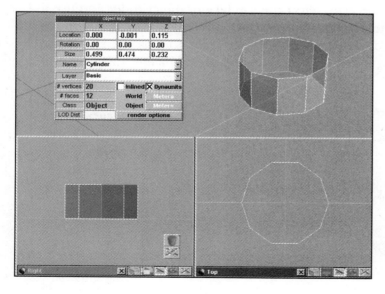

Figure 4.30

Start the arm off with a 10-sided cylinder primitive.

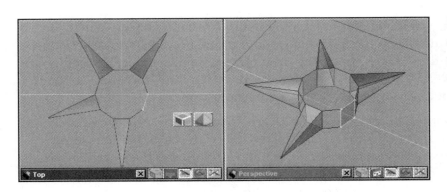

Figure 4.31 *Select every other face of the cylinder and apply the Tip tool.*

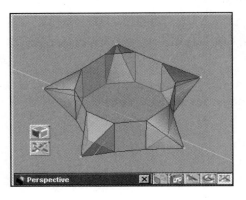

Figure 4.32 *Select all the tips and scale them down.*

5. To create the rest of the arm, select the top face of the cylinder and use the Sweep tool to extrude it. Continue sweeping this face, scaling each time, until you get a general shape of the arm. Remember to use the slogre sketch as a guide—his arms are massive with huge, bulging biceps. Just like mine.

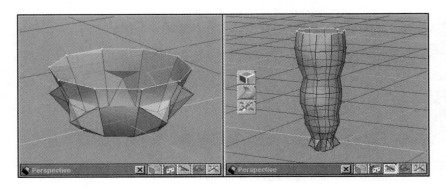

Figure 4.33 *Use the Sweep tool repeatedly to extrude the top face of the cylinder into the entire arm.*

6. Make minor adjustments to the arm by selecting a face or multiple faces (by holding down Ctrl and clicking) and moving/scaling them appropriately. In Figure 4.34, I'm selecting a patch of the bicep area and augmenting it.

7. Now for the hand—just as you did with the arm, select the face on the other side of the cuff and sweep it several times, adjusting the width to conform to a hand shape as I have done in Figure 4.35.

8. Select a pad of faces on the inside of the hand and move, rotate, and/or scale them to make a palm (see Figure 4.36).

9. When the palm portion of your hand is complete, start adding fingers by first breaking the end face into four smaller sections. To do so, use the Add Edges tool (part of the tool group that pops up when you enter point-edit mode) to create an edge between opposite vertices on the face (see Figure 4.37).

10. The fingers can't just be extruded from these new faces you've just created. Instead, select each face and apply the Bevel tool (Figure 4.38).

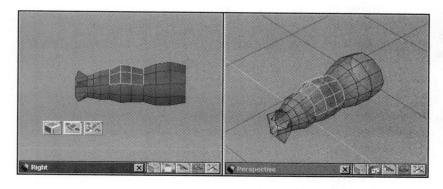

Figure 4.34
Enhance the muscles of the arm by selecting faces and moving or scaling them to size.

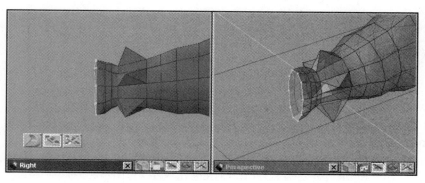

Figure 4.35 *Begin sweeping the hand on the other side of the cuff.*

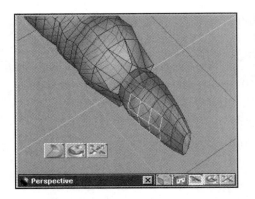

Figure 4.36 *Form the palm of the hand by manipulating a small set of faces.*

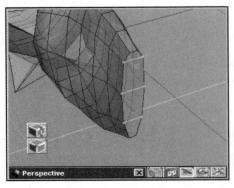

Figure 4.37 *Start the fingers by creating new edges at the end of the palm.*

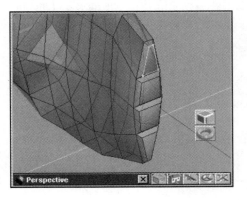

Figure 4.38 *Bevel the new faces so you can add the fingers.*

11. With the new bevels in place, the fingers can be pulled out of them.
    However, the faces are too square for my standards—use the Add Vertex tool
    to add four new vertices to the edges of each face, and move each new vertex
    away from the center to round it out. When you're finished with each face,
    create the fingers by using the Sweep tool on each (see Figure 4.39).

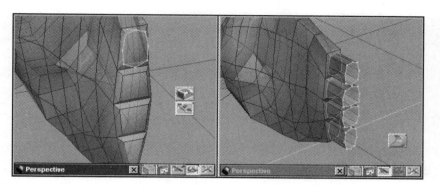

Figure 4.39 *Add vertices to the square faces and round them out. Sweep them to start the fingers.*

12. Continue sweeping the faces of each finger, scaling them as you get closer to the tip. In Figure 4.40, I also moved the faces away from each other so that from a short distance, a player can discern each individual finger.

13. To form the long, slashing nails that embellish your behemoth, add a small edge at the tip of each finger, effectively creating a triangular face, and use the Tip tool to pull that out. Then, grab the tip and pull it out further—the nails should be long, according to the sketch, about the length of the entire hand (see Figure 4.41).

14. Form the thumb the same way you created the fingers in steps 11, 12, and 13—though there's no need to bevel the first face. Make the thumb curve outward slightly so it can hold the RF-9 plasma gun (see Figure 4.42).

That's it for the arm. Notice that this took much longer than the other body parts, but the tradeoff is in the face count–to-smoothness ratio. In Figure 4.43, my arm model shows only 341 faces, even with all of the minute detail, whereas the leg object was more than 600; that said, the leg looks much more organic and realistic

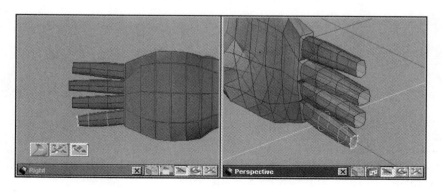

Figure 4.40 *Continue sweeping the faces to form the fingers.*

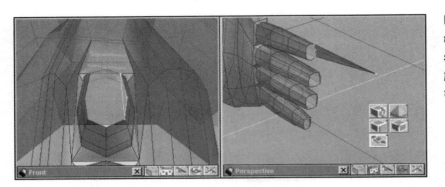

Figure 4.41 *Form the nails by adding small edges to the fingertips and tipping them.*

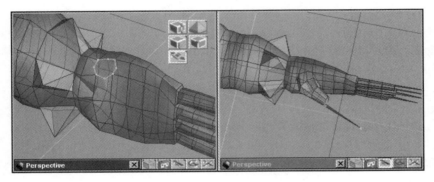

Figure 4.42 *Create the thumb using the same steps as you did with the other fingers.*

than this arm. (You'll fix the choppiness in 3D Studio using a Smooth modifier—more on that in Chapter 6, " U-V Mapping the Slogre with DeepUV," when you import the slogre model and prepare to unwrap the U-V coordinates.) For now, save this object as **arm.cob**.

Step 4: Complete the Model (Well, Half of It)

Now it's time to bring the fruits of your labor together into a working slogre model. There are a number of ways to finish up a model, but I think the best way to handle this one is to create only half of it since this beast is basically symmetrical. If you were to union the legs and arms to both sides of the object and then optimize it in 3D Studio Max, however, the mesh would be smooth but the polygons would be a jumbled mess—that is, the optimization process in Max would make the mesh uneven throughout the character's body. Instead, let's union one arm and one leg to the body, slice the sucker in half, and let Max take care of the rest, since its suite of optimization tools is far more advanced.

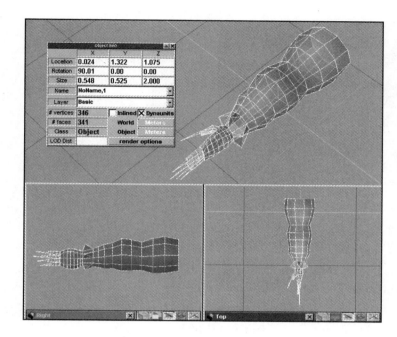

Figure 4.43 *The completed arm. Notice the low polygon count and high detail, but sacrifice in smoothness.*

To load into one scene the three separate body components that you created in previous sections, start a new scene and choose File, Load, Object to load each component individually. (If you like, you can load my components instead of the ones you created by choosing the **arm.cob**, **leg.cob**, and **body.cob** files from the Chapter 4 Data section on the CD-ROM.) Once these components are loaded, the scene should consist of two NURBS objects (the body and leg) and a regular polyhedron object (the arm). Your job is to align the ends of the appendages to the body and Boolean Union them together. First, however, you need to resize the body parts and adjust the NURBS resolution.

1. Click on the body object to select it, and then right-click on the NURBS Patch to Polyhedron tool to bring up the Patch Options panel. I have the Static Res set to 0.3, which will result in the body object having just over 1,100 faces. Click on the Patch to Polyhedron tool to permanently convert the body to a regular mesh (see Figure 4.44).

TIP
When you convert a **NURBS** object to a regular polygon, the operation *is not undoable!* Be sure to save your work before performing this action!

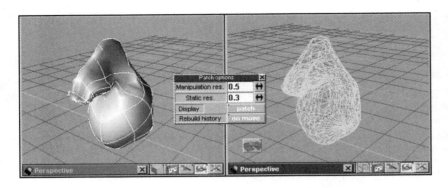

Figure 4.44 *Use the Convert Patch to Polyhedron tool to turn the NURBS object into an ordinary mesh.*

2. Repeat step 1 for the leg object, only set its Static Res to 0.2. This will make it contain just over 600 polygons.

3. After the leg object is converted, scale it evenly so its proportion is accurate when placed next to the slogre's body, and rotate it into position where it should protrude.

4. Repeat step 3 for the arm object (it doesn't need to be converted; you built it from an existing polyhedron mesh). Figure 4.45 shows my arrangement.

5. Make sure the arm and leg objects extend fully into the body of the slogre, or you'll get holes in the final mesh. To do so, rotate around the body and zoom in close to be sure they're all the way in. (If you have your rendering environment set to Solid mode you can see the mesh move in and out of one another much more easily.)

6. When you're satisfied that the appendages are, indeed, all the way in, save your scene, and use the Object Union tool to fuse the three body parts together.

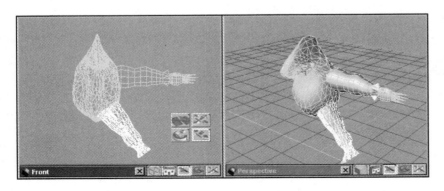

Figure 4.45 *Convert the NURBS leg, and scale and position it—and the arm—on the body.*

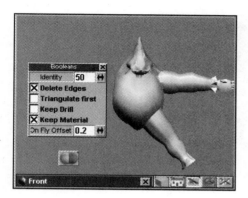

Figure 4.46 *Fuse the arm and leg to the body using the Object Union tool.*

> **NOTE**
>
> Should trueSpace proclaim that an error has occurred, right-click on the Object Union tool to bring up a Booleans options panel (see Figure 4.46). In this panel, you can adjust the Identity value and try the union operation again. This value represents a distance in 1/100ths of a millimeter between near coincident vertices—that is, vertices that happen to be on top of one another. Adjusting this value will tell trueSpace to recalculate the operation and try to avoid invalid geometric fusion.

7. If the union operation was successful, you should have one solid, goofy-looking mesh with a single arm and leg sticking out of it; the next step is to split the slogre's body in half. To begin, create a cube primitive in the scene and scale it so it's much bigger than the slogre itself.

8. Position the cube so it intersects the half of the body that has no arm or leg (see Figure 4.47). Be sure that the edge of the cube is as close as possible to the middle seam of the body.

9. Select the slogre mesh, click the Object Subtraction tool, and click the cube. You should end up with a half mesh.

> **NOTE**
>
> If trueSpace issued a warning, right-click the tool and change the Identity value a bit, and then try again.

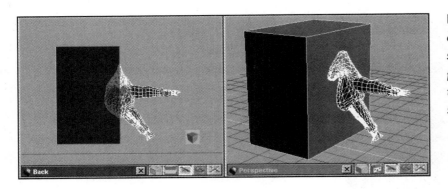

Figure 4.47 *Add a cube primitive to the scene, scale it, and position it so it covers the entire half of the slogre's mesh.*

10. Rotate around to the foot. When you created the leg, the foot was extruded from a spline curve and had no end cap; notice that in solid-render mode, it appears open. To fix this, right-click on the mesh to enter point-edit mode, choose the Point Edit: Add Face tool, and click on this open area to close it up (see Figure 4.48).

11. Rotate around to the flat side of the slogre, where it was cut; as a result of the Boolean operation, there's a solid face there. For you to be able to fuse a copy of the finished side of the slogre to the other side, the slogre mesh needs to be a hollow object. To make it so, select the Point Edit: Delete Face tool and click once on the abovementioned flat area to remove it (see Figure 4.49). As soon as you delete the face, right-click to deselect the Delete Face tool.

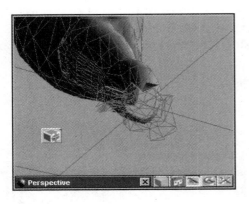

Figure 4.48
Subtract the cube object from the slogre, and cap the hole on the foot using the Add Face tool.

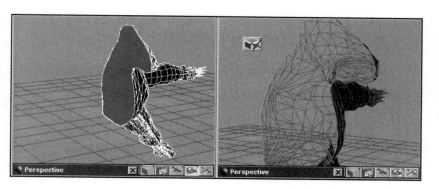

Export the Mesh

You're finished with your half-shell slogre mesh and are ready to save it as an STL file and bring it over to Max for completion and U-V mapping, just as you did with the RF-9 plasma gun. To do so, choose File, Save As, Object; from the Save As Type list, select Stereolithography (*.STL). To finalize the slogre mesh and continue mapping, move on to Chapter 6.

Summary

In this chapter you learned how to create a character mesh object using new and powerful NURBS modeling techniques that allow your creation to look very realistic, with a more natural, organic feel. There are pros and cons to using NURBS; on the positive side the resulting model can be created in only a fraction of the time it would take using older modeling techniques such as shaping with primitives and point editing. The negative side is the resulting polygon count, which, for now, can be fairly high. However, with the steadily evolving computing technology, the need to be keenly aware of polygon counts in models will no doubt diminish.

PART TWO

Unwrapping the UVs with DeepUV

CHAPTER 5

U-V Mapping the RF-9 Plasma Gun with DeepUV

Every 3D model you create consists of a finite set of vertices, or points, defined in 3D space by X, Y, and Z Cartesian coordinates. These points are connected by lines, or edges, which then define the faces of the object, giving the object the appearance of a solid surface. When you finish creating a model, you have a choice: Either paint the faces with plain, boring colors (which any 3D modeling program can do using simple paint tools), or *texture* the model by utilizing a special set of points called *U-V coordinates*.

When you paint the faces of a mesh object, all you're doing is telling the vertices what colors to become, and to fill in the spaces between them with a blend of their neighboring vertices' colors. If you want to wrap a texture, or *skin*, around the object, you must use U-V coordinates to align it properly so it wraps without smearing, tearing, or generally looking bizarre. All 3D models are created with a default set of these U-V coordinates, which are simply invisible duplicates of the model's mesh vertices. Your modeling program of choice will use these U-V coordinates to dictate how a texture map should be applied to the surface.

The way this process works is, you create a 3D object, unwrap *only the U-Vs*, lay them out flat on a blank bitmap surface, and arrange them in a way that makes the texture creation process easy. Then you paint the texture according to the newly adjusted U-V map, and finally apply the texture map to the model. Sound confusing? It really isn't!

In this chapter, you will

- Enter the realm of texture-coordinate manipulation with DeepUV.
- Learn to use rudimentary projection techniques to unfold complex 3D texture coordinates.
- Practice by example unfolding the texture coordinates of a simple widget object.
- U-V map the texture coordinates of the RF-9, step-by-step, in preparation for its texturing.

TIP

If you're totally new to this U-V stuff, see Appendix A, "A 3D Modeling Primer," for more detailed information on the basics of U-V coordinates.

This chapter assumes you've finished creating your model from Chapter 3, "Modeling the RF-9 Plasma Gun with trueSpace 6," and are moving along the logical route of game-object creation, as shown in Figure 5.1. This chapter represents the next step in creating a 3D game asset: manipulating the U-V coordinates of your mesh object in preparation for texturing.

Installing the Software

Included in the Programs section on the CD-ROM is a demo version of DeepUV (although the demo has a 30-day expiration period, it does feature all of the functionality of the full version). If you haven't done so already, go ahead and install it. When you do, make sure the plug-in for 3D Studio Max is installed as well. The option for installing the plug-in for Max is part of the installation routine.

> **NOTE**
>
> Depending upon your video card and driver, you may need to adjust a setting in DeepUV for it to work properly. Do this by clicking File, Preferences, and in the Rendering tab, select the mode you want DeepUV to use. I have a GeForce 3 card, and have both 3D and 2D rendering set to Software. This allows DeepUV to rely directly on my video card's driver software. Only experiment with these settings if you're having graphics problems when running this program.

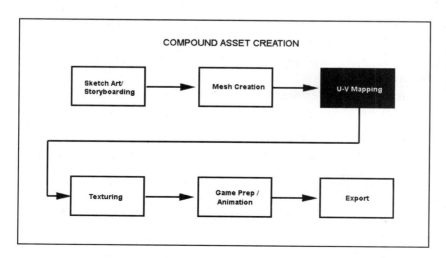

Figure 5.1 *This phase in the sequence of 3D game-object creation.*

TIP

If you have trouble installing the demo, or need software patches or other support, visit http://www.righthemisphere.com.

Introduction to DeepUV 1.0

The great thing about the U-V coordinates of an object is that you can move them around and position them so that your texture will align itself nicely and look great during render time. The downside is, it's nearly impossible to manually move the U-Vs around so your texture fits correctly. That's why the company Right Hemisphere has developed specialized software, DeepUV, to aid in manipulating the U-Vs to your liking.

On the surface, DeepUV is a very simple, easy-to-use program (what it does behind the scenes is a different story). It presents you with a modest set of tools to analyze small parts (or the entirety) of your mesh object's U-V coordinates, and to unfold them flat on a texture map's surface—without affecting the actual shape of your 3D mesh. These tools allow you to view your U-Vs *planarly, cylindrically, spherically, or polarly*. Using primarily the first three of these techniques, you can easily and quickly unwrap any object's texture coordinates, no matter what shape it has.

Confused? Pretend that DeepUV has a specialized camera that you can position around your 3D model. You tell DeepUV what technique—planar, cylindrical, spherical, or polar—the camera should use to view the texture coordinates of the area in question; the camera then displays whatever it's looking at only as a 2D unwrapped map. When you specify a technique other than planar, such as cylindrical, the camera, all-at-once, views the entire selection in a cylindrical fashion, and displays what it sees as a flattened 2D map.

For instance, suppose you're trying to unwrap the U-Vs of the forearm of a character model. You can tell DeepUV to look at the arm *cylindrically*, since the forearm has that general shape, and the camera simultaneously wraps itself around the entire forearm to display the UVs nice and flat.

Still confused? Don't worry. The best way to see all of this is by example.

Example: Unwrap the Widget

Before you jump into unwrapping the RF-9 plasma gun (or whatever cool object you've created), let me give you a quick example that uses the three most common U-V unwrapping techniques in DeepUV: planar, cylindrical, and spherical.

Start by firing up DeepUV. When the program starts, it displays a blank interface, with a Tools box and a Command Panel to the right (see Figure 5.2). Notice that there are only a few tools available; they're all you'll need to get the job done. Notice also that DeepUV's tools appear to be very similar to Photoshop's; as it happens, they work the same way. I'll go over these and the other features as we use them.

For this example, I used trueSpace to create a simple object (I'm calling it a widget) that contains most of the shapes you'll encounter when unwrapping. Because DeepUV only opens 3D Studio Max (.3ds), Lightwave (.lwo), and Wavefront (.obj) file formats, I saved it as **widget.3ds** in the Chapter 5 Data section on the CD-ROM. Go ahead and open it (click File, Open); you should see the screen that appears in Figure 5.3.

Figure 5.2 *The default DeepUV 1.0 interface.*

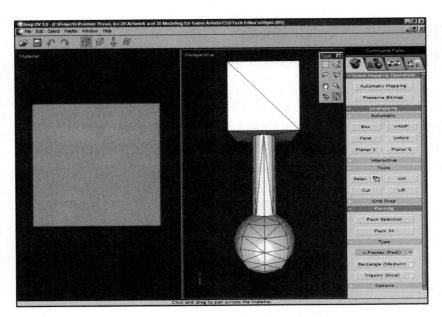

Figure 5.3 *Open the **widget.3ds** file on the CD-ROM.*

Notice that the screen splits into two halves. On the left is the Material screen, which represents your U-V coordinates as they will eventually be laid out flat and bounded by the gray square in the middle. The gray square will contain the final layout of the texture-mapping coordinates, which you will then export to a painting program to begin your texturing. On the right is the Perspective view of the widget, which allows you to rotate your model in 3D space and select coordinates for unwrapping. Notice that the Mapping tab under the Command Panel has expanded to offer you a suite of options for unwrapping your object.

Click and drag the widget; notice that it rotates around, letting you view it from any angle. The blue lines of the object represent the portions that are not selected, whereas red signifies an active selection. Also notice that there appears to be a clumpy, blue dot on the upper-left hand of the corner of the Material map—this is the unorganized, jumbled mess of U-V coordinates you need to sort through.

Automatic Mapping

Your objective is to lay out the U-V coordinates within the Material area so that painting a texture map in a paint program will be a snap. DeepUV offers an

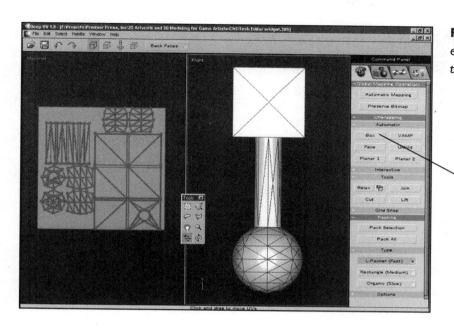

Figure 5.4 *Select everything and click the Box button.*

The Box button

Automatic Mapping feature, which unwraps your selection based on several mapping techniques and tries to figure out what makes the most sense. To use it, start by pressing Ctrl+A to select all the points of the mesh. (Note that the widget becomes entirely red, indicating that all texture coordinates have been selected.) Then, under the Automatic section of the Mapping panel, click Box. In a few short seconds, you should see something like what's shown in Figure 5.4.

As plausible as automatic mapping may seem, it almost never unwraps things the way you want it to—although it didn't work too badly in this case. You can clearly see in the Material screen at the left that the U-V coordinates have been neatly unwrapped, and then packed into the gray square. The cube portion of the widget is nicely unfolded (that's because you chose the Box unwrapping method), and the cylinder portion (laid out in the upper-left corner) has been flattened, but the sphere portion got chopped up a bit—the result of the Box procedure doing its best to unfold a sphere like a box.

From here, you could simply export the map for texturing, but it would be difficult to do a decent texture for the sphere portion because it's spread all over the place. Instead, click Edit, Undo to undo the mapping operation so you can do it manually.

Manual Mapping: Isolate and Unfold

Just as you did when Point Edit modeling in trueSpace, you need to select coordinates using one of DeepUV's selection tools in order to map it manually. Let's start with the box at the top of the widget (it'll be the easiest to map), followed by the cylinder, and lastly the sphere:

1. In the widget's Perspective view screen, right-click to open the View menu.

2. Select View, Front to reveal an orthogonal view of the object, as shown in Figure 5.5.

3. Click on the Rectangular Selection tool (the first tool in the Tools group, as shown in Figure 5.6).

4. Notice the four selection-mode options near the top-left of the screen; each one represents a different way of making U-V selections on your object. Click on the Point Selection Mode option so you can select individual coordinates. (The other modes let you select in groups if your object has subobjects and the like, which yours doesn't.)

5. Enable the Back Faces option, to the right of the selection-mode buttons. This allows you to make selections that include all points, front and back, in the box.

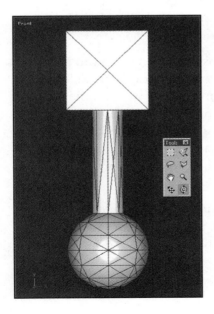

Figure 5.5

View the object with the Front view.

6. Click to the left and slightly above the cube, and drag a rectangular selection around the cube portion of the widget. The selected area becomes red; because the points contained at the end of the cylinder are selected as well, the red fades to blue towards its other end. This simply indicates that your selection is attached to another part of the widget (see Figure 5.6).

7. With the cube portion selected, it's time to excise its U-Vs from the rest of the object. Under the Tools section of the Mapping panel, click Cut. This isolates your selection, so you can proceed with unfolding it.

8. Because the shape you want to unfold is a cube, click the Box button under the Mapping panel's Automatic section. Your selection will neatly unfold, as shown in Figure 5.7. Notice that one side of the flattened cube has a hole in it; that's where the cylinder portion of the widget attaches.

NOTE

It won't matter that your selection boundary invades the cylinder because the cylinder contains no selectable points in there—except for the cylinder's end (more on that in a moment).

NOTE

None of what we're doing has anything to do with the mesh object's vertices, only the U-V coordinates.

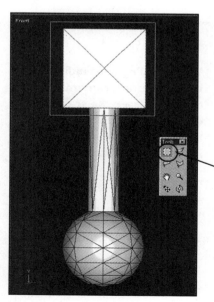

Figure 5.6 *Use the Rectangular Selection tool to select all points of the cube end of the widget.*

The Rectangular Selection tool

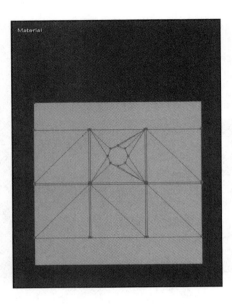

Figure 5.7 *Cut the selection away from the rest and click the Box button.*

9. As it stands, the cube's U-Vs consume too much space on the Material map—space that you need for the cylinder and sphere portions of the widget. To scale the cube down, you can press Ctrl+T to use the Free Transform tool, or click Edit, Transform, Scale By, . . . and scale the cube by whatever percentage will shrink it adequately (I scaled by 50 percent).

10. Select the Move tool and move the selection to the upper-right corner, as shown in Figure 5.8. (You can scale and move the cube however you want, as long as the U-Vs stay within the gray area.)

> **TIP**
>
> **When scaling your individual U-V selections, remember that the larger the scale, the more detail you will be able to have in the texture map for that particular area.**

11. Moving on to the cylinder portion of the widget, use the Rectangular Selection tool to select the cylinder, going slightly over the edges into the cube and sphere.

12. Click the Cut button in the Tools section of the Mapping panel to separate the selection from the other U-Vs.

13. Because the shape you want to unfold is a cylinder, click the Cylinder button in the Interactive section of the Mapping panel.

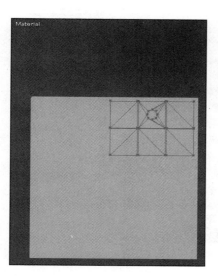

Figure 5.8 *Scale and move the U-V selection to fit within the texture map and allow room for the rest of the widget's U-Vs.*

14. In the same area of the Mapping panel, click the Selection button to center the mapping on your selection. You should end up with an unfolded selection as I have in Figure 5.9.

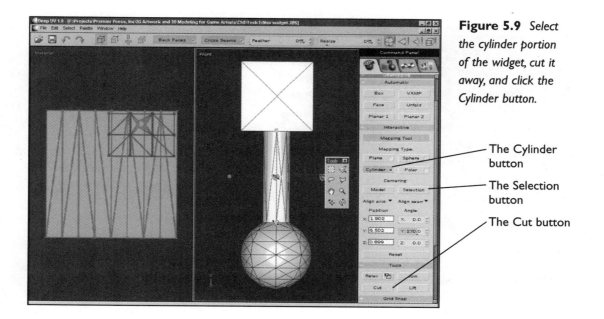

Figure 5.9 *Select the cylinder portion of the widget, cut it away, and click the Cylinder button.*

— The Cylinder button

— The Selection button

— The Cut button

NOTE

When you use the Interactive options to map a selection, you'll notice little multicolored gadgets that hover around the selection. These represent the X, Y, and Z (or, more appropriately, U, V, and W) axes of the mapping technique. You can change the way the mapping technique observes your model's U-Vs by clicking and dragging them—this creates the same effect as rotating the camera around your model. This enables you to position the unwrapping technique so that it unwraps weird- or odd-shaped areas more effectively, and allows you to align and hide texture seams. I'll discuss that in more detail later, particularly when I cover unwrapping the slogre model.

15. With the cylinder area unwrapped, scale and position it so it fits on the map, just as you did in steps 9 and 10 (see Figure 5.10).

16. Now for the sphere. As with the cube and the cylinder, use the Rectangular Selection tool to select the sphere.

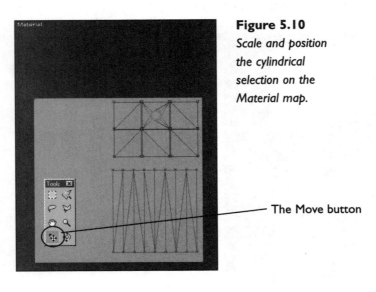

Figure 5.10
Scale and position the cylindrical selection on the Material map.

The Move button

17. Click the Cut button in the Tools section of the Mapping panel.

18. In the Interactive section of the Mapping panel, click the Sphere button.

19. In the same section of the Mapping panel, click the Selection button to center the mapping technique on the selection.

20. Scale and move your newly unfolded U-Vs; the result is shown in Figure 5.11.

That's it! You've successfully unwrapped and nicely aligned the U-Vs for the widget object. From here, you'd typically export the map to a program such as Deep Paint 3D and begin texturing; alternatively, you can send the updated U-V coordinate arrangement to a program like 3D Studio Max, which is what you'll do for the RF-9 plasma gun.

To give you a better understanding of where this operation goes from here, I exported this U-V arrangement to Deep Paint 3D and Photoshop (see Chapter 11 for detailed information on exporting and painting texture maps) and painted a texture on it, using the U-V lines as a guide. Then I placed the texture map back onto the widget model as shown in Figure 5.12.

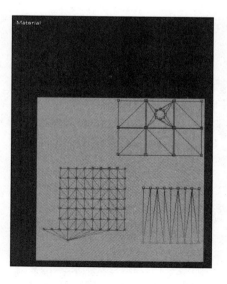

Figure 5.11 *Select and unfold the sphere portion, then scale and move it so it fits on the Material map.*

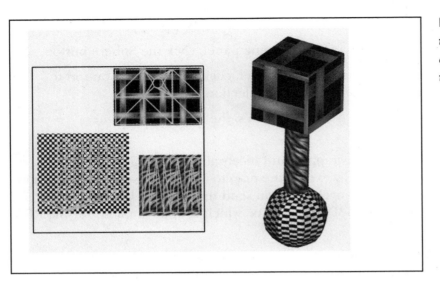

Figure 5.12 *Using the new U-V map to add a skin texture to the widget.*

Mapping the RF-9

Ah, the section you've been waiting for! I hope the previous section helped acquaint you with DeepUV. I didn't touch on every aspect of the program, but I think it was enough to get your feet wet and help you to understand what's involved with texture mapping. The RF-9 is a bit more complicated, so you'll have to isolate and unpack it with more finesse.

Preparing the Model for Texturing

Before you dive into unwrapping and texturing the RF-9, you need to import the STL version of the weapon you created in Chapter 3, check it for problems, optimize it, and map it. (If you don't have this file, you can find it in the Chapter 5 Data section on the CD-ROM; it's named **RF9.stl**.) Instead of using DeepUV to do this, however, you'll use 3D Studio Max.

NOTE

If you don't have 3D Studio Max installed on your machine, you'll be glad to know that the CD that comes with this book includes a demo version, located in the Programs section. Install it, as well as the DeepUV plug-ins that come with the DeepUV demo.

Import the STL

To import the STL file into 3D Studio Max, do the following:

1. Start the program.

2. Click File, Import.

3. Select StereoLitho (.STL) from the Files of Type drop-down list.

4. Browse for the **RF9.stl** file (or whatever you named your model), and click Open.

5. The Import STL File dialog box opens, with various default settings selected. Click on the Quick Weld option (see Figure 5.13).

6. Click OK when you're ready for 3D Studio Max to do its job.

You should now have successfully imported the model into Max.

> **NOTE**
>
> The Import STL File dialog box's default settings allow the program to sniff out any errors such as duplicate vertices, open faces, and the like, and fix them on-the-fly.

> **TIP**
>
> If you're new to 3D Studio Max, or need some guidance using it, see the 3D Studio Max tutorials on the CD-ROM that accompanies this book.

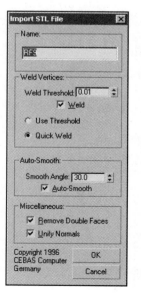

Figure 5.13
Importing the **RF9.stl** *file in 3D Studio Max.*

Apply the STL Check Modifier

Even though the STL Import feature did its best to check your model for problems, you need to further verify that the model is clean by using the STL Check modifier. (If the model does contain errors, such as having holes and whatnot, it may cause DeepUV or the game's engine to crash.)

To use the STL Check modifier, do the following:

1. Click once on the RF-9 to make sure it's selected, then click on the Modifiers tab at the top-right of the screen.

2. Pull down the modifier list and click on STL Check (see Figure 5.14).

3. When the STL Check modifier has been added to the modifier stack, you'll see a panel below it displaying the modifier's options. By default, the modifier will check everything possible within your object, which is fine. To complete the check operation, click the Check button. In a flash the program does its job, and any errors are reported in the Status location (see Figure 5.15). In addition, if any errors are detected, they will show up in red on your mesh object.

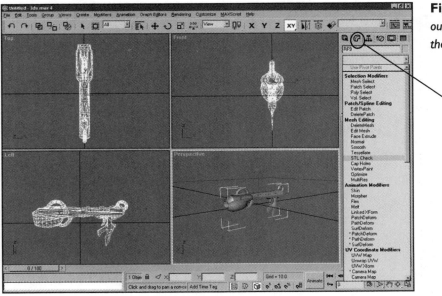

Figure 5.14 *Pick out STL Check from the modifier list.*

The Modifiers tab

Figure 5.15

Applying the STL Check modifier to detect errors in the mesh.

> **NOTE**
>
> If, after running STL Check, you discover that your mesh has problems, you must return to trueSpace (or use 3D Studio Max) and clean up your model. If the model is clean but STL Check still detects a problem, re-import the STL file and adjust some of the options in the STL Import dialog box to see if that fixes the problem.

4. If all goes well (and it did for mine), you should have no errors; go ahead and save your scene as a MAX file by clicking File, Save.

Run a Polygon Check

Notice that since you imported the RF-9 into 3D Studio Max, its mesh no longer appears nice and clean. In fact, there are new lines added all over the place! This is the result of the *triangulation* I mentioned in Chapter 3. When the model is triangulated, all of its faces are broken down into constituent triangles that represent the elementary faces (three-sided polygons) of the model. This effectively doubles, if not triples, the polygon count, but is necessary because all 3D objects must be processed at the triangular level.

To determine just how many polygons your model now has, right-click on it to open the Transform menu, and select Properties. The Object Properties dialog box opens. It relays a number of details about the model, including the total vertices and faces (see the top-left portion of the dialog box). My model chimes in at more than 1,300, which could be better, but will work just fine in a game's engine.

Besides, when it comes time for final preparation of your model for use in a game (see Chapter 13), you'll generate several different Levels of Detail (LOD's) for the model, so its polygonal count drops dynamically with distance from other players.

Gone are the days of the slow computer, when you needed to pay attention to every little polygon. Because computers are (finally) picking up the processing pace, we can stop being so finicky and make higher-resolution models. That said, you can, if you like, clean up your model a bit by applying the Optimize modifier, located in the modifier panel's drop-down list. This will shave off another 50 or so polygons, thus speeding up game play even more!

Map the Selection

Finally, you're ready to export the U-Vs to DeepUV! If you've installed DeepUV correctly, including the Max plug-in, it should be available in 3D Studio Max's Utilities panel (see Figure 5.16). To access it, click on the Utilities tab and, in the list that appears, click Right Hemisphere. Below that, you'll see a DeepUV section. With your model selected, click Map Selection. Because you haven't yet applied any materials to the model in Max, you'll get a warning to that effect; just click OK. 3D Studio Max applies a default solid-color material to the object just so there's something to work with. If your programs and plug-ins were installed correctly, DeepUV should pop up and import the RF-9.

TIP

Even after you've imported the RF-9 to DeepUV, it's a good idea to keep 3D Studio Max open; when you finish laying out the U-Vs, you'll want to send a U-V update back to Max. That way, after you send the model's U-Vs to DeepUV, a dynamic link is established between the programs that allows you to bounce back and forth between the two as you work. If you're low on system memory, however, don't fret; this is not an absolute necessity; you'll just need to manually fetch the updated U-Vs in Max after you finish with them in DeepUV. (I'll show you how to update both ways.)

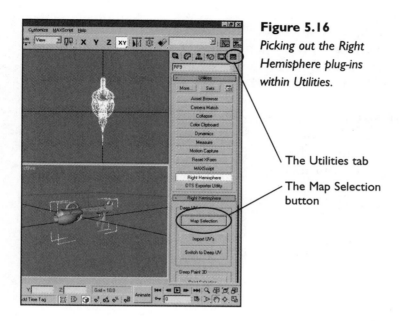

Figure 5.16
*Picking out the Right
Hemisphere plug-ins
within Utilities.*

The Utilities tab

The Map Selection
button

Plan of Attack

In keeping with the U-V mapping example earlier in this chapter, I'd like to break down the RF-9 plasma gun model in the same primitive-style manner. Looking at the weapon, you can see that it is mostly a bunch of spheres, cylinders, and planes all glued together. Even the hoop-shaped objects protruding at the ends are simply bent cylinders. Because the RF-9 is one complete mesh, instead of a bunch of sub-objects all glued together, you'll need to pick off individual components, unwrap them appropriately, and organize the Material map. Here's my plan of attack (although you can do this in any order):

1. Unwrap the grip and trigger.

2. Unwrap the rear hoop.

3. Unwrap the barrel.

4. Unwrap the front hoop and hose.

5. Unwrap the muzzle.

6. Pack the map.

7. Update the U-Vs.

> **NOTE**
>
> I've designed this section to be easy and workable, as opposed to efficient. This also applies to the actual model of the weapon; it will have mesh and texture details that won't be noticed in a video game, but might in up-close shots outside of a game. That's just to keep things simple as you learn the ropes.

First, however, you should set up your workspace for easier mapping. Chances are, when you imported the RF-9 into DeepUV, you probably ended up looking at the weapon according to the original axial orientation as established in trueSpace. To switch to Right view, right-click on the RF-9, and select View, Right (Shift+F). You should end up with a screen as in Figure 5.17. Whatever your model's orientation, the rest of this tutorial operates under the assumption that the Front view looks at the side of the model; depending on the axes of your model, you may need to make a view adjustment by choosing View, Front or View, Back.

NOTE

If you open the **start.rh3** file on the CD-ROM, you can start fresh with the model and see things happen exactly as I explain them. If not, do your best to follow along as I suggest in the figures.

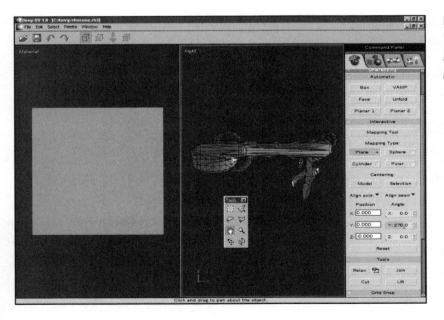

Figure 5.17
The Right view of the RF-9 after importing it into DeepUV.

Step 1: Unwrap the Grip and Trigger

The gun's grip and trigger are two components that will be easy to unfold, because they consist of flat, planar faces joined together like a box (hint, hint!); let's start with the grip.

For starters, notice that the screen is split up into two parts: a Mapping section and the object viewport. As you can see, there's a tiny blue cluster at the top-left of the Mapping area; that represents every U-V coordinate of the RF-9 all clumped together. It'll be your job to slowly detangle this cluster and lay it out nice and neat on the texture map (the large gray square in the middle of the Mapping area). Here's how:

TIP

Before you do anything whatsoever, get in the habit of saving your work in DeepUV (and every other program for that matter!). Just click File, Save As; then, within the Save As Type list, select Scene File (.rh3). Give the file a name and click OK. That way, if something goes wrong, you can always reload your scene just as it is now.

1. Using the Pan and Zoom tools, zoom up close to the gun's grip area.

2. Click on the Rectangular Selection tool; several options appear at the top of the screen.

3. Click the Point Selection Mode button. This allows you to make individual coordinate selections.

4. Click the Back Faces button; that way, you'll be able to grab those coordinates that are hidden on the other side of the RF-9.

5. Using the Rectangular Selection tool, click and drag over the entire handle. Try to include only points that make up the grip and trigger as I have in Figure 5.18.

6. Using the Rotate tool, twirl the gun over a bit so you can see underneath.

7. As you can see in Figure 5.19, there are red (selected) areas that include points that don't belong to the grip and trigger. To eliminate them, click the Rectangular Selection tool again, and, while holding down the Alt key on your keyboard, drag an area over the bogus points to deselect them. Notice that Rectangular Selection tool has a tiny minus sign next to it, indicating that it will subtract from the existing selection. (Conversely, if you hold down the Shift key instead of the Alt key, you can add to your selection.)

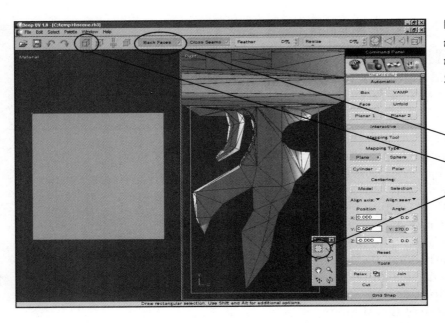

Figure 5.18 *Select the RF-9's grip with the Rectangular Selection tool.*

The Back Faces button

The Rectangular Selection tool

The Point Selection button

NOTE

Don't worry too much if you've accidentally selected and cut away points outside the grip area; you can always detach and rejoin these points back to their proper portions of the weapon later. Remember, you're only affecting the U-V points, and not the actual vertices of the object!

8. When satisfied with your selection, look at the upper-left corner of the texture map. A small red dot within the blue cluster is displayed, indicating that you've made a selection among those points. Your next step is to cut the points away so you can unfold your selection. Do so by clicking Cut in the Tools section of the Mapping panel (see Figure 5.20).

9. Using the Move tool, drag the red dot to the center of the texture map.

NOTE

If you don't cut the points away before trying to move them, they'll remain attached to the rest of the group.

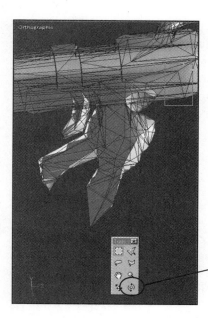

Figure 5.19
Rotate the model to view the underside, and deselect any points not belonging to the grip and trigger.

The Rotate tool

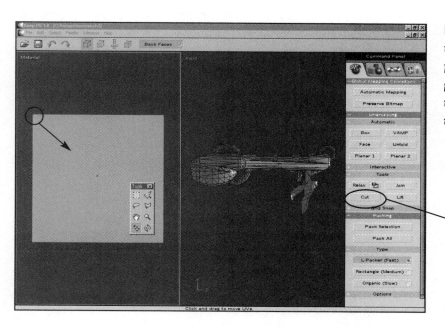

Figure 5.20 *Cut the selection away from the rest of the points and move it to the middle of the texture map.*

The Cut button

10. Your selection is ready to be unfolded. Because the grip is somewhat boxy, click Box under the Automatic section of the Mapping panel. DeepUV does its best to unfold everything (as you would a cardboard box) and lay it out flat, as shown in Figure 5.21. Notice that you can clearly see both sides of the grip, but that there's a mess of other pieces lying around it. Those are the back and front faces of the grip, along with pieces of the trigger. You'll organize those in a moment.

11. Using the Pan and Zoom tools, zoom in to the area containing the back and front faces of the grip.

12. With the Lasso tool, drag your mouse to draw a selection around one side of the grip. When you release your mouse button, only those points belonging to that side of the grip in the 3D view should be highlighted (see Figure 5.22).

TIP

If you accidentally select points not belonging to the face, just press and hold the Alt key and drag a circle around the bogus point with the Lasso tool to deselect it. Just as with the Rectangular tool, holding Shift will add points.

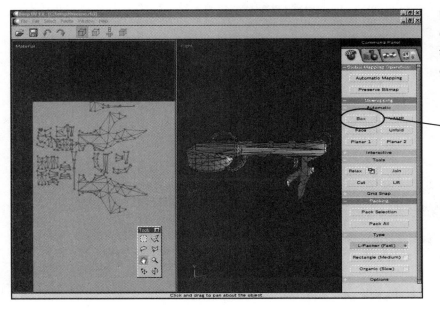

Figure 5.21
Click the Box button to unfold the grip and trigger.

The Box button

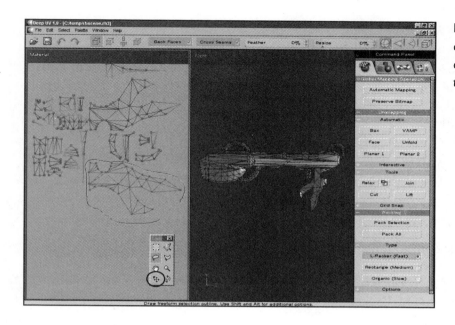

Figure 5.22 *Make a Lasso selection around one face of the grip.*

13. To keep your workspace uncluttered, use the Move tool to move the selection away from the map, as I have done in Figure 5.23.

14. Repeat the Lasso selection process for the other side of the grip, and move it next to its kin.

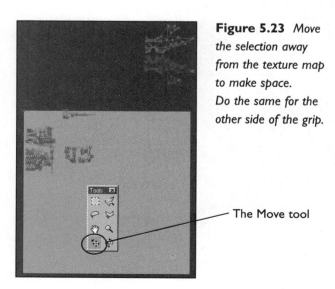

Figure 5.23 *Move the selection away from the texture map to make space. Do the same for the other side of the grip.*

The Move tool

15. Now for the trigger. Use the Lasso tool to circle the trigger area, but this time within the 3D viewport (see Figure 5.24).

16. Notice that several areas in the texture map have become highlighted, indicating the pieces that belong to the trigger. If you accidentally grabbed a portion of the barrel, it will show up as a red dot in that little blue cluster at the top-left of the Material map. To subtract them, hold down the Alt key on your keyboard and use the Rectangular Selection tool to deselect them.

17. Notice the small portion of the trigger's selection that's attached to the rest of the grip. To cut the group away, click Cut under Tools in the Mapping panel.

18. Using the Move tool, move the selection away, as I have in Figure 5.25.

19. Your trigger components are already isolated and unfolded; let's pack them together and set them aside using the Packing and Type section in the Command Panel. Click on the Rectangle (Medium) option in the Type section, and then click Pack Selection above it. You should now have a packed selection, as shown in Figure 5.26.

20. Choose Edit, Transform, and scale the huge selection down to size to make it small and manageable.

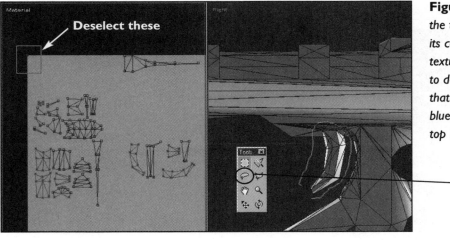

Figure 5.24 *Lasso the trigger to display its components in the texture map. Be sure to deselect any red that shows up in the blue clump at the top left.*

The Lasso tool

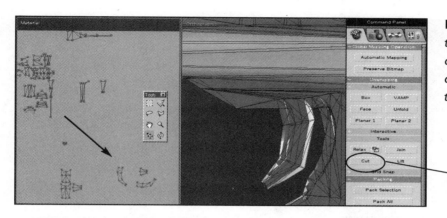

Figure 5.25 *Cut the trigger selection away from the group and move the selection away.*

The Cut button

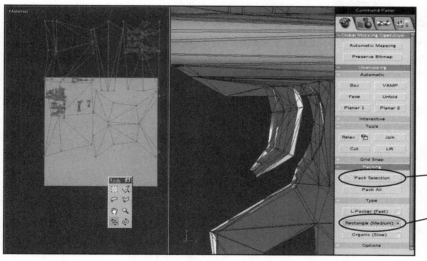

Figure 5.26 *Pack the selection using the Rectangle option in the Command Panel.*

The Pack Selection button

The Rectangle (Medium) button

21. Using the Move tool, move the scaled selection over to the grip's location (see Figure 5.27).

22. Rotate the RF-9 so you can see the back side of the grip.

23. Use the Rectangular Selection tool to select the area (see Figure 5.28). If you grabbed bogus points by accident, deselect them in the texture map.

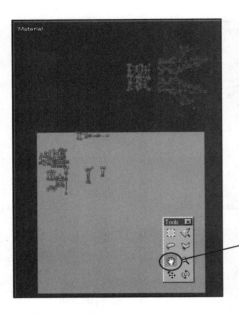

Figure 5.27 *Scale the trigger selection down to size and move it next to the grip's faces.*

Scale and move

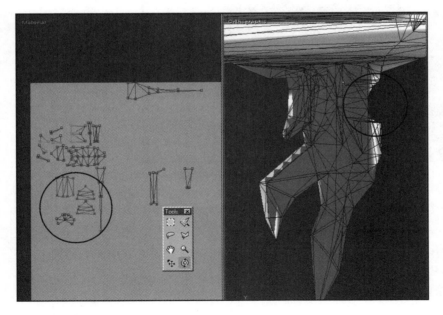

Figure 5.28 *Select the curved notch in the back side of the grip.*

24. Click Unfold in the Automatic section of the Command Panel to lay the selected area out flat, as in Figure 5.29.

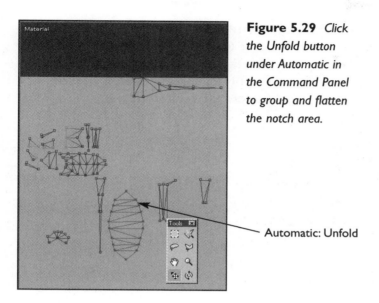

Figure 5.29 *Click the Unfold button under Automatic in the Command Panel to group and flatten the notch area.*

Automatic: Unfold

25. Rotate the RF-9 so you can see the front of the grip.

26. Repeat steps 23 and 24 for the notch in the front, just behind the trigger (see Figure 5.30).

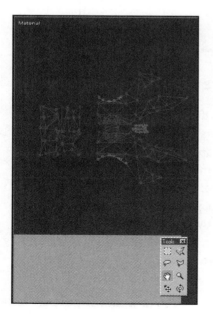

Figure 5.30 *Scale and position the curve selection, and do the same for the front of the grip.*

27. Using any of the selection tools, select the remaining bits and pieces all at once, and pack, scale, and move them over to the rest of the grip and trigger group (see Figure 5.31). These pieces represent texturing detail so minute that you don't need to do much except apply a general painting later on, so don't bother trying to organize them (unless you really want to).

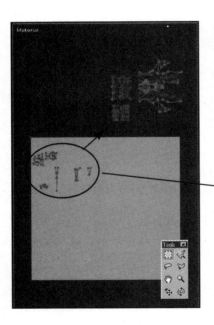

Figure 5.31 *Select the remaining pieces, and pack, scale, and move them to the rest of the group.*

Pack, scale, and move

Sharing U-V Space

Notice that the two halves of the grip are nearly, if not perfectly, identical. In such cases, if any texture coordinates cross or overlap each other, the texture at that point on the texture map will duplicate (or smear, if the points are crossed) itself on the 3D model once the texture is applied. This is known as sharing U-V space. In the case of identical coordinate sections, like the sides of the grip, you could flip one side to match the other, and then place one exactly on top of the other. That way, you only have to texture one side, and the texture would be placed onto both. Although this will save space on your texture map, I'd rather have a model that has unique texture on all sides.

That concludes the unwrapping of the grip and trigger! No doubt you're freaking out about now due to all the steps required to unwrap such as small area. Most of the U-V mapping from here on out involves the same repetitive stuff, but you'll get the hang of it in no time.

> **NOTE**
>
> In case you're having trouble, I've saved each of the steps as individual .rh3 files in the Chapter 5 Data section on the CD-ROM.

Step 2: Unwrap the Rear Hoop

It's time to unfold the top hoop at the back of the barrel. Because this is one of those goofy shapes that's one solid piece, I'd like to keep the U-V map for it together. The problem is, because DeepUV doesn't come with a torus-style unwrapping technique, you'll need to split the hoop into two parts, flatten the sections, and then re-attach them. Here's how:

1. Pan and zoom over to the rear hoop.

2. Use any one of the selection tools to select all points of the hoop (make sure the Back Faces option is checked), up to and including where the hoop meets the barrel.

3. Using the Rotate tool, rotate around the model, selecting/deselecting points until you're satisfied.

4. Click Cut in the Tools section of the Command Panel, then drag the red clump away from the rest at the top-left corner of the texture map (see Figure 5.32).

> **TIP**
>
> Before you unwrap the rear hoop, remember to save your work. Clicking File, Save, doesn't do the trick if the program bails for any reason; instead, click File, Save As, and overwrite your previous .rh3 file. Make sure you save it to this format so all information is retained!

> **NOTE**
>
> Even though it's most efficient to have both 3D Studio Max and DeepUV open at the same time, both of these programs are memory hogs. If you're running low on space, try shutting down all other programs. Otherwise, you can always manually fetch the updated U-V coordinates later, but only if you've saved your .rh3 file!

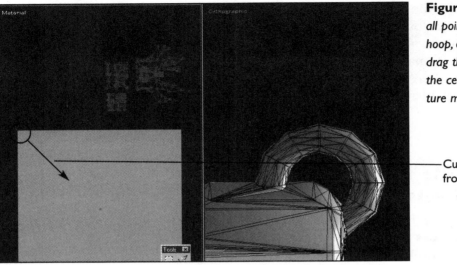

Figure 5.32 *Select all points of the rear hoop, click Cut, and drag the cluster to the center of the texture map.*

—Cut hoop from group

5. There are two ways to map this selection: Interactive: Planar and Automatic: Planar 2. For the sake of expediency, let's use the Automatic: Planar 2 method. To do so, click Planar 2 in the Automatic section. You should end up with a side view of the selection, as in Figure 5.33.

6. Select only one half of the hoop, and cut it away from the other half. To do so, start by right-clicking on the RF-9 in the 3D viewport, and selecting View, Right (or whatever view will produce a perpendicular view to the hoop).

> **NOTE**
>
> When you map interactively, you perform the operation manually. The great thing about interactive mapping is that you can manually specify the way DeepUV uses the selected technique when viewing the U-Vs. The Interactive mapping options, like their Automatic counterparts, are located in the Command Panel, but may be collapsed; just click the + sign in the section's top-left corner to view them.

7. Pan and zoom over to the hoop.

8. Click the Rectangular Selection tool, and uncheck the Back Faces option at the very top of the screen. This enables you to grab only those points that are visible in the viewport.

9. Drag a rectangle around the entire hoop, thereby selecting one half of the hoop (see Figure 5.34).

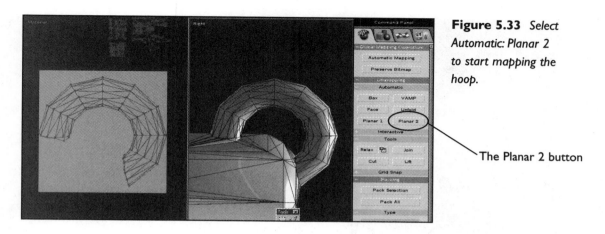

Figure 5.33 *Select Automatic: Planar 2 to start mapping the hoop.*

The Planar 2 button

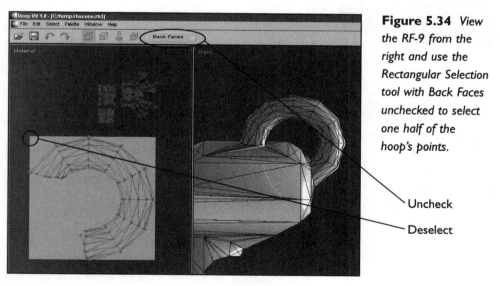

Figure 5.34 *View the RF-9 from the right and use the Rectangular Selection tool with Back Faces unchecked to select one half of the hoop's points.*

Uncheck

Deselect

10. In selecting the hoop, you may have grabbed points on the barrel, which will show up as a tiny red dot in the tiny blue cluster in the top-left portion of the texture map. To deselect them, hold down the Alt key and apply any of the selection tools to that area.

11. Notice that the hoop in the texture map is now red and blue, indicating that half of the points have been selected. Click Cut in the Command Panel to separate them from the other side of the hoop.

12. Using the Move tool, drag one half away from the other (see Figure 5.35).

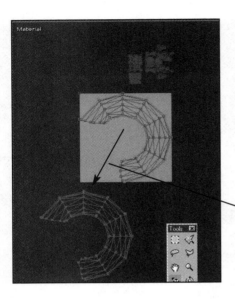

Figure 5.35

Deselect any bogus points, excise half of the hoop from the other half, and move it away.

Cut half and move

13. The two halves of the hoop are the U-Vs as viewed by DeepUV straight on from the right, in a planar fashion, but they are not relaxed—that is, the halves are not taking on their natural volumetric form as they would in 3D space. To see what I mean, with all points of only one half selected, click Relax in the Tools section of the Command Panel. In a few seconds you'll see DeepUV gently relax the points so they even out.

> **NOTE**
>
> Relaxing the points at this time is not required; I just wanted you to see the Relax feature in action. Relaxing is a way to get your U-V mapped portions to rest naturally on the texture map. That way, when it comes time to actually texture, the bitmap won't distort or smear when applied to the model.

14. Repeat step 13 for the other half (see Figure 5.36).

15. Next, join the two halves to create a single, 2D map representing the hoop. To begin, with the top half selected, choose Edit, Transform, Flip Horizontal. This flips the back portion of the hoop, so it faces toward you.

16. Position both halves as I have in Figure 5.37. You want to join the outer edges of both halves, because these represent the top of the hoop.

17. Use the Lasso tool to select the points at the joined edges of both halves.

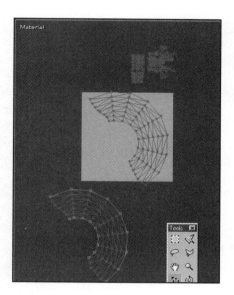

Figure 5.36

Choose Relax for each half so the points spread themselves proportionately.

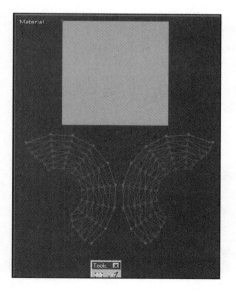

Figure 5.37

Select the outer points of each half. These points represent the top of the hoop.

18. Here's the cool part: With the edge points selected, click Join in the Tools section. Because the selected points actually neighbor/belong to each other, DeepUV will allow them to re-join each other, just as they were joined before you cut the one half away from the other. Figure 5.38 shows the halves joined as one.

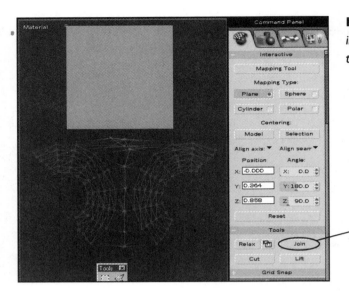

Figure 5.38 *Click Join in the Tools section to join the two halves together.*

The Join button

19. Select the entire hoop in the texture map area, and once again click Relax. This will relax all the points naturally, and you should end up with a nicely unfolded hoop as shown in Figure 5.39.

20. That's it for the hoop; scale it down and move it aside. (Just try to keep track of where things are so you know what's what when you arrange your texture map at the end!)

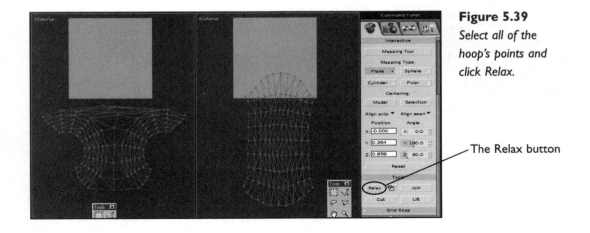

Figure 5.39
Select all of the hoop's points and click Relax.

The Relax button

Seams

Now is a good time to quickly explain seams. When you paint the textures on your completed texture map, the U-Vs as laid out will correspond to locations on your 3D model. In the previous example, the hoop's halves were joined at the *top halves*, and not the bottom halves. That way, when DeepUV relaxed them and the whole thing became flat, the outer edges represented the *seam*, underneath the hoop. You could just as well have joined the halves together using the bottom points, but that would leave a noticeable seam at the top half. It's better, if you have the option, to re-join halves in a way that puts the seam in a location that's difficult to see, if not totally invisible, to the players in the video game.

Step 3: Unwrap the Barrel

The barrel is the long shaft that connects the front muzzle to the grip and back hoop. Normally, for a shape like this, you could use Interactive: Cylinder mapping to quickly unwrap the thing, but I'd rather iso-late and unfold the back and bottom first, because they will get separate texture detail, before unfolding the rest of the barrel.

TIP

Remember, before you unwrap the barrel, save your work by clicking File, Save As, and over-writing your previous .rh3 file.

1. Select the Rectangular Selection tool, and check the Back Faces option to select it so you can see all points of the barrel.

2. In the 3D window, switch to a side view of the RF-9 so you can see it perpendicularly.

3. Create a rectangular selection around the entire barrel.

4. Chances are, your selection includes points from the grip and rear hoop (and muzzle, but hold off on that a second). Deselect them by dragging around them while holding down the Alt key, as I have done in Figure 5.40.

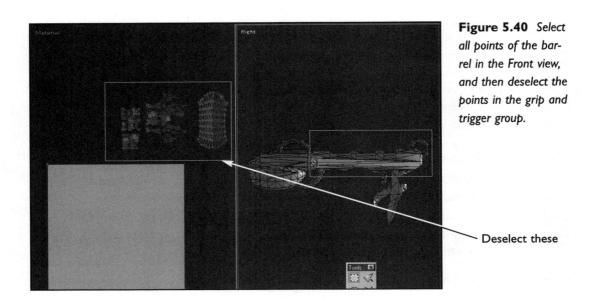

Figure 5.40 *Select all points of the barrel in the Front view, and then deselect the points in the grip and trigger group.*

Deselect these

5. Zoom into the model and deselect any other bogus points that are part of the muzzle (remember, press and hold the Alt key as you click to deselect, or press and hold the Shift key as you click to add to your selection). Be sure to rotate the model around and zoom in close so you don't miss anything.

6. When you're satisfied with your barrel's selection, click Cut to separate it from the rest of the weapon.

7. Use the Move tool to drag the red clump that represents the barrel's U-V coordinates away from the small blue dot at the top-left of the texture map.

8. In the Right view, zoom in on the back of the barrel.

9. Using the Rectangular Selection tool, select the back end of the barrel.

10. Deselect any points of the grip or top hoop that you may have inadvertently selected.

11. When satisfied with your back selection, click Cut (see Figure 5.41).

12. The back end can be planarly mapped, but the Automatic: Planar 1 and Planar 2 options won't know to project the planar mapping toward the rear of the gun. For this reason, you'll need to map the back end interactively. To begin, expand the Interactive section and click the Plane button.

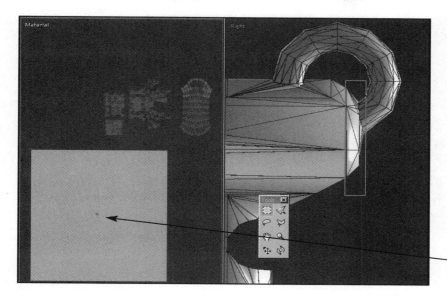

Figure 5.41 *Cut the barrel selection away from the rest of the gun; select the back end and cut it away too.*

Cut and move
barrel group

13. You'll see three gizmos float along the X, Y, and Z, axes of the gun; these allow you to manually rotate the projection to your liking. Because the rear face of the gun is along the Z axis, however, all you need to do is tell it to look along that axis. To do so, click the Selection button under Centering in the Command Panel.

14. Pull down the Align axis drop-down list and select +Z (see Figure 5.42). You should end up with a nice planar mapping of the back end along the positive Z axis.

15. Relax, scale, and move the newly unfolded rear face away from the texture map.

16. The rest of the barrel is now essentially a hollow tube with no end caps—or, more precisely, a cylinder. To map it, click the Cylinder button in the Interactive section of the Command Panel.

> **NOTE**
>
> If your model's axial orientation is different from mine, you may need to align your mapping techniques along axes other than those I've specified. For this reason, if I tell you to align the axis on a particular coordinate, such as −X, you may need to experiment with other axes, such as +Z, to get the same results.

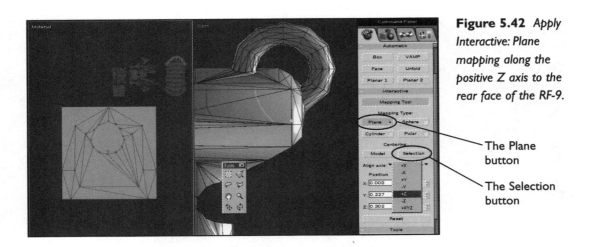

Figure 5.42 *Apply Interactive: Plane mapping along the positive Z axis to the rear face of the RF-9.*

The Plane button

The Selection button

17. Click the Selection button under Centering to tell DeepUV to center its analysis on the selection.

18. Pull down the Align axis drop-down list and select +Z to tell DeepUV to perform the cylindrical projection along the positive Z axis. You should end up with a nicely unwrapped barrel, as in Figure 5.43.

19. The barrel has unwrapped itself wonderfully. Thinking ahead, however, I'd like to texture this weapon such that both sides of the barrel are attached to

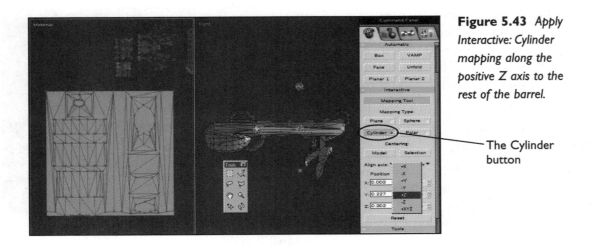

Figure 5.43 *Apply Interactive: Cylinder mapping along the positive Z axis to the rest of the barrel.*

The Cylinder button

either side of its top, leaving the bottom portion dangling off to one side. You can accomplish this by clicking and dragging the Y axis's control handle (the green dot with two arrows encircling it in the 3D model) to rotate the projection along the Z axis. As you're dragging, look to the left of the screen at the unwrapped barrel; you should see the map slowly shift. Stop when the bottom portion of the gun is all the way to one side (see Figure 5.44).

20. Scale and move your unwrapped barrel away from the texture map.

NOTE

The Y-axis control rotates itself perpendicularly to the Z axis, which is why you're rotating that one instead of the other two. If you were to rotate the Z-axis control, all hell would break loose and your mapping would be ruined.

TIP

If you're scaling this stuff using the Free Transform method, make sure to hold down Ctrl during the scaling. That way it will scale proportionally without distorting the mapping.

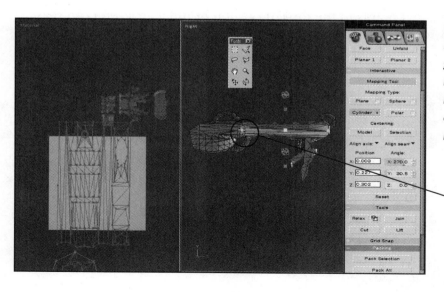

Figure 5.44
Rotate the Y-axis gizmo so that the bottom face of the barrel is positioned on the outside of the barrel's U-V map.

Click and drag to reorient the seams

Step 4: Unwrap the Front Hoop and Hose

The front hoop and hose are just two bent cylinders, like the rear hoop; you can isolate and unfold them in the same manner. (I'll walk you through this one quickly since you already know how to do it.)

1. Create a rectangular selection around the top hoop (be sure the Back Faces option is checked).

2. Deselect any bogus points not belonging to the hoop.

3. Choose the Cut button in the Command Panel's Tools section.

> **TIP**
>
> Before you unwrap the front hoop and hose, save your work by clicking File, Save As, and overwriting your previous .rh3 file.

4. Move the red dot away from the group at the upper-left of the texture map.

5. You'll need a planar view of the hoop from the side; I clicked the Planar 2 button in the Automatic section of the Command Panel (see Figure 5.45).

6. There will be shared points that bridge both ends of the hoop; these belong to the top of the muzzle. Carefully select the points on both ends and cut them away.

7. Move the excised points to the top-left portion of the map so you can reassign them with the rest of the muzzle in the next section (see Figure 5.46).

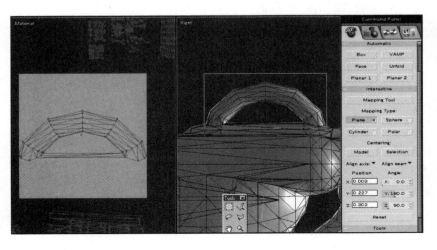

Figure 5.45

Select the top hoop, cut it away, and choose Automatic: Planar 2 as a mapping technique.

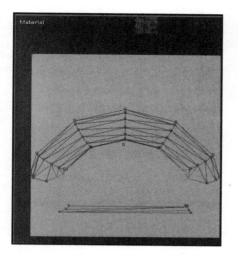

Figure 5.46
Select and cut away the bogus points belonging to the top of the muzzle.

8. Click the Rectangular Selection tool.

9. Uncheck the Back Faces.

10. Select half of the hoop in a perpendicular 3D view, just as you did with the back hoop.

11. Cut the hoop in half, moving one half of it away from the other.

12. Relax both halves of the hoop (see Figure 5.47).

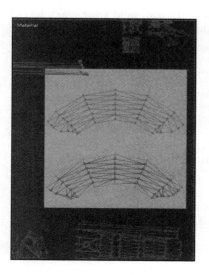

Figure 5.47 Select half of the hoop in a perpendicular 3D view, cut it away, and relax it. Relax the other side as well.

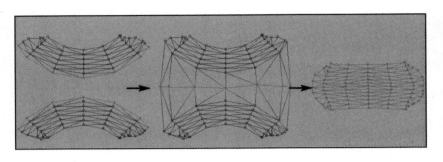

Figure 5.48 *Select the edge points of each side, join them, and then relax the entire structure.*

13. Click Edit, Transform, Flip Vertically to flip one side of the hoop upside down so you can get the edges to meet.

14. Using the Lasso tool, select the edge points of both sides, and click Join.

15. Select the entire hoop and click Relax (see Figure 5.48).

16. Repeat the steps in this section to unwrap the hose.

Step 5: Unwrap the Muzzle

The remaining, unmapped points all clumped together at the top-left of the texture map represent the muzzle. This is the most difficult portion of the RF-9 to unwrap, because it's awkwardly shaped and has an inner area representing the plasma chamber. After you've removed and mapped the front portion, however, the remaining part of the muzzle is somewhat cylindrical, which dictates what type of mapping technique you'll use.

> **TIP**
> Before you unwrap the front hoop and hose, save your work by clicking File, Save As, and overwriting your previous .rh3 file.

1. Select the clump that represents the muzzle, along with those stray points from the top of the muzzle.

2. Move the selection to the center of the texture map and click Join. This will re-join all those stray points of the muzzle.

3. Click the Plane button in the Interactive section of the Command Panel.

4. Click Selection to center the mapping on the selection.

5. Pull down the Align axis drop-down list and select −X to have the projection aim at the muzzle from the side, or X axis. (I selected −X instead of +X to flip the muzzle upside down, as shown in Figure 5.49.)

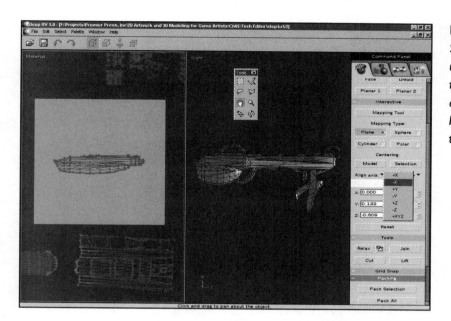

Figure 5.49

Select the remaining, unmapped points of the muzzle and apply Interactive: Plane mapping along the X axis.

6. Before you unwrap the muzzle like a cylinder, let's remove the front face so it can be textured separately. Zoom in on the front points, select them, and click Cut.

7. Apply Automatic: Planar 1 mapping to the excised points. You should end up with the front face of the muzzle.

8. Click Relax to put the muzzle's face in its natural form, scale it, and move it away from the map (see Figure 5.50).

9. The cone inside of the muzzle is next. Zoom in close to the single point that makes the tip of the cone and select it.

10. The point fades from red to blue as it shoots out toward the end of the muzzle; this gives you a good indication as to what points to select at the front.

11. With the inner cone's points selected, click the Cut button.

12. Apply an Automatic: Planar–style mapping to the inner cone (see Figure 5.51). It won't be necessary to relax this cone section, since it represents the inside of the weapon and will get textured mostly with black color anyway.

13. Select the rest of the muzzle.

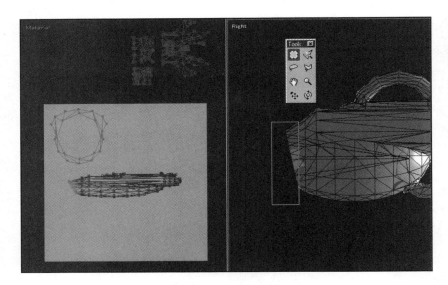

Figure 5.50
Select the front points of the muzzle and cut them away. Then, choose Automatic: Planar 1 to map the front face flat.

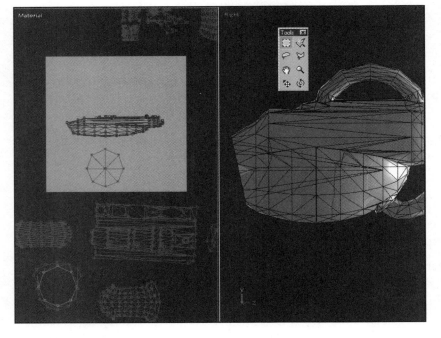

Figure 5.51 *Select and cut away the inner cone of the muzzle, and apply an Automatic: Planar mapping to it.*

14. Click the Cylinder button in the Interactive section of the Command Panel, and center the mapping on the selection.

15. I'd like to use the seam instead of hiding it this time, so let's put it on top (that is, the outer edges of the mapping should represent the top of the gun). To make the top of the muzzle visible, pull down the Align axis drop-down list and select −Z (because you're looking at the z-axis underneath).

16. You may need to roll the cylindrical mapping over so that the bottom of the muzzle is in the center of the flattened map. To do so, click and drag one of the gizmos that's aligned with the long axis of the barrel (mine's the green Y-axis gizmo) in the 3D view. You should end up with a map that looks like the one in Figure 5.52.

17. That's it! Now, just relax the muzzle selection and move it out of the way.

Step 6: Pack the Map

Now it's time to arrange all of the unfolded pieces of the RF-9 into the gray square (this square, remember, represents the actual texture map you'll be painting later on). The tough part is getting everything to fit within the area! You can do this one of two ways:

> **TIP**
>
> Of course, you should save your work by clicking File, Save As, and overwriting your previous .rh3 file before you pack the map into the texture-map area!

either let DeepUV automatically pack them in for you (which I don't recommend, because it might not arrange things to your liking) or do it yourself.

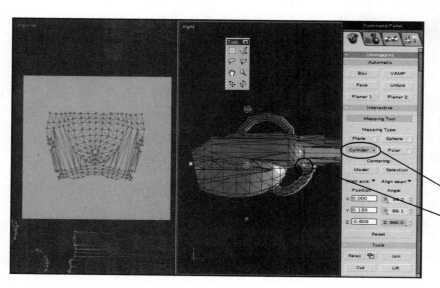

Figure 5.52

Map the rest of the muzzle with Interactive: Cylinder mapping. Align the projection so that the seam is on the top of the gun.

The Cylinder button

Drag to rotate seam

For the sake of example, click the Pack All button in the Command Panel to instruct DeepUV to pack the model automatically. Notice in Figure 5.53 how DeepUV crammed everything together into the map? Of course, you have some say in how DeepUV packs your model—namely, those settings found in the Type and Options sections. For instance, choosing Rectangle- or Organic-style packing instructs the program to take more time arranging the pieces to fit better (but it's much slower). Even so, at the end of the day, I'd rather just do it all myself!

By arranging and scaling the pieces manually, you can determine how you'll paint the texture on the various pieces, as well as decide which pieces will get the most texturing detail. (To apply more detail to a particular piece, just scale it up in the texture map to provide more area on which to paint.) In the RF-9's case, most of the detail will reside on the barrel and muzzle, so those two pieces can take up most of the map.

To arrange the pieces manually, simply select each item that you unwrapped, scale and rotate it if necessary, and place it on the map to your liking. You don't have to fill every little gap; in fact, having some space will make it easier when texturing. (Figure 5.54 shows how I packed my map; if you want to see how it looks in DeepUV, just open the **step6.rh3** file on the CD-ROM.) Take your time with this step, because the way you pack your map will determine how you texture your model.

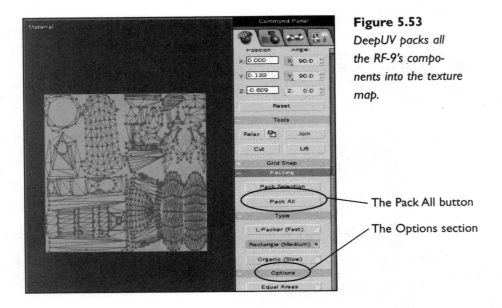

Figure 5.53

DeepUV packs all the RF-9's compo- nents into the texture map.

The Pack All button

The Options section

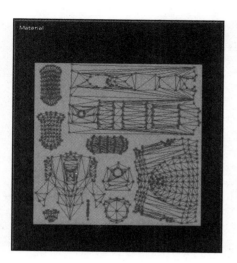

Figure 5.54
Packing the RF-9 my way.

Take one last moment here to note the way I arranged the weapon's grip and trigger. You could still keep just the sides and back of the grip neatly arranged as you did earlier in this chapter, but I decided to put in a little more effort and join the remaining pieces to the grip's edges. This way, the grip itself is now unfolded as one entire piece, which will help to provide some extra detail when texturing.

Step 7: Update the U-Vs

It's time to update the model! You can do this one of two ways. If you've kept 3D Studio Max open from the beginning, and nothing went awry, you can simply click File, Export, Send UV Update. This will update the U-V mapping for the RF-9 model in Max by adding a DeepUV modifier onto the stack. Switch back over to Max to see that in action.

If, however, you had to close and reopen Max during the mapping process, you'll need to fetch the map manually. Here's how:

1. Start 3D Studio Max and load the RF-9 file. (If you don't have it, there's an **RF9.max** file on the CD-ROM.)

2. In the Utilities panel, choose Right Hemisphere from the list.

3. Click on the Import UV's button; as shown in Figure 5.55, a second DeepUV modifier is added to the Modifier stack, containing the updated U-Vs. (Click on the Modifier section to see this.)

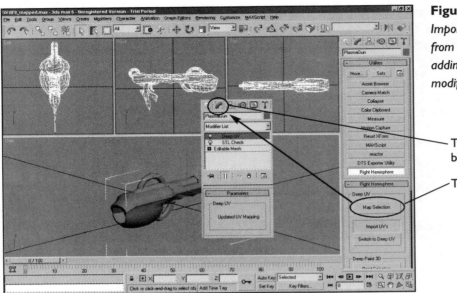

Figure 5.55

Importing the U-Vs from DeepUV and adding them to the modifier stack.

The Import UV's button

The Modifier tab

Time Count

Once you've established your skills with unwrapping and manipulating U-V coordinates, you should keep track of how long it takes you to complete this task for a particular model. As an example, the first time I unwrapped the RF-9, which included several instances of back-tracking because I found one or two better techniques as I worked, I spent a total of one hour from the time I sent the model's coordinates over to DeepUV to the time I finished organizing the texture map. The map-packing portion of it took the longest because I wanted it to be neat and well organized (for the most part). Once you get into this stuff, you'll find a regular pace; then, when it comes time to handle your workload at a game-development company, you can properly budget your time.

4. Save the Max scene file.

You can always bounce back to DeepUV by
clicking Map Selection in the Utilities tab. Do
make sure, however, that your U-Vs were, in
fact, updated properly in Max by adding an
Unwrap UVW modifier to the stack, and clicking Edit in that modifier's parameter section
below (see Figure 5.56). You should see an
identical map to that in DeepUV.

NOTE

I've saved my updated model
as **RF9_mapped.max** on
the CD-ROM for your convenience.

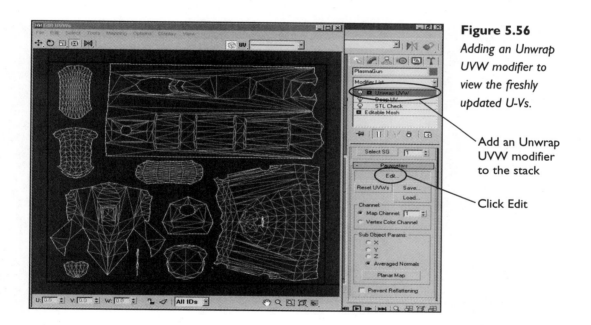

Figure 5.56
*Adding an Unwrap
UVW modifier to
view the freshly
updated U-Vs.*

Add an Unwrap
UVW modifier
to the stack

Click Edit

Summary

U-V mapping is an essential part of preparing your 3D models for texturing. U-V
coordinates are invisible points that correspond 1:1 with the actual vertices of a 3D
model, and programs like DeepUV allow you to isolate portions of the U-V points
and unfold them nicely on a texture map. There are many different ways these
pieces can be manipulated, and DeepUV offers a suite of projection techniques
that aid you in this process.

The next step in creating your model is to texture it based on the new U-V map. You can texture one of several ways. The poor man's way is to take a screen shot of the UVW map in 3D Studio Max and paint over it in a program like Photoshop. Alternatively, you can export the U-Vs to Deep Paint 3D and use that in conjunction with Photoshop to paint your map. To proceed with this technique, skip to Chapter 11, "Skinning the RF-9 Plasma Gun with Deep Paint 3D and Photoshop."

CHAPTER 6

U-V Mapping the Slogre with DeepUV

Now that you've finished creating your slogre model (that is, half of it), it's time for the next logical step in game object creation, as shown in Figure 6.1. In this chapter, you'll learn how to manipulate the U-V coordinates of your mesh object in preparation for texturing. The difference between this chapter and the previous one ("U-V Mapping the RF-9 Plasma Gun") is that you need to unify and optimize your character model in 3D Studio Max before pushing it over to DeepUV.

In this chapter, you will

- Use 3D Studio Max to complete the slogre model.
- Use Max to fix, optimize, and smooth the model's mesh.
- Import and efficiently texture map the U-V component of the slogre model using DeepUV.

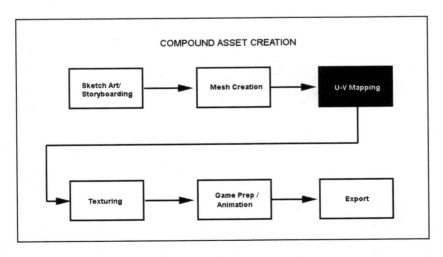

Figure 6.1 *The next phase in the sequence of 3D game object creation.*

Completing the Slogre Model in 3D Studio Max 5

The first thing you need to do before unwrapping the U-Vs of your slogre character is to, well, have a complete mesh. If you recall, you created precisely 50 percent of the character model in Chapter 4, "Modeling the Slogre Character with trueSpace 6." To complete your mesh, fire up 3D Studio Max (the demo of which is on the CD-ROM) and choose File, Import. Choose the Stereolitho (*.STL) file type and import the **slogre.stl** file you exported from trueSpace (alternatively, use the **slogre.stl** file in the Chapter 6 Data section on the CD-ROM). The first screen to pop up will be an Import STL File menu, shown in Figure 6.2.

> **NOTE**
>
> The 3D Studio Max demo on the CD-ROM is version 5. However, the tutorials in this book work the same in 3D Studio Max 4.

In this menu, select the Quick Weld option in the Weld Vertices section and click OK. Quick Weld fuses any vertices that are reasonably close to one another; you should end up with a screen that displays the slogre half, as shown in Figure 6.3.

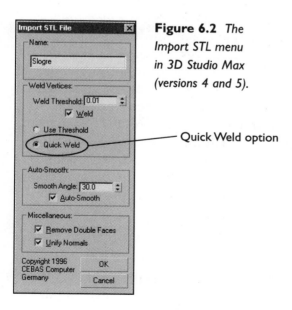

Figure 6.2 *The Import STL menu in 3D Studio Max (versions 4 and 5).*

Quick Weld option

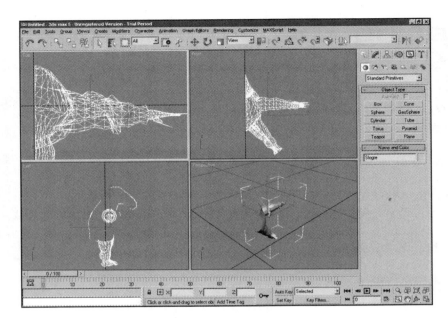

Figure 6.3 *The Max interface containing the imported slogre half.*

Optimize the Mesh

When your slogre half is in Max, locate the Command Panel at the far right and click on the Modifier tab (if it isn't selected already). This panel is called the Modifier Stack, and offers the best way to make changes to your mesh objects. Any operation you perform on your model gets stacked in this list, allowing you to peruse the model's history and remove or add changes simply by deleting items from or adding items to the stack. Click the Modifier List down arrow, and select the Optimize modifier (see Figure 6.4) to instruct Max to examine your slogre half and remove any unnecessary vertices, edges, and/or faces. The results of this operation are displayed in the Last Optimize Status area at the bottom of the panel; the Before/After area indicates how many polygons appeared before the operation versus after it. In this example, the modifier has effectively reduced the polygon count from more than 2,100 faces to about 1,600, without removing any noticeable detail in the model.

Edit the Mesh

The default settings for the Optimize modifier are quite satisfactory (you could play around with some of the settings to push the envelope on the optimization, but it's not necessary). You're targeting around 3,000 polygons for this character,

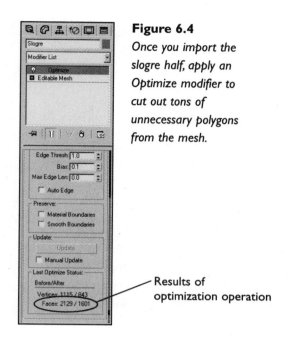

Figure 6.4

Once you import the slogre half, apply an Optimize modifier to cut out tons of unnecessary polygons from the mesh.

Results of
optimization operation

and so far you're pretty much on par. Your next step is to edit the mesh a bit further, because the Optimize modifier is slightly indiscriminate when it comes to deciding how to perform the optimization. For instance, your model might contain extraneous vertices—particularly along the seams where the arm or leg meet the body—that could be welded together. In order to manipulate the vertices directly, however, you need to convert the mesh back to its editable mode. The only problem is, the Optimize modifier is sitting on top of the Editable Mesh modifier (which is the default), and if you return to that modifier, you'll lose the optimization. Instead, make the mesh editable by adding an Edit Mesh modifier (located in the same list as the Optimize modifier) to the stack. Once on the Edit Mesh modifier is in the stack, expand it and select Vertex from its list (see Figure 6.5).

With the Edit Mesh modifier in place on top of the Optimize modifier, you can now edit the already optimized mesh. Using the Pan, Arc Rotate, and Zoom tools in the bottom-right portion of the screen, zoom in close to areas where the appendages meet the body of the slogre and check for vertices that are simply not needed. When you spot a cluster that should just be combined as one vertex, right-click to exit pan/rotate/zoom mode, and then Ctrl+click each vertex in the cluster to select it. Then, in the Edit Mesh modifier's panel, click the Weld: Selected button (see Figure 6.6).

Figure 6.5
Apply an Edit Mesh modifier to the stack so you can edit the vertices of the mesh.

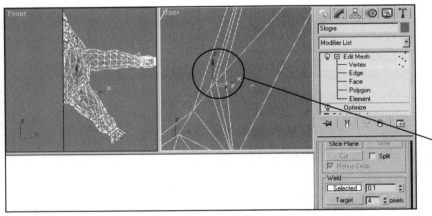

Figure 6.6 *Zoom into the mesh at the seams and weld clumps of unnecessary vertices.*

Weld unnecessary vertices at body joints

TIP

Don't go nuts welding vertices all over the place. Take your time, and be sure that what you're welding is two or three vertices that simply don't add any noticeable detail to the model. You can jump back and forth between wireframe and smooth-render mode by pressing F3; that way, you can see if your weld negatively affected the area.

NOTE

The joint between the leg/arm and the body needs to have a nice, even number of vertices around the entire seam, so when you deform the mesh during animations the seams won't crease bizarrely. Think of it this way: If the shirt you're wearing only had a few rigid stitches around the seam where the sleeve met the body part, what would happen when you flexed your arm? The portions not stitched would bulge awkwardly away from the rest of the shirt and expose your skin underneath.

Clone and Attach

Once you're finished combing through the model half and welding vertices, it's time to make your big guy feel complete. First, however, save your work. Then, compile your changes, including the optimization, by right-clicking the top-most item on the stack and choosing Collapse All from the menu that appears. You might get a warning; just click OK. The stack should now be reset to its default, but will retain all the results of your work.

Next, with the mesh selected, make a mirrored copy of it by choosing Tools, Mirror, and, in the Mirror Options dialog box, select Copy and click OK. A mirrored copy will be placed in your scene; use the Move, Rotate, and Scale tools (located at the top of the screen) to move it so its seam lines up with the other half (see Figure 6.7) — use the Zoom tool to align them as tightly as you can.

TIP

When you move the item in any orthogonal view, make sure you select the axis on which you'd like to move it so it stays in the same line as the other half. The axis gizmo will light up when you place your cursor over it.

Now it's time to attach the two mesh pieces so they become one single mesh. Notice that the only item in the list in the Modifier panel is Editable Mesh; below it is an Attach button. Click it, and then click the other, non-selected half to weld them together. Once they are attached, apply an STL Check modifier to the list (this option is located in the same Mesh Editing section as the modifiers you've already used) and click the Check option at the bottom of the STL Check modifier's panel to execute the operation. This will check the mesh for errors, which is

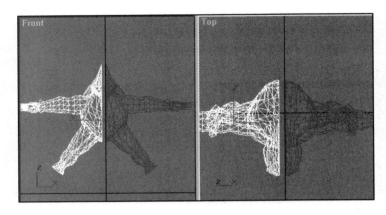

Figure 6.7 *Use the Mirror tool to create a mirrored clone of the other half, and move it directly next to its twin.*

an absolute necessity! If your mesh has holes, open edges, and the like, there's a 99.9-percent chance it won't work properly in any game engine. Due to the complexity of the welding process, you'll almost certainly end up with a bunch of errors (errors are indicated by red areas, as shown in Figure 6.8). No big deal; you'll fix that in a flash with another modifier.

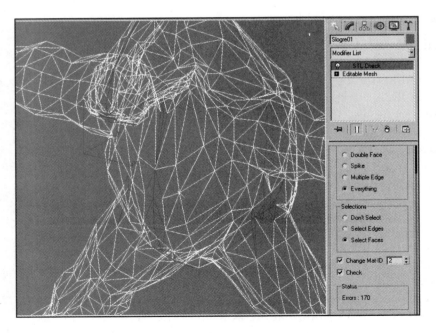

Figure 6.8 *Attach both sections of the slogre together, and then apply an STL Check modifier to check for errors.*

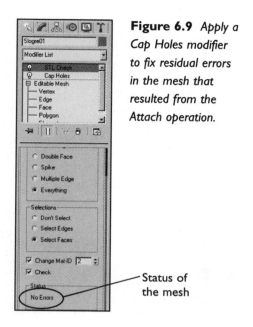

Figure 6.9 *Apply a Cap Holes modifier to fix residual errors in the mesh that resulted from the Attach operation.*

To fix errors resulting from the attach operation, apply a Cap Holes modifier to the stack. To see if this fixed the errors, apply yet another STL Check modifier on top of the Cap Holes modifier, and re-run the check. Figure 6.9 shows my fixed mesh. If you still have errors, you might need to zoom into the red problem errors and manually weld coincident vertices, or possibly apply another Optimize modifier. The attach operation will most definitely have generated another handful of unnecessary vertices along the center seam of the mesh; just take a few minutes to go along them and weld vertices.

Add Some Tusks

The original slogre sketches included some versions of the slogre character without tusks and some with. I really liked them, but decided not to include them until this point. If you wish, import the **tusk.stl** file located in the Chapter 6 Data section on the CD-ROM, or create your own. In Figure 6.10, I aligned the tusks to the front area of the slogre mesh and attached them. I think this model looks great with them. (Ever see the movie *Relic?* Your slogre character looks somewhat like the hideous monster in that movie with these menacing things sticking out of its face.)

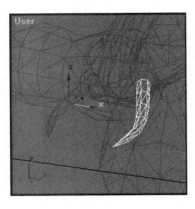

Figure 6.10 *If desired, attach tusks to the character to highlight its ferocity.*

Smooth Out the Bumps

To complete the mesh portion of your model, apply a Smooth modifier to tone down the harsh angles inherent with the way the faces of the model neighbor each other, particularly along the point-edited arm. With the Smooth modifier in place, a Smoothing Groups cluster will be presented in that modifier's panel. Just click button #1 in the cluster to see its beautiful results (see Figure 6.11).

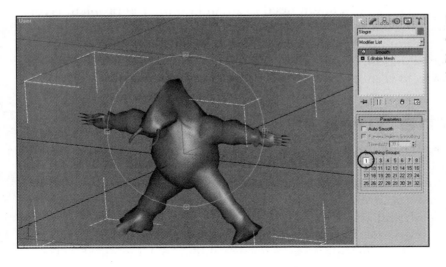

Figure 6.11 *Apply a Smooth modifier to finalize and beautify the slogre mesh.*

Export to DeepUV!

With your slogre mesh looking awesome, you can now U-V map the model. First, fire up DeepUV, the demo of which is on the CD-ROM. Make sure this program is properly installed, along with the 3D Studio Max plug-ins that come with it. Then click on the Utilities tab in the Command Panel, and click the Map Selection button under the Right Hemisphere utility (see Figure 6.12).

Note that you must have DeepUV started in order for 3D Studio to send the mapping information over to it. Once the model is successfully imported into DeepUV, you should see the slogre floating comfortably in the right of the scene, with the fresh new blank Material map on the left. The small blue cluster at the top-left of the Material map contains all the unmapped U-V points that you need to sift through (see Figure 6.13).

> **NOTE**
>
> If you're new to U-V mapping, please read the beginning of Chapter 5, "U-V Mapping the RF-9 Plasma Gun with DeepUV," where I explain the essentials of mapping with DeepUV.

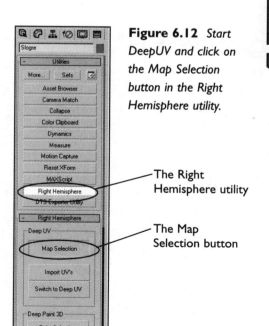

Figure 6.12 *Start DeepUV and click on the Map Selection button in the Right Hemisphere utility.*

The Right Hemisphere utility

The Map Selection button

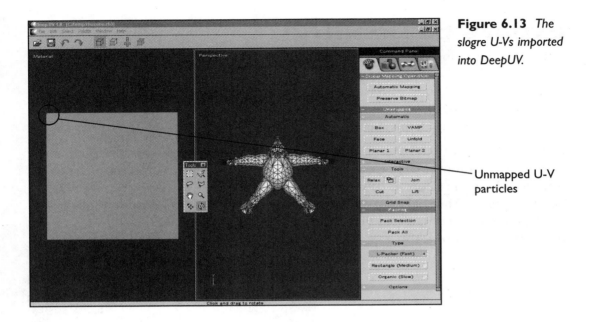

Figure 6.13 *The slogre U-Vs imported into DeepUV.*

Unwrap the Slogre's U-Vs

Now it's time to create the U-V texture map. I'll break this process down by focusing on one body part at a time, and since the slogre is symmetrical, all you have to do is repeat the process for the other side of him. Then it's just a matter of stacking the identical U-Ved sections on top of one another to make the texturing job in Chapter 12 much easier.

Step 1: Unwrap the Legs

Let's start by getting the feet and legs unfolded and stashed away. The entire model can be symmetrically stacked for texturing—that is, you can unwrap both sides of the model, and place each unfolded part on top of the other so in Chapter 12, "Skinning the Slogre with Deep Paint 3D and Photoshop," you only have to texture half of the model.

1. Zoom in to one of the legs of the slogre and click on the Lasso tool.

2. At the top of the screen, activate the Back Faces button so your selection will include points on the other side of the model as well.

3. Draw a selection completely around the leg (see Figure 6.14).

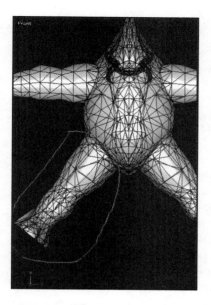

Figure 6.14 *Use the Lasso tool with the Back Faces option checked to select a leg of the slogre.*

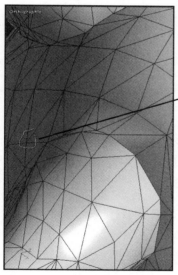

Figure 6.15 *Deselect points that don't belong to the leg.*

Deselect points from body

4. Zoom in very close to where the leg meets the body and, again using the Lasso tool, press and hold down the Alt key as you circle points that aren't part of the leg to subtract them from the selection. As shown in Figure 6.15, the red areas are selected, while the blue are deselected. (Note that a selected point causes the edge between itself and a deselected point to fade from red to blue).

5. With the entire leg selected, choose Cut in the Command Panel to cut those points away from the rest of the group.

6. Use the Move tool to move the red cluster away from the general group of points (see Figure 6.16).

7. Repeat steps 1–6 for the other leg.

8. Before you attempt to unfold the newly isolated legs, let's cut and unfold the bottom of the feet. (That way, the legs can be unfolded purely with cylinder-style mapping.) Zoom in close to one of the feet and create a lasso selection along the end as I have in Figure 6.17.

9. If your selection of the bottom of the foot included points on the foot itself, deselect them.

> **TIP**
>
> Remember that anything you do to the texture points in this program does not physically affect the actual vertices of the mesh model itself. You're only messing with the model's texture coordinates, which, before unwrapping, represent a 1:1 correspondence with the mesh's vertices.

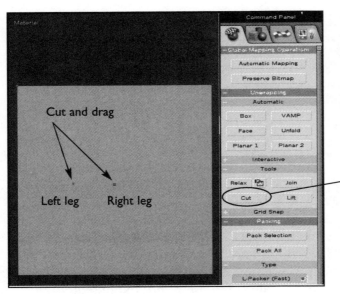

Figure 6.16 *Cut and move the leg points away from the group. Repeat for the other leg.*

Cut and drag

Left leg   Right leg

The Cut button

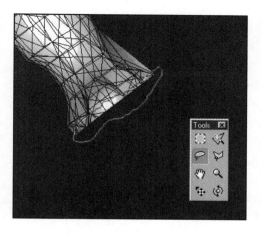

Figure 6.17
*Create a lasso selec-
tion around the bot-
tom of one foot.*

10. Click Cut to cut the points of the bottom of the foot away from the rest of the leg, and click the Planar 1 mapping button in the Command panel to unfold it as in Figure 6.18.

11. Click the Relax button so the coordinates settle naturally and prevent texture streaking.

NOTE
The Planar 1 and 2 mapping buttons offer two simple orthogonal mapping techniques that you'll use occasionally. If one doesn't do the trick, try the other.

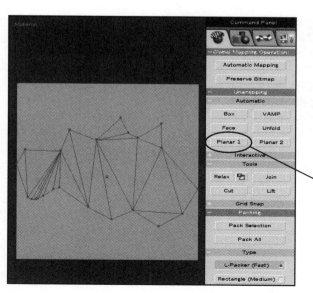

Figure 6.18 *Cut the bottom of the foot away and choose Planar 1 mapping to unfold it. Relax the points when finished.*

The Planar 1 button

12. Repeat steps 8–11 for the bottom of the other foot, and then position one piece on top of the other as shown in Figure 6.19 (you'll have to click Edit, Transform, Flip Vertical to get both pieces to match).

13. When the pieces are aligned, choose Edit, Transform, Scale, and scale the group down so it isn't so big, and then move it out of the way.

14. Now for the feet. I'd like to unwrap the feet separately since they're awkwardly shaped and won't unwrap nicely along with the rest of the leg. Notice, however, that there's a long, unbroken face that runs from the foot to the leg. I like that detail, but it will make it difficult to select the foot evenly (see Figure 6.20). Here's where the advantage to working between 3D Studio and DeepUV comes into play; let's go back to Max and create an edge that breaks this face in half. First, choose File, Export, Send UV Update to send your changes to the U-V coordinates back to Max (assuming you've kept Max and the slogre model open during this entire procedure).

15. When the update is complete, switch to 3D Studio Max and expand the Editable Mesh item in the Modifier stack. Select Edge and, in the stack's panel, click on the Cut button.

16. Click on the middle of the obnoxious edge and drag to a nearby perpendicular vertex. Right-click to close the edge.

17. Repeat step 16 for the other side of the edge. While you're at it, break the faces below this edge to make them nice and continuous (see Figure 6.21).

18. Repeat steps 16 and 17 for the other foot.

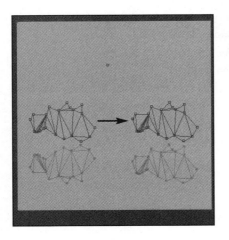

Figure 6.19
Repeat steps 8–11 for the other foot, and flip/align the two.

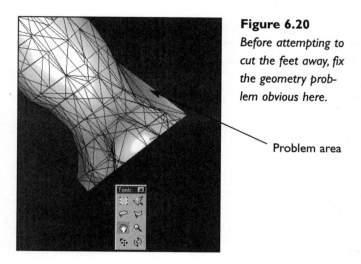

Figure 6.20
Before attempting to cut the feet away, fix the geometry problem obvious here.

Problem area

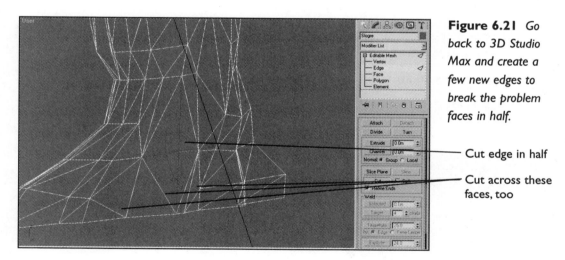

Figure 6.21 *Go back to 3D Studio Max and create a few new edges to break the problem faces in half.*

Cut edge in half

Cut across these faces, too

19. When you're finished creating the new edges, go to the Utilities tab and click Map Selection. (Remember, you've altered the mesh by adding new edges and vertices, and therefore have changed the U-V map slightly—the U-V points correspond to the physical locations of the model's vertices.)

20. The newly fixed map should now appear in DeepUV; zoom in and lasso the foot (see Figure 6.22).

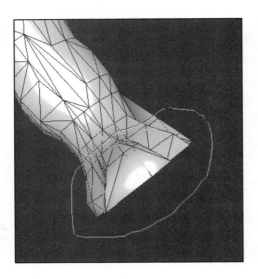

Figure 6.22 *With each foot's geometry fixed, lasso a selection around one.*

21. After you've selected a foot, cut it away and apply Planar 1 mapping. When finished, relax this area.

22. Repeat steps 20 and 21 for the other foot.

23. Align both maps and set them aside (see Figure 6.23).

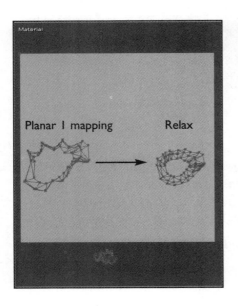

Figure 6.23 *Cut the foot away and apply a Planar 1 mapping.*

CAUTION

If at any point you try to relax your cut selection and something out of the ordinary happens (for instance, the selection suddenly becomes enormous, or DeepUV crashes), then something is wrong with the mesh of the object itself. The only thing you can do is return to 3D Studio Max and fix the problem. Usually, the problem is something as simple as an open face, an isolated vertex that's attached to nothing, and so on. Just zoom close to the mesh and you'll usually see the problem.

24. Now for the legs. Select one of the two small clumps that represent the legs in the middle of the Material map.

25. Click the Interactive: Cylinder button.

26. Click the Centering: Selection button to center the mapping gizmos on the center of the leg.

27. Because the leg is off at an angle, you'll have to interactively align the projection along the long axis of the leg as I have done in Figure 6.24. Do so by clicking and dragging any of the x-, y-, or z-axis gizmos to rotate them. Also, look to the left at the unfolded map of the leg—you want to make sure that the map is unfolded in a way that makes the seam (that is, the edges of the texture map) align itself with the *inside* of the leg. That way, when you apply your texture to the model, the seams are placed in the most unnoticeable location. See Table 6-1 for a quick guide on mapping techniques and where to align seams for most character models.

28. When you're satisfied with your leg's mapping, click the Relax button. Notice that the U-V map relaxes weirdly, away from the nice and rectangular shape it once had. That's because the relaxed shape now appears natural, as if you took a pair of scissors and cut the mesh down the seam, like a pants leg, and laid it out on a table. This is exactly what you're trying to achieve here, so when you texture the map, none of your work will smear or distort.

29. Repeat step 28 for the other leg, and align the maps of both legs and move them out of the way (see Figure 6.25).

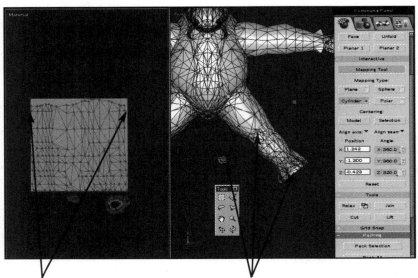

Figure 6.24 *Use Interactive: Cylinder mapping for the legs. Make sure the seams are aligned with the inside.*

Outer edges of map represent seam inside of leg

Rotate gizmos to align to leg, then align to seam

Table 6.1 Seam-Alignment Suggestions

Mesh Portion	Mapping Technique	Seam Location
Head (normal)	Spherical	Top/back
Head (oblong)	Planar/Cylindrical	Top
Face	Planar	n/a
Body	Planar/Cylindrical	Sides
Tail	Cylindrical	Bottom
Arms/Legs	Cylindrical	Inside, facing body
Feet	Planar/Cylindrical	Inside, facing body
Bottom of feet	Planar	n/a

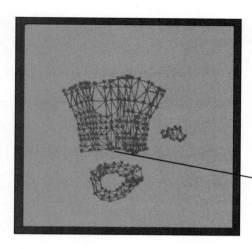

Figure 6.25 *Relax the leg's mapping and repeat for the other leg. When finished, align both maps and move them out of the way.*

Both leg components, completed and overlapped

This concludes the mapping of the legs. Normally, I'd just say "Repeat for the arms." Your character's arms, however, are quite different from those of other characters, so you'll need to handle them a bit differently. Before you continue, though, choose File, Export, Send UV Update to transfer your work back to 3D Studio Max. It's also a good idea to switch back over to Max and save your file so you won't lose your work.

Step 2: Unwrap the Arms

The most complex part of the slogre's arms are its fingers. There's a lot going on there, what with the long fingernails and all. But because there won't be a whole lot of texture detail on them, you'll just stack 'em and skip 'em. After all, nobody will notice the itsy bitsy finger detail in a video game, so why bother?

1. Right-click on the 3D view of the slogre and select View, Front.

2. Zoom in close to one of the slogre's hands and use the Rectangle selection tool to select it (see Figure 6.26).

3. Make sure the Back Faces option is checked so you get all the points, and then cut the hand away.

4. Apply Planar 2 mapping to the newly cut hand (see Figure 6.27).

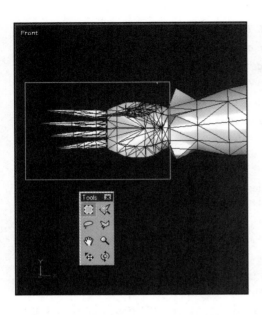

Figure 6.26 *Select and cut away one of the hands in the Front view.*

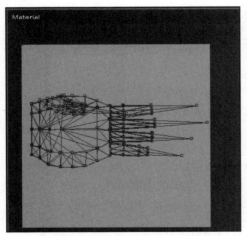

Figure 6.27 *Apply Planar 2 mapping to the hand.*

5. The top and bottom of the hand itself are what you're interested in here, so you'll need to isolate them. In a Top view of the model, select and cut away the thumb (see Figure 6.28). With the thumb away, you'll have an easier time tackling the rest of the hand.

6. Switch to a Back view of the model and zoom in close to the back side of the hand (where the nails face you).

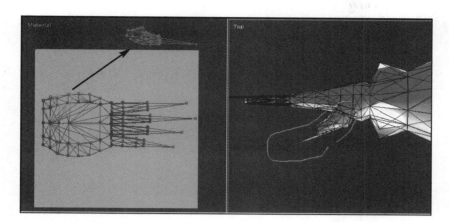

Figure 6.28 *Cut the thumb away in the Top view.*

7. Uncheck the Back Faces option, and create another rectangular selection around the hand. Do this in the 3D view, and *not* in the Material view. That way, you'll get all the points on the back of the hand and not on the front.

8. Deselect any points that were wrongfully selected in the thumb and arm (see Figure 6.29), and cut the selection away.

9. Once the back side of the hand is cut away, move it next to the other side of the hand so you can work on both (see Figure 6.30).

CAUTION

Don't relax the hands yet, or everything will get messed up.

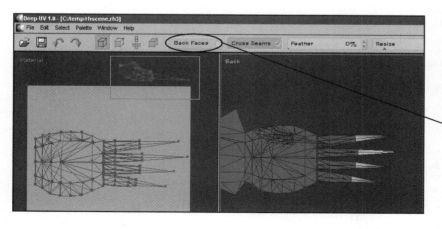

Figure 6.29 *In the Back view, select the points on the back of the hand.*

Back Faces button

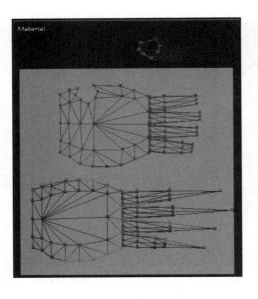

Figure 6.30 *Move the front and back of the hands away from each other.*

10. Use the Rectangle selection tool to select and cut the fingers away from each part of the hand (see Figure 6.31). After the fingers are away, select each part of the hand and relax it.

11. Notice that after you relax the top and bottom of the palm, a small piece sticks out of one that apparently belongs to the other. Select the piece, cut it away, and move it over to the other part of the palm like a jigsaw puzzle. Then, select the points that each piece shares, click the Join button, and re-select the hand and relax it, as shown in Figure 6.32. (This operation is exactly the same as the one I described in Chapter 5 when operating on the RF-9's hoops.)

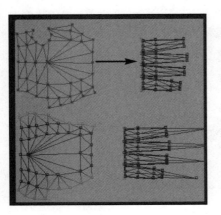

Figure 6.31 *Cut the fingers away from each part of the hand.*

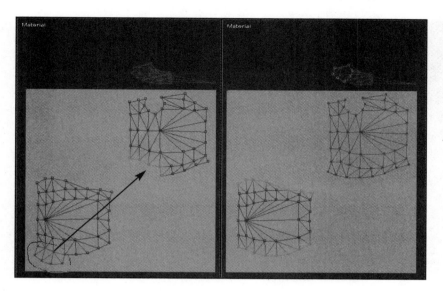

Figure 6.32

Relaxing the palms displays a piece of one palm that belongs to the other. Cut it away and re-join it to its rightful owner.

12. Repeat steps 1–11 for the other hand.

13. Stack the top parts of the two palms together as one piece, and repeat for the bottom parts. That way, you can texture the top and bottom of the hand separately. (The fingers can all be stacked in one clump, to which you'll apply subtle detail.)

14. Use the Rectangle selection tool to select the cuff on one arm—be sure to check off the Back Faces option at top.

15. Apply Interactive: Cylinder mapping, centering it on the selection, and align it along the x axis (see Figure 6.33).

16. Repeat steps 14 and 15 for the other cuff.

17. Relax the cuffs, and stack them on top of the other.

18. Select the arm in the same manner as you did the leg, and apply Interactive: Cylinder mapping to it.

19. Align the seam on the –y axis (see Figure 6.34).

NOTE

To get a handle on the axial alignments, look at the xyz axes in the lower-left corner of the 3D Perspective screen, and note that the arm is pointing down the x axis. Note, too, that the y axis is up and down, so if you want the seam of the arm on the inside, you'd tell DeepUV to align the seam along the –y axis.

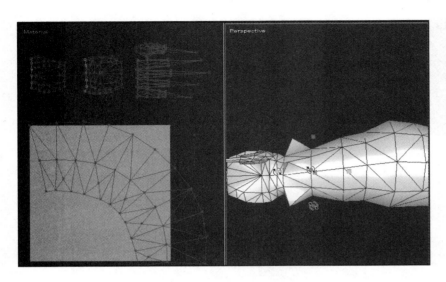

Figure 6.33 *After stacking the hand parts, unwrap the cuffs of the arm using Interactive: Cylinder mapping.*

20. Relax the arm.

21. Repeat steps 18–20 for the other arm.

22. Stack these two arm pieces on top of each other (one side will have to be flipped to match).

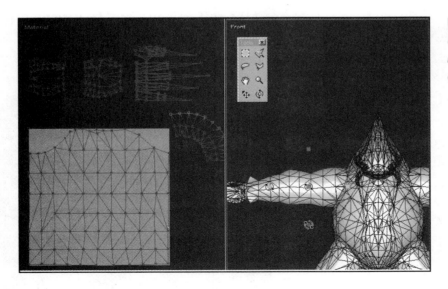

Figure 6.34 *Unwrap the arms using Interactive: Cylinder mapping.*

That completes the arms. Just move the components away for now, and at the end you'll organize the map neatly. Before you continue, choose File, Export, Send UV Update to transfer your work back to 3D Studio Max. It would also be a good idea to switch back over to Max and save your file so you won't lose your work. Now let's move on to the head portion of the slogre, which represents the most detail of the model.

Step 3: Unwrap the Head and Body

Normal human characters have fairly spherically shaped heads, and therefore an Interactive: Sphere mapping would suffice. However, 'tis not this case for this lovely beast, which will require a combination of Interactive: Sphere mapping plus some cutting and stitching to get it just right. I also want to get more of the neck in there because, according to the sketches in earlier chapters, the underside has a very snake-like appearance.

1. In a Top view, lasso one of the tusks as shown in Figure 6.35 and cut it away. Be sure to deselect any points of the head that you may have accidentally grabbed; if you cut the wrong points, however, you can always re-join them with the rest of the head's U-V mesh and try again.

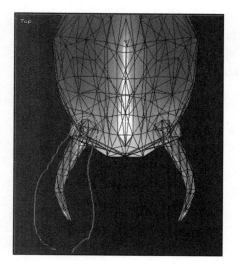

Figure 6.35 *Select a tusk in the Top view.*

2. Once the tusk is cut away, apply Planar 2 mapping. Because the tusk won't get much detail other than a cloudy, off-white texture, you don't have to unwrap or relax it.

3. Repeat steps 1 and 2 the other tusk, stack them, and set them aside (see Figure 6.36).

4. The remaining cluster of points at the top-left of the Material map represents the entire head and body. Select that, and apply Planar 2 mapping (see Figure 6.37). This will give you a nice profile of the character with which to work.

5. Use the Lasso tool to select the forward portion of the head, which will require the most detail on your behalf. Zoom in to the neck region and select the points that spill downward from the head as well (see Figure 6.38); just be sure to uncheck the Back Faces option when doing this or you'll grab points through the mesh. Once it is selected, cut and move the head away.

6. Apply Interactive: Sphere mapping to the head, again centering it on the selection. Align the mapping technique along the +z axis, and align the seam along the −y axis. (Don't do this manually; use the alignment control panel in that mapping section!)

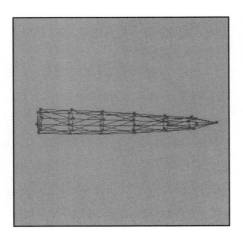

Figure 6.36

Apply Planar 2 mapping to the tusk. Repeat steps 1 and 2 for the other tusk, and stack them.

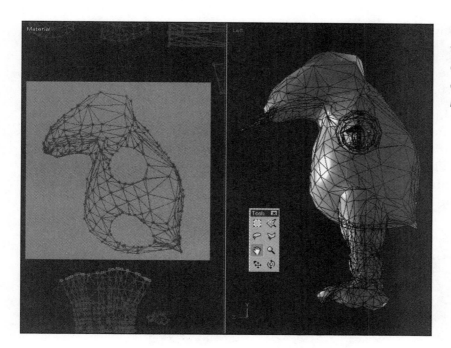

Figure 6.37 *Select the remaining points on the Material map and apply a Planar 2 mapping.*

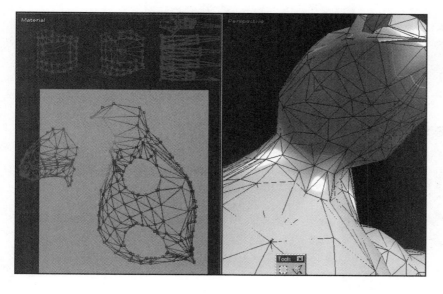

Figure 6.38 *Select the forward portion of the head and cut it away.*

7. Relax the selection (see Figure 6.39).

8. The lower portion of the map has points that could be joined, so select them and click the Join button. Then, reselect the entire head and relax it again (see Figure 6.40).

9. The face in the center of the map may be a little scrunched, even after relaxing. This is due to the fact that there is a sharp transition between the face points and the rest of the head, and DeepUV is doing its best to relax it all proportionally. This is why I kept the top portion of my map unjoined, so DeepUV didn't have to wrestle with it. Zoom into the face area and select it, and click the Relax button again to see it smooth out a bit (see Figure 6.41).

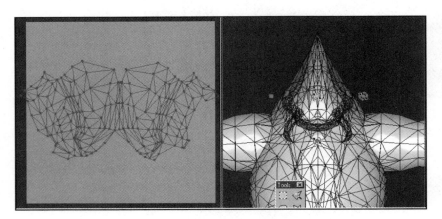

Figure 6.39 *Apply an Interactive: Sphere mapping to the head and relax the selection.*

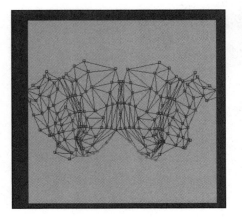

Figure 6.40 *Join the broken portion of the neck area and relax the head again.*

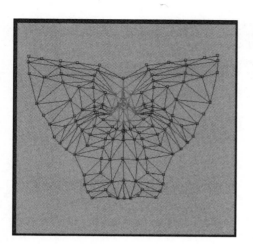

Figure 6.41 *Select the face portion of the map and relax it.*

10. You're finished with the head and face; move that map out of the way for now.

11. Select the rest of the body in the Left view, with Back Faces unchecked (this allows you to select just one half of the body, as shown in Figure 6.42).

12. Cut the selection away from the other half of the body and relax it.

13. Select the other half, and relax it as well. Stack the two pieces together (see Figure 6.43).

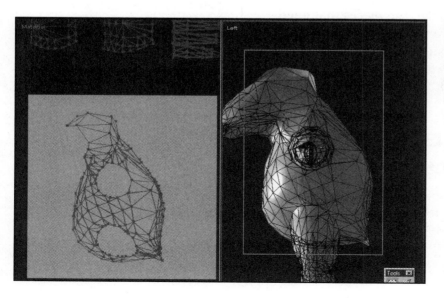

Figure 6.42 *In the Left view, select one half of the body with Back Faces unchecked.*

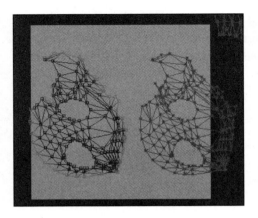

Figure 6.43 *Cut, relax, and stack the two body halves together.*

Pack the Map

As I mentioned in the previous chapter, it's best to pack these maps manually so you can give preference to items that need more detail. The logic is thus: The larger the scale of an individual map item on the Material map, the more texture detail you'll be able to apply to it. If you were to scale the head portion of the map down to a tiny little piece, how much texture detail would show up once the texture skin was reduced to 256×256 pixels? Not a lot, my friend. So in this case, the pieces that need the most detail are the head, followed by the body, arms, legs, and so on. Figure 6.44 shows my map, packed with preferences to those pieces mentioned.

> **TIP**
> When you place and scale the pieces on the map, use Edit, Free Transform in conjunction with the Shift key to scale the pieces uniformly.

Update and View the Results in Max

Once your map is packed, choose File, Export, Send UV Update to send your completed work back to 3D Studio Max. Then, switch back to Max and click on the Modifier tab to see all the stacked updates you've sent. The topmost update is the

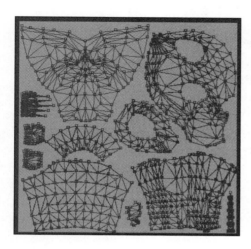

Figure 6.44 *The completed slogre U-V mapped, packed, and ready to texture.*

latest—to view it, add an Unwrap UVW modifier to the stack, and in its panel, click the Edit button (see Figure 6.45). Now you're ready to texture the slogre. To commence this process, save your scene in Max, then skip to Chapter 12.

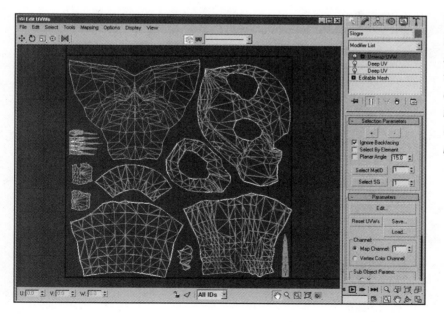

Figure 6.45
Export the final version of the map back to Max. View the completed mapping in Max using an Unwrap UVW modifier.

Summary

In this chapter, I showed you how to import your slogre mesh from Chapter 4 and complete it using 3D Studio Max attaching, optimizing, and smoothing techniques. The U-V coordinates, which represent the way the skin texture for the model will be wrapped around it, were exported to DeepUV. This program allowed us to isolate and unwrap individual portions of the slogre's U-V's, thereby generating a two-dimensional and easily texturable skin map. The combination of Max and DeepUV rendered this entire operation painless and swift and prepared the model for its texturing phase, which is covered in Chapter 12.

PART THREE

TEXTURING THE UV'S WITH DEEPUV

CHAPTER 7

GAME
TEXTURING

In this chapter I'll introduce you to the vast world of game texturing. This will be a primer, so to speak, for the chapters that follow. Specifically, this chapter covers

- The game texturing arena
- Different types of textures
- Texturing techniques
- Application of textures

Introduction to Game Texturing

I think you'll find that the art of designing textures for games has become a field in itself. (In fact, my next book might be solely about game textures.) I wish I had more room in this book to cover every gritty detail, but I'm going to do my best to show you the median of what you should be familiar with in each of the texturing categories. You see, a good game (especially a 3D one) has quite an amalgam of different types of textures, from ones made from scratch, to "scripted" ones via filters, to photo-based . . . all to deliver some eye candy to the player.

Types of Textures

Even though we're headed towards pure photorealism in games (hmmm, I'd say around the year 2012), not every game that's developed now or in the future will require an environment that appears purely photorealistic. In fact, sometimes it's cool to create a game that appears cartoon-like or bizarrely unreal—so don't panic too much when trying to make things look perfectly real. I'll be covering many different types of textures as this book progresses, many of which simulate the real world, but also others that would fit nicely with Hanna-Barbera! That said, let's discuss the various texture categories:

- Hand-drawn textures
- Photo-based textures
- Compositing textures
- Seamless textures
- Animated textures

Hand-Drawn Textures

For the most part, I'll show you how to create textures from scratch using either Photoshop versions 6 or 7 (both are nearly identical in general functionality and tool locations). Of course, it's easier to get a picture of something real, clean it up, and make a texture out of it; however, I want you to be able to make just about anything by hand should the need arise.

Inorganic Versus Organic

Throughout this book, I tend to categorize models and textures as *inorganic* and *organic*. By *inorganic*, I mean that, whatever it is, it's most likely portraying something carved from steel, wood, or even rock—mostly inanimate objects. By *organic*, I mean objects or other entities that have fluidity to their shape, or are in fact alive. Organic, to me, are things that relate directly to living things. Rock-based textures I like to contain within the inorganic category, despite their worldly origins, because they represent materials used more for building things.

I believe inorganic textures (rocks, metals, walls, floors, and the like) to be the easiest and most fun, as well as being the most realistic. For example, I made the Mars rock texture shown in Figure 7.1 in under a minute using only a handful of the default filters that come with Photoshop. I couldn't believe how realistic it was; I honestly didn't expect it to look that good (I'll show you how to make it in the next chapter).

Figure 7.1 *A quick Mars rock texture.*

Organic textures—that is, any living (or once alive) carbon-based life form or part of something living—can be either unbelievably easy or a total pain to create. Animal and reptile skins are usually easy to make by hand because they take the same path as rock-texture creation—usually you can achieve a great base texture for them using only a handful of Photoshop's filters. Textures for humans, insects, or anything else with complex detail, however, can be a real challenge for someone like me who has limited freehand artistic ability. Figure 7.2 shows a weak example of a texture map I made for a butterfly . . . I'll show you how to make skin textures for the Slogre model later on in Part III.

Photo-Based Textures

No doubt you'll encounter many occasions when using a photograph of a brick wall, tree bark, a rusted pipe, or whatever to create your texture will be easier than creating it from scratch. A good example would be if your game called for you to create a texture for the side of an old train car. Just get a really good snapshot of the car in broad daylight, clean it up a bit, and slap it on the side of a 3D model—it's much easier than spending a couple hours trying to make something real.

The most common case of photo-based texture usage probably is with brick walls. Games sometimes have a gazillion of them, and you want the widest variety possible. So grab your digital camera, head into the big city, and go nuts. Figure 7.3 shows a seamlessly tiled brick wall texture I made from a picture I took of the side of a building. I toned it down and cleaned it up a bit so it would be more appropriate for a video game.

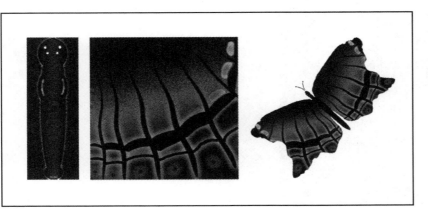

Figure 7.2 A freehand texture map applied to the skin of a butterfly model.

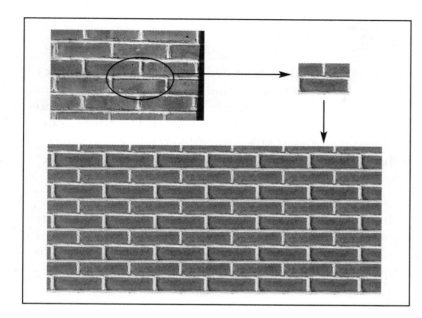

Figure 7.3 *A brick texture created from a photograph.*

Compositing Textures

Compositing is simply mashing two or more textures together, but typically it's the careful combination of a photo and a hand-drawn image. I like to make composites, often because a flat-out photo can be too, well, dorky. Integrating a part of a live picture with something you've created by hand or adding some layer effects to a picture can make a texture work very well in a game. Check out Figure 7.4—I took the brick texture from Figure 7.3 and, in Photoshop, applied a stucco look to parts of it. Now it looks like someone tried to cement over the wall, and over time it broke away.

Figure 7.4
Compositing a real picture with a hand-drawn image to make a viable texture.

Seamless Textures

Seamless textures are an art form in themselves. I don't think there's a 3D video game out there that doesn't have hundreds of seamless textures—that is, textures that can be tiled side-by-side (and sometimes above and below) each other without a noticeable seam. The basic technique for making a texture seamless is to first create the texture, and then offset it evenly using the Offset filter in Photoshop. But here's the trick: A good seamless texture has little noticeable repetition in the overall pattern. That is, when the texture is tiled, nothing stands out to make you say, "Oh, I see. It's just a simple brick wall copied over and over again."

Making a 256 × 256-pixel wall texture for a game is fairly easy—however, a good artist will spend time weeding out the "sore thumbs" in the image. For instance, the top seamless brick wall texture in Figure 7.5 has obvious shadows that stand out as its tiled—every other row seems much darker and has a brick with stains where its ends meet. After playing with it a bit, toning down some of the colors here and there, I managed to make the wall look nice, smooth, and even.

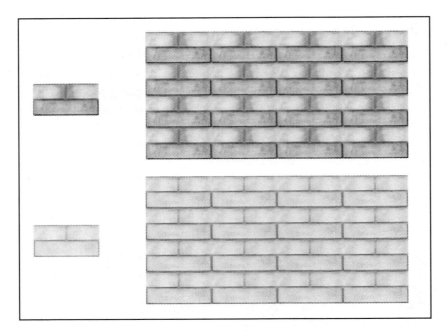

Figure 7.5
A seamless brick wall fixed for proper continuity.

Animated Textures

Often in games you'll see random belches of steam coming out of a pipe, or a flow of water gushing down a drain. Both are cases of texture animation, but the first might be considered a *sprite*, or a series of 2D textures (with transparency, meaning that all areas surrounding the smoke are transparent in a game engine) chained together to give the illusion of steam. The latter could simply be a flat-out AVI of rushing water that's overlaid onto a 3D object in the shape of water, then looped ad infinitum. Animated textures can also be as simple as a blinking light on a control panel—two textures are created; one for the light being on, and one for off. The game engine will handle alternating the two during game play (see Chapter 9, "Advanced Texturing Examples," where I show a simple on-off animation of two textures that creates the illusion of a power switch being activated).

Summary

The texturing world is truly divided between two different categories: inorganic and organic. Inorganic textures are those that represent man-made objects in this world, such as metal, whereas organic textures are those that represent living or natural things. As most artists paint images based on real life, textures are many times the result of compositing photographs with filtering effects in Photoshop. Whether your texture is seamlessly tileable for a large wall, or animated as a sprite to simulate steam, the next few chapters will guide you through these detailed processes so you can generate your own outstanding game textures.

CHAPTER 8

Inorganic Texture Tutorials with Photoshop

Just what are inorganic textures anyway? Inorganic textures are those textures that resemble materials such as stone or wood that may or may not be carbon-based, but are not "alive"—at least, not in their final building-material stage. All the textures I'll cover here can be created by using the filters that come by default with Photoshop versions 6 and 7, and by using images of real objects I took with my digital camera.

NOTE

Unfortunately, I can't detail every little inorganic texture that might go into a typical video game. Fear not, though; by the time you're finished practicing the textures in this chapter, you'll be saturated with information to get you rolling with your own texture creations.

TIP

This chapter assumes you're proficient in Photoshop; for this reason, the instructions in each tutorial may not spell out the details of how to accomplish each task. If you have trouble following along, check out the Photoshop tutorials found on this book's CD-ROM.

This chapter starts with some simple procedures, which you may find a bit boring. Soon, though, things will speed up. (Try to pay attention to the particular details of each tutorial, because I'll be going over some of the advanced features that Photoshop has to offer.) In particular, you will learn

- How to create the base material for most types of textures
- How to use Photoshop's default filters, pictures, or combinations of both to create inorganic textures
- How to create seamlessly tileable textures
- How to create tileable texture sets
- How to prepare textures for games
- How to Automate texture procedures using actions
- How to combine and composite images

Texture Creation

Texture creation is not a random process. A good artist will spend time creating and organizing textures to fit a particular scene or level so that everything comes together somewhat fluently, and that nothing will seem out of place. Textures are usually created in sets—that is, if you're creating a dungeon, you'll create a "dungeon set" by grouping appropriate artwork for the stone walls, floors, and ceilings; and wood textures for the doors, stretching racks, torches, and the like.

Here's a quick guideline/overview of what you should think about before embarking on any texture-creation projects:

- The more time you spend on a texture, the better (or more realistic) it will look. On the other hand, as with any business, time is money. Work fast, but work well.

- There's more than one way to skin a cat. Always think of the fastest or best way to do any particular step while creating your textures. No one way is the absolute correct way!

- Work large and reduce. Don't try to create a tileable stone wall that starts off the size of your thumb. By putting in details on a large image and then reducing the whole thing, you'll get how-did-you-do-that results.

- Understand everything that each room or scene is trying to convey. Is it happy or sad? What decade or era is it set in? Have detailed knowledge of what your game company wants, and then research the materials you'll be creating before you begin. If you're not sure, don't just try to come up with a texture in your head. Use life as your reference! Break out your camera and go to town. Literally.

- Group and work with textures in sets. Don't work randomly.

- Don't make any texture stand out unless it needs to. Blend it nicely with its surroundings.

- Be patient. A game's graphic content can make it sell.

- Don't re-invent the wheel. If a texture exists in some picture, use that instead of recreating it from scratch.

- Don't be too detailed unless the game's engine calls for it. In fact, the average game's texture is around 256×256 pixels in size; not a whole lot of detail can be crammed into that.

With that in mind, all the following procedures can be mixed and matched and placed just about anywhere in a room, on an outside surface, or on an object. Use this chapter to get a good feel for creating the base material for things; then, in the next chapter, you'll bring it all together and make some blue-ribbon textures.

TIP

As you begin to develop your own games, you'll probably discover that you use certain textures on a routine basis. Rather than re-creating those textures from scratch each time, try recording the creation process in the Actions palette. Then, the next time you need to use that texture, you can simply re-play the procedure.

Brick Textures

Brick textures are among the most often created of all textures, and there are a gazillion ways of doing every type. In this section, I'll show you the foundations for texturing brick, give you some cool tricks and examples, and let you fly on your own. In no time, you'll make the transition from texturing bricks like the ones in Figure 8.1 to creating walls like the one in Figure 8.2.

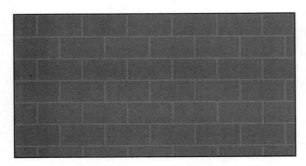

Figure 8.1 *A rudimentary brick wall.*

Figure 8.2 *A brick wall that's far cooler.*

Brick Procedure #1: From Scratch

To texture the type of brick typically found on the outside of houses, buildings, stores, and whatnot, do the following (note that rather than making an entire brick wall, you'll make a single, seamlessly tileable pattern to fill any 2D space with a brick texture):

1. In Photoshop, choose File, New Image to open a new 7×4-inch image (see Figure 8.3).

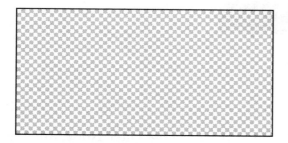

Figure 8.3 *Start a new 7×4-inch image.*

File, New Image

Width:	7 inches
Height:	4 inches
Resolution:	72
Mode:	RGB
Contents:	Transparent

2. Using the Color Picker, set the new image's foreground to bright red (hex# CE0000) and its background to dark red (hex# 900202), as shown in Figure 8.4.

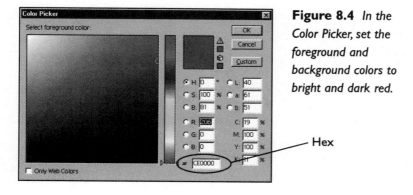

Figure 8.4 *In the Color Picker, set the foreground and background colors to bright and dark red.*

3. Choose Filter, Render, Clouds. The Clouds filter creates a cloudy blend of the foreground and background colors, as shown in Figure 8.5.

Figure 8.5 *Apply the Clouds filter to a canvas with a bright red foreground and dark red background.*

Filter: Render, Clouds
Foreground: hex# CE0000
Background: hex# 900202

4. To add some noise to break up the pattern, choose Filter, Noise, Add Noise (see Figure 8.6).

Figure 8.6 *Apply the Noise filter.*

Filter: Noise, Add Noise
Amount: 22%
Distribution: Uniform
Monochromatic: (checked)

5. Choose Filter, Texture, Craquelure to add some, er, texture to the texture (see Figure 8.7).

Figure 8.7 *Apply the Craquelure filter.*

Filter:	Craquelure
Crack Spacing:	12
Crack Depth:	3
Crack Brightness:	10

6. You now have the base of the brick texture; now it's time to put in some mortar, which is usually a medium-gray color. To begin, use the Color Picker to set your foreground to hex# 767676.

7. Add a new layer. This is important, because you'll be adding an effect to the mortar to make it appear to have depth.

8. Turn on your rulers by choosing View, Show Rulers (or pressing Ctrl+R).

9. Select the Line tool, and make sure its options are set as follows, from left to right (this will enable you to draw a thick gray line on the image):

Create Filled checkbox (third from left)	Enabled
Weight	25 pixels
Mode	Normal
Opacity	100%

10. Using the rulers as a guide, draw a horizontal line across the middle of the image at the 2-inch mark. Draw another line from the horizontal line's center (the 3.5-inch mark) to the bottom of the canvas, as shown in Figure 8.8.

TIP

To constrain the Line tool to 45-degree increments, press and hold down the Shift key on your keyboard as you drag to draw the line.

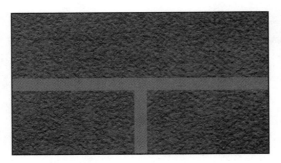

Figure 8.8 *Use the Line tool to draw dividing lines in the texture.*

11. Draw four more lines along top, bottom, and *top sides* of the image, but this time draw them so that only half of the line's width is displayed. (That way, when the texture is tiled, the opposite edges will combine to form a whole width.) To do so, align your cursor along each edge of the image, press and hold down the Shift key, and drag (see Figure 8.9).

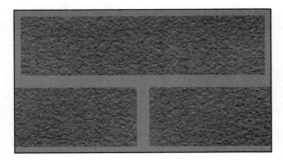

Figure 8.9 *Draw half-width lines along the top, bottom, and top sides of the image.*

12. Double-click the mortar's layer to bring up the Layer Styles screen, click the Bevel and Emboss effect, and add an inverted outer bevel (see Figure 8.10).

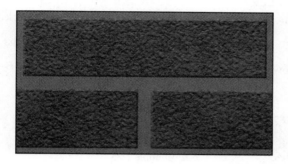

Figure 8.10 *Add an inverted outer bevel to the mortar's layer.*

Style, Bevel and Emboss

Style:	Outer Bevel
Technique:	Smooth
Depth:	100%
Direction:	Down
Size:	5 pixels
Soften:	10 pixels

13. Still in the mortar layer, choose Filter, Noise, Add Noise, using the same noise settings as before.

14. Choose Filter, Texture, Craquelure, using the same settings as before (see Figure 8.11).

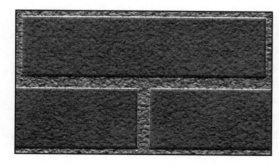

Figure 8.11 *Finish the mortar by adding Noise and Craquelure.*

15. Flatten the image (that is, combine the layers) by clicking Layer, Flatten Image.

16. That's it! The pattern is complete. It is, however, really big, so you'll need to click Image, Image Size and change the width to 128 pixels (or however small you want). When you change the width, the height will proportionally adjust automatically, so long as the Constrain Proportions option is checked.

17. Choose Edit, Define Pattern to add the pattern to the existing pattern list.

18. Fill any blank space on any new or existing image with the pattern; Figure 8.12 shows the result.

Figure 8.12

Reduce the image to a reasonable size and add it to your pattern list. Finally, try filling a blank space in an image with it.

> **TIP**
>
> You could have created the brick wall shown in **Figure 8.12** by simply drawing all the mortar lines in the wall by hand instead of tiling a smaller image, but doing so would be quite time consuming. Tiling is a great way to save time as you create textures, but not all objects tile evenly the way the bricks in this image do. To figure out how uneven patterns tile, just look at the real-world object you're trying to create to determine how the elements in the pattern repeat.

If you think this first tutorial seems a bit lengthy, wait until you start doing some of the high-end stuff. Instead of 18 steps and 10 minutes, try 500 steps and two days! Good textures take some time.

Brick Procedure #2: From an Existing Image

More often than not, you'll create a texture using a photograph of the real McCoy—or at least using portions of a photograph to create a seamless pattern, and then combining that with patterns you've made by hand. In this example, you'll isolate the repetitious pattern in a digital photograph, and then fill a blank canvas with it to see it in action.

1. In Photoshop, open the **brick01.jpg** file in the Chapter 8 Data section on the CD-ROM (see Figure 8.13).

Figure 8.13 *Open the brick01.jpg image on the CD-ROM.*

2. Notice that the image is slightly tilted clockwise by about 1 degree. To fix this, click Image, Rotate Canvas, Arbitrary. Then, type 1 in the Angle field, select CCW (counter-clockwise), and click OK. The bricks (not the canvas) should be somewhat level now (see Figure 8.14).

Figure 8.14 *Straighten out the image using the Rotate Canvas feature.*

3. Using the Crop tool, select an area in the image that includes a single brick on top with two half bricks beneath, like the pattern you created in the preceding section. Remember to include one-half of the mortar that surrounds these bricks so when the pattern is tiled, the halves will constitute a whole (see Figure 8.15).

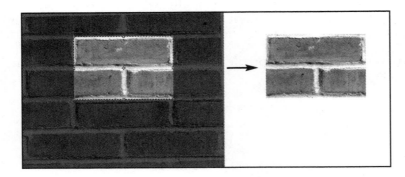

Figure 8.15 *Use the Crop tool to isolate a tileable pattern from the brick wall.*

4. Click Edit, Define Pattern, give the pattern a name, and click OK.

5. Open a new, big, blank image—say, 1024×1024.

6. Click Edit, Fill.

7. Under Contents, select Pattern. In the Custom Pattern list, select your new brick pattern, and click OK. You should now have a filled image similar to the one in Figure 8.16.

Figure 8.16
Define your brick selection as a pattern and fill a blank image with it.

8. In my filled image, I see a handful of imperfections that repeat all over the place (see Figure 8.17). To eliminate these flaws in your image, return to the first image from which you created the pattern, and use the Clone Stamp tool to cover the blemishes. In addition, you can use the Clone Stamp tool to eliminate the shadows on the mortar (copy over shadowed areas with non-shadowed mortar). Alternatively, you can use the Dodge tool with a low exposure setting to do the trick.

9. As you make adjustments and clean up your pattern, re-define the pattern and fill your test image with it to see your progress (see Figure 8.18).

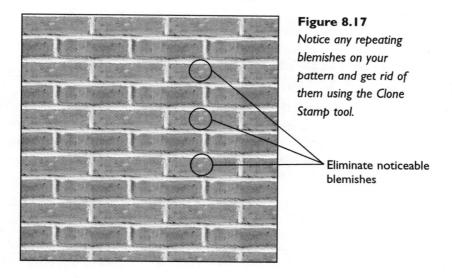

Figure 8.17
Notice any repeating blemishes on your pattern and get rid of them using the Clone Stamp tool.

Eliminate noticeable blemishes

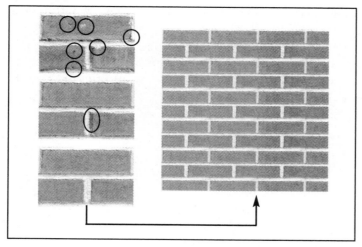

Figure 8.18 *Keep cleaning up your pattern until it's nice and even. Fill the pattern on an image to make sure it looks good.*

Of course, the more time you spend cleaning up the texture, the better it will look. That said, don't go overboard—just make sure nothing sticks out like a pimple on your nose! Here are some things to keep in mind when creating tiling textures like this:

- Use the Clone Stamp tool avidly to copy good areas and paste them over bad ones.
- Use the Clone Stamp tool to even out the texture itself.
- Dodge (and burn) shadows and highlights out of (or into) the image.
- Zoom in on your work to aid in detailed operations.
- Take your time. This is a small piece of work to make a huge wall!

Brick Procedure #3: A Quick Composite (Yeah, Right)

As I mentioned earlier, you'll often use part of a real image (or images) in combination with an object you've created from scratch in Photoshop to produce a final texture. In this section, you'll take your brick texture from the last example and add a cement/stucco look over portions of it—kind of like you'd see chipping away from brick walls in big cities:

1. The pattern you made in the last example is too big for tiling onto a typical game-texture image. To resize it, begin by clicking Image, Images Size.

2. Under Pixel Dimensions, set the width to 64 pixels. The height will proportionally readjust as long as the Constrain Proportions checkbox is checked.

3. Click Edit, Define Pattern, and add the new pattern to your pattern list.

4. Create a new 512×512 canvas.

5. Click Edit, Fill, and fill the image with the custom brick pattern you just created. This will be your base wall, which on its own would fit (or scale down and fit) nicely for a video game (see Figure 8.19).

Figure 8.19 *Fill a blank 512×512 image with the reduced brick pattern you created earlier.*

6. This brick wall is way to bright, perfect, and hazy for my tastes; to fix it, begin by clicking Image, Adjust, Levels.

7. A histogram of the input levels (the general balance of shadows, midtones, and highlights) appears. Slide the left black triangle toward the center of the histogram. Notice that the wall takes on a nice, rich, crisp red texture, much like a normal brick wall (see Figure 8.20).

> **NOTE**
>
> Levels are a very important feature in Photoshop to aid you in adjusting your images and channels. You'll use levels more as you progress.

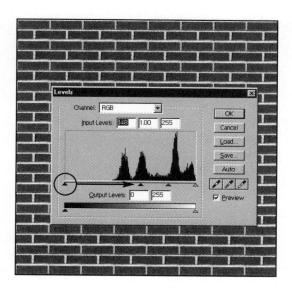

Figure 8.20 *Enrich your texture by read-justing the shadows using levels.*

8. Now that the color is okay, desaturate it a bit by clicking Image, Adjust, Hue/Saturation.

9. Drag the Saturation slider to −30 or so; the results are shown in Figure 8.21.

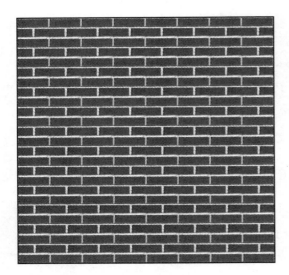

Figure 8.21
Desaturate the texture so it won't burn a hole in your eye.

10. Save your image so you can use it later as a plain brick wall. I recommend you save the image as a PSD file in a separate folder called \Textures\Brick\ or something similar.

11. Start a new layer. This will be your cement/stucco layer.

12. You could use a cement sample from a digital photo, but let's fool around with filters so you can have some fun instead. To begin, set your foreground to a grayish cement color, like hex# 7D7D7D, and set your background to a pukey yellow-green, like hex# 525035. This will constitute the disgusting blend of your cement mix (feel free to use whatever colors you want, however).

NOTE

If the wall you just created were ready for a game, you'd typically reduce it, if needed, to your game's wall proportions and save it as an 8-bit bitmap. I'll go into that in the next example.

TIP

Finding the right colors for a texture can be difficult;
that's why when you do find a color that works, you
should save it. Try storing colors in the Swatches palette
as you go, or keeping a color list (with each color's hex#);
that way, you can easily locate the colors you want.

13. Choose Filter, Render, Clouds to blend the colors on your new layer (see Figure 8.22).

Figure 8.22

*Render clouds using
cement colors.*

Filter:	Render, Clouds
Foreground:	hex#7D7D7D
Background:	hex# 525035

14. Choose Filter, Noise, Add Noise to make the texture grainier.

15. Choose Filter, Texture, Grain to break the texture up even more (see Figure 8.23).

Figure 8.23 *Add noise and grain to break up the texture.*

Filter:	Noise, Add Noise
Amount:	5%
Distribution:	Uniform
Monochromatic:	(checked)
Filter:	Texture, Grain
Intensity:	6
Contrast:	13
Grain Type:	Horizontal

16. Now you have the base composition of the cement mixture. (This doesn't have to be perfect, by the way!) From here, you want to hack away at the cement to expose the underlying brick, as though the cement has been there for a while and now it's falling away. Using the Lasso tool, select a jaggy, diagonal pattern from the bottom-left to the top-right of the canvas. Once you get to the top-right edge, move your cursor outside the image and up, over, and back down to your starting point (see Figure 8.24).

TIP

If you mess up, just press Ctrl+Alt+Z to undo the selection and try it again.

Figure 8.24 *Use the Lasso tool to select a diagonal pattern across the cement.*

17. The selection represents what will be hacked away in a moment, but it's too clean at the edges. To roughen things up, begin by pressing Q to enter Quick Mask mode. The pink area represents the non-selected area of your texture.

18. Apply a filter to the mask itself to re-define the selection boundary. To do so, choose Filter, Brush Strokes, Spatter (see Figure 8.25). This is a good technique for chipping the edges on just about anything.

Figure 8.25 *Enter Quick Mask mode and apply the Spatter filter.*

Filter: Brush Strokes, Spatter
Spray Radius: 15
Smoothness: 4

19. Exit Quick Mask mode by pressing Q again.

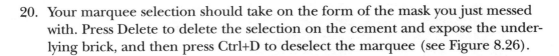

20. Your marquee selection should take on the form of the mask you just messed with. Press Delete to delete the selection on the cement and expose the underlying brick, and then press Ctrl+D to deselect the marquee (see Figure 8.26).

Figure 8.26 *Exit the Quick Mask mode and delete the selection.*

21. Switch to the background layer (the brick wall).

22. Press Ctrl+A to select the entire layer.

23. Press Ctrl+C to copy the layer to the Windows buffer.

24. In the Channels palette, click on the Create New Channel icon to create a new Alpha channel that you can use as a bump map. (I'll get more into that later).

25. Press Ctrl+V to paste the brick wall into the new channel (see Figure 8.27).

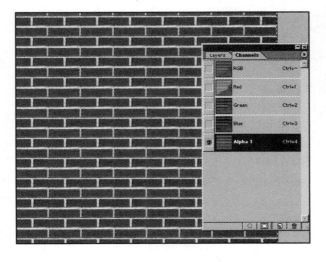

Figure 8.27 *Copy the contents of the brick-wall layer and paste them into a new Alpha channel.*

26. Click Image, Adjust, Invert to invert the black-and-white colors on the Alpha channel. The white areas represent the raised portions of the brick wall, and the black areas represent the lower portions.

27. Click Image, Adjust, Levels, and slide the middle (midtones) slider way over to the right so that most of the white in the image is washed out; all that's left should be a vague representation of the brick wall (see Figure 8.28).

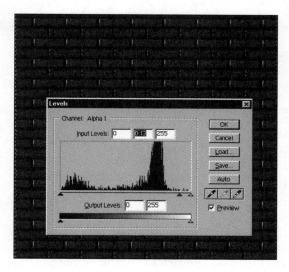

Figure 8.28 *Invert the colors and adjust the midtone levels so that most of the white is washed out.*

28. The darkened Alpha channel represents the bumps in the cement created by the underlying bricks. Any white you see will define these bumps. To apply this effect, return to the Layers palette and click on the cement layer to select it.

29. Click Filter, Render, Lighting Effects to begin rendering the layer using a light source and the Alpha channel as a bump map.

30. Choose Directional from the Light Type list.

31. Check the preview area on the left side of the dialog box to view the effect. The preview area also illustrates the light source, which, in this case, is a line with a white circle on one end and a square at the other. By grabbing either end, you can position the light source to point in the direction you wish, and by elongating it you can intensify it. (See Figure 8.29 to see how I set mine up.)

32. Pull down the Texture Channel list at the bottom of the dialog box and choose Alpha 1 (this is the Alpha channel you made a few steps ago).

33. Adjust the Height slider to 7 or something similar; you want the cement to appear as though the bricks beneath it are just slightly pushing it up. Then click OK.

NOTE

Notice the White is high checkbox near the bottom of the Lighting Effects dialog box. As I mentioned earlier, any white in your Alpha channel represents the raised portion in the final rendering with the filter. The more intense the white, the higher things will appear.

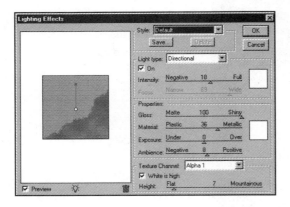

Figure 8.29 *Apply the Lighting Effects filter to the cement layer to give the texture an aligned bump map.*

34. The cement appears to be very thin, and the bricks' surfaces are pushing it up. To break up the repetition of the cement, choose Filter, Brush Strokes, Spatter and use the settings noted near Figure 8.30.

35. To give the entire texture a more realistic masonry look, choose Filter, Noise, Dust & Scratches.

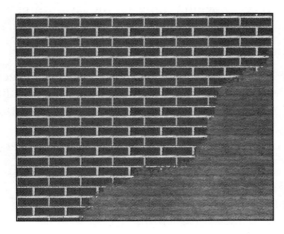

Figure 8.30 *Apply the Spatter filter to the cement to break up the pattern a bit.*

Filter:	Brush Strokes, Spatter
Spray Radius:	5
Smoothness:	7
Filter:	Noise, Dust & Scratches
Radius:	9
Threshold:	35

36. If you like, you can give the chipped edges of the cement a bit of a 3D effect to make it look rather thick; simply apply an outer-bevel style to the cement layer. (I changed the Highlight Mode setting to a grayish color, set it to Normal, and set the Opacity to 100%, as shown in Figure 8.31.) Click OK. Figure 8.32 shows the final texture, ready to be plopped into a game.

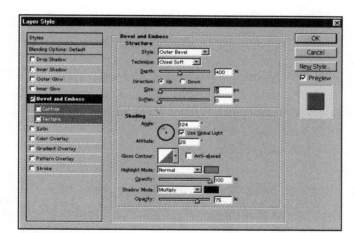

Figure 8.31 *Apply an outer bevel to the cement layer to give the edges a 3D look.*

Figure 8.32 *The final texture panel.*

Fini! I know this example may seem a bit tedious, especially if you haven't done texturing like this before, but get used to it. If it makes you feel better, the steps you took constitute a large portion of techniques that normally go into most textures.

> **NOTE**
>
> None of the settings in any step are cast in stone; try adjusting things all over the place to vary your results to your satisfaction!

Here's a quick recap of some of the things that went into this texture, and that comprise most textures I create:

- My textures almost always have some photograph of the real thing from which to extract a tangible base layer, either from directly copying portions of the picture or recreating the texture using the picture as a reference.

- Textures are generally highly detailed. It's not uncommon to apply a dozen filters just to get the base of a texture working.

- Almost every texture has some sort of 3D effect to make it look real and not flat. Alpha channels can be used extensively in this respect to give textures realism.

- Edges of objects within my textures usually have a 3D look. Beveling and embossing are commonly applied to achieve that.

- Drop shadows can be used to pull objects in textures away from others.

Setting Up Textures for a Game

I'd like to give you a heads up on how you might prepare your textures for whatever game engine you're working with (I'll be showing you how to bring your work into the *Torque* engine, but most other engines work similarly).

I said earlier that your textures should be evenly divisible by some multiple of 8 or 16. This is a good rule to follow for several reasons. For one, game engines are coded following certain rules spawned by the language in which they are generated. The language (most probably C++) works with variables to store numbers that are powers of two (binary), and typically these variables are 8- and 16-bit. You therefore want your engine to deal with external assets, such as textures, that have dimensions that are at least divisible by two or by a factor of two, like 16.

Another reason to keep your textures dimensionally consistent is for placing them in the level you're designing. It would be cumbersome to have to constantly tweak and adjust textures for walls and other objects if the textures had all sorts of weird measurements. It would be much better if, for instance, your wall textures were all 256×256 pixels in size. Then all you would have to do is create walls that were 256 pixels high, make your editing environment snap to multiples of 16, and easily place the texture map(s) on the walls.

Finally, in many cases, game engines require that your bitmap be constrained within a maximum size and that it also be divisible by some binary multiple. For instance, if you are developing textures for Half-Life, your texture bitmaps are limited to a maximum size of 256 × 256 pixels, must be 8-bit BMPs, and the length and width must be divisible by 2. On the other hand, the Unreal engine's ceiling allows for a maximum size of 1024 × 1024 pixels (although you'll find that most of the textures in Unreal are not much bigger than 256 × 256), either the length or the width must be divisible by 2, and the images themselves must be 8-bit PCXs. Newer engines and newer graphics cards will allow for higher-resolution textures, but I think a 1024 × 1024-pixel image is as much eye candy as I want to ingest!

Resize and Palletize

If you've played any 3D first-person game since the turn of the new millennium, the walls that constitute the boundaries of your environment were probably adorned with 256 × 256-pixel textures either seamlessly tiled using just one image or using a tileable set. From analyzing these games, I've noticed that the lead character's height is typically in the ballpark of 128 to 177 pixels, or just over half the height of a texture panel (in level-editor measurements, this generally translates to a character height of around two meters). Therefore, using the brick image you just created,

> **NOTE**
>
> Keep in mind that I'm dishing out advice and settings based on what I work with using *Torque-*, *Quake-*, and *Unreal*-based engines. Make sure you check with the documentation or the programmers of the game engine you're working with to determine what your textures need to be. Even if you're reading this to learn how to make artwork for something like *Unreal Tournament*, read up on texture specs that come with the level editor. You're most likely going to have to finagle things to make them work just right!

choose Image, Image Size, and set the dimensions to 256 × 256. For consistency, you can also set the resolution to 256 pixels per inch, making the overall image size one square inch. (Don't worry about that too much. Only affects the output if you print it.) You might have to uncheck the Constrain Proportions checkbox to keep the numbers the way you want them.

The next thing you need to do is palletize the image. You're currently working in RGB (24-bit) color mode, which is typical for any texture creation, but the image will have too much color information for a typical game engine to handle (although some game engines, like the *Torque* engine, will accept it). The programmers of games like *Half-Life* and *Unreal* force artists to *palletize* their textures, or convert their artwork to use a self-contained palette consisting of only 256 (8-bit) colors. This will help to dramatically speed up the game without much loss of texture quality (sort of).

To palletize your image, click Image, Mode, Indexed Color. Set your palette to Local (Selective) and Colors to 256. This will make Photoshop analyze your image and select the best matching 256 colors to stick in an accompanying palette, which is subsequently stored in the BMP or PCX file when you save the texture. Also, set Forced to None. Later on, you can do something advanced like force your texture groups to use a common palette for game optimization, but let's not go overboard for now. When everything is set, click OK. Now your image has only 256 colors, and is ready to be saved as a BMP or PCX file (see Figure 8.33). You can see the actual palette your file will use by clicking Image, Mode, Color Table.

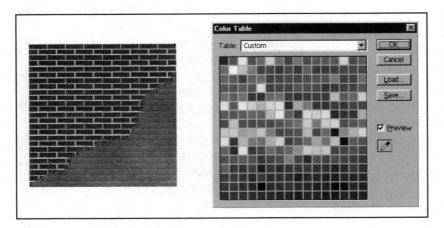

Figure 8.33 *The brick texture resized for a 3D game engine. Note the color table (palette) that the image uses.*

I know the image now looks small and silly, but once brought into a game, it will regain its proportions. In Figure 8.34, I took my 256×256 brick texture, including a few similar ones, and made a simple street corner using the *Unreal* game level editor. It could use a bit of finesse, but it'll work, don't you think?

Figure 8.34
Importing and applying the finalized brick texture into the Unreal game engine.

Cement Textures

In the last section, you created a cement-like texture that was smeared over brick. This section rehashes what you learned somewhat, but also shows you how to take an image without a pattern and make it tileable.

Plain and Boring Cement

This will constitute the base of the architectural textures. As usual, start with a new white canvas, RGB, at 512×512. Then, do the following:

1. Select a medium-gray foreground and a dark-gray background.
2. Choose Filter, Render, Clouds (see Figure 8.35).

Figure 8.35 *Apply the Clouds filter with medium and dark gray.*

Filter:	Render, Clouds
Foreground:	525252
Background:	3B3B3B

3. To churn up the texture, choose Filter, Artistic, Sponge (see Figure 8.36). You can tone it down a bit by choosing Filter, Blur, Gaussian blur.

Figure 8.36 *Apply the Sponge filter.*

Filter:	Artistic, Sponge
Brush Size:	0
Definition:	1
Smoothness:	3
Filter:	Blur, Gaussian Blur
Radius:	2 pixels

4. If you try to tile this texture in any game, you'll get horizontal and vertical seams around each tile because the opposing edges aren't fluent with each other (see Figure 8.37). To rectify this, click Filter, Other, Offset. Offsetting is a way of making an image shift a user-defined number of pixels in one direction. The excess that gets shifted off the one edge ends up being wrapped around the opposite edge. Then, when the image is tiled next to its duplicate, the edges blend smoothly. To create an even tile in all directions, make the filter shift the image one-half of the image's length and width—in this case, 256 pixels for both horizontal and vertical directions.

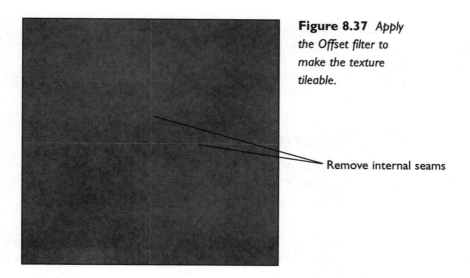

Figure 8.37 *Apply the Offset filter to make the texture tileable.*

Remove internal seams

Filter:	Other, Offset
Horizontal:	256 pixels
Vertical:	256 pixels
Undefined Areas:	Wrap around

5. Now that the texture is offset, the edges that would have originally put noticeable seams in when tiling are visible in the center of the image. To get rid of them, use the Clone Stamp tool to copy other areas of the texture over the internal seams (see Figure 8.38).

Figure 8.38
Use the Clone Stamp tool to get rid of the vertical and horizontal seam in the middle of the cement texture.

Not that this is anything exciting yet, but if you were to reduce this texture to 256x256, define it as a pattern, then fill a wall, the texture would tile itself smoothly in all directions. However, rarely do you see a large, smooth, cement wall anywhere—there's usually some sort of beveled pattern, form, or intentional seam where the slabs of concrete meet.

Not So Plain and Boring Cement

The next few sections use the previous example's image as a base. In this section, let's make the texture contain a quad of beveled edges so that when the texture is tiled, it will appear as though the wall was built by stacking slabs of preformed cement blocks:

1. With the image you created in the preceding section (if you haven't created it, just open the **cement.jpg** texture located in the Chapter 8 Data section on the CD-ROM), create a new layer. This will be an effect layer for creating the bevels.

2. Click Image, Canvas Size, and double the width and height of the canvas (you'll find out why in a moment). If you're using the image created earlier, this should now be a 2×2-inch canvas (see Figure 8.39).

Figure 8.39
Create a new layer.
Enlarge the canvas
by a factor of 2.

3. On the new layer, add a thick gray cross directly through the middle of the texture to simulate how the four corners of slabs of cement would come together. To do so, first turn on the rulers to guide you. Then, using the Line tool with a weight of 10 pixels and a foreground color of medium gray (hex# 525252), draw a horizontal and vertical line across the exact center of the texture (press and hold down the Shift key to keep the lines straight). Go a bit outside of the texture; this will get hacked away when you restore the canvas size (see Figure 8.40).

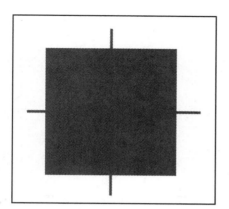

Figure 8.40 *Draw a 10 pixel-wide cross through the center of the texture.*

4. Double-click the layer to open the Layer Styles dialog box and add an inverted (down) inner bevel.

5. Note that once a bevel is applied, the edges of the beveling effect (when tiled) have a bit of a hiccup where the seams meet; restoring the canvas to its original size will eliminate this problem. To do so, flatten the image; click Image, Canvas Size; and set the canvas dimensions back to 1×1 inch (see Figure 8.41). Photoshop will warn you that some clipping will occur when the canvas is reduced, but that's what you want, so click Proceed to continue. What's happening here is, you're telling Photoshop to reduce the overall canvas size, which in turn crops the image for you automatically, effectively eliminating the edge bevels.

Figure 8.41 *Add an inverted inner bevel to the cross and restore the original canvas size.*

Style:	Bevel and Emboss
Style:	Inner Bevel
Technique:	Chisel Hard
Depth:	50%
Direction:	Down
Size:	5 pixels
Soften:	5 pixels

Now the texture is ready for finalization for your game's level. Reduce the image to 256×256 pixels, set it as a pattern, and fill a large blank canvas with it. The end result is a nice, even texture that has a more realistic look to it. In Figure 8.42, I made a simple room with a long wall and slapped this texture on it. The wall is 512 pixels high by 2048 pixels wide.

Figure 8.42 *The finalized texture tiled on the wall of a simple room.*

Try using the beveling technique to create other patterns like I've done in Figure 8.43. The first one shows simple holes, called *form ties*, commonly seen in large buildings. These holes are the byproduct of the cement formers holding the form itself together, but architects and designers decided to keep the holes since it gives a bit style to the walls. The others have fancy patterns that might look good in a spaceship or something. Have fun.

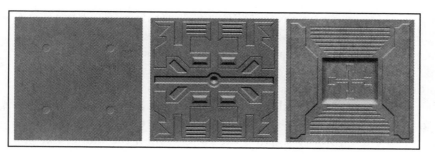

Figure 8.43
Other bevel patterns I created that look interesting when properly placed.

Creating Randomly Tileable Sets

Many game engines allow you to create and import a sequence of textures that the game will randomly tile on the wall, floor, or whatever object of your choice. This can greatly improve upon the monotony of a wall that has the same texture tiled all over it, as well as speeding up the process of skinning large walls at the same time.

For instance, if you applied the texture from Figure 8.38 onto a large wall and stood back to view it entirely, you'd easily notice that it is a single tileable texture repeated in all directions (see Figure 8.44). To avoid this, you can create a randomly tileable set of textures (typically somewhere from four to 10), each of which is just a bit different but seamlessly blends with any of the others in any direction.

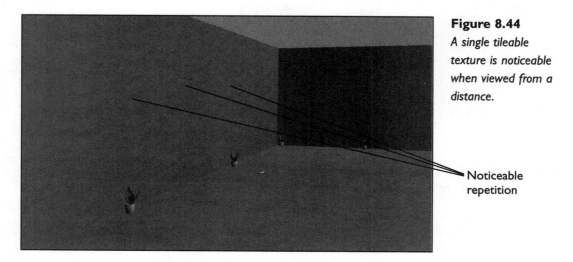

Figure 8.44
A single tileable texture is noticeable when viewed from a distance.

Noticeable repetition

Making a randomly tileable set can be easy or difficult, depending on what type of texture you're dealing with. In the case of Figure 8.38, slightly modifying the inner portion of the image, and then saving it as another filename is easy enough. The set could then appear as in Figure 8.45, in which each image is similar to and tileable with the others. To instigate the set, all you have to do is follow whatever level editor's proper nomenclature to indicate that it is in fact a randomly tileable set. For example, in the case of *Half-Life*, simply start each texture's name with a – sign, followed by a sequence number starting with 0, and then the name, like so:

–0 cementwall.bmp

–1 cementwall.bmp

–2 cementwall.bmp

–3 cementwall.bmp

Figure 8.45
A randomly tileable set of textures applied to a wall is more realistic than using a single texture.

Creating Seamlessly Tileable Cement from an Image

Using digital images of real-world items to create textures of those items for your game is usually the way to go if you're trying to make your environment realistic. There are, however, advantages to making textures completely from scratch. For one, you have complete control of the texture's constitution—that is, the texture will be thoroughly uniform, the lighting will be the way you want it, and so on.

When you take a picture of something in the real world, however, you have to work around your environment. Maybe the sun wasn't splashing evenly on your brick wall, and you got weird shadows all over the place. Or maybe the flash from your camera made a lovely but unwanted halo smack in the middle of the stop sign you were snapping. The point is, there are ups and downs to both ways of accomplishing texture creation, which is why I'm trying to show you both.

For this section, I used a digital image (**cement_pic.jpg** on the CD-ROM) of an area of cement that had a bit of personality, thinking it might look nice when adjusted and offset for tiling:

1. Isolate an area that seems relatively uniform (I'm eyeballing an area in the upper-right portion of the image).

2. Select the Rectangular Marquee tool and set its options to Style: Fixed Size with a selection size of 128×128 pixels.

3. Select a portion that you think might tile smoothly and evenly, copy the selection, and paste it into a new document (see Figure 8.46).

> **TIP**
> A quick trick to finding areas of an image that are somewhat balanced (that is, finding a norm that has few highlights or shadows) is to use levels (Ctrl+L) in Photoshop. In the Levels dialog box, just slide the Midtones slider all the way to the right; the nasty areas will either be brightly highlighted or darkly shadowed. Then click the dialog box's Cancel button and pick an area that seems to be in between those areas.

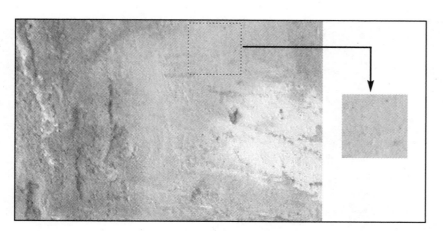

Figure 8.46
*Isolate a homogenous area of cement of the **cement_pic.jpg** image.*

4. The texture (and the original image) is very hazy and bright, and should be adjusted before you continue. Press Ctrl+L to open the Levels dialog box, and slide the Midtones slider to the right a bit, and click OK. Now it looks a bit more like cement (see Figure 8.47).

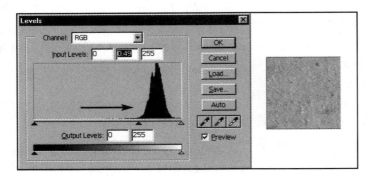

Figure 8.47
Adjust the midtones of the image with the Levels dialog box.

5. Set the texture as a pattern and fill a blank image with it to see how it looks. Even without the Offset filter applied, it looks pretty good! Still, it's a good idea to offset it to make sure the colors blend smoothly. Click Filter, Other, Offset, and enter one-half the amount of the length and width of the image (64×64 pixels).

6. Use the Clone Stamp tool to copy homogenous areas of the texture over any internal seams, areas that contain blemishes, or other items that stand out. (As you make adjustments, preview your work by making it a pattern again and again and filling a large canvas with it.) Figure 8.48 shows a before and after of this step.

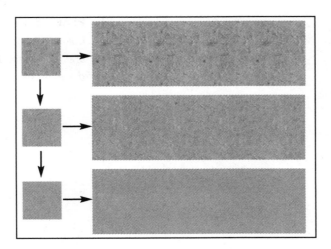

Figure 8.48 *Offset the texture and use the Clone Stamp tool to get rid of things that stand out.*

Now you have a good tileable base texture of cement to work with. Try adding bevel effects and whatnot, and creating tileable sets to add to your collection. Also try making a cinderblock pattern using the brick technique you practiced at the beginning of this chapter.

TIP

It's good to know the makeup of real-world materials when building your textures. For example, when making formed cement walls, engineers don't just take a batch of plain, smooth cement and pour it into a form to make the wall block. If they did, the mildest of vibrations or pressure over time would cause the cement to become very unstable or even break apart. Instead, they mix the cement with cracked stones and put a thick grid of ribbed steel rods, called *rebar* (reinforcement bar), into the center of the cement formers. That means that if you decide to make a cement wall that has been blasted away in one area by, say, a 50mm shell, you'll want keep in mind that in the real world, cement walls contain stone and rebar, and render them accordingly.

Rock and Stone Textures

Creating stone textures from scratch is a little more complicated, but it opens up a world of fun with alpha-channel bump mapping. The most difficult part, I think, is making them seamless, especially when dealing with pictures.

Mineral Rock

Let's start off with a basic rock-base tutorial that you can use for almost any type of rock on any planet—just try changing the foreground and background colors for different results.

1. Start a new 512×512-pixel RGB image.

2. Select any foreground and background you want; this will be the mineral representation in the rock. I typically use earthy colors that involve some sort of reddish-brown, like hex# 751C00 and hex# 4C2901.

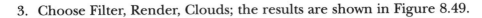

3. Choose Filter, Render, Clouds; the results are shown in Figure 8.49.

Figure 8.49
*Apply the Clouds
filter with an earth-
colored foreground
and background.*

Filter: Render, Clouds
Foreground: hex# 751C00
Background: hex# 4C2901

4. Using the Channels palette, start a new channel.

5. Choose Filter, Render, Difference Clouds, and then press Ctrl+F a few times
    to repeat this action. Do this until the black and white mix is somewhat even
    (see Figure 8.50). This will be your displacement map when you render the
    mineral layer—that is, the whiter areas will represent the high spots on the
    texture, while the blacker areas will represent the low spots.

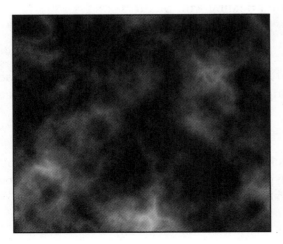

Figure 8.50 *Start
a new channel and
apply the Difference
Clouds filter several
times.*

6. In the Layers palette, click on the background layer to make it is the current working selection.

7. Click Filter, Render, Lighting Effects, and adjust the settings as I have in Figure 8.51 (make sure the directional light is positioned as mine is). Also, make sure Alpha 1 is selected in the Texture Channel list—this is the black and white alpha channel you just made, which this filter will use as a displacement map.

> **TIP**
>
> Later on, try playing around with all the sliders to produce an enormous variety of effects, from making the texture rock-like, to bubbly plastic, to lizard skin.

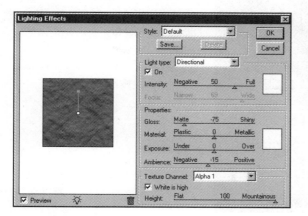

Figure 8.51 *Click the Lighting Effects filter and use the Alpha 1 channel as a displacement map.*

8. Click OK; Figure 8.52 shows the results. Try going back and forth between this new texture and the Alpha 1 displacement channel in the Channels palette to see how the map was used to create all the bumps and valleys. You'll use maps like this when making 3D terrain meshes later on in this part.

Figure 8.52 *The resulting rock texture, post Lighting Effects.*

9. Before you offset the image for tiling and use the Clone Stamp tool to get rid of the internal seams, I want you to see the power of the Alpha displacement channel in a bit more depth. Press Ctrl+Z to undo the Lighting Effects filter, and go back to the Channels palette. Click on the Alpha 1 channel to select it.

10. Let's tighten up the channel a bit to further enhance the ridges and valleys. Click Image, Adjust, Levels (Ctrl+L), and slide the Midtones and Highlights markers over to the left a little. This will enhance and sharpen the white areas and subsequently will make the resulting texture much more mountainous (see Figure 8.53).

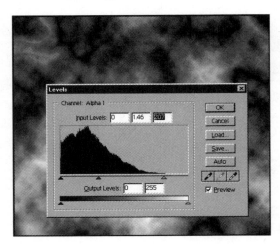

Figure 8.53 *Adjust the levels of the alpha channel to enhance the white areas.*

11. Select the background layer in the Layers palette, and apply the Lighting Effects filter as you did in step 7. Figure 8.54 shows the updated results with respect to the new alpha map.

Figure 8.54 *Apply the Lighting Effects filter once more using the new Alpha 1 map.*

These textures aren't the best for making walls and whatnot, but work well when wrapped around boulders and such. For more on U-V mapping and skinning objects, see Part II, "Unwrapping the U-Vs With DeepUV," and Chapters 11 and 12, where I show you how to create skin textures for a weapon and character model.

Granite

This texture uses the same displacement technique as the last, only you'll apply a few other filters to bring out the quartz-like sparkles you see in granite.

1. Start a new 512×512-pixel RGB image. (These dimensions aren't cast in stone, no pun intended. It's just convenient to start things off big, square, and divisible by 16.)

2. Fill the canvas with black, or near-black.

3. Press D, and then press X. This sets the foreground to white and the background to black.

4. Choose Filter, Pixelate, Pointillize. Set the Cell Size to 6 and click OK (see Figure 8.55). This provides that quartz-type look to the texture.

Figure 8.55 *Fill the canvas with black, then apply the Pointillize filter.*

5. Create a new channel in the Channels palette.

6. Choose Filter, Render, Difference Clouds a few times. Enhance the midtones and highlights by adjusting their levels (Ctrl+L) a bit to the left (see Figure 8.56).

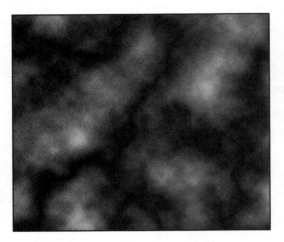

Figure 8.56 *Apply the Difference Clouds filter to a new Alpha channel, then adjust the levels.*

7. To the Alpha channel, apply Filter, Texture, Grain. This blotches up the displacement map (see Figure 8.57).

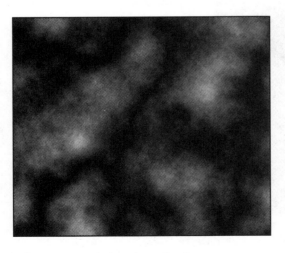

Figure 8.57 *Apply the Grain filter to the Alpha channel.*

Filter: Texture, Grain
Intensity: 25
Contrast: 50
Grain Type: Clumped

8. In the Layers palette, click on the background layer to select it (alternatively, remain in the Channels palette and click on the RGB channel—this will do the same thing).

9. Click Filter, Render, Lighting Effects, making sure Alpha 1 is selected in the Texture Channel list (see Figure 8.58). My settings are attached to the image; try playing around to get different effects. I also cranked down the height of the map to make the rock smoother.

Figure 8.58 *Apply the Lighting Effects filter to the background layer, using the Alpha 1 map for displacement.*

Filter:	Render, Lighting Effects
Light Type:	Directional
Intensity:	35
Focus:	69
Gloss:	−25
Material:	0
Exposure:	0
Ambience:	−18
Texture Channel:	Alpha 1
Height:	35

I think granite has a gazillion variations, and is usually more black and white, but this could suffice. Try doing a final levels adjustment to enhance the texture.

Sandstone

Here's an easy one that makes a great base for a raised pattern:

1. Start a new 512×512 RGB image.

2. Set the foreground color to a light yellow-orange, like hex# EBC459, and fill the canvas with it.

3. Choose Filter, Noise, Add Noise (see Figure 8.59).

Figure 8.59 *Fill the canvas with an off-yellow and apply the Noise filter.*

Filter:	Noise, Add Noise
Amount:	5%
Distribution:	Gaussian
Monochromatic:	(checked)

4. Start a new channel in the Channels palette.

5. Choose Filter, Render, Difference Clouds, and repeat a few times (see Figure 8.60).

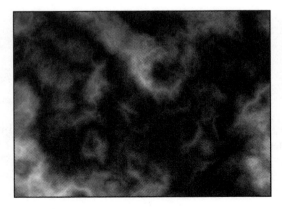

Figure 8.60 *In a new Alpha channel, apply the Difference Clouds filter a few times.*

6. Choose Filter, Blur, Gaussian Blur to decrease the map's displacement strength.

7. Apply the Noise filter with the same settings as before (see Figure 8.61).

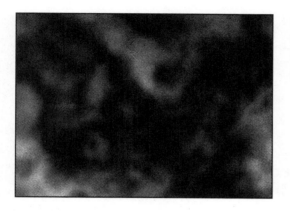

Figure 8.61 *Apply the Gaussian Blur and Noise filters to the Alpha channel.*

Filter:	Blur, Gaussian Blur
Radius:	4.0 pixels
Filter:	Noise, Add Noise
Amount:	5%
Distribution:	Gaussian
Monochromatic:	(checked)

8. In the Layers palette, click on the background layer to select it. Then apply the Lighting Effects filter using Alpha 1 as a texture channel (see Figure 8.62).

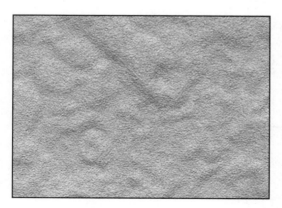

Figure 8.62 *Apply the Lighting Effects filter to the background layer.*

Filter:	Render, Lighting Effects
Light Type:	Directional
Intensity:	21
Focus:	69
Gloss:	−25
Material:	0
Exposure:	0
Ambience:	0
Texture Channel:	Alpha 1
Height:	21

Sandstone with a Pattern

Now let's make a worthwhile pattern out of this base texture. You'll need to have View, Snap, and View, Show, Grid, enabled. You'll also need to adjust the increments of the grid to coincide with the thickness of the pattern's lines. Click Edit, Preferences, Units and Rulers, and change both Rulers and Type to Pixels. Then, under Edit, Preferences, Guides and Grid, change Gridlines to every 21 pixels, and Subdivisions to 1. I had to do a little math to figure out the right amounts for this pattern; you'll understand when we're finished.

1. With the sandstone texture you just created (which should include the Alpha displacement channel), click Image, Image Size, and change the Width and Height settings to 504 pixels. This will align the grid precisely onto the texture (see Figure 8.63).

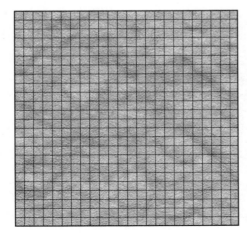

Figure 8.63

Enable Grid and Snap, and adjust the grid values as shown. Resize the image to 504 pixels.

2. Offset the texture for tiling. To do so, click Filter, Other, Offset, and set the Horizontal and Vertical values to one-half of the image's dimensions—in this case, 252 pixels for both.

3. The detail is so fine in this image that you can hardly notice the internal seams, but try using the Clone Stamp tool to get rid of any that are noticeable.

4. Start a new layer. This will be the pattern layer to which you'll add a style to raise it away from the base.

5. Set the foreground color to a maroon color, like hex# BA6F1F.

6. Using the Rectangular Marquee tool, make and fill selections with the foreground color as I have in the top-left quadrant of the image (see Figure 8.64).

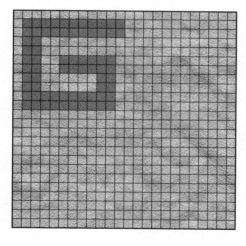

Figure 8.64 *Use the Rectangular Marquee tool to create and fill the first quarter of the pattern.*

7. Make a copy of this layer.

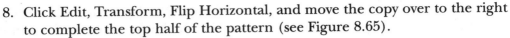

8. Click Edit, Transform, Flip Horizontal, and move the copy over to the right to complete the top half of the pattern (see Figure 8.65).

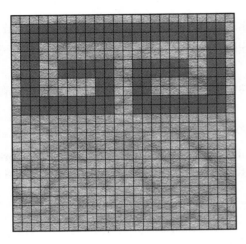

Figure 8.65
Duplicate the pattern layer, flip it, and move it to the right.

9. Press Ctrl+E to merge the two pattern layers.

10. Make a duplicate of the top pattern.

11. Click Edit, Transform, Flip Vertical, and then move the duplicate to the bottom to complete the pattern (see Figure 8.66).

12. Merge the two pattern layers again so just one layer exists above the background layer.

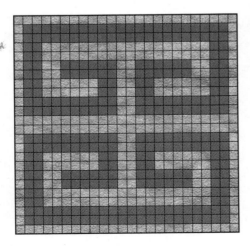

Figure 8.66
Complete the pattern by duplicating the top, flipping it, and moving it to the bottom.

13. Turn off the grid by clicking View, Show, Grid (Ctrl+Alt+').

14. To add some texture, click Filter, Noise, Add Noise, using the same settings as before.

15. Click Filter, Render, Lighting Effects, again using the same settings as before (use the Alpha map you created earlier for the texture channel).

16. Click OK. Not to shabby, eh? You could stop here and use this as a tileable texture if you want (see Figure 8.67).

Figure 8.67 *Add Noise and apply the Lighting Effects filter to the pattern's layer.*

17. Here's where you can go nuts with styles. Double-click the pattern's layer to bring up the Styles screen, and apply a bevel of your choice. In Figure 8.68, I applied an outer bevel with Contour checked. Not bad, eh?

Figure 8.68 *Apply a bevel to the pattern's layer.*

Style:	Bevel and Emboss
Style:	Outer Bevel
Technique:	Chisel Hard
Depth:	100%
Direction:	Up
Size:	4
Soften:	4
Angle:	90 degrees
Style:	Contour
Contour:	Cone - Inverted
Range:	50%

I think this is quite nice now. Just reduce the image to suit your needs and tile it. I used this pattern along the walls in the room in Figure 8.69.

Figure 8.69 The final texture, reduced and tiled on walls in a room.

Hot Lava

I invented this texture by accident; here's how it's done:

1. Fill a new 512 × 512-pixel RGB canvas with pure black.

2. In the Channels palette, start a new channel.

3. Press D to reset the foreground and background colors to white and black, respectively.

4. Click Filter, Render, Clouds.

5. Click Filter, Render, Difference Clouds. Press Ctrl+F several times to reapply this filter until you get a nice mix of black and white (see Figure 8.70).

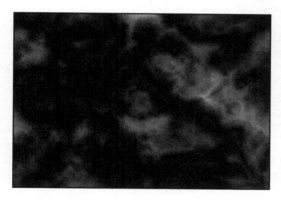

Figure 8.70 *Apply the Clouds filter, then apply the Difference Clouds filter several times to a new Alpha channel.*

6. Click Image, Adjust, Levels.

7. Slide the Shadows marker to the right a bit to flood out the black areas (you want a nice, thick filling of black, which you'll fill with molten-hot colors (see Figure 8.71).

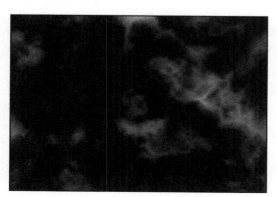

Figure 8.71 *Adjust the levels in the Alpha channel to enhance the shadows.*

8. In the Layers palette, click on the background layer to select it.

9. Click Filter, Render, Lighting Effects, making sure Alpha 1 is the selected texture channel (see Figure 8.72).

10. Scale the directional light source down a bit in the filter's preview area (this will make the light source shine more overhead, eliminating unnecessary shadows). Click OK.

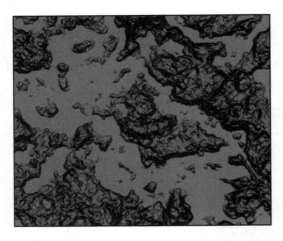

Figure 8.72 *Apply the Lighting Effects filter to the background layer, using the Alpha channel as a displacement map.*

Filter:	Render, Lighting Effects
Light Type:	Directional
Intensity:	47
Focus:	69
Gloss:	−36
Material:	−64
Exposure:	0
Ambience:	0
Texture Channel:	Alpha 1
Height:	100

11. Now to make a proper fill selection for the molten lava. I frequently use Alpha channels to store selections, so we'll do that here. Using the Channels palette, make a copy of the Alpha 1 channel (click and drag it to the Create New Channel icon).

12. Invert this new copy by clicking Image, Adjust, Invert. The black areas of the map are now white (you need the white in order to make a selection).

13. Click Image, Adjust, Levels, and slide the Shadows marker (at the far left) all of the way to the far right. This will create 100% contrast between black and white (see Figure 8.73).

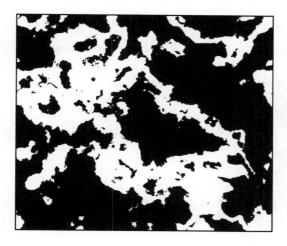

Figure 8.73 *Make a copy of the Alpha 1 channel, invert it, and adjust the levels to bring out all the white.*

14. Ctrl+click the new Alpha channel to select all of its white.
15. Using the Layers palette, start a new layer.
16. The selection should now be on the new layer; fill the selection with a reddish-orange color, like hex# FB2900 (see Figure 8.74).

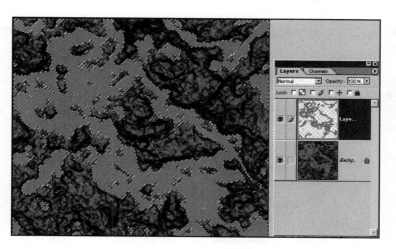

Figure 8.74 *Select the opacity of the new Alpha channel and fill this selection with a reddish color on a new layer.*

17. Now let's make the center of the molten lava appear very hot. With the selection still active (you can always go back to the new Alpha channel and

Ctrl+click it to restore the selection area), click Select, Modify, Contract, and enter a value of 5.

18. Fill this new area with an orange color, like hex# FB5900.

19. Again, click Select, Modify, Contract, and type a value of 5.

20. Fill this selection with a bright yellow, like hex# FBF200 (see Figure 8.75).

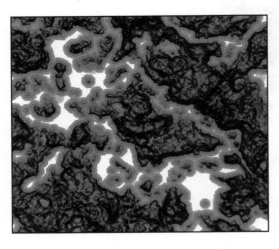

Figure 8.75
Reduce the selection area, fill with orange, reduce again, then fill with yellow.

21. To the molten-lava layer, apply Filter, Blur, Gaussian Blur, with a radius of 3 pixels.

22. Double-click this layer to bring up the Styles screen, and add a red-colored Outer Glow style (see Figure 8.76).

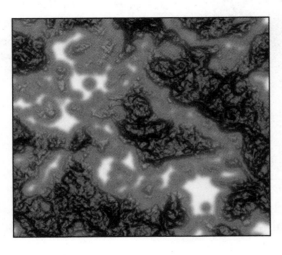

Figure 8.76 *Blur the molten lava layer, then add an Outer Glow style.*

Filter:	Blur, Gaussian Blur
Radius:	3.0 pixels
Style:	Outer Glow
Blend Mode:	Screen
Opacity:	75%
Noise:	0
Glow Color:	hex# FF2A00
Technique:	Softer
Spread:	0
Size:	35 pixels

This is a very effective technique for reproducing lava, both hot and cold. You might think that offsetting this for a tile will be a bit cumbersome, because it has so much detail, but in fact, this isn't the case. When you applied the Difference Clouds filter to the first Alpha channel, the filter applied itself as a tileable offset; the rest of the texture was based on that original channel. It's just up to you to fix the colors in an offset—try merging the layers, then choosing Filter, Other, Offset. Then just Clone Stamp the seams in the hot lava. Voilá!

This texture works great when tiled on a 2D plane that has some type of vertex-displacement effect applied to it. In Figure 8.77, the lava is applied to the ground in the *Realm Wars* demo, which accompanies this book's CD-ROM.

Figure 8.77 *The lava texture applied to the floor of the Realm Wars demo.*

Cold Lava

You could create cold lava by repeating steps 1–10 of the last example, but you might have to make a slight modification with step 6. Instead of flooding out the black with the Shadows slider, you could mess with the Midtones and Highlights sliders a bit to enhance the ridges in the final rendering.

The next tutorial, composed of just a few quick steps, produces another type of cooled lava flow that appears somewhat elegant:

1. Start a new 512×512-pixel image.

2. Press D to reset the Color Control Panel to black and white.

3. Choose Filter, Render, Clouds (see Figure 8.78).

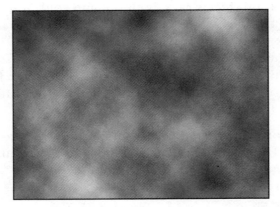

Figure 8.78 *Apply the Clouds filter onto a new canvas using black and white.*

4. Choose Filter, Stylize, Find Edges (see Figure 8.79). This tells Photoshop to create significant borders where there are definitive transitions in the image.

Figure 8.79 *Apply the Find Edges filter to trace out the significant color transitions in the image.*

5. Adjust the levels to bring out your texture—first slide the Midtones marker almost all the way to the right, then slowly slide the Shadows marker to the right until you get something like what's shown in Figure 8.80.

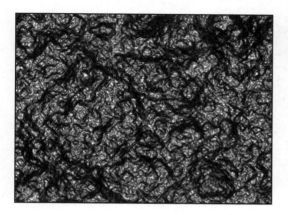

Figure 8.80 *Finish the texture by adjusting the levels.*

Marble

Marble varies in appearance from a cloudy multicolor obelisk (like the kind you make with Photoshop's Marble filter) to a monotone slate penetrated with sharp, contrasting veins. To create the latter, do the following:

1. Start a new 512×512-pixel RGB image.

2. Pick a dark green foreground, say hex# 214819, and a slightly lighter green background, like hex# 18230E.

TIP

Record this procedure in your Actions palette. I'm going to wrap it up by making a nice, big floor tile whose repetition is barely detectible.

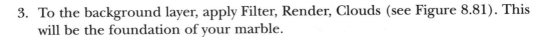

3. To the background layer, apply Filter, Render, Clouds (see Figure 8.81). This will be the foundation of your marble.

Figure 8.81 *Apply the Clouds filter using dark and medium green colors.*

4. Using the Channels palette, create a new channel.

5. Choose Filter, Render, Clouds.

6. Choose Filter, Render, Difference Clouds. This will create the veins. (You could keep applying this filter to get the veins you prefer, but since you're recording this action, it's best not to.) The veins in the final marble texture are represented by the thin dark scraggly lines in the new channel (see Figure 8.82).

Figure 8.82 *In a new channel, apply the Clouds filter, then the Difference Clouds filter. The black lines will be the veins in the final image.*

7. In the new channel, choose Image, Adjust, Invert (Ctrl+I). This inverts the grayscale range and makes the black veins white for your selection.

8. Choose Image, Adjust, Levels.

9. In the Levels dialog box, slide the Shadows marker toward the right. Play around with it to make the veins either fuzzy or very sharp (see Figure 8.83).

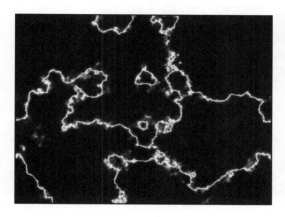

Figure 8.83 *Invert the channel and adjust the levels to bring out the veins.*

10. You now have a stored selection in your Alpha channel. Ctrl+click this channel to create a selection.

11. In the Layers palette, start a new layer.

12. The selection should still be active; fill it (Alt+Backspace) with the dark-green foreground color (see Figure 8.84).

13. Press Ctrl+D to deselect the selection.

14. Adjust the layer using the Levels dialog box to enhance the veins.

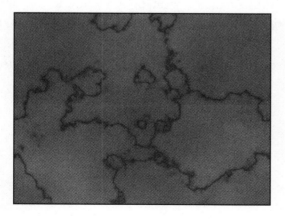

Figure 8.84 *Load the selection from the Alpha channel and fill a new layer with the dark-green foreground color. Use the Levels dialog box to enhance the veins.*

15. You could probably stop here and classify this as marble, but I want to apply
    a worn effect and a grout-like border. To begin, apply a Pillow Emboss style
    to the veins layer with the settings outlined in Figure 8.85.

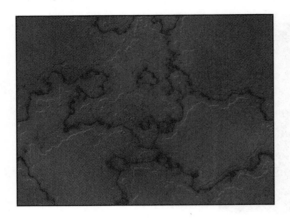

Figure 8.85 *Apply a Pillow Emboss style to the vein layer.*

Style:	Bevel and Emboss
Style:	Pillow Emboss
Technique:	Chisel Hard
Depth:	100%
Direction:	Up
Size:	0
Soften:	0

16. Now the marble looks like the thin surface is wearing away due to the pres-
    ence of the veins. For the border, go to the Channels palette and start a new
    channel.

17. Press Ctrl+A to select the entire channel, then click Select, Modify, Border,
    and enter a value of 20.

18. Press Alt+Backspace to fill the border; notice that you've now got a feathered, frame-like border (see Figure 8.86). Press Ctrl+D to deselect.

Figure 8.86 *Start a new channel and create and fill a border selection.*

19. Adjust the levels in the channel to sharpen the inner edges. In the Levels dialog box, slide the Shadows and Highlights markers toward the center (see Figure 8.87).

Figure 8.87 *Adjust the levels to sharpen the edges of the channel's border.*

20. Ctrl+Click this channel to load a selection, then start a new layer in the Layers palette.

21. Fill this selection with a dark gray-green, like hex# 222B20.

22. Choose Filter, Noise, Add Noise to make the border appear more grout-like (see Figure 8.88).

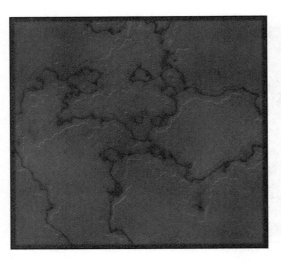

Figure 8.88 *Load a selection using the channel, start a new layer, and fill it with a grayish color. Apply noise to break it up.*

Filter:	Noise, Add Noise
Amount:	10%
Distribution:	Uniform
Monochromatic:	(checked)

23. Apply an inverted outer bevel to the border layer. This will make the marble appear raised and polished (see Figure 8.89).

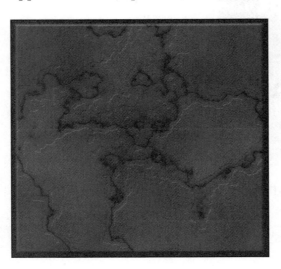

Figure 8.89 *Apply an outer bevel to the border layer.*

Style:	Bevel and Emboss
Style:	Outer Bevel
Technique:	Smooth
Depth:	100%
Direction:	Down
Size:	3
Soften:	5

24. You could save this as a single working tile, but to complete the tiling texture, flatten the image and reduce the dimensions to 256×256 pixels.

Hopefully, you've been recording this entire procedure on your Actions palette. If so, press the Stop button to stop recording. With the marble tile fully recorded in the Actions palette, you can quickly produce any number of marble tiles, each having a unique pattern to its veins.

To make a nice tileable floor pattern, start a new 512×512-pixel image and add four of these tiles to it. This texture will tile nicely in a large room (see Figure 8.90). If you like, make several of these quad-tiled textures for a tileable set.

NOTE

The steps you took to make the base portion of the marble are very similar to the steps that programmed shaders use in 3D programs. Remember the levels adjustments you made to vary the vein thickness? Look for that in a marble shader in any 3D modeling program like trueSpace or 3D Studio Max.

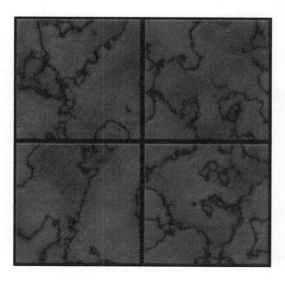

Figure 8.90 *Add four tiles to one 512×512-pixel image for a nice tileable texture.*

Asphalt

This is a quick base material for any street, spaceship deck, or what have you; it'll get more interesting when I show you how to add painted lines to the material.

1. Start a new 512×512-pixel RGB image.

2. For the background layer, choose Filter, Render, Clouds, using two dark gray colors as the mix. (I used hex# 212121 and hex# 343434.)

3. In the Channels palette, create a new channel.

4. To the new channel, apply Filter, Noise, Add Noise (about 50%).

5. To the same channel, apply Filter, Noise, Median, with a setting of 1 pixel.

6. Adjust the levels of the channel to bring out the white speckles (see Figure 8.91).

Figure 8.91 *Adjust the levels to enhance the choppy noise.*

7. To the background layer, apply Filter, Render, Lighting Effects, using the Alpha 1 map as a texture channel (see Figure 8.92).

Figure 8.92 *Render the texture using the Alpha 1 channel as a displacement map.*

Filter:	Render, Lighting Effects
Light Type:	Directional (vertically)
Intensity:	21
Focus:	69
Gloss:	13
Material:	50
Exposure:	18
Ambience:	21
Texture Channel:	Alpha 1
Height:	100

You might want to adjust the levels again to sharpen or darken the grain in the texture. Also, there's no need to run an offset to make it tileable—the grain is too tight and random to make any noticeable seams, so there's a load off!

Space Deck with Caution Lines

This tutorial is very effective, but make sure you retain the Alpha 1 map—you'll use that to bump the paint that's been sprayed on the floor. These steps assume that you just completed the previous tutorial.

1. Start a new channel.

2. Press Ctrl+A to select the entire channel.

3. Fill the selection with pure white.

4. Choose Edit, Stroke, and stroke the inside of the selection with pure black with a thickness of 40 pixels (see Figure 8.93).

Figure 8.93
Create a new channel that has a 40-pixel border around the edges.

5. Choose Filter, Blur, Gaussian Blur (see Figure 8.94).

Figure 8.94 *Apply the Gaussian Blur filter to the channel.*

Filter: Blur, Gaussian Blur
Radius: 20.0 pixels

6. Choose Image, Adjust, Levels, and slide the Shadows and Highlights markers toward each other until the white area has nice, crisp, round edges (see Figure 8.95). This is the same effect as applying the Threshold command.

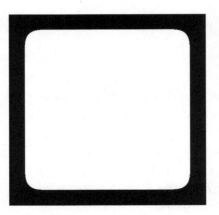

Figure 8.95 *Adjust the levels, or apply the Threshold command, to sharpen out the channel.*

7. Ctrl+click this channel to create the edge selection.

8. Choose Select, Modify, Expand, and enter a value of 20. Click OK.

9. Choose Select, Inverse.

10. Make sure your background color is pure white, and press Delete.

11. Press Ctrl+D to deselect.

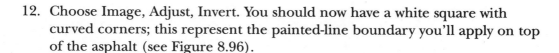

12. Choose Image, Adjust, Invert. You should now have a white square with curved corners; this represent the painted-line boundary you'll apply on top of the asphalt (see Figure 8.96).

Figure 8.96 *The completed white boundary that will represent the painted areas.*

13. Make a copy of this channel by dragging and dropping it onto the New Channel button. This way, if you mess up the pattern, you can always revert back to the original.

14. Choose Image, Canvas Size, and change the Width and Height settings to 1024 pixels each.

15. The channel must be rotated before you can perform the diagonal cuts on the lines. To do so, click Edit, Transform, Rotate. Then press and hold down the Shift key and rotate the channel 45 degrees (see Figure 8.97).

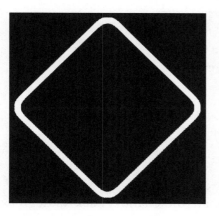

Figure 8.97 *Increase the size of the canvas and rotate the channel 45 degrees.*

16. Enable Photoshop's Snap and Grid functions.

17. Choose Edit, Preferences, Guides and Grid to adjust the grid settings; I placed my gridlines every 16 pixels, with only 1 subdivision. This way, selections will snap to the grid and be somewhat uniform.

18. Create a single, vertical, rectangular marquee selection that is one grid square wide, and taller than the entire image. Position it to the left, as shown in Figure 8.98.

Figure 8.98
Enable the Snap and Grid features and create a single rectangular marquee selection.

19. With the first selection in place, make sure your background color is pure black and press Delete. This will delete a chunk from the white square. Continue this process all the way to the far right (see Figure 8.99). Notice that I left the elbows of the square intact.

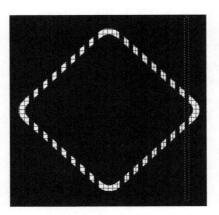

Figure 8.99 *Use the marquee selection to create the "caution line" look around the white square.*

20. Choose Edit, Transform, Rotate, and rotate the channel back 45 degrees.

21. Choose Image, Canvas Size, and restore the Width and Height settings to 512 pixels each.

22. Turn off the Grid feature (Ctrl+Alt+').

23. The caution-line channel is now complete. Ctrl+click this channel to load the selection (see Figure 8.100).

Figure 8.100
Restore the canvas and load the channel's selection.

24. With the selection loaded, go back to the Layers palette and start a new layer.

25. Fill the selection on the new layer with pure yellow (hex# FFFF00), as shown in Figure 8.101.

Figure 8.101 *On a new layer, fill the selection with pure yellow.*

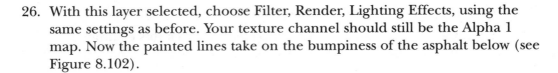

26. With this layer selected, choose Filter, Render, Lighting Effects, using the same settings as before. Your texture channel should still be the Alpha 1 map. Now the painted lines take on the bumpiness of the asphalt below (see Figure 8.102).

Figure 8.102
Apply the Lighting Effects filter using the Alpha 1 map as a texture channel.

You might want to make a final levels adjustment to the painted layer. Also, try changing the layer's properties to something like Hard Light; this will give it a worn look. In addition, try applying the Spatter filter to the second Alpha channel before you load its selection; this will make the paint appear to be chipped away. I did that, in addition to using the Eraser tool, in the image shown Figure 8.103.

Figure 8.103 *Play around with the painted lines to make them appear more worn.*

Creating a Set that Shares the Same Palette

You could make a ton of different textures based on the previous example. For instance, say you have a spaceship deck, or many decks, that have those caution lines tracing all over the place. Maybe they're a path for a robot or something. It might be a good idea to make a nice set of textures that can be flipped and arranged to create any number of caution-line patterns. In Figure 8.104, I made six different patterns and tiled them to create a floor map.

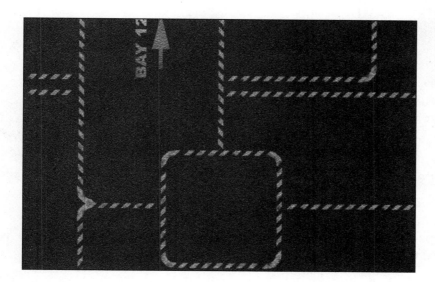

Figure 8.104 *Create a tileable set of caution lines to make a variety of patterns.*

When you create each tile, reduce the image, and then palletize the image for final import into a game, you might want to force these tiles to share the same color palette—after all, how much different are the colors between each texture? If tiles share the same palette, the game's engine can load a single palette (hence making the game run faster).

To see what I mean, using the previous example, click Image, Image Size, and make both the width and the height 256 pixels. Change the Resample Image setting to Bilinear–this will avoid a halo effect that can be generated otherwise if you stay with the default Bicubic resampling–and click OK. Next, palletize the image (click Image, Mode, Indexed Color). Set the Colors to 256, then pull down the Palette list and select Custom. You'll get a Color Table dialog box like the one in Figure 8.105. Finally, click the Save button to save this palette (pick whatever file-name you wish).

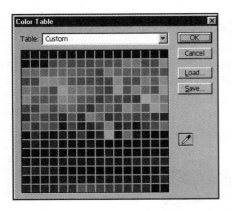

Figure 8.105

Creating a custom palette for your texture set to share.

The next time you create another space-deck texture and change the mode to Indexed Color, just click Custom Palette again and load the palette you saved. The textures will share the same palette without loss of color data, and the game will be optimized.

Stone Wall Set

If you've ever played *Return to Castle Wolfenstein,* you may have noticed that many of the textures present in that game are stone-based. It has rustic medieval castle embattlements, ramparts carved from granite or limestone, cement-formed gargoyles, keystones, and archways; it's quite a texturing dream come true.

If you have indeed played that game, or similar games whose architecture revolves around the early- to mid-second millennia, you've probably noticed that walls are massive and/or extensive, terrains seem endless, and any efforts you make to create decent, seamlessly tileable textures for those scenarios will be unwieldy. This section shows you how to circumvent this situation in three steps:

- Via a stone-texture procedure whose recorded action is called (nested) within a wall procedure
- Via a mildly complex wall-texture procedure that's recorded in the Actions palette
- Via a final action that generates seamlessly tileable set members based on the wall texture

The Medieval Brick Texture

Let's start with a simple stone texture so you can see what I mean. This must be recorded in the Actions palette, because the second wall procedure will be calling this routine.

1. Start a new 512×512-pixel RGB image.

2. Set your foreground color to a dark green, like hex# 102800, and your background to a dark tan, like hex# 635826. This will be the base-color blend for the rock. (You can use whatever colors you want, but these make your rock look algae-riddled and weathered, especially when you apply mortar to the seams.)

3. Open the Actions palette (F9).

4. It's a good idea to group all your game textures into a single folder set; I have a folder called "Game Textures" that contains all my actions. Within whatever folder you've created to hold your texture actions, start a new action called "Medieval Stone."

> **NOTE**
> It's important that you record this procedure because it will be called over and over.

5. Once you've entered the name, press Record.

6. Choose Filter, Render, Clouds (see Figure 8.106).

Figure 8.106
Apply the Clouds filter to the background layer.

7. Go to the Channels palette and start a new channel. Double-click this channel to bring up its options, and change its name to "temp."

8. To this channel, apply Filter, Render, Clouds. Then choose Filter, Artistic, Paint Daubs to clump some white areas together (see Figure 8.107).

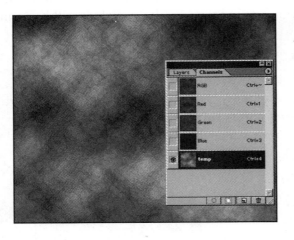

Figure 8.107
Apply the Clouds and Paint Daubs filter to the temp channel.

Filter:	Render, Clouds
Filter:	Artistic, Paint Daubs
Brush Size:	5
Sharpness:	40
Brush Type:	Simple

9. Select the RGB channel (this is the same as selecting the background layer).

10. Choose Filter, Render, Lighting Effects, using a vertical directional light and the temp channel as a texture channel (see Figure 8.108).

Figure 8.108
Apply the Lighting Effects filter using the temp channel as a bump map.

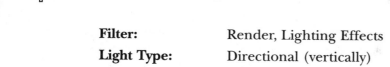

Filter:	Render, Lighting Effects
Light Type:	Directional (vertically)
Intensity:	35
Focus:	69
Gloss:	0
Material:	69
Exposure:	0
Ambience:	8
Texture Channel:	temp
Height:	100

11. Select the temp channel again and delete it. That way, every time this proce-dure gets called from another procedure, you won't have a mess of channels being created all over the place.

12. Select the RGB channel and click the Stop Playing/Recording button on the Actions palette.

Now you have a procedure that will fill any canvas or selection with a stone pattern, based on whatever foreground and background colors you've set in the Color Control Panel. Try it out: Start a new image or make a marquee selection, then play the Medieval Stone action you just recorded. This will be the basis for creating the individual stones in your next wall procedure.

Now the Wall Procedure

In this section, you'll record a procedure that will create a stone wall based on the Medieval Stone texture. When you're finished recording this procedure, you'll probably think that all this is way too complicated. To generate a completely differ-ent wall texture every time, however, all you need to do is click the Play button for the action. Here's what to do:

1. Start a new action—preferably within the same folder as the one in which you created the Medieval Stone action—called "Stone Wall."

2. With the action recording, start a new 512×512-pixel RGB image. I usually set the resolution to 512 as well, and keep the base transparent.

3. Make sure the Snap and Grid features are enabled. You'll need these to quickly align the stone patterns (click View, Snap, and View, Show, Grid).

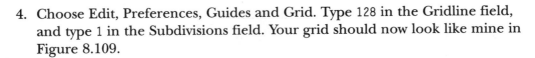

4. Choose Edit, Preferences, Guides and Grid. Type 128 in the Gridline field, and type 1 in the Subdivisions field. Your grid should now look like mine in Figure 8.109.

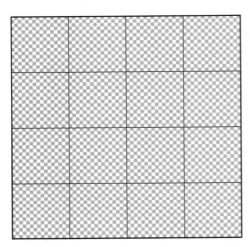

Figure 8.109
Enable the Snap and Grid features, and type 128 *in the Gridlines field.*

5. Using the Rectangular Marquee tool, create a 256×128-pixel rectangular selection in the upper-left corner. This dimension represents a stone selection two squares wide by one square high on the grid.

6. Click on the Medieval Stone action in the Actions palette, and click Play. This fills the selection with the stone procedure (see Figure 8.110).

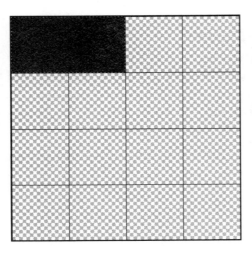

Figure 8.110
Create a 256×128-pixel rectangular selection at the top-left of the image and play the Medieval Stone action to fill it.

7. With the selection still active, use the Channels palette to start a new channel.

8. Choose Edit, Stroke, and stroke the *inside* of the selection, 8 pixels wide, with white (which should be the default color), as shown in Figure 8.111. By stroking the selection in the new channel, you're storing the shape of the mortar you'll fill later on.

Figure 8.111

Stroke the marquee selection in a new channel. This will store the shape of the mortar.

Edit:	Stroke
Width:	8 pixels
Color:	White
Location:	Inside
Mode:	Normal
Opacity:	100%

9. Click on the RGB channel to select it (this is the same as clicking on the background layer).

10. Using the Rectangular Marquee tool, select the top-right portion of the image (or move the existing selection over to it).

11. Play the Medieval Stone action to fill the selected area.

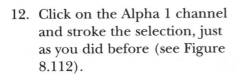

12. Click on the Alpha 1 channel and stroke the selection, just as you did before (see Figure 8.112).

> **NOTE**
> You'll be bouncing back and forth between the **RGB** channel and the **Alpha 1** channel as you create the wall texture.

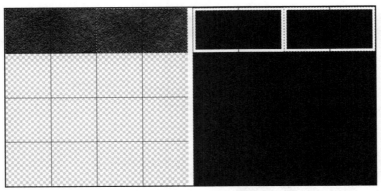

RGB channel (background layer)   Alpha 1 channel

Figure 8.112
Create and fill a selection at the top-right with the Medieval Stone action. Stroke the selection again in the Alpha 1 channel.

13. Now for the next row of stones. This one is a bit trickier, because you want to make this texture inherently tileable with others of its kind. To do so, the edge stones must be manually split in half and positioned. To begin, use the Rectangular Marquee tool to select the area centered and below the top two stones.

14. Play the Medieval Stone action to fill the selected area (see Figure 8.113).

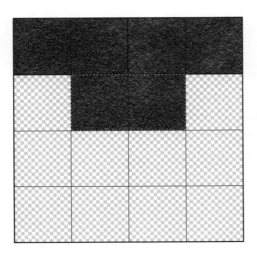

Figure 8.113
Create a selection centered and below the top two stones. Fill it with the Medieval Stone action.

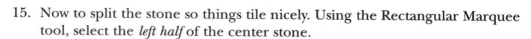

15. Now to split the stone so things tile nicely. Using the Rectangular Marquee tool, select the *left half* of the center stone.

16. Press and hold down the Ctrl key and drag the selection over to the *right edge*.

17. Move the remaining half to the *left edge* (see Figure 8.114). Now when the texture tiles up against itself, the edge tiles will come together as one.

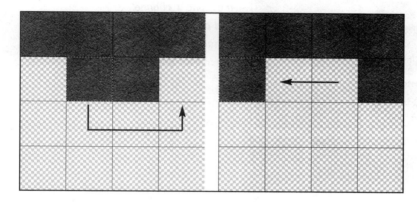

Figure 8.114
Split the center stone and move the halves to the opposite edges.

18. Create another selection in the center (between the edge stones) and fill it with the Medieval Stone action. This will complete the row.

19. With the center selection still active, click on the Alpha 1 channel to select it.

20. Stroke the inside of this selection as before.

21. This is important: Move the selection to the left edge, stroke it, and then move it to the right edge and stroke it again (see Figure 8.115). By moving the center selection to the edges instead of creating square selections, you avoid stroking the edge itself. If you did, the mortar at the end would slice through the middle of certain stones.

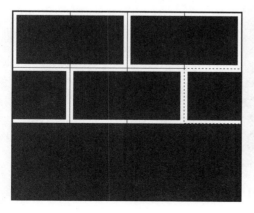

Figure 8.115
Stroke selections for the second line of stones in the Alpha 1 channel. Make sure the edges aren't stroked by moving the full stone selection left and right.

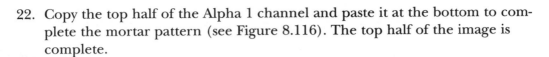

22. Copy the top half of the Alpha 1 channel and paste it at the bottom to complete the mortar pattern (see Figure 8.116). The top half of the image is complete.

Figure 8.116
Copy the top half of the Alpha 1 channel and paste it at the bottom to complete the mortar pattern.

23. You could just duplicate the top to the bottom, but this wouldn't give you a nice variety of unique stones. Instead, repeat the previous steps to fill in the bottom portion of the image, making sure the last row has split stones at the edges. Because you've already completed the mortar pattern in the Alpha channel, however, you don't have to include the stroking steps (see Figure 8.117).

Figure 8.117
Repeat the previous steps to fill the bottom half of the image with stones.

24. Press Ctrl+Alt+' to disable the Grid feature.

25. Old mortar tends to display itself as crumbly and chipping, while rounding out the corners of the stone. To mimic this effect, begin by selecting the Alpha 1 channel.

26. Choose Filter, Blur, Gaussian Blur, and set Radius to 8 pixels (see Figure 8.118).

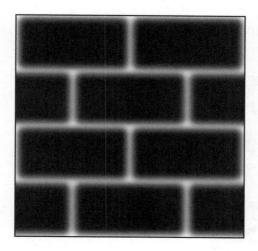

Figure 8.118
Apply the Gaussian Blur filter to the Alpha 1 channel.

Filter: Blur, Gaussian Blur
Radius: 8 pixels

27. Still in the Alpha 1 channel, choose Image, Adjust, Levels, and slide the Shadows and Highlights markers toward each other to sharpen the channel (use the other settings shown in Figure 8.119). This redefines the mortar's selection with rounded corners.

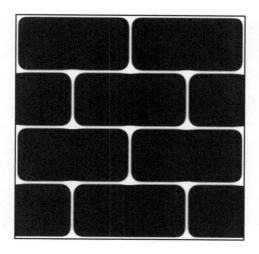

Figure 8.119
Adjust the levels to sharpen the Alpha 1 channel.

Image:	Adjust, Levels
Input Levels:	151, 1.00, 173
Output Levels:	0, 255

28. Ctrl+click the Alpha 1 channel to load the selection.

29. Create a new layer in the Layers palette, and fill the selection with the dark-green foreground color (see Figure 8.120).

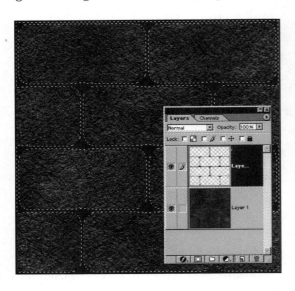

Figure 8.120
Select the Alpha 1 channel's opacity to load the mortar selection. Fill the selection with the foreground color on a new layer.

30. Choose Select, Inverse (Ctrl+Shift+I).

31. Press Q to enter Quick Mask mode.

32. In Quick Mask mode, choose Filter, Brush Strokes, Spatter (see Figure 8.121).

Figure 8.121
Invert the selection and enter Quick Mask mode. Apply the Spatter filter to chop it up.

Filter:	Brush Strokes, Spatter
Spray Radius:	19
Smoothness:	5

33. Press Q to exit Quick Mask mode.

34. Press Delete to create the choppy effect on the top layer. Then press Ctrl+D to deselect it.

35. Choose Filter, Noise, Add Noise (about 10%).

36. Choose Filter, Texture, Craquelure to enhance the mortar (see Figure 8.122).

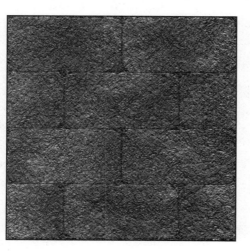

Figure 8.122
Apply the Noise and Craquelure filters to the mortar layer.

Filter:	Noise, Add Noise
Amount:	10%
Distribution:	Uniform
Monochromatic:	(checked)
Filter:	Texture, Craquelure
Crack Space:	20
Crack Depth:	7
Crack Brightness:	8

37. Click Stop on the Actions palette to stop recording.

That's the wall texture in a nutshell. By itself, it will tile seamlessly; when viewed from a short distance, however, a player will see the same bricks repeating themselves. You need to record a final routine that will simply make a copy of the base texture, start a new image, and replace *only the whole stones* in the image. By retaining the split edge stones, you retain the ability to tile other textures with each other.

To accomplish this, record a new action that does the following:

1. Selects the first layer of the stone wall.

2. Copies the layer to a new image.

3. Copies the mortar layer to the new image.

4. Applies the Medieval Stone action to each of the six whole stones in the texture.

In Figure 8.123, the first texture is the one you just did. The second stems from an action I made to replace only the six whole stones using the Medieval Stone action. Now I have two textures whose edges tile seamlessly and whose stones are different from each other. To complete the set, I created four different tiles using this Medieval stone action (see Figure 8.124).

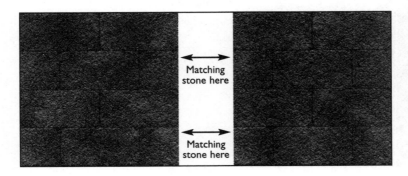

Matching
stone here

Matching
stone here

Figure 8.123 *The second texture is based on the first; only the six whole stones have been replaced.*

Figure 8.124
A completed stone wall set. Any texture in the set can be randomly tiled with any set member.

NOTE

From now on, creating any color wall in seconds is just a matter of setting new foreground and background colors, then playing the Stone Wall action. I make tiles for my set by playing a stone-replacement action called "Patternize," consisting of the steps I mentioned just before.

TIP

Notice that some of the stones in the set have cracks in them—try adding a stop just before the call to the Gaussian Blur in the Stone Wall action. When you play the action, the stop will pause the action at that point; just spray thick lines in your Alpha 1 channel where some cracks would go. Click Play to resume the action.

Metal

Being a very high-tech kind of guy, most of the video games I appreciate are fully loaded with heavy machinery, futuristic equipment, spaceship hulls, underground research labs, you name it. As with the other textures you've made, metal textures can be hand-made, taken from photograph, and more often than not, a composite of both. What I find most striking about texturing metal is how sharp and effective beveling styles and displacement channels can be. Let's start with a few simple tutorials, then add to them as we go.

Basic Metal

This is a simple filter-based brushed metal procedure that can be applied to any object requiring a finished metal look, like elevator doors or a control panel.

1. Start a new 600 × 600-pixel RGB image. (You'll reduce it to 512 × 512 pixels on the last step to get rid of the smearing effect.)

2. Set your foreground color to a medium gray, like hex# A7A6A6. Press Alt+Backspace to fill the canvas with it.

3. Choose Filter, Noise, Add Noise (about 25%), as shown in Figure 8.125.

Figure 8.125 *Fill the image with gray and apply the Add Noise filter.*

Filter:	Noise, Add Noise
Amount:	25%
Distribution:	Uniform
Monochromatic:	(checked)

4. Choose Filter, Blur, Motion Blur (about 50 pixels), as shown in Figure 8.126.

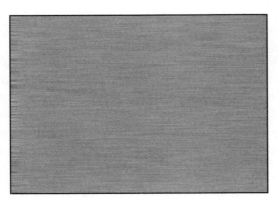

Figure 8.126 *Apply the Motion Blur filter.*

Filter:	Blur, Motion Blur
Angle:	0 degrees
Distance:	50 pixels

5. See the smearing/streaking that's going on at the left and right edges? Crop it by clicking Image, Canvas Size, and entering 512 for both the width and height. Now you have basic metal.

> **NOTE**
>
> You can play around with the Distance amount; setting it anywhere from 10 to 60 pixels yields a texture that looks like real brushed metal (the type you see on elevator doors, panels, and whatnot).

Shiny Metal

To the texture you created in the previous section, you can apply the Lighting Effects filter coupled with a Curves adjustment to illuminate the metal texture's surface and enhance its specularity.

1. Using the completed metal texture from the previous example, choose Filter, Render, Lighting Effects.

2. Use a spotlight for this one, making sure the light is pointing straight down and high above, encompassing the entire texture. Don't make the top of the texture too bright; you only want to vary the surface shine so the Curves function can do its job (see Figure 8.127).

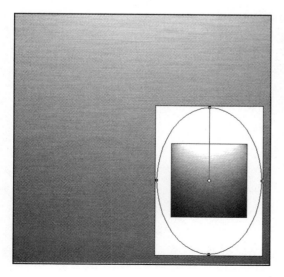

Figure 8.127

Apply the Lighting Effects filter to the basic metal texture, using a semi-distant spotlight.

Filter:	Render, Lighting Effects
Light Type:	Spotlight (vertically)
Intensity:	28
Focus:	69
Gloss:	0
Material:	69
Exposure:	0
Ambience:	8
Texture Channel:	(none)

3. To enhance the specularity, click Image, Adjust, Curves.

4. Adjust the curve you see so that it looks like the one in Figure 8.128.

> **NOTE**
>
> Feel free to play around with this to get the shininess you want. Curves can be a pain, and in most cases, only a seasoned art pro will quickly know how to set the Curve function appropriately. If you're having a hard time getting a curve just right, try loading the **shinymetal.acv** file in the Chapter 8 Data section on the **CD-ROM**.

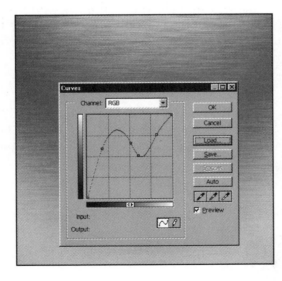

Figure 8.128
Adjust the Curves function to enhance the texture's specularity.

5. Choose Image, Adjust, Levels, and adjust the levels a bit to suit your taste (see Figure 8.129).

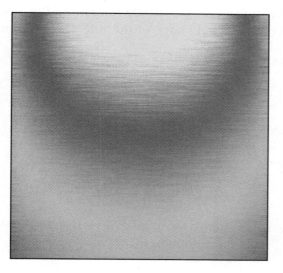

Figure 8.129
Adjust the levels to suit.

Metal from an Image

The next time you go to any type of building that houses a public business, bring your camera (of course, tell the people at the front desk what you're doing before you take any photos lest they nix you from the place). The countertops, bathrooms, and elevators are bound to be trimmed out with brushed metal. These images make outstanding base materials with which to work because their general composition is linear but slightly heterogeneous, ideal for beveling operations.

NOTE

Why am I going into so much detail with textures? After all, most games have textures that average at best 256×256 pixels! Well, when you do concept art for the characters, box cover, posters, and what have you, the artwork will need to be *at least* the detail and resolution we start with, and averaging 3000×3000 pixels at 300 pixels/per inch! Start that image in Photoshop. Blank, it's 25 MB. By the time you're finished, it might be well over 100.

For this next example I want to give you some ideas for beveling metal. You'll create a set of institutional doors with some personality.

1. Open the **brushedmetal.jpg** file in the Chapter 8 Data section on the CD-ROM (see Figure 8.130). This is a cropped image of the side of a gas pump (see gaspump.jpg to view the original).

Figure 8.130 *The* **brushedmetal.jpg** *image.*

2. Make a copy of the background layer so there are two layers of metal.

3. Click on the bottom layer and fill it with black. That way, when a player punches or tears through the metal, a void will be revealed. You can then put other stuff between the background and the metal layers, like pipes and wires.

4. Select the top layer.

5. Using the Rectangular Marquee tool, select the entire left half of the image. (This might be easiest if you set the tool to Fixed Size, and enter 256 pixels for the width and 512 pixels for the height.)

6. Right-click on the selection and choose Layer Via Cut (see Figure 8.131). This places the door halves on separate layers.

Figure 8.131
Select half of the image and cut it onto its own layer.

7. To raise the surface of the doors, double-click one of the door's layers to bring up the Styles screen and apply an inner bevel. Apply this same style to the other door (see Figure 8.132).

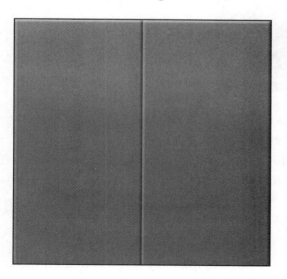

Figure 8.132
Apply inner bevels to both doors.

Style: Bevel and Emboss
Style: Inner Bevel

Technique:	Smooth
Depth:	100%
Direction:	Up
Size:	7
Soften:	0

8. Using the Rectangular Marquee tool, create a window by selecting the upper half of one of the doors and pressing Delete to knock it out.

9. Click on the other door's layer, move the selection, and delete it as well (see Figure 8.133). Notice that the inner bevel applies itself to the windowed area.

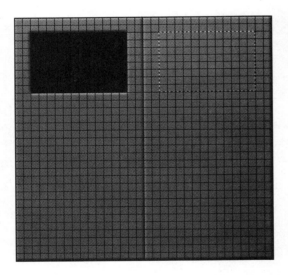

Figure 8.133
Make windows in the doors.

10. With the rectangular selection still active, create a new layer between the black background and the door halves.

11. Using the Gradient tool, fill the selection diagonally with a linear gradient. If you go to the Gradient Editor, use the Copper gradient for this fill; this will give the window a glass look—except that it's brown (you'll fix that in a minute).

12. Move the selection to the other side and fill it again.

13. Click Image, Adjust, Desaturate. This gives the copper gradient a grayish look.

14. To simulate that shatter-proof look, add some little black lines to the windows (see Figure 8.134).

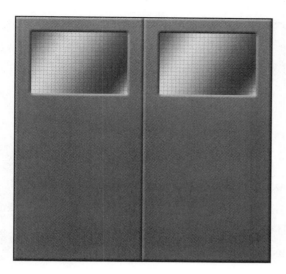

Figure 8.134
Create windows by filling the rectangular selections with a copper gradient, then desaturate.

15. Merge the doors and windows onto a single layer by linking each layer (except for the background layer), then clicking Layer, Merge Linked. This way, you won't disturb the individual layer styles.

16. Let's put a sign on the doors. Open the **authorized.psd** file on the CD-ROM, make a copy of it, and paste it into your image on the bottom-half of each door.

17. Double-click each sign's layer to bring up the Styles screen, and apply a downward outer bevel (see Figure 8.135). (Add whatever bevel you think looks best. Sometimes, no bevel is good too!)

Figure 8.135 *Add the authorized.psd signs to both doors and apply an outer bevel to each.*

Style:	Bevel and Emboss
Style:	Outer Bevel
Technique:	Chisel Soft
Depth:	200%
Direction:	Down
Size:	5
Soften:	0

18. Click on the layer with the doors and add a new layer directly above it.

19. Create rectangular selections on each door to represent impact shields, or the spot where people most frequenty push the doors open.

20. Fill the selections using the Basic Metal technique from earlier in the chapter.

21. Apply a bevel of your choice. I applied a small upward outer bevel, then added rivets to the edges. (Don't worry, rivets, screws, and the like are coming up soon.) This will represent the basic, completed set of doors (see Figure 8.136).

Figure 8.136 *Add impact shields to the doors using the Basic Metal as a texture. Apply a bevel for a 3D effect.*

Rusted Metal

Rust varies greatly from bubbly dark brown spots to solid dark orange smears to . . . well, you've seen it. It's downright nasty (but quite delicious for texturing spaceship interiors, I must add). The Photoshop default actions come with a rusted metal procedure that's alright, but let's try this instead:

1. Start a 600×600-pixel RGB image. (You'll crop the image back to 512×512 when you're done to get rid of the edge bevels.)

2. Set the foreground to a reddish-brown, like hex# 2C0C01, and the background to a brownish-orange, like hex# 2C1407.

3. Choose Filter, Render, Clouds (see Figure 8.137).

Figure 8.137
Apply the Clouds filter using red-brown and brown-orange colors.

Filter:	Render, Clouds
Foreground:	hex# 2C0C01
Background:	hex# 2C1407

4. Choose Filter, Noise, Add Noise (see Figure 8.138).

Figure 8.138
Apply the Noise filter.

Filter:	Noise, Add Noise
Amount:	12%
Distribution:	Uniform
Monochromatic:	(checked)

5. Choose Filter, Noise, Median (see Figure 8.139).

Figure 8.139
Apply the Median filter.

Filter:	Noise, Median
Radius:	1 pixels

6. The base rusted panel is done. Now let's add a bolted rail that spans the width. To begin, use the Rectangular Marquee tool to select the upper half of the texture.

7. Right-click on the selection, and choose Layer Via Copy (see Figure 8.140).

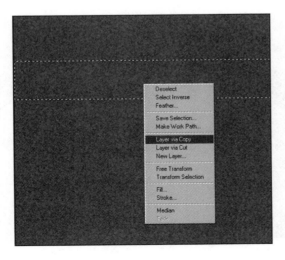

Figure 8.140
Make a rectangular selection and copy it.

8. The copy of the selection you just made should be on its own layer now. Double-click this layer to open the Styles screen, and apply an inner bevel to raise the surface.

9. Change the Highlight Mode setting's color from white to something dark orange or it'll look silly (see Figure 8.141).

Figure 8.141

Apply an inner bevel to the new layer to raise the surface.

Style:	Bevel and Emboss
Style:	Inner Bevel
Technique:	Chisel Soft
Depth:	100%
Direction:	Up
Size:	5 pixels
Soften:	0
Highlight Mode:	Normal, dark-orange

10. Now for the bolts. To begin, start a new layer above the rail.

11. Select the Polygon tool, set its options to six sides, and create a large solid hexagon in the middle of the screen.

12. Ctrl+click the layer to select the hexagon, then run through the basic Rusted Metal routine to fill it (Clouds, Noise, Median).

13. Apply an outer bevel to the hexagon to give it depth, as shown in Figure 8.142. (I also added the Contour option to sharpen the depth a little.)

Figure 8.142 *Add a hexagon and fill it with basic rust. Apply an outer bevel to give the hexagon depth.*

Style:	Bevel and Emboss
Style:	Outer Bevel
Technique:	Chisel Soft
Depth:	100%
Direction:	Up
Size:	5 pixels
Soften:	0
Highlight Mode:	Normal, dark-orange
Style:	Contour
Contour Shape:	Linear
Range:	50%

14. Scale the bolt down to size and position it on the middle of the rail.

15. Make copies of the bolts and position them as you see fit. (I rotated a couple of mine as well to make it more natural.)

16. Click Layer, Flatten Image.

17. Click Image, Canvas Size, and change the canvas to 512×512 pixels to crop out the edge bevels, if any (see Figure 8.143).

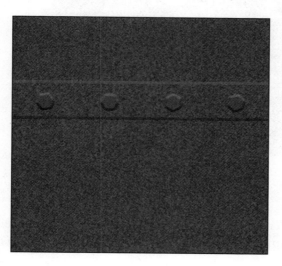

Figure 8.143
Scale, position, and copy the bolt. Resize the canvas to crop the edge bevels.

This is a good base panel for some type of equipment, or the outside of a boiler. Notice that I placed the bolts so that when duplicates of the texture are placed side-by-side, the bolts are evenly spaced (see Figure 8.144). I hope this texture will inspire you to create some other designs—try making other marquee selections and applying inner or outer bevels.

Figure 8.144 *The rusty panel wrapped around pipes.*

> **NOTE**
>
> A word about bevels, drop shadows, and styles in general: Assume, when making textures, that the global light for your game is a light source positioned high overhead and not off at an angle—unless your game company tells you otherwise. Just make sure that the **Use Global Light** option is always checked in any **Styles** dialog box, that the default (unless specified) light source is at **90 degrees** high, and that your work is saved as a **PSD** before you merge layers with styles. That way, you can always retrieve your texture and readjust the global light in one go.

Dripping Rust

Dripping rust is a popular texture. To render it, you simply create some type of selection and apply the Wind filter when in Quick Mask mode to get your selection to drip.

1. Start a new 512×512-pixel RGB image.

2. Repeat steps 1–5 of the Rusted Metal procedure.

3. Start a new layer.

4. Fill this layer with the entire Basic Metal procedure. The top layer should now be metal, and the bottom layer should be rust.

5. Start a new layer on top of the Basic Metal layer.

6. Using the Lasso tool, create a selection in the shape of a crack or tear and fill it with black (see Figure 8.145).

Figure 8.145

Create a Lasso selection on a separate layer and fill it with black.

7. To the black tear's layer, apply an inner bevel to give it a little depth (see Figure 8.146).

Figure 8.146
Apply an inner bevel to the tear to give it depth.

Style:	Bevel and Emboss
Style:	Inner Bevel
Technique:	Chisel Soft
Depth:	200%
Direction:	Down
Size:	2 pixels
Soften:	0

8. With the crack still active, press Q to enter Quick Mask mode. This is where you'll apply a dripping effect to the selection (see Figure 8.147).

Figure 8.147
Enter Quick Mask mode with the crack's selection active.

9. Press Ctrl+A to select the entire layer.

10. Choose Edit, Transform, Rotate 90 degrees CCW (counter-clockwise).

11. Choose Filter, Stylize, Wind, and make sure the wind is blowing from the left (see Figure 8.148). Repeat this filter (Ctrl+F) several times to extend the dripping effect.

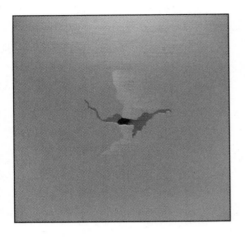

Figure 8.148
Rotate the mask and apply the Wind filter several times.

Filter:	Stylize, Wind
Method:	Wind
Direction:	From the Left

12. Choose Edit, Transform, Rotate 90 degrees CW (clockwise) to restore the mask.

13. Press Q to exit Quick Mask mode.

You have transformed the crack into one that drips. From here, you could either punch out the metal's layer with this selection to reveal the rust, or click on the rust's layer, press Ctrl+C to copy the dripping portion, and then paste it back between the metal layer and the crack (see Figure 8.149). Finally, you can complete the rust effect by blurring the dripping layer with the Blur tool (see Figure 8.150).

Figure 8.149 *Fill the selection using the rust layer.*

Figure 8.150 *Use the Blur tool on the dripping rust to finish the effect.*

This technique is fairly useful for other things like bolts, screws, dripping slime, and blood. It also makes a cool effect when you Quick Mask some type and make the letters drip with something. Check out some of the dripping effects I applied to the panel in Figure 8.151.

Figure 8.151 *Various dripping effects applied to objects on a control panel.*

Rusted Catwalk with an Alpha Channel

In most 3D games, there are times when an object (or *brush*, in level-design lingo) is present that the player must be seen through, such as a catwalk, ladder, or chain-link fence. Instead of making a high-poly mesh model, you can simply create a texture with an alpha channel as its see-through portion. The game's engine will interpret a predefined color (typically either pure blue or black) as the color that won't be displayed.

1. Start a new 512×512-pixel RGB image.

2. Fill the background layer with pure blue.

3. Create a new layer, and fill it with the entire Rusted Metal procedure.

4. Enable Photoshop's Snap and Grid features, with the gridlines set to every 16 pixels. This will help you align your selections.

5. Using the Rectangular Marquee tool on the Rusted Metal layer, select a 3×3 grid square in the top-left area of the image.

6. Press Delete to remove the selection. Move the selection over so that one grid unit is skipped and repeat. Do this for the entire layer (see Figure 8.152).

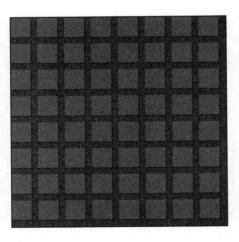

Figure 8.152
Use the Rectangular Marquee tool to delete selections of the Rusted Metal layer, forming a cat-walk grid.

7. Turn off the Grid feature.

8. Apply an inner bevel to the Rusted Metal layer to raise the surface (see Figure 8.153). You might want to change the gloss color of the Highlight Mode from white to orange-ish.

Figure 8.153
Apply an inner bevel to raise the surface.

Style:	Bevel and Emboss
Style:	Inner Bevel
Technique:	Chisel Hard
Depth:	100%
Direction:	Up
Size:	13 pixels
Soften:	0
Highlight Mode:	Normal, dark-orange

This is your finished catwalk texture. If this image were imported into the *Half-Life* engine, the blue areas would be transparent. Not all engines are the same, however, so you'll have to find out what is specified within your game engine's parameters. For example, some engines require that your images have an embedded alpha channel instead of a color to represent transparency. Here's how you would do this with the previous example:

1. Ctrl+click the catwalk layer to select its opacity.

2. Click Select, Inverse to select the transparent regions.

3. Start a new channel and fill the selection with white.

4. Click File, Save As, and choose TGA, TIF (or whatever the engine requires).

5. Make sure Alpha Channel is selected and click Save.

If the Alpha Channel option is not present in the Save As screen, you may have to go to the Preferences section (Ctrl+K) to enable the advanced save options. See Figure 8.154 to see this texture in action.

Figure 8.154 *The finished catwalk texture applied to a level. Notice how the blue areas are now transparent, allowing objects behind them to show through.*

Diamond-Plated Metal

The term *diamond-plated metal* refers to that classic raised, anti-slip pattern that fits well on metal stairs. You'll be doing this on rusted metal, but it'll work well with anything else.

1. Start a new 512×512-pixel RGB image.
2. Fill the canvas with the entire Rusted Metal texture.
3. Enable Photoshop's Snap and Grid features, with the gridlines set to every 16 pixels.
4. Using the Polygonal Lasso tool, create a six-sided selection that looks like the one in Figure 8.155. Use the gridlines to guide you.

Figure 8.155 *Use the Polygonal Lasso tool to create a six-sided selection.*

5. The diamond divots that stick up can be a bit rounded on the edges, so let's use the Channels palette to round them. With the selection still active, go to the Channels palette, start a new channel, and fill the selection with white.

6. Choose Filter, Blur, Gaussian Blur (about 7 pixels).

7. Choose Image, Adjust, Levels, and move the Shadows and Highlights markers towards each other to make the edges of the white boundary more crisp (see Figure 8.156).

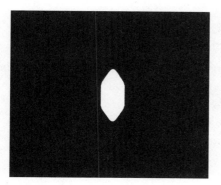

Figure 8.156 *Use an Alpha channel to round the selection by blurring it and using the Levels dialog box.*

Filter: Blur, Gaussian Blur

Radius: 7 pixels

8. Ctrl+click this channel to load the selection.

9. With the revised selection loaded, go back to the Layers palette and click on the background layer.

10. Press Ctrl+J (Layer Via Copy). The shape now has its own layer.

11. To the new layer, apply an inner bevel (see Figure 8.157).

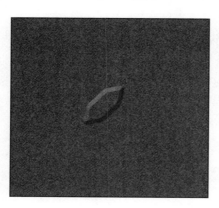

Figure 8.157 *Use the selection to copy the contents of the rusted-metal layer. Apply an inner bevel to it.*

Style:	Bevel and Emboss
Style:	Inner Bevel
Technique:	Chisel Hard
Depth:	630%
Direction:	Up
Size:	10 pixels
Soften:	0
Highlight Mode:	Normal, dark-orange

12. Make a copy of the raised diamond layer.

13. Rotate the copy 90 degrees and position it as shown in Figure 8.158. This represents the base pattern of the diamond-plated metal.

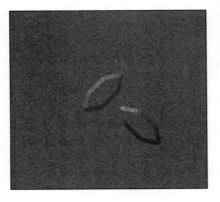

Figure 8.158 *Copy the diamond and rotate it 90 degrees.*

14. Link the two diamond layers, and choose Layer, Merge Linked. This will preserve their styles and allow them to be scaled without consequently scaling the styles as well.

15. Choose Edit, Transform, Scale to scale down the newly merged diamond layer. Press and hold down the Shift key to make the scaling uniform.

16. Position the layer at the top-left of the image, and make copies of it across, then down. Figure 8.159 shows how mine ended up.

Figure 8.159
Merge the diamond layers, and then scale, position, and copy them to complete the pattern.

You might have to crop your image to make the pattern smooth and seamless. For an odd-shaped repeating pattern like this, I didn't feel like hassling with measurements; it's okay to just eyeball it and crop it appropriately. Figure 8.160 shows this texture applied to metal stairs.

Figure 8.160 *The completed diamond-plated metal texture applied to stairs in a level.*

Peeling Paint on Metal

This one takes a little work, but I think you'll like it. In this tutorial, you'll add paint to a rusted-metal layer, and then chip some of the paint away.

1. Start a new 512×512-pixel RGB image.

2. Fill the background layer with the entire Rusted Metal texture. (I guess it'd be good to have this as an action by now, eh?)

3. Start a new layer.

4. Apply the Clouds filter with two dark-yellow colors, like hex# 5A4D2A and hex# 292718 (see Figure 8.161). This will represent paint.

Figure 8.161
Apply the Clouds filter on a new layer.

Filter: Render, Clouds
Foreground: hex#5A4D2A
Background: hex#292718

5. Make a copy of the paint layer.

6. With the copied layer selected, choose Filter, Noise, Add Noise (about 6%).

7. Set the Blending Mode of this layer to Color Dodge.

8. Merge the two paint layers (see Figure 8.162).

Figure 8.162
Copy the paint layer, add Noise, change the Blend mode to Color Dodge, and merge the layers.

Filter:	Noise, Add Noise
Amount:	6%
Distribution:	Uniform
Monochromatic:	(checked)
Blend Mode:	Color Dodge

> **NOTE**
> You can adjust the levels of the paint layer to your liking if you want, but I'm keeping mine as is.

9. Use the Lasso tool to create a curvy, closed selection that will represent where the paint has peeled away (see Figure 8.163).

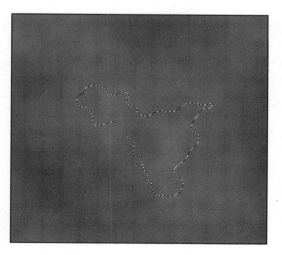

Figure 8.163 *Use the Lasso tool to create a selection where the paint will be removed.*

10. With the selection active, press Q to enter Quick Mask mode.

11. Choose Filter, Brush Strokes, Spatter to apply this filter to the mask.

12. Press Q again to exit the mask.

13. Press Delete to remove the paint (see Figure 8.164).

Figure 8.164
Apply the Spatter filter to the selection in Quick Mask mode. Delete the selection from the paint layer.

Filter:	Brush Strokes, Spatter
Spray Radius:	10
Smoothness:	5

14. Using the Dodge tool at 25% exposure, dodge out highlights on all the areas where the paint curves in or creates tips. The highlights will eventually appear to make the paint peel upwards.

15. Using the Burn tool at about 12% exposure, burn shadows a bit just behind the white portions you just dodged, as well as on the portions where the paint curves away from the inside (see Figure 8.165).

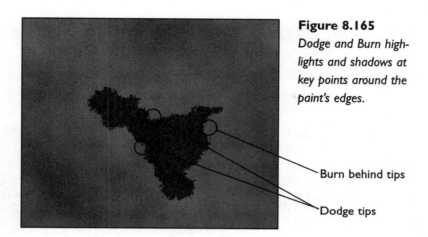

Figure 8.165
*Dodge and Burn high-
lights and shadows at
key points around the
paint's edges.*

Burn behind tips

Dodge tips

16. To the paint layer, apply an inner bevel and a drop shadow (see Figure 8.166).

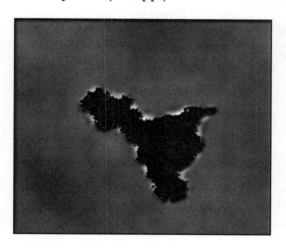

Figure 8.166
*Apply an inner bevel
and drop shadow to
the paint layer.*

Style:	Bevel and Emboss
Style:	Inner Bevel
Technique:	Smooth
Depth:	81%
Direction:	Down
Size:	8 pixels
Soften:	0
Highlight Mode:	Screen, gray-green
Style:	Drop Shadow
Distance:	7 pixels

Metal Panels (and Spaceship Hulls)

You probably already have an idea about how to create a metal panel. These can look really cool, especially when you put painted stuff on top. I'm going to make several panels out of this texture, but I'm only going to show you one; I'll let you do the rest.

1. Start a new 512×512-pixel RGB image.

2. Apply the Clouds filter with two dark military-green colors like hex# 141A00 and hex# 292602 (see Figure 8.167).

> **NOTE**
>
> If you want to make a spaceship hull, ignore step 2; I'm going for a panel that could go on the side of some Army equipment.

Figure 8.167
Apply the Clouds filter using two dark-green colors.

Filter: Render, Clouds
Foreground: hex# 141A00
Background: hex# 292602

3. Start a new layer.

4. Apply the entire Basic Metal procedure to the new layer.

5. Set the layer's Blend mode to Soft Light (see Figure 8.168). This will give the overall texture a painted-steel look.

Figure 8.168
Add a new layer and apply the Basic Metal procedure. Set its Blend mode to Soft Light.

6. Merge the two layers.

7. Enable Photoshop's Snap and Grid features.

8. Using the Polygonal Lasso tool, create a shape that will become a panel (see Figure 8.169).

Figure 8.169 *Use the Polygonal Lasso tool to create a shape that will be a panel.*

9. Panels like this are generally curved, so let's curve it! With the selection still active, go to the Channels palette and create a new channel.

10. Fill the selection with white.

11. Press Ctrl+D to deselect the selection.

12. Choose Filter, Blur, Gaussian Blur, with a radius of about 3.0 pixels.

13. Use the Levels dialog box to sharpen the white area, then Ctrl+click the channel to load the selection (see Figure 8.170).

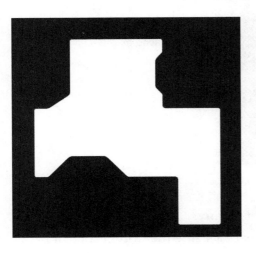

Figure 8.170
Fill the selection in a new channel. Apply the Gaussian Blur filter, and adjust the levels to sharpen it.

Filter: Blur, Gaussian Blur
Radius: 3.0 pixels

14. With the revised selection loaded, go back to the Layers palette and select the painted-metal layer.

15. Press Ctrl+J (Layer Via Copy) to copy the metal within the selection boundary.

16. To this new layer, apply an inner bevel with an inverted-cone contour (see Figure 8.171). Adding the contour will give the panel a recessed look.

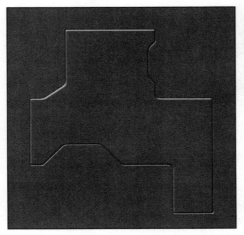

Figure 8.171
Apply an inner bevel with contour to the metal panel.

Style:	Bevel and Emboss
Style:	Inner Bevel
Technique:	Smooth
Depth:	100%
Direction:	Up
Size:	5 pixels
Soften:	0
Style:	Contour
Contour Shape:	Cone - Inverted
Range:	50%

17. Repeat steps 8 through 16 to add more panels. Then, drag and drop the bevel effect from the first panel's layer onto the new ones (see Figure 8.172).

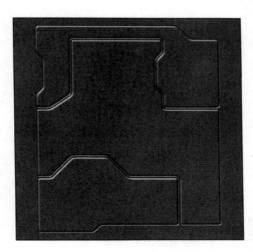

Figure 8.172 *Add more panels to the scene using the same beveling effects as before.*

18. If you want, link all of the panel layers and merge them. This is only to de-clutter your Layers palette.

19. To add a cool paint effect, begin by selecting a light yellow-green foreground color, like hex# C3C44E, to be the paint color.

20. Using the Text tool, type some text, preferably in huge, fat letters.

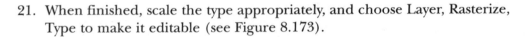

21. When finished, scale the type appropriately, and choose Layer, Rasterize, Type to make it editable (see Figure 8.173).

Figure 8.173

Add text to the panels and then rasterize the type to make it editable.

22. Ctrl+click the text layer to select its opacity (that is, this will select the pixel contents of the text layer).

23. Choose Select, Inverse.

24. Press Q to enter Quick Mask mode.

25. Choose Filter, Brush Strokes, Spatter to apply the Spatter filter to the mask. This chops it up.

26. Press Q again to exit Quick Mask mode.

27. Press Delete. Now the text has a bit of a worn look (see Figure 8.174).

Figure 8.174

Select the text and use the Spatter filter in Quick Mask mode to chop it up.

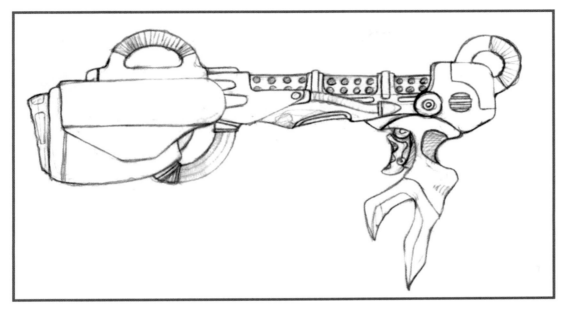

The RF-9 Plasma Gun developed in this book starts off as a concept sketch
(courtesy Lars Ricaldi).

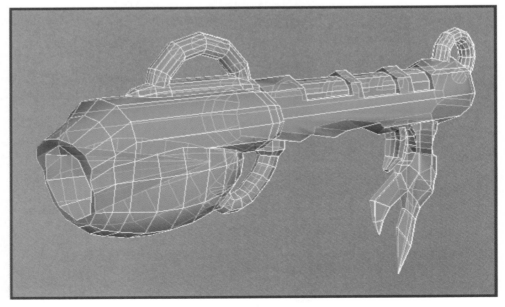

From sketch to mesh creation with trueSpace 6.

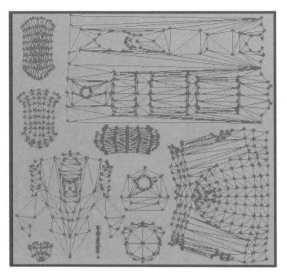

The plasma gun's U-Vs are unwrapped next, using DeepUV.

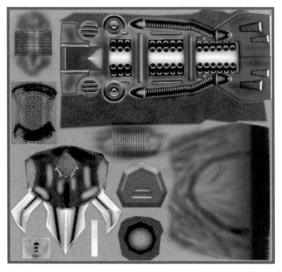

A futuristic skin for the weapon is created using Deep Paint 3D and Photoshop 7.

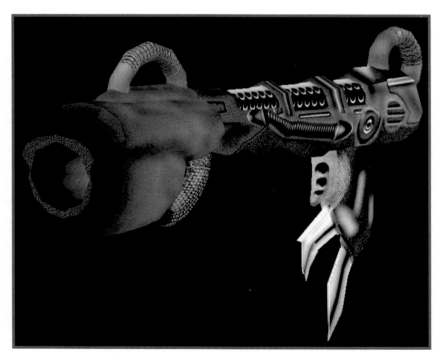

The final RF-9 plasma gun, skinned and prepared using 3D Studio Max 5.

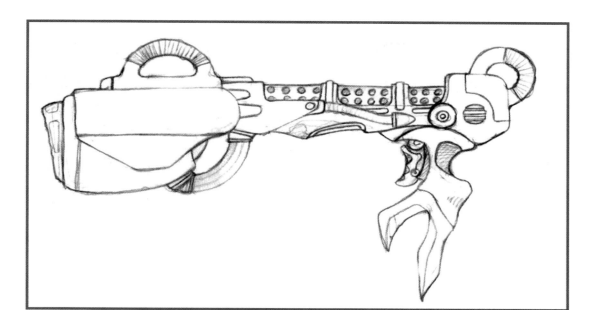

The RF-9 Plasma Gun developed in this book starts off as a concept sketch (courtesy Lars Ricaldi).

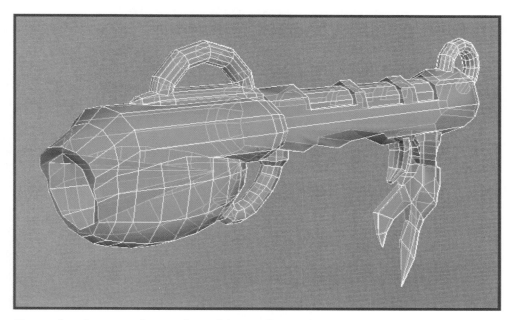

From sketch to mesh creation with trueSpace 6.

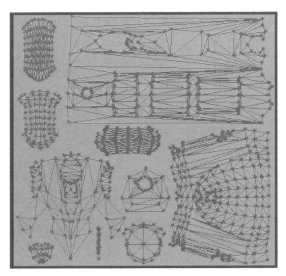

The plasma gun's U-Vs are unwrapped next, using DeepUV.

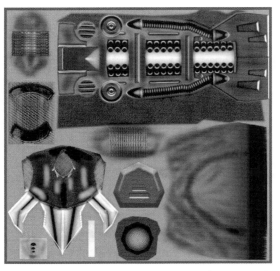

A futuristic skin for the weapon is created using Deep Paint 3D and Photoshop 7.

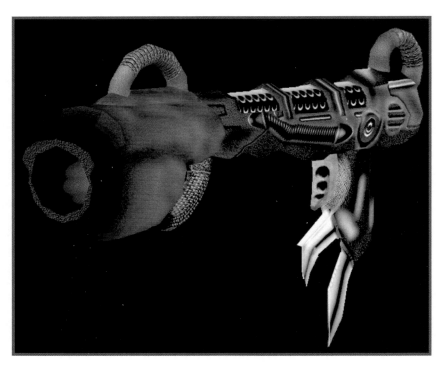

The final RF-9 plasma gun, skinned and prepared using 3D Studio Max 5.

The slogre character developed in this book starts off as a concept sketch
(courtesy Lars Ricaldi).

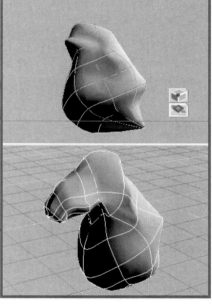

Using trueSpace 6's powerful NURBS modeling tools, the slogre mesh comes to life.

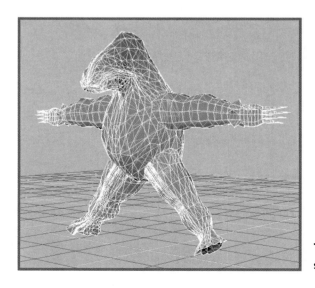

The completed slogre mesh.

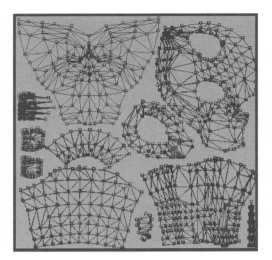

The U-Vs for the slogre are
unwrapped using DeepUV.

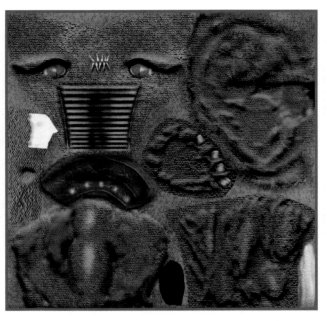

Next, a skin is developed using Deep Paint 3D and
Photoshop 7.

Finally, the slogre
is skinned and
prepared for a
game using 3D
Studio Max 5.

Another nice pose for the slogre—concept art is vital when developing models for games (courtesy Lars Ricaldi).

The final output of hard work: the slogre character blasting away enemies in the Torque game engine.

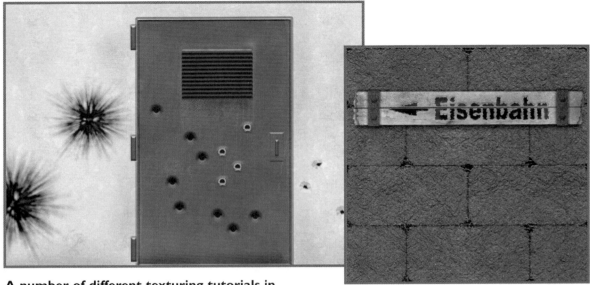

A number of different texturing tutorials in Chapter 8 can be used to make this bullet-riddled wall.

Stone and wood textures in Chapter 8 used to make a rustic stone wall.

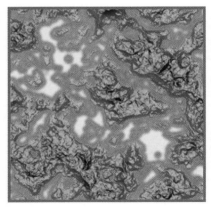

Lava texture also developed from scratch using a number of Photoshop's filters.

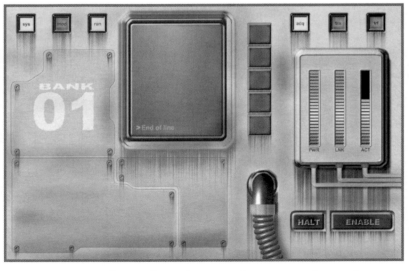

Metal textures, pipes, wires, rivets, and screws make cool control panels.

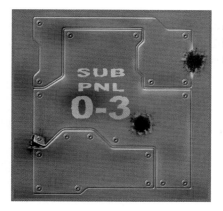

Another military texture. This type of texture only takes an hour or so to make using the texturing tutorials in this book.

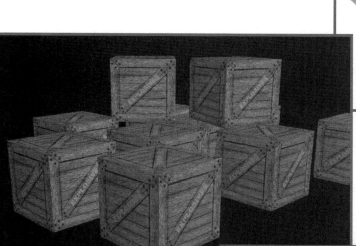

Bullet holes and peeling paint on a sign. Everything here was created from scratch.

A single wooden crate texture can be wrapped around dozens of boxes (see Chapter 9).

More advanced texturing using composites of real pictures and other texturing techniques in this book.

A cool, futuristic texture, created in **Chapter 9**, made entirely from scratch in only a couple of hours.

A landscape texture, seamlessly tileable and spread across a rocky terrain in the Torque engine.

A water texture, seamlessly tileable and applied to water in the Torque engine. The water here is in motion as well.

Filter:	Brush Strokes, Spatter
Spray Radius:	10
Smoothness:	10

Try using the Dodge and Burn tools to add more realism to the edges and whatnot. In Figure 8.175, I also added some inset hex screws to the corners, and some sustained shell damage.

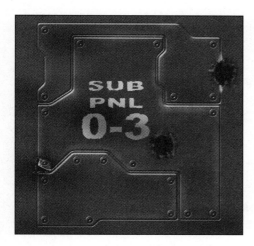

Figure 8.175
Added details to the texture to enhance realism.

Pipes, Wires, Rivets, and Screws

In the rest of this section, I'd like to show you how to add the little details that can complete a metal texture. Some of this stuff is good when done in 3D, then exported as a 2D image—especially things like elbow joints and couplings.

Basic Metal Pipes

Creating metal pipes is easy and effective. It's best to view your creations when the base layer is metal as well.

1. Start a new 512×512-pixel RGB image.

2. Fill the base layer with the Basic Metal texture.

3. Create a new layer.

4. Using the Rectangular Marquee tool, create a selection that spans the width of the image (see Figure 8.176). This will be the pipe itself.

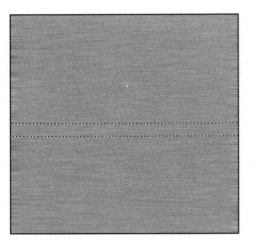

Figure 8.176
Create a rectangular selection in the shape of a pipe.

5. Press D to reset the swatches to black and white.

6. Click on the Gradient tool and, in the tool's options, select Reflected Gradient. (It's the button on top that looks like the top of a pipe.) Also enable the Reverse option.

7. Create a gradient as shown in Figure 8.177. The gradient should start in the selection area's mid point, and extend upward beyond the selection; the total height of the gradient should be the same as the height of the selection. (It might help to press and hold down the Shift key when creating the gradient to keep the line snapped to 90 degrees.)

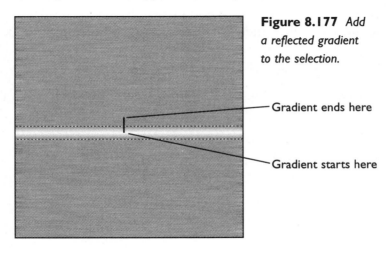

Figure 8.177 *Add a reflected gradient to the selection.*

Gradient ends here

Gradient starts here

8. Press Ctrl+D to deselect the selected area.

9. Choose Image, Adjust, Levels, and slide the Shadows marker to the right a bit to darken the top and bottom edges of the pipe.

10. To enhance the pipe's shininess, adjust the curves as I have in Figure 8.178. I also added a drop shadow to make it look like it's floating above the metal surface.

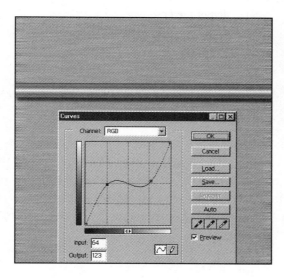

Figure 8.178
Adjust the levels and/or curves, and add a drop shadow to complete the effect.

To quickly make a pipe fitting, do the following:

1. Create a small rectangular selection surrounding any portion of the pipe.

2. Right-click on the selection and choose Layer Via Copy.

3. The fitting's layer will have a copy of the drop shadow; delete it.

4. Choose Edit, Transform, Scale, and scale the fitting so it's slightly larger than the pipe itself.

5. Apply a very slight drop shadow to the fitting's layer to complete the effect (see Figure 8.179).

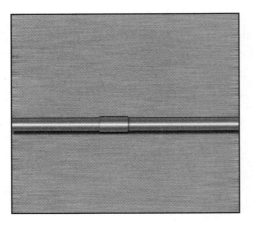

Figure 8.179
Create a pipe fitting by copying and transforming a small portion of the base pipe.

Making pipes can get somewhat interesting. Try creating a pipe within a pipe, then cut notches into the outer pipe to create a futuristic effect. On a layer below a pipe, put another pipe perpendicular to the first, and use the Elliptical Marquee tool to cut a semi-circle out of the base pipe (where the two pipes meet) to make them look joined (see Figure 8.180).

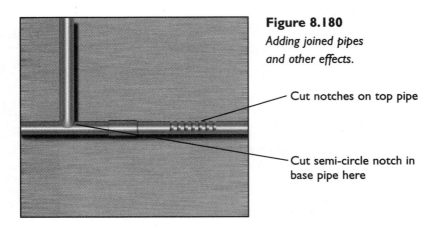

Figure 8.180
Adding joined pipes and other effects.

Cut notches on top pipe

Cut semi-circle notch in base pipe here

Bent Pipes

The Reflected Gradient tool is good only when you want to create a straight pipe; creating a similar effect on a curved pipe is somewhat more difficult. Here's how:

1. Start a new 512×512-pixel RGB image.

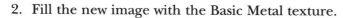
2. Fill the new image with the Basic Metal texture.

3. Enable Photoshop's Snap and Grid features.

4. Use the Polygonal Lasso tool to create a selection for your pipe to follow. Figure 8.181 is mine.

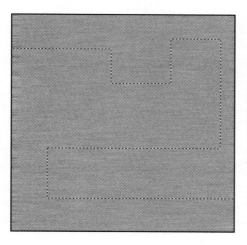

Figure 8.181 *Use the Polygonal Lasso tool to make a selection that your pipe will follow.*

5. Create a new channel in the Channels palette.

6. Choose Edit, Stroke, and stroke the center of the selection with white, about 25 pixels. The thicker your stroke, the thicker the pipe will be (see Figure 8.182).

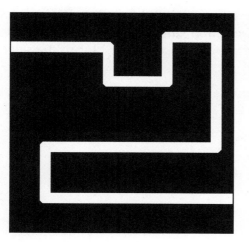

Figure 8.182 *Stroke the selection with white in a new channel.*

7. Press Ctrl+D to deselect the selection.

8. Still with the new channel open, choose Filter, Blur, Gaussian Blur (about 7.0 pixels).

9. Choose Image, Adjust, Levels, and pull the Shadows and Highlights markers together to make the image more crisp. This will create rounded corners (see Figure 8.183). The pipe is starting to come into view!

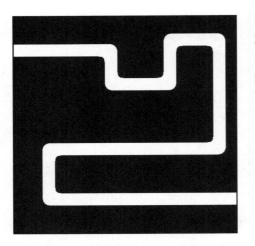

Figure 8.183
Apply a Gaussian Blur to the channel, then adjust the levels to sharpen it.

Filter: Blur, Gaussian Blur
Radius: 7.0 pixels

10. Now that you have a rounded-edge selection, let's bring the pipe back. Ctrl+click the channel to load the selection, and apply the Gaussian Blur filter again. Having the selection loaded will constrain the blur to the selection boundary.

11. Press Ctrl+C to copy the pixels in the selection.

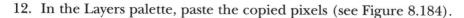

12. In the Layers palette, paste the copied pixels (see Figure 8.184).

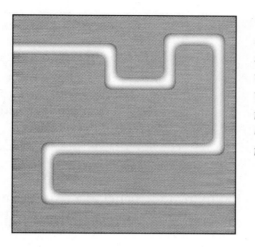

Figure 8.184
Load the channel's selection and apply the Gaussian Blur filter again. Copy and paste this selection into the Layers palette.

13. Desaturate the new bent pipe layer by choosing Image, Adjust, Desaturate. This causes the colors to revert to grayscale.

14. Adjust the levels and curves like you did in the section "Basic Metal Pipes," and add a drop shadow. In Figure 8.185, I crowned it off by enlarging the elbows and adding some end fittings to give the corners that "elbow pipe" look.

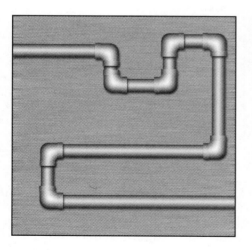

Figure 8.185
Desaturate the layer, and adjust the levels and curves. Add a drop shadow and fittings to complete the bent pipe.

Wires

Wires are quick and easy; here's how you make them:

TIP

If you want something very thick, such as a hose, make your selection with the Path tool, and then continue with the Bent Pipes example.

1. Start a new 512×512-pixel RGB image.

2. Fill the image with black.

3. Create two new layers.

4. To the top layer, apply the Basic Metal texture. Leave the middle layer alone.

5. Just as you did with the Metal Panel procedure, create a panel outline, but apply a Layer Via Cut (instead of copy) to treat the panel as a separate unit.

6. Apply an inner bevel to the removed panel, and move it out of the way to expose the black void beneath.

7. Apply an outer bevel to the base metal layer to give it some depth (see Figure 8.186).

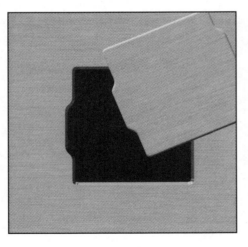

Figure 8.186 *Cut out a panel from the metal layer and bevel both.*

8. Click on the blank layer that should be directly above the black background layer.

9. Using the Pen tool, create a curved path selection that reflects the shape you want your wire to be. Make sure the path crosses the hole where the panel used to be.

10. Click the Load Path as Selection button in the Paths palette (see Figure 8.187).

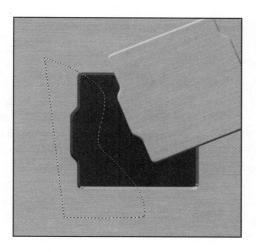

Figure 8.187 *Use the Pen tool to create a curved selection that will represent the wire.*

11. Click Edit, Stroke, and stroke the selection with pure red (hex# FF0000), 5 pixels wide.

12, Apply an inner bevel with a Linear Contour style to the wire layer (see Figure 8.188). Now you have a wire! (This will only work with small stroked selections.)

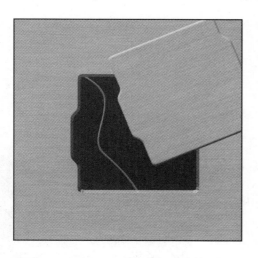

Figure 8.188 *Stroke the selection with red, then apply a contoured inner bevel.*

Style:	Bevel and Emboss
Style:	Inner Bevel
Technique:	Smooth
Depth:	100%

Direction:	Up
Size:	5 pixels
Soften:	0
Style:	Contour
Contour Shape:	Linear
Range:	50%

I went nuts and put a whole bunch of wires in the image shown in Figure 8.189, making them appear to have been ripped out with utter vengeance.

> **TIP**
> Use masks in layers to help expose hidden elements that exist behind other layers. See the Photoshop tutorials if you're rusty on masks.

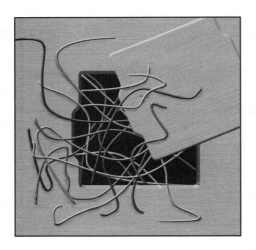

Figure 8.189 *Fun with adding wires.*

Rivets and Screws

Rivets and screws are just about the same thing, and are fairly simple to create. If I were you, I'd set up a handful of actions to automatically generate different types of rivets and screws.

> **NOTE**
> This section describes how to make shiny steel rivets and screws, but they look good in rusted form as well.

1. Start a new 512×512-pixel RGB image.

2. Fill with the Basic Metal texture.

3. Start a new layer.

4. Use the Elliptical Marquee tool to make a circular selection, about the size of a silver dollar, on your screen (see Figure 8.190). Holding down both Ctrl and Shift while creating the marquee will make the circle uniform.

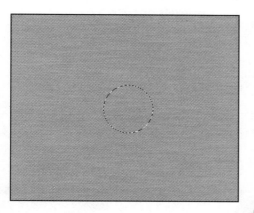

Figure 8.190
Create a circular selection on a new layer.

5. Set your foreground to medium-gray, like hex# 828282, and your background to pure white.

6. Select the Gradient tool. In the tool's options, choose Radial Gradient.

7. Create an angled gradient so that a white spot appears at the upper-left or -right portion of the circle (see Figure 8.191).

NOTE

Bear in mind the overall direction of light being cast on your textures when you add these rivets and screws. Rotate the rivets to match that direction. It's good to make several versions of the same thing featuring light being received from different angles so you have options of more suitable objects to place in your scene.

Figure 8.191 *Add a radial gradient to the circle using medium-gray and white colors.*

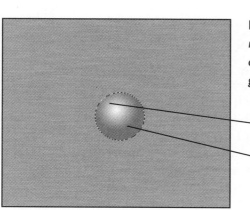

Gradient starts here

Gradient ends here

8. This could pass as a rivet head as it is, but I'd like to take it one step further. Apply an inner bevel with a cone contour to give it extra 3D curvature (see Figure 8.192).

TIP

If you want, you can adjust the levels or curves to enhance the rivet's shininess.

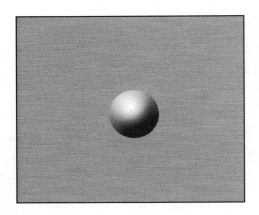

Figure 8.192
Apply an inner bevel with contour to polish it off.

NOTE

Note the style parameters I've set in the Settings dialog box; if you play around with the function curve of the cone contour itself, you can achieve better results, but probably not necessary.

Style:	Bevel and Emboss
Style:	Inner Bevel
Technique:	Smooth
Depth:	21%
Direction:	Up
Size:	87 pixels
Soften:	0
Style:	Contour
Contour Shape:	Cone
Range:	50%

9. You can finalize the effect in a couple of ways. One way is to add a simple drop shadow to make it look flush with the metal panel. Or, add a blank layer between the background and the rivet, link and merge the two to flatten the rivet's layer but retain the style, and then apply an outer bevel with a contour to make the rivet look like it's been tightened down firmly and is warping the metal. Figure 8.193 shows both types.

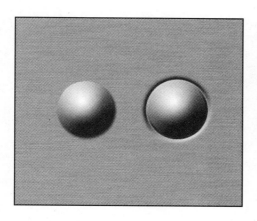

Figure 8.193 *Add a drop shadow to complete the rivet, or flatten out the rivet and add an outer bevel with a contour for a realistic effect.*

Style:	Bevel and Emboss
Style:	Outer Bevel
Technique:	Smooth
Depth:	100%
Direction:	Up
Size:	16 pixels
Soften:	0
Style:	Contour
Contour Shape:	Cone - Inverted
Range:	50%

10. Turning a rivet into a Phillips-head screw is just a matter of flattening the layer, then adding and beveling a dark cross. First, insert a layer behind the rivet, link the two, and then choose Layer, Merge Linked. This will preserve the layer styles but keep the rivet on its own layer.

11. Add a new layer on top of the rivet.

12. Use the Rectangular Marquee tool to select a vertical and a horizontal slot in the middle of the rivet.

13. Fill the selection with dark gray.

14. Apply an inner bevel to the cross to complete the effect (see Figure 8.194).

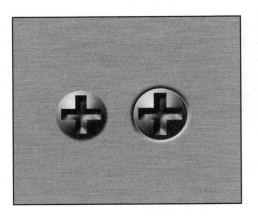

Figure 8.194

Add a dark cross on a new layer, and apply an inner bevel to turn the rivet into a Phillips-head screw.

Style:	Bevel and Emboss
Style:	Inner Bevel
Technique:	Smooth
Depth:	510%
Direction:	Down
Size:	16 pixels
Soften:	0

The rivets and screws will look much better once you've scaled them down to size. In the image shown in Figure 8.195, I added a bunch of them, then applied the dripping-rust effect that we did earlier.

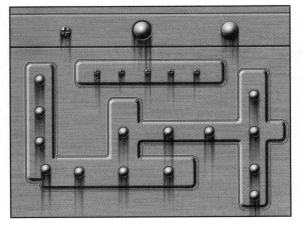

Figure 8.195

Scaling down the rivets and screws will make them look very real. Add dripping-rust effects to crown it all off.

. . . And the Rest

There's only a handful of stuff left that I want to show you, so I didn't bother to try to sort everything into separate main categories.

Wood

I know, wood is technically an organic texture. But this chapter focuses on textures that make up all types of building materials for a scene, so I decided to squeak it in here. As with other textures, you can create wood one of two ways: by taking a picture of the real thing, or by making it from scratch via filters. I've tried to re-create wood from scratch, but the best I've come up with is something that looks like those snap-together, faux-finish plastic pieces kids get for G.I. Joe karate boards (see the Crate tutorial in Chapter 9).

I'll show you a couple filtering techniques for creating wood, but only for fun (using pictures of wood is by far the best way to go):

> **NOTE**
> If you did any of my Photoshop tutorials, the **sampler.psd** file had a piece of fake wood I made.

1. Start a new 512×512-pixel RGB image. (Dimensions aren't critical here, since most of the time you're only interested in slivers of wood for boards.)

2. Press D to reset your swatches.

3. Choose Filter, Render, Clouds.

4. Start a new layer and fill it with the foreground color (black).

5. Choose Filter, Sketch, Graphic Pen. Use a Vertical setting; this will be the wood grain (see Figure 8.196)

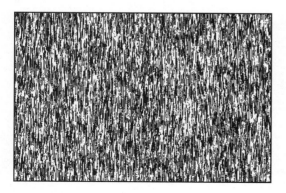

Figure 8.196
Apply the Graphic Pen filter for wood grain.

Filter:	Sketch, Graphic Pen
Stroke Length:	15
Light/Dark Balance:	50
Stroke Direction:	Vertical

6. Select the Magic Wand tool and make sure you uncheck Contiguous in the tool's Options panel.

7. Click a portion of the grain layer that's black to select all the black parts of the layer.

8. Right-click on the selection, and choose Layer Via Cut.

9. Delete the middle layer that has the white stuff that got cut out.

10. The grain is now isolated on a transparent layer above the background layer. Apply a slight outer bevel to the grain layer to raise its surface (see Figure 8.197).

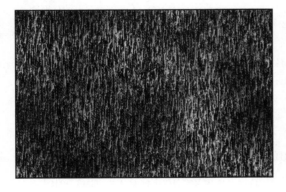

Figure 8.197
Apply an outer bevel to the grain layer.

Style:	Bevel and Emboss
Style:	Outer Bevel
Technique:	Smooth
Depth:	100%
Direction:	Up
Size:	3 pixels
Soften:	0

You can now flatten this image and take long rectangular selections as boards. Kind of sucks, doesn't it? Your best bet is to play around with colors, or even try the Liquify command (Ctrl+Shift+X) on the grain layer to produce knots and the like. Like I said, though, the absolute best way to make anything out of wood is from an image. Let's go ahead and make a wooden sign based on wood from a picture:

1. Start a new 512×512-pixel RGB image.

2. Fill the background layer with black.

3. Open the **woodpic.jpg** file in the Chapter 8 Data section on the CD-ROM (see Figure 8.198).

Figure 8.198 *The* **woodpic.jpg** *image from which you'll extract some wood.*

4. Using the Polygonal Lasso tool, select a board from the image, copy it, and paste it into a new layer. Repeat for a second board (pasting it into a new layer as well), as shown in Figure 8.199. Scale each board so it fits in the image.

TIP

You don't have to do a perfect job with the selection. In fact, it's better to keep your selection boundary within the border of the wood so you don't have to clean up the edges.

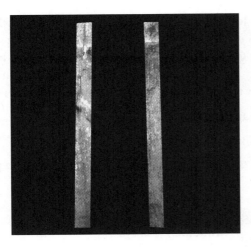

Figure 8.199 *Copy and paste two boards from the picture into your new image. (I'm using the two vertical boards on top.)*

5. Rotate the two boards horizontally and align them so they are parallel to each other with just a slight gap in between. (This is going to be a rustic old sign, so don't be too finicky.)

6. Merge the two board layers when finished (see Figure 8.200).

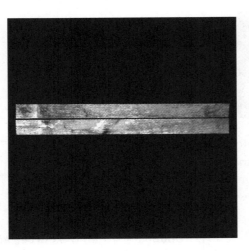

Figure 8.200 *Rotate and align the boards with a slight gap.*

7. Let's tear up and then apply a 3D effect to the left and right edges of the boards to give it some depth. Using the Lasso tool, make a jagged selection along the left edge and choose Layer Via Cut. As shown in Figure 8.201, my selection is only slightly inside of the edge of the wood.

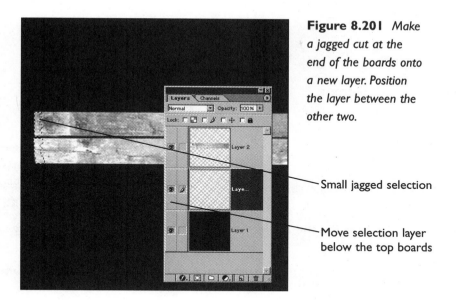

Figure 8.201 *Make a jagged cut at the end of the boards onto a new layer. Position the layer between the other two.*

Small jagged selection

Move selection layer below the top boards

8. Move the new cut layer from the top of the layer stack to the middle.

9. Apply a drop shadow to the top layer (the one with the boards).

10. In the jagged cut layer, use the Lasso tool to make *another* jagged cut to its outside border to match the inner jagged cut. Now the board's overall edge looks three-dimensional and chopped up (see Figure 8.202).

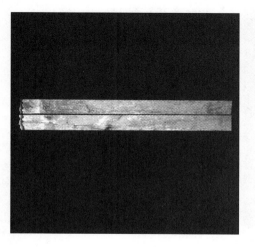

Figure 8.202 *Apply a drop shadow to the top boards, and cut up the edge to complete the 3D effect.*

Style:	Drop Shadow
Blend Mode:	Multiply
Opacity:	75%
Angle:	0 degrees
Distance:	0
Spread:	45
Size:	8

TIP

Later on, you can use the Burn tool to further darken areas that stand out, particularly the sharp edges at the ends of the boards.

11. Repeat the jagged look for the right side of the board.

12. Link all layers except for the background layer, and choose Layer, Merge Linked.

13. Let's bind the two boards with a rusty iron, er, binder. First, create a new layer.

14. On the new layer, use the Rectangular Marquee tool to create a selection near the left end that's slightly thicker than the two boards combined.

15. Fill the selection with the Rusted Metal texture.

16. Apply a drop shadow to the binder with the same settings as before (see Figure 8.203).

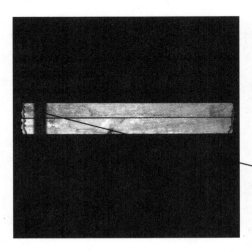

Figure 8.203 *Make a rectangular selection on a new layer and fill it with Rusted Metal. This will be the metal that binds the two boards together.*

Binder slightly thicker than both boards

17. On a new layer above the binder, add two rusty rivets using the Rivet procedure outlined earlier in this chapter.

18. Link and merge the rivet layer with the binder layer, then copy it to the right side of the boards (see Figure 8.204).

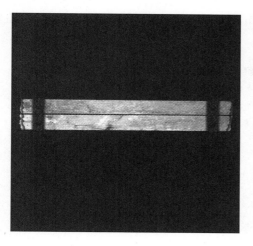

Figure 8.204
Add rivets to the binder, and copy the binder to the right side.

19. Add and scale some dark text to the wood with a font of your choice. I masked and spattered my text selection before filling it, as demonstrated earlier in this chapter, to give it a weathered look.

20. Apply a contoured outer bevel to recess the text into the wood.

21. Rasterize the type and cut out a selection where the gap between the boards exists (see Figure 8.205).

Figure 8.205
Add text to the wood and apply a contoured outer bevel. Split the text where the gap exists between the boards.

Now just add some finishing touches to your work. In the image shown in Figure 8.206, I put the sign on the stone wall we made a while ago, then added some dripping-rust effects from the iron binders. Also, add a drop shadow for the entire sign on a wall to give it depth, and use the Burn tool to burn out those annoying highlights everywhere.

Figure 8.206
The completed wood sign on the stone wall.

Glass

Doing the actual texturing for glass is very simple if you think of glass in terms of alpha transparency, dealing strictly with a grayscale range. Pure black represents 100% transparency, whereas pure white is 100% opaque. For instance, Figure 8.207 shows a texture with a linear grayscale gradient applied, and how it would look when rendered in the game's engine. Notice that behind the window you can see objects, but things get more opaque towards the bottom.

Figure 8.207 *A grayscale gradient texture applied to a window. Notice that the window becomes more transparent towards the darker end.*

A typical window, for example, would be completely transparent (all black), featuring very light gray streaks to represent the reflection of light. Let me show you a quick one:

1. Start a new 512×512-pixel RGB image.

2. Fill the background with pure black (hex# 000000).

3. Create a new layer.

4. Use the Rectangular Marquee tool to make a small rectangular selection.

5. Fill the selection with pure white (hex# FFFFFF).

6. To skew the area for that "glass" look, choose Edit, Transform, Skew, and skew the white area up about 45 degrees or so (see Figure 8.208).

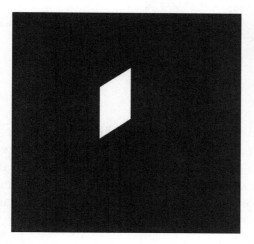

Figure 8.208

Make a rectangular selection and fill it with white. Skew it for that "glass" look.

7. Here's where the transparency comes into effect. Adjust the opacity of the layer to 10%. This opacity will correlate almost directly to the game engine's translation of transparency.

8. Make a few other skewed rectangles and fill them with white; make sure they're all on the same layer. Overlap one or two for an added effect (see Figure 8.209).

Figure 8.209

Adjust the opacity of the white layer to 10%, making it see-through. Notice the effect it has on the room's window.

Decals

Decals are simply small images, usually coupled with an alpha channel, that are placed on top of existing textured objects in a game. If you've ever blown something away that was near a wall, for instance, and seen blood or slime splatter all over the place, those images were decals overlaid dynamically by the game's engine. A decal can also be a simple metal sign or something that needs to be placed anywhere.

The only thing special about these game assets is that they sometimes have transparent sections to them, requiring a single color to represent transparency. The channel that represents transparency is a parameter you need to find out—consult the engine's specifications. For instance, if you're creating a decal for *Half-Life* (using the Worldcraft/Hammer editors), the transparent color will be pure white (hex# FFFFFF), whereas a decal in *Unreal* (using UnrealEd) will be medium gray (hex# 808080). See Table 8.1 for what to think about when generating images that have some sort of transparency, particularly for *Half-Life*, *Unreal*, and the *Torque* engine. Note that levels in Torque may be created using the Worldcraft or Hammer level editor.

Table 8.1

Game/engine	Texture Type	Transparency Color
Half-Life	Decals	White (hex# FFFFFF)
Half-Life	Brush objects (catwalks, etc.)	Blue (hex# 0000FF)
Half-Life	Sprites	Black (grayscale, where hex# 000000 is 100% transparent)
Unreal	Decals	Gray (hex# 808080)
Unreal	Brush objects	Black (grayscale variable)
Unreal	Sprites	Black
Torque	Decals	none (uses Photoshop's transparency in .png format)

The only other thing you should keep in mind when creating this stuff is what will be the base material to which they are applied. You'll be doing bullet holes here, but not every hole will look good on every surface. Hence, it might be necessary to make an arsenal of bullet-hole decals that can be put on a wide range of objects.

Bullet Holes

People (like me) make a big stink about this type of decal, when most of the time it's just a silly, feathered or splotchy black hole. One quick squirt with your Airbrush tool will usually do the job, and the resultant texture is an overall 8×8 pixels. But, seeing as you're an artist, you'll want to look at it in more detail.

Bullet Holes on Metal, Inward

This is one of the two most common types of bullet holes: The lead has made a penetrating entry mark that has curved the metal inward. Here's how to create this effect:

1. Start a new 512×512-pixel RGB image.

2. Fill the background layer with pure white (hex# FFFFFF). This will be the alpha (transparency) channel (for the *Half-Life* engine).

NOTE

If you're doing this texture for *Unreal* (or a similar engine), fill the background layer with pure gray (hex# 808080). Make sure you check the engine's specifications for alpha-channel colors for decals.

3. Start a new layer.

4. Enable Photoshop's Snap and Grid features.

5. Select the Elliptical Marquee tool, and in its Options panel, type 20 in the Feather field.

6. Create a circular selection in the middle of the image, about 350 pixels wide, and fill it with the Basic Metal texture (see Figure 8.210).

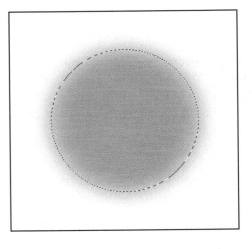

Figure 8.210 *Fill a feathered selection with the Basic Metal texture on a new layer.*

7. Start another new layer. This is important, because you'll be applying an inner bevel to this to make the hole curve inward.

8. With the previous selection still active, choose Select, Transform Selection, and scale the selection down about 100 pixels. It will help to hold down Shift and Alt at the same time to make the selection scale down uniformly.

9. Press Enter to commit the change, and with the 20-pixel Feather option still set, fill the selection with black (see Figure 8.211).

Figure 8.211
*Reduce the selection
and feather-fill it with
near black on a new
layer.*

10. You should now have three layers; the top is the bullet hole, the middle is the curved metal, and the bottom is the pure black background. To the top bullet-hole layer, apply an inner bevel. I set the Highlight Mode color to dark yellow at a 90-degree light angle to give it some finesse (see Figure 8.212).

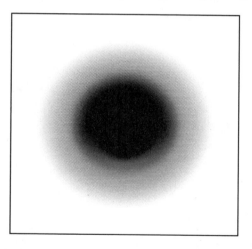

Figure 8.212
*Apply an inner bevel
to the bullet hole to
give it depth.*

Style:	Bevel and Emboss
Style:	Inner Bevel
Technique:	Chisel Soft
Depth:	500%
Direction:	Down
Size:	20 pixels

Soften:	5
Shading Angle:	90 degrees
Highlight Mode Color:	dark yellow, hex# 8E8D34

If you want to see the results of this hole, just fill the background layer with any metal material to see the effects. To keep things more real, modify the curved-metal layer (the middle layer) to suit different types of metals. When you're ready to apply this texture as a decal, you need to flatten the image and make it very small. Check out Figure 8.213; these are multiple holes on a sign applied in combination with the Peeling Paint procedure.

TIP

Group a cluster of different-sized bullet holes onto a decal for shotgun effects. Dust the areas between the holes using a black airbrush to simulate the blast powder.

Figure 8.213
Bullet holes applied to a sign in combination with the Peeling Paint procedure.

Bullet Holes on Metal, Outward

This is the second most common type of bullet hole. In this case, the shot was fired from behind the metal, rupturing the metal outward. The actual physics involved are like this: The bullet was traveling around the speed of sound. After piercing the metal, the bullet's speed would cause the metal to whip open, creating intense heat and fatigue in a very short period of time. This might cause the metal to curl, distort, and discolor . . . so here we go:

1. Start a new 512×512-pixel RGB image.

2. Fill the background layer with pure gray (hex# 808080).

3. Start a new layer.

4. Press D to reset the swatches.

5. Choose Filter, Render, Clouds.

6. Choose Filter, Render, Difference Clouds (see Figure 8.214).

> **NOTE**
>
> I'm pretending this is a decal for *Unreal*. If this were for *Half-Life*, I'd use pure white (hex# FFFFFF).

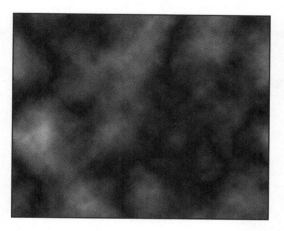

Figure 8.214
Apply the Clouds, then the Difference Clouds filter to a new layer.

7. Choose Filter, Blur, Gaussian Blur, with a radius of 4.0 pixels.

8. Choose Filter, Sketch, Chrome.

9. Adjust the levels by sliding the Highlights marker to the left. This will give the texture the appearance of fatigued (or liquid) metal (see Figure 8.215).

Figure 8.215
Apply the Gaussian Blur and Chrome filters. Adjust the levels to make the texture look like fatigued steel.

Filter:	Blur, Gaussian Blur
Radius:	4.0 pixels
Filter:	Sketch, Chrome
Detail:	10
Smoothness:	0

10. With the fatigued-metal layer active, choose Edit, Transform, Scale, and scale the image down evenly about 50% (see Figure 8.216).

Figure 8.216
Scale the metal layer down 50%.

11. Start a new layer.

12. Set your foreground color to black.

13. Using the Airbrush tool (with its brush type set to Soft Round 100 pixels), spray a hole in the middle of the metal. (The paint should be on a separate layer.)

14. Apply an inner bevel to this layer with a medium-gray Highlight Mode color (see Figure 8.217).

Figure 8.217
Spray an off-black circle on a new layer, and apply an inner bevel to it.

Style:	Bevel and Emboss
Style:	Inner Bevel
Technique:	Chisel Soft
Depth:	500%
Direction:	Down
Size:	10 pixels
Soften:	0
Shading Angle:	90 degrees
Highlight Mode Color:	medium-gray, hex# 757373

15. Select the metal layer (it should be the one in between the background and the bullet hole).

16. Use the Lasso tool to create a jagged selection around the bullet hole. This will be the pattern of the outwardly bent metal (see Figure 8.218).

Figure 8.218
Use the Lasso tool to select a jagged border around the bullet hole.

17. Choose Select, Inverse. You'll be deleting the outside portion of the metal from this selection.

18. Now let's chop up the edges of the selection. First, press Q to enter Quick Mask mode.

19. With the mask active, choose Filter, Brush Strokes, Spatter.

20. Press Q to exit Quick Mask mode.

21. Press Delete to remove the outside metal (see Figure 8.219).

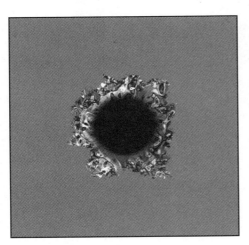

Figure 8.219
Spatter the selection in Quick Mask mode, then delete the outer portion of the metal.

Filter: Brush Strokes, Spatter
Spray Radius: 10
Smoothness: 5

22. Apply a small drop shadow to the metal layer to give it some height off the surface.

23. Use the Dodge tool to add highlights around the rim near the hole, and use the Burn tool to darken the edges where the metal appears torn (see Figure 8.220). This will make the metal appear to be curving up and down.

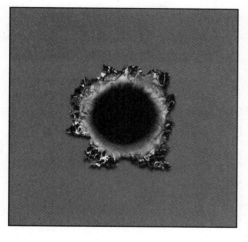

Figure 8.220
Apply a drop shadow to the metal, then dodge and burn the inside and outside to give it a curved feel.

Style: Drop Shadow
Blend Mode: Multiply
Opacity: 75
Angle: 90
Distance: 7
Spread: 0
Size: 5

And there you have it! You can merge the hole and metal layers, then scale everything to size. Try filling the blue background layer with a metal texture to see the end effect.

Bullet Holes on Cement

This is the last one I'll do, since it is a bit different from the others. When a projectile hits something like cement, stucco, mortar, tiles, or whatever, it doesn't just leave a clean hole like it might on metal. Instead, the substance appears to crumble in a cone-shaped pattern that has several layers.

1. Open the **cement_pic2.jpg** file from the Chapter 8 Data section on the CD-ROM. This is a 512×512-pixel RGB image cropped from a picture of a classic cement/stucco wall.

2. Use the Lasso tool to create a misshapen circle that takes up a good portion of the image (see Figure 8.221). This will be the outer shape of the erosion.

TIP

I highly recommend you record this as an action at this point, since you'll want to make several variants of the same technique.

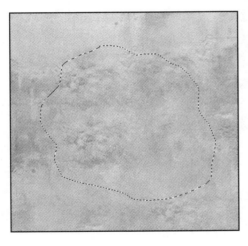

Figure 8.221
Create a circular selection with the Lasso tool.

3. Press Q to enter Quick Mask mode.

4. Apply the Spatter Filter to the selection to chop up the edges.

5. Press Q again to exit the mode.

6. Right-click on the selection and choose Layer Via Copy. This will separate the selection onto its own layer, preserving the background layer.

7. Apply an inner bevel to this new layer to recess the cement (see Figure 8.222).

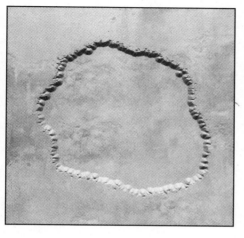

Figure 8.222
Spatter the edges of the selection, copy the selection to a new layer, and apply an inner bevel to recess it.

Filter:	Brush Strokes, Spatter
Spray Radius:	15
Smoothness:	5
Style:	Bevel and Emboss
Style:	Inner Bevel
Technique:	Chisel Hard
Depth:	200%
Direction:	Down
Size:	10 pixels
Soften:	0
Shading Angle:	90 degrees

8. Ctrl+click this layer to reload the selection.

9. Choose Select, Modify, Contract, and enter a value of 15 pixels. This will reduce the selection.

10. Repeat steps 3–9 several times until you have several layers, creating a cone- or bowl-shaped erosion mark (see Figure 8.223).

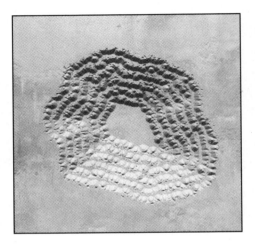

Figure 8.223

Contract the selection and repeat the previous steps several times to recess the bullet hole.

11. Ctrl+click the smallest layer to load the selection, then fill it with black.

12. Choose Filter, Blur, Gaussian Blur, with a radius of 1.0 pixel, to complete the effect (see Figure 8.224). You can now link the erosion layers (except for the background layer), merge them, and scale the bullet hole to size.

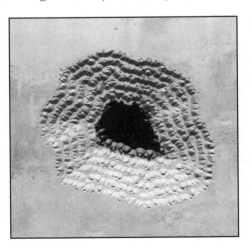

Figure 8.224

Fill the smallest erosion layer with black, then apply the Gaussian Blur filter.

When scaled down appropriately, this will work. Remember to fill the background layer with the transparency color of choice. Try playing around with other types of selections to achieve different results. Check out Figure 8.225; here, I've combined the various bullet-hole techniques onto a single texture, making it appear as though someone was shooting at a door, and the assailant behind it shot back.

Figure 8.225

Various bullet-hole techniques being applied to a texture.

Blast Marks

Blast marks are just smoky radial marks of varying transparency using either a grayscale range (like from white to black) or within an alpha channel. I'm going to do a quick effective one with a white background for a game like *Half-Life*, where hex# FFFFFF is completely transparent.

1. Start a new 512×512-pixel RGB image.

2. Fill the image with pure white (hex# FFFFFF).

3. Start a new layer.

4. Select the Airbrush tool. For the tool's Brush type, choose a blotchy, radial pattern like Spatter 58 Pixels. (If it's not on the Brush type list, you need to add brushes to your list under Edit, Preset Manager.)

5. Spray a black spot directly in the center of the new layer. Use the guides or grid to align the spot (see Figure 8.226).

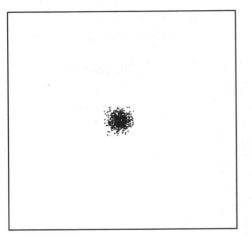

Figure 8.226
Spray a small blotchy pattern in the center of the layer.

6. With this top layer still active, choose Edit, Transform, Scale. Scale up the pattern equally until it covers about 70 percent of the image (see Figure 8.227).

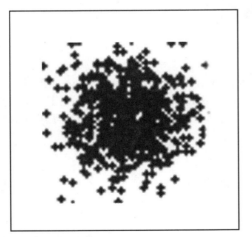

Figure 8.227
Scale the blotch up until it fills a good portion of the image.

7. Choose Filter, Blur, Radial Blur, using the Zoom method. Not too bad for a blast mark, eh? See Figure 8.228.

Figure 8.228.

Apply the Radial Blur filter for the final effect.

Filter:	Blur, Radial Blur
Amount:	100
Blur Method:	Zoom
Quality:	Good

Experiment with different base blotch patterns for various blast marks. When you want to see the effect in action, replace the blue background layer with something like the Stone Wall texture (see Figure 8.229).

Figure 8.229 *The blast mark on the Stone Wall texture.*

Blood Splats

Okay, so blood is another organic texture, and this chapter is supposed to cover inorganic textures, but blood fits nicely here since it's a decal. Although you might be able to get away with using a red-shaded blast pattern for blood, blood (or other liquids, for that matter) tends to drip and/or bead. (By the way, this is so totally gross.)

1. Start a new 512×512-pixel RGB image and fill it with gray (hex# 808080). (This will be for *Unreal.*)

2. Repeat the procedure for generating a blast mark, only use a deep red color, like hex# 5A0330, instead of black (see Figure 8.230).

Figure 8.230

Create a blast mark using a dark-red color.

3. This could be a blood splat as it is, but I want it to look more, er, splat-like. To do so, Ctrl+click the top, splat-mark layer to load its selection.

4. In the Channels palette, start a new channel, and fill it with white. You should have an identical blast mark in a new channel.

5. With the new channel active, choose Filter, Artistic, Paint Daubs.

6. Choose Filter, Sketch, Plaster (see Figure 8.231).

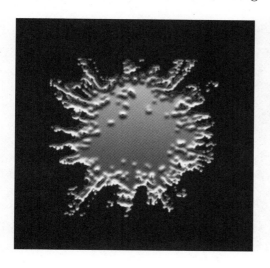

Figure 8.231
*Load the splat selec-
tion, then fill it on a
new channel. Apply
the Paint Daubs and
Plaster filters to the
channel.*

Filter:	Artistic, Paint Daubs
Brush Size:	5
Sharpness:	40
Brush Type:	Sparkles
Filter:	Sketch, Plaster
Image Balance:	50
Smoothness:	1
Direction:	Top

7. See the splotchiness? Now Ctrl+click the channel to load the selection, go back to the Layers palette, and click on the blood-splat layer.

8. Alt+Backspace to fill this selection with the deep-red color (see Figure 8.232).

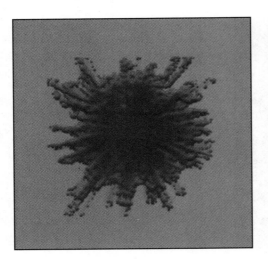

Figure 8.232
*Load the channel's
selection and fill the
blood layer with deep
red to complete the
effect.*

Try filling the gray background layer with a wall texture to see the final effect (but remember to retain the gray for the game). A good image-reduction size for this decal is something around 128×128 pixels.

CHAPTER 9

Advanced Texturing Examples

Now that you've absorbed a good deal of basic, general texturing examples from the previous chapter, it's time to further your skills and take game texturing to the next level. In this chapter you will learn how to use advanced Photoshop techniques to create the following textures:

- A wooden crate, to be applied to a cube primitive
- A medieval wood and iron gate, by compositing textures with a digital photograph
- A high-tech, futuristic wall, with an associated animation frame to alter the texture's state in a game

Wood Crate with Explosives

This is a standard, but very useful, prop that typically adorns those big empty rooms found on loads of game levels out there. (If you're addicted to *Half-Life* like I am, you know exactly what I'm talking about.) To make a crate, I'd typically just grab wood samples from images, but I'll show you how to do this one entirely from scratch. Figure 9.1 shows the completed crate texture, applied to cube primitives.

Figure 9.1 *The texture we'll create in this section. Not a safe room to be in, eh?*

1. Start a new 512×512-pixel RGB color image.

2 Set the Resolution to 512.

3. Activate Photoshop's Grid and Snap features by choosing View, Show, Grid (Ctrl+Alt+') and choosing View, Snap (Ctrl+;).

4. Choose Edit, Preferences, Guides and Grid and configure the grid in increments of 64 pixels. This represents the width of the boards on the crate texture.

5. Set your foreground and background to medium and dark browns, like hex# 7C5004 and hex# 492A03, respectively.

6. With the background layer active, choose Filter, Render, Clouds.

7. Choose Filter, Noise, Add Noise, about 5%.

8. Choose Filter, Noise, Median, 1 pixel (see Figure 9.2). This represents the base of the wood texture.

Figure 9.2 *Fill the background with the Clouds filter, using medium- and dark-brown colors. Add some noise to break it up.*

9. Using the Rectangular Marquee tool, create a selection across the image that's only one 64-pixel cell wide. This will be our board shape.

10. Right-click on this selection and choose Layer Via Copy. The board will now be on a separate layer.

11. With the new layer active, choose Filter, Sketch, Graphic Pen. In Figure 9.3, I've hidden the background layer to show you the results.

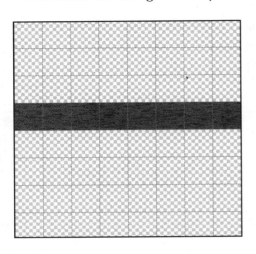

Figure 9.3 *Copy the selection to a new layer and apply the Graphic Pen filter.*

Filter:	Sketch, Graphic Pen
Stroke Length:	15
Light/Dark Balance:	80
Stroke Direction:	Horizontal

12. The image already looks like wood, but let's make the surface look a bit more three-dimensional, using the wood itself as a displacement map. Ctrl+click the board's layer to load its selection, and press Ctrl+C to make a copy of it.

13. In the Channels palette, start a new channel.

14. Press Ctrl+V to paste the copied selection. This will be the texture channel you'll use for the Lighting Effects filter in a moment (see Figure 9.4). (Note that the channel is black and white; the lighter areas represent the higher portions, while the darker areas are recessed.)

TIP

If you're having trouble following along with using layers, channels, or other tool functions, review the Photoshop tutorial on the CD-ROM. Also, if you haven't read it yet, Chapter 8, "Inorganic Texture Tutorials with Photoshop," is a good place to start, particularly when it comes to Alpha channels and rendering textures.

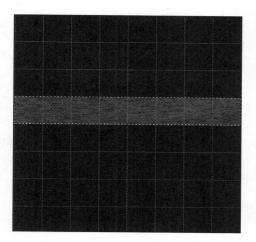

Figure 9.4 *Copy the contents of the board's layer and paste it into a new channel.*

15. Select the Layer 1 channel in the Layers palette. This should be the isolated board's layer.

16. Choose Filter, Render, Lighting Effects, using the Alpha 1 channel as a displacement map (see Figure 9.5).

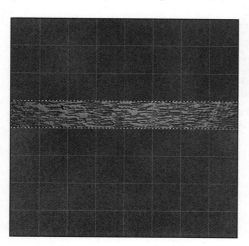

Figure 9.5 *Render the board's layer with the Lighting Effects filter, using the Alpha 1 channel as a displacement map.*

Filter:	Render, Lighting Effects
Light Type:	Spotlight, encompassing the entire board, from the top right
Intensity:	35
Focus:	69
Gloss:	0

Material:	69
Exposure:	0
Ambience:	8
Texture Channel:	Alpha 1
Height:	50

17. To give the board a bit of depth, apply an outer bevel style to it by double-clicking the board's layer to bring up the Styles screen, and applying the outer-bevel style with the settings listed alongside Figure 9.6.

Figure 9.6 *Apply an outer bevel to the board's layer.*

Style:	Bevel and Emboss
Style:	Outer Bevel
Technique:	Chisel Hard
Depth:	1000%
Direction:	Up
Size:	2
Soften:	0
Shading Angle:	90 degrees
Highlight Mode:	Dark Yellow (hex# 51451F)

18. Move this board up to the top edge and repeat steps 9–17 to create other boards, filling the image vertically (make sure you begin each board taking a sample from the background layer). Figure 9.7 shows my first layer of wood slats.

TIP

Try recording the board-making steps in the Actions palette to help speed things up.

Figure 9.7 *Repeat steps 9–17 to make different boards, and position them next to each other.*

19. Now it's time to build the rest of the box panel. To begin, link all the layers except for one board layer, including the background layer, and press Ctrl+E to merge them. You should end up with one isolated board on its own layer, and the rest of the boards all on the background layer.

20. The top board will still have its outer bevel style active, which should be flattened. Do this by creating a new layer, linking the new layer with the board's layer, and merging the two.

21. You should now have a background layer with all the boards, less one on its own layer. Make a copy of this board's layer.

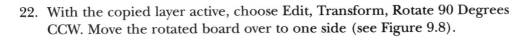

22. With the copied layer active, choose Edit, Transform, Rotate 90 Degrees CCW. Move the rotated board over to one side (see Figure 9.8).

Figure 9.8 *Copy the layer with the single board on it, and rotate it 90 degrees. Move it over to one side.*

23. Make both boards meet at a 45-degree angle. To do so, use the Polygonal Lasso tool to draw a selection that slices the tip off of each board at 45 degrees where they meet. This will create that stereotypical wooden-frame look (see Figure 9.9).

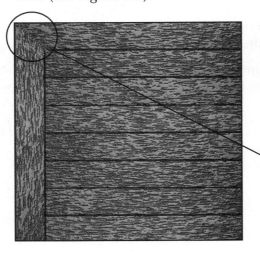

Figure 9.9 *Slice the ends of each board where they meet at 45 degree angles.*

Cut each board at a 45-degree angle

24. Merge the two board layers and make a copy of this new layer.

25. Rotate the copy 180 degrees so that you complete the frame as shown in Figure 9.10. (You might have to chop off another end or two at 45 degree angles to make the frame look right.)

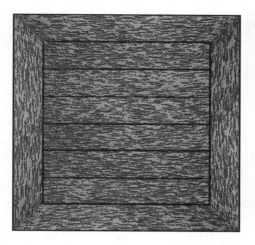

Figure 9.10 *Merge the two board layers, make a copy of the new layer, and rotate it 180 degrees.*

26. You should now have two layers on top of the background layer, each containing two boards joined at an angle; merge these two layers now.

27. To add a cross-bracing board diagonally between the frame, begin by using the Rectangular Marquee tool to select one of the boards in the background layer, and then press Ctrl+C to copy it.

28. Paste the copied board into the image, then choose Edit, Transform, Rotate, and rotate and move it into place.

29. Hack off the ends of the copied selection using the Polygonal Lasso tool.

30. When you're satisfied, merge that layer with the frame's layer; at this point, you should have only the background layer and the frame above it (see Figure 9.11).

Figure 9.11 *Create a cross-bracing board by making a copy of one of the boards in the background layer, rotating and positioning it, and hacking off the ends at 45-degree angles.*

31. Add a drop shadow to the frame's layer. This gives the frame excellent depth in contrast to the background layer's boards.

32. Flatten the entire image.

33. The boards are way too saturated with color; fix this by choosing Image, Adjust, Hue/Saturation, and sliding the Saturation slider down until the wood looks more dull and worn (see Figure 9.12).

34. Use the Burn tool with a very low setting (like 5%) and, with a large brush, burn in shadows all over the wood.

Figure 9.12 *Apply a drop shadow to the frame, and then desaturate its ends at 45-degree angles.*

35. Add some large screws to the ends of all of the visible, whole boards. (See the section "Pipes, Wires, Rivets, and Screws" in Chapter 8 for details on making 3D screws.) The ones I made here are simple, featuring a single flathead slot, and a darker shade to make them appear a bit rusty (see Figure 9.13).

Figure 9.13 *Add screws to the edges of the whole boards for added realism.*

36. Lastly, add some painted text to the outside board using the Text tool. I used the Spatter filter to break up the edges of the text, causing the paint to appear chipped (see Figure 9.14).

Figure 9.14 *Finish the crate with some painted text.*

I'm excited about this texture—it's very realistic, and you didn't even use pictures of real wood! If you can get away with using filters, then why not? Try reducing this texture down to 256×256 pixels, a more appropriate size for a game texture, and painting the faces of a simple cube primitive in your favorite 3D program.

A Quick Note on the Crate's U-V Map

You might be wondering how I textured the crate objects using the completed texture in Figure 9.14. This can be done in several ways. The easiest is to first create a cube primitive in any 3D program like trueSpace or 3D Studio Max and simply paint the faces of the cube with the texture, assuming the object's U-Vs (texture coordinates) are projected cubically. However, this would generate a lower resolution bitmap, because there are six sides to a cube, and therefore the bitmap would require six individually placed textures on the unfolded U-Vs (see Figure 9.15).

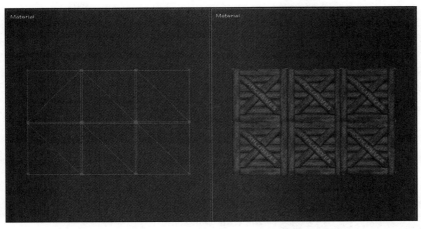

Figure 9.15 *An inefficient way of applying the crate texture onto the crate's U-V map.*

U-V map (unfolded)   Texture applied to map

A better way to increase your texture's resolution while still placing the texture on each face of the cube would be to isolate each U-V face of the cube, scale it to the extents of the entire bitmap, and apply a single instance of the bitmap on top of them all. This is called *U-V overlapping*, which is wonderfully practical in applications such as this. Figure 9.16 shows each face of the cube's U-V coordinates stacked on top of each other; I simply put the texture down on top of it all. When it's time to render, the overlapping will cause the single texture to project itself through to all the other faces. The single downside to this approach is that the cube will be homogenous on all sides (not unique).

For details on U-V mapping, see Chapter 5, "U-V Mapping the RF-9 Plasma Gun with DeepUV."

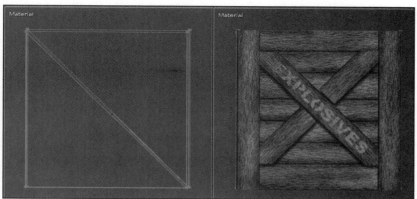

U-V map, faces overlapped   Texture applied to map

Figure 9.16
Placing all the cube's U-V faces on top of one another allows you to apply a single instance of the bitmap, resulting in a higher-texture resolution.

Medieval Castle/ Haunted House Gate

This texture is fairly easy but takes a while—much of it is just pure repetition. For it, I picture those huge English oak doors bound by wrought iron so commonplace in the 13th century, particularly during the Crusades. Nearly everything was adorned by a cross or crucifix of some sort. The doors I'd like to see also have huge drop handles (knockers) that weight a gazillion pounds. Figure 9.17 shows the completed texture you'll create.

Figure 9.17 *The completed, monstrous doors applied to a castle wall.*

This texture could easily port itself over to the modern haunted-house genre, so let's get to it!

1. You'll be building a single door in its entirety, then at the very end making a copy of it and flipping it over as the other door. Instead of creating the wood for the door from scratch, as we did in the previous example, you'll create it from a digital photograph of a table, courtesy yours truly. To begin, open the **wood_table.jpg** file located on the CD-ROM; it's shown in Figure 9.18.

Figure 9.18 *Open the wood_table.jpg file.*

TIP

When acquiring digital images for texture composites, it's best to get full sunlight shots, particularly in the mid-morning or late afternoon where the sun's rays can hit the objects straight on, or perpendicularly. Sunlight is one of the best light sources around for illuminating your props, because it contains the full spectrum of colors and then some. Just try your best to avoid getting shadows in your image, for they relay improper depth cueing when composited with the rest of your texture.

2. Let's grab all the vertical boards that make up the face of the table; this will represent the entire door. To begin, create a selection around the boards using the Rectangular Marquee tool, and then rotate the selection slightly so the rectangular outline matches the outer edges of the vertical boards using Select, Transform Selection.

3. Copy the selection, close the image, and paste the copied selection to a new canvas (see Figure 9.19). The new canvas will inherit the copied image's dimensions.

Figure 9.19 *Create a selection around the vertical boards of the table, copy the selection, and paste it to a new image.*

4. Get rid of the hole in the center of the table using the Clone Stamp tool with a medium Opacity setting, like 70%. (I Alt+clicked a point about a half inch above the hole, then sprayed with a small brush over the hole until it was gone.)

5. Adjust the levels a bit to sharpen/darken the image.

6. Choose Image, Adjust, Hue/Saturation to desaturate the wood's tones (see Figure 9.20). (Nobody in the 13th century had a bright yellow door!)

TIP

It's a good idea to use low spray settings for tools, as they allow your work to blossom gradually.

Figure 9.20 *Use the Clone Stamp tool to get rid of the hole in the table. Adjust the levels and hue/saturation to suit.*

7. Each of the boards needs to be isolated onto its own layer so you can apply a bevel style to each one. Using the Rectangular Marquee tool, create a selection around one, right-click the selection, and choose Layer Via Copy.

8. Repeat step 7 for the remaining seven boards.

9. Space the boards apart so a small gap exists between each one (see Figure 9.21). This way, the bevels will have room to present themselves.

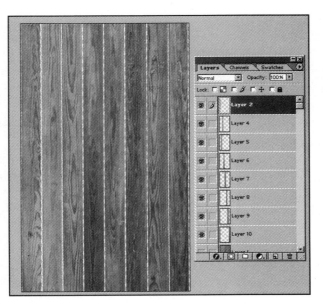

Figure 9.21 *Select each board with the Rectangular Marquee tool and create a copy onto its own layer. Make space between each for beveling.*

10. You should have eight layers in the Layers palette that contain individual boards; Go ahead and merge them all together, *excluding the background layer.*

11. With the layer that contains the boards active, apply an inner bevel style to raise the wood, as shown in Figure 9.22. (I added a Contour style as well.)

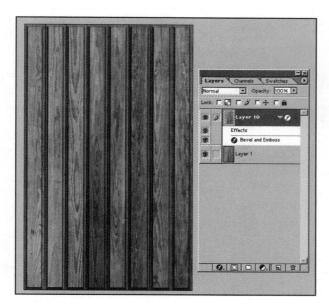

Figure 9.22
Merge the board layers onto a single layer, and apply an inner-bevel style to them.

Style:	Bevel and Emboss
Style:	Inner Bevel
Technique:	Chisel Soft
Depth:	600%
Direction:	Up
Size:	4
Soften:	0
Shading Angle:	72 degrees
Highlight Color:	hex# 6B580B
Contour:	Cove—Deep contour
Range:	20%

12. Flatten all the layers in the image. You now have the base for your door!

13. From here, let's create the rusty, riveted bindings that hold the boards together. I recommend using a picture of something rusty to create the best effect; for this reason, I've provided the file **rusty_metal.jpg** on the CD-ROM (see Figure 9.23); you can take samples from this image to create the metal bindings.

Figure 9.23
*Open the **rusty_metal.jpg** image on the CD-ROM, which you'll use to create the metal bindings.*

14. Using the Rectangular Marquee tool, make a horizontal, thin selection— roughly the shape of a binding—on any part of the rusty area in the **rusty_metal.jpg** image (see Figure 9.24).

15. Copy the selection from the **rusty_metal.jpg** image and paste it on the door.

16. Adjust the levels to sharpen/darken the image a bit.

Figure 9.24
Create a selection of rust in the shape of a metal binding, copy it, and paste it to the door.

17. You can make the metal binding appear slightly raised by applying an outer bevel to it. It doesn't take much; just a subtle bevel will do.

18. Using the metal as a base material, use the Elliptical Marquee tool to make a circular rivet (see Figure 9.25).

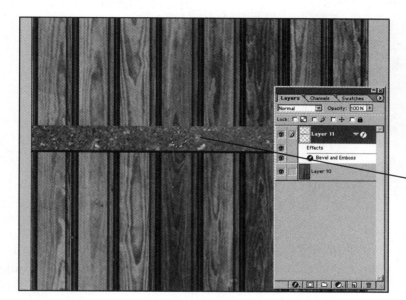

Figure 9.25 *Bevel the metal binding to make it a bit 3D. Begin creating a rivet by making a small circular selection on top of the binding.*

Make rivet from strap

19. Right-click the rivet selection and choose Layer Via Copy.

20. Apply an inner bevel style to the new layer (the one with the rivet).

21. Add a blank layer and merge it with the rivet's layer to get rid of the inner bevel style in the Layers palette, but retaining the style in the image. This way, you can duplicate the rivet over and over without caking up the styles.

22. Make copies of the rivet and position them as I have in Figure 9.26.

NOTE

You'll need to play around with the inner bevel style's settings a bit to make it appear raised. Just make sure the lighting angle is consistent—that is, the light sources for all styles come from above.

TIP

See the section "Pipes, Wires, Rivets, and Screws" in Chapter 8 for detailed information on creating rivets.

Figure 9.26 *Copy the circular rust selection to its own layer and apply an inner-bevel style to raise it. Position multiple copies of the newly created rivet as shown.*

23. Repeat steps 14–22 to continue forming metal bindings with rivets all around the door as I have done in Figure 9.27. Notice the left side of the door; I applied the same rivet style to a thin rectangular selection, simulating hinges of a sort. (By the way, you don't have to do this *exactly* as I have done . . . by all means, have fun and do it your way!)

Figure 9.27 *Repeat the last few steps to continue adding bindings around the door.*

24. Merge all the metal bindings to one layer, but keep them separate from the door itself so that you can make drop shadows and other adjustments later.

25. Let's add a drop handle to the top-center of the door. You can do this in several ways—some people like to use the Path tool to create designs and then fill them with textures; I, on the other hand, use the Alpha channels extensively (outlined here). To begin, create a circular selection using the Elliptical Marquee tool as I have done in Figure 9.28. This will be the base shape of the pattern you'll create.

Figure 9.28 *Start a drop handle by creating a circular selection with the Elliptical Marquee tool.*

26. In the Channels palette, start a new channel.

27. The selection should still be active in this new channel; fill it with white.

28. Make a cross pattern by using the Rectangular Marquee tool to cut horizontal and vertical slots out of the shape.

29. Choose Filter, Blur, Gaussian Blur, about 7 pixels.

30. To sharpen the image, choose Image, Adjust, Levels and drag the Shadows and Highlights markers together until the edges of the shape are nice and crisp, as shown in Figure 9.29. (This technique is a great way to create smooth, curved objects.)

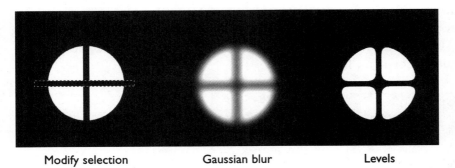

Modify selection   Gaussian blur   Levels

Figure 9.29 *Start a new channel and fill the selection with white. Carve the selection to your liking, then Gaussian Blur it. Use the Levels command to sharpen it back up.*

31. Make another circular selection around the existing pattern.

32. Choose Image, Adjust, Invert; you should end up with a white pattern that looks like the one in Figure 9.30. Remember, the white areas in the channel represent the selection boundaries.

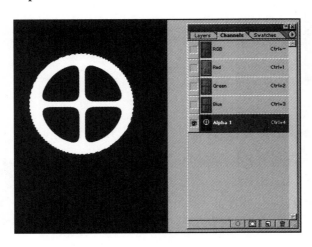

Figure 9.30
Create another circular selection around the existing object and invert it. Ctrl+click the channel to load the selection.

33. When the shape in the Alpha channel looks good, Ctrl+click the channel to load the selection.

34. With the selection active, go back to the Layers palette and start a new layer.

35. Fill the selection with a sample of rust from the **rusty_metal.jpg** image.

36. As you did in steps 17–22, finish the pattern with an outer bevel and some smaller rivets (see Figure 9.31).

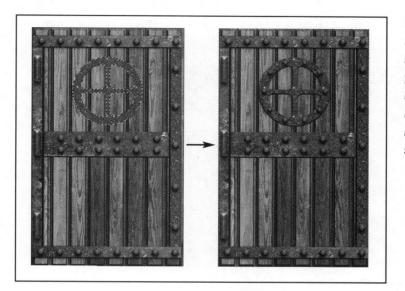

Figure 9.31 *On a new layer, fill the selection with rust from the* **rusty_metal.jpg** *image. Apply an outer bevel and some smaller rivets.*

37. Merge the pattern you just created with the metal binding's layer.

38. In the same way you created the rivets, create two small raised objects that will support the actual drop handle itself; Figure 9.32 shows mine.

Figure 9.32 *Create two small raised surfaces that will support the drop handle (or knocker).*

39. Now for the handle—you're essentially going to make a 3D hoop from scratch (a technique you learned in the section "Pipes, Wires, Rivets, and Screws" in Chapter 8). Create a circular selection in the shape of a hoop that barely touches both of the raised objects you created in the last step (see Figure 9.33).

Figure 9.33
Create a circular selection in the shape of a hoop, where the handle will be.

40. In the Channels palette, create another new channel.

41. The hoop's selection should still be active; choose Edit, Stroke, about 8 pixels wide.

42. Stroke this selection with white.

43. Ctrl+click the channel to reload the selection.

44. Choose Filter, Blur, Gaussian Blur, about 5 pixels.

45. With the selection still loaded, adjust the levels (slide the Midtones and Highlights markers together) until your start seeing a 3D shaded hoop appear (see Figure 9.34).

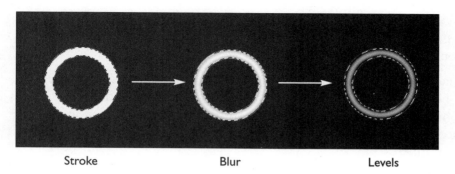

Figure 9.34 *Stroke the selection in a new channel. Use the blur-levels technique to create a 3D appearance, and then make a copy of the selection.*

Stroke   Blur   Levels

46. Press Ctrl+C to copy the selection.

47. In the Layers palette, start a new layer.

48. With the new layer active, press Ctrl+V to paste the contents from the channel.

49. Adjust the levels again to darken the hoop.

50. Choose Filter, Noise, Add Noise, about 10% (see Figure 9.35). Now it looks like a beautiful, weathered, wrought-iron drop handle.

51. Add a finishing touch by applying a drop shadow to the drop handle.

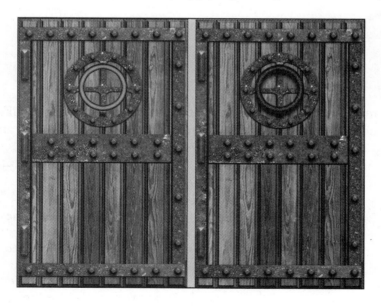

Figure 9.35 *Paste the hoop onto a new layer, adjust the levels, and add some noise. Finish it off with a drop shadow.*

52. Link and merge the handle's layer and the metal binding's layer. You should now have only two layers: the bindings and drop handle on one layer, with the wooden door on the background layer.

53. Choose Image, Adjust, Curves to correct the colorization and specularity of the metal binding's layer. In Figure 9.36, you can see how I adjusted the graph in the Curves command to tone down the metal and make it look much more real. The Curves function is very handy for adjusting specular highlights in images.

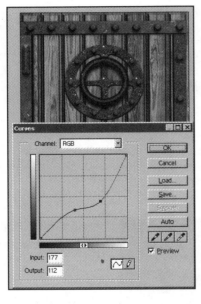

Figure 9.36 *Merge the metal layers and adjust the specularity of the layer using the Curves command.*

54. Touch up the entire image using the Burn tool with a very low setting, like 5% exposure, and a splatter-like brush. I went over the wood doors too, and made sure the bottoms of the image were darker than the tops, indicating a high-noon sun.

55. Flatten the image, and increase the canvas width by 100%.

56. Make a copy of the door, paste it into the same image, and click Edit, Transform, Flip Horizontal.

TIP

If you burn shadows into the top areas of the wood, it'll make the bindings appear to be floating away from the door. Correct this by undoing it, or using the Dodge tool.

57. Position the copy next to the original (see Figure 9.37). Finally, you're finished!

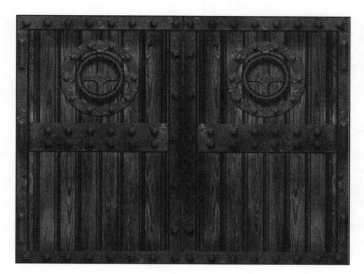

Figure 9.37 *Touch up the image using the Burn tool with a low setting. Make a copy of the door, flip it, and align it next to the original.*

High-Tech

Making textures suitable for any space ship or futuristic otherworld is my forte. This type of texture involves nothing less than creating lots of pipes, wires, lights, metal panels, and anything else that makes you feel as far as possible from quaint. In addition, this texture will have an animation frame associated with it—a couple of the lights will go on and off, depending on the actions of the player (once the texture is in a game engine, that is). Figure 9.38 shows the texture whose creation I'll demonstrate now.

NOTE

I'm going to pick up the pace here and assume that you already know the basics of the general filters Photoshop has to offer, as well as applying styles, adjusting levels, and so on. If you find that you get lost quickly, you might want to go over Chapter 8 in more detail, where these essentials are thoroughly covered.

Figure 9.38 *The futuristic, high-tech texture you'll create in this section.*

1. Start a new 1024×1024-pixel RGB color image with a resolution of 1024.

2. Fill the image with the Clouds filter, using pure black and medium gray (hex# 808080).

3. Choose Filter, Render, Difference Clouds.

4. Add noise, 10%.

5. Choose Filter, Stylize, Emboss. This will make the surface appear slightly bumpy (see Figure 9.39).

Figure 9.39 *Use the Clouds, Noise, and Emboss filters to make a uniquely textured background.*

Filter: Stylize, Emboss
Angle: 135 degrees
Height: 1 pixel
Amount: 118%

6. Using the Polygonal Lasso tool, with both the Grid and Snap features enabled, create a selection as shown in Figure 9.40.

7. Right-click on the selection and choose Layer Via Copy.

Figure 9.40 *Create a polygonal selection on the background layer and copy it to a new layer.*

8. With the selection on its own layer, apply an inner bevel.

9. Notice that the style causes bevels on the left, right, and bottom edges, which you don't want. To get rid of them, flatten the layer (that is, add a new layer, link the two, and press Ctrl+E to merge them); click Edit, Transform, Scale; and scale out the sides and bottom.

10. Adjust the levels on all layers to darken the image (see Figure 9.41).

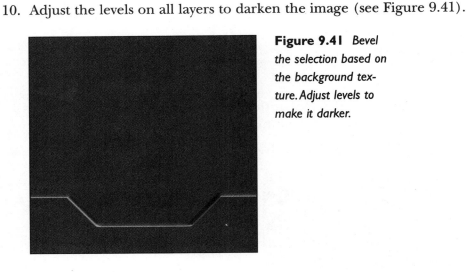

Figure 9.41 *Bevel the selection based on the background texture. Adjust levels to make it darker.*

Style:	Bevel and Emboss
Style:	Inner Bevel
Technique:	Smooth
Depth:	1000%
Direction:	Up
Size:	20
Soften:	0
Shading Angle:	75 degrees
Style:	Linear Contour
Range:	50%

11. The large, circular furnace thing (in the middle of Figure 9.38) is simply a pattern I created using an Alpha channel in the Channels palette. To begin, create a circular marquee selection, and then fill it with white in a new channel.

12. Continue making the pattern by deleting and filling other circular selections, as I have done in Figure 9.42. (I used the Line tool to make the straight lines of fixed width.)

13. Once the pattern is about what you want, use the Gaussian blur/levels technique, as mentioned in the previous example, to round the corners.

14. When you're finished, Ctrl+click the channel to load the selection.

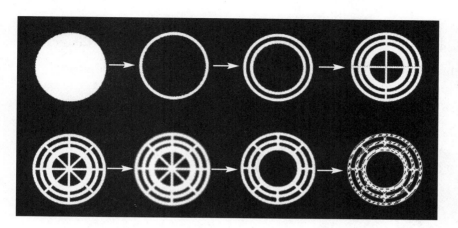

Figure 9.42
Create a cool grate pattern in a new Alpha channel.

15. With the pattern's selection loaded, right-click the background layer and choose Layer Via Copy.

16. Apply an inner bevel to the new layer to make the surface look 3D (see Figure 9.43).

17. Start another layer below the grate.

NOTE

I don't have any set preferences for bevels; I usually just play around with the settings to get the look I want. The most important thing to do is to use the Global Light feature, which is usually enabled by default.

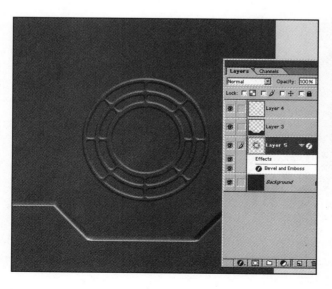

Figure 9.43 *Use the pattern selection to copy the material from the background layer, and apply an inner bevel to this layer.*

18. Create a circular marquee selection that is almost as big as the grate; its border should be placed right in the middle of the outside border of the grate.

19. Fill the selection with a foreground-to-background radial gradient, using black as the foreground color and a deep red, like hex# 6F0707, as the background. You should end up with the illusion that the grate stands in front of a very hot, deep furnace (see Figure 9.44).

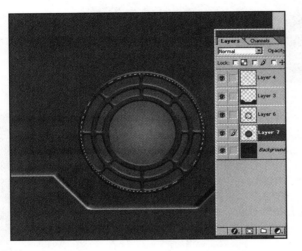

Figure 9.44 *Fill a circular marquee selection with a Radial Gradient using black and deep red colors.*

20. Repeat the techniques in steps 11–16 to make another grate pattern in the same shape as the lower portion of the wall (see Figure 9.45).

Figure 9.45 *Repeat steps 11–16 to create another grate pattern for the lower portion of the wall.*

21. Invert the selection, start a new layer below the grate, and fill it with a black-to–deep red linear gradient, indicating that that area is some form of vent for the furnace (see Figure 9.46).

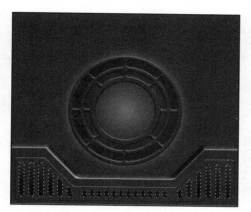

Figure 9.46 *Invert the selection and fill it with a Linear Gradient, using the same colors as before. Add an Outer Glow to the radial gradient's layer.*

CAUTION

During this tutorial, try not to flatten layers that have any type of glow styles applied to them. Near the end, you'll need to turn them on and off to simulate the texture animation during game play.

22. Add an outer-glow style to the layer that contains the furnace's radial gradient. (Make sure the glow color is the same as before—in this case, hex# 6F0707.)

23. Break up the top portion of the background layer a bit by creating Polygonal Lasso selections, making a copy of that portion of the background layer, and applying a small, downward, outer bevel to them. In Figure 9.47, I created my general patterns and rounded the corners using an Alpha channel and the blur-levels technique.

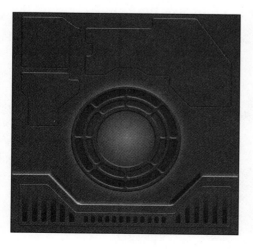

Figure 9.47 *Add panels to the top portion of the background layer using Polygonal Lasso selections.*

24. Now for the pipes that run a course through the texture. With Photoshop's Grid and Snap features enabled, create a Polygonal Lasso selection as I have done in Figure 9.48.

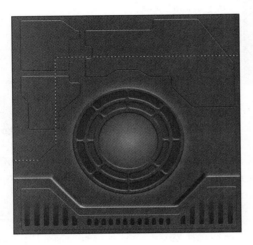

Figure 9.48 *Start a pipe by first making a Polygonal Lasso selection*

25. In a new Alpha channel, stroke the selection with white, entering a width of about 25 pixels.

26. Apply the Gaussian Blur filter to the channel, and then tighten it up again with the levels command. This will smooth out the edges.

27. Ctrl+click the channel and reapply the Gaussian Blur filter.

28. Adjust the levels a bit to make the 3D pipe come into focus (see Figure 9.49). (Note that this is the same technique you used in the previous example for the door's drop handles.)

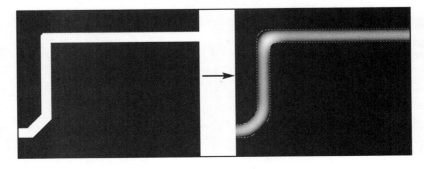

Figure 9.49 *Stroke the selection in a new channel, and use the blur/levels technique to create the pipe.*

29. Copy and paste the pipe from the Alpha channel over to a new layer.

30. Apply noise (about 10%), and adjust the levels to darken the image and bring out the pipe's highlights (see Figure 9.50).

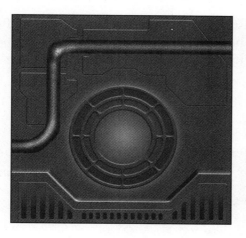

Figure 9.50 *The new pipe copied over from the Alpha channel.*

31. Create collars on the pipe by making a Rectangular Marquee selection around a small portion of the existing pipe, copying the selection, and pasting it back into the scene. Then just scale the small piece so it's slightly larger than the pipe itself to give the illusion of a collar.

32. After all the pieces have been added, merge them to the pipe's layer.

33. Add a drop shadow to the pipe. Make sure the lighting direction is the same as the bevel styles—that is, the shadow drops down and away to the left a bit (see Figure 9.51).

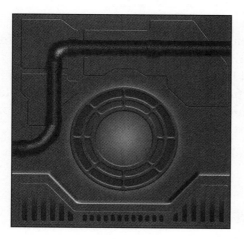

Figure 9.51 *Make collars using copies of a small portion of the existing pipe. Drop-shadow the whole thing when finished.*

34. Make a copy of the pipe's layer and move it so it's right next to the first. The copy's edges won't be long enough, so just make a Rectangular Marquee selection around the long end, copy it, and position it to make the pipe run off of the image.

35. The portion of the pipe that's closest to the furnace could use a little reflective glow underneath it. Ctrl+click the pipe's layer to select it, and then use the Airbrush tool with a very low setting (like 3%) to brush in a deep red along its length (see Figure 9.52).

36. Make a hidden copy of this pipe so that when the lights are off, you can recall the copy to get rid of the glow.

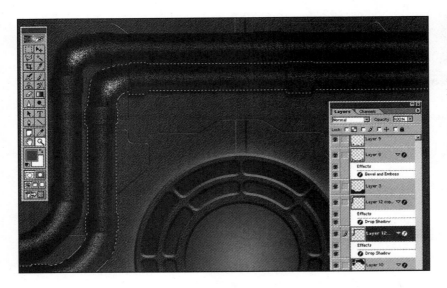

Figure 9.52 *Copy the pipe and move it next to its parent. Add a bit of red glow to the bottom pipe to simulate reflectance of the furnace.*

37. Next, make an on/off panel that a player could approach and activate. In the image shown in Figure 9.53, I simply made a rectangular selection, copied a portion of the background layer, and applied an inner bevel to it just like the lower front portion of the wall. Then, I added another smaller panel, this time with a downward inner bevel. The combination makes for a raised panel with another that's inset.

38. Ctrl+click the top-most beveled panel to reload its selection.

39. Fill the selection with a dirty yellow color, and add a bit of noise.

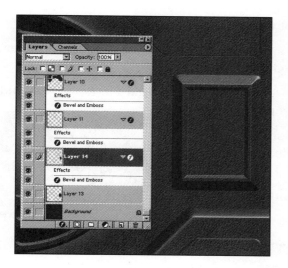

Figure 9.53
Create a raised panel using rectangular selections of the background layer and applying bevels to them.

40. Change the Blending Mode of this layer to Hard Light. This allows you to retain much of the color, and bring out the texture of the panel behind it.

41. Adjust the levels to enhance the panel.

42. Use the Line tool to create black diagonal stripes across the selection (enabling Photoshop's Snap and Grid features helps this procedure). Hold down the Shift key while making the lines to keep them at 45-degree angles (see Figure 9.54).

Figure 9.54
Make a caution-style texture on the topmost panel using a medium-yellow background with black lines.

43. Create another layer on top of the panel.

44. Make two black vertical lines, and apply an inner bevel to both. These serve as the rails for the on/off switch.

45. Make a handle using the pipe technique described earlier. Round the ends of the handle and paste it into position.

46. Choose Image, Adjust, Variations to change the color of the handle to red (see Figure 9.55).

47. Add a drop shadow to the handle to pull it away from the panel.

NOTE

Keep the handle on a separate layer so you can move it down to the "off" position later.

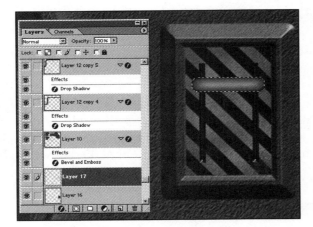

Figure 9.55 *Make rails and a red handle to complete the panel.*

48. Make an illuminated light that represents the "on" state of the entire texture. To begin, create a small rectangular panel, as before, based on the background.

49. On a new panel (above the rectangular panel), fill the inside of the panel with a reflected gradient, using a medium-light blue and white (see Figure 9.56).

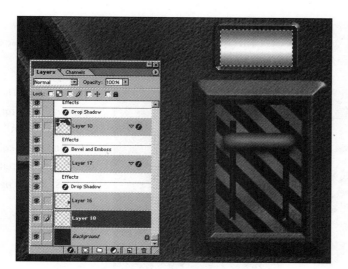

Figure 9.56
Create another small panel for the on/off light. Fill the inside with a blue-to-white Reflected Gradient.

50. Enhance the light by adding some light gray horizontal lines, and then go over the light with the Dodge tool until the center and edges are fairly white.

51. Use the Burn tool to darken the edges, making the light appear almost rounded and 3D.

52. Apply a blue outer glow to the light, as shown in Figure 9.57. (As with the handle you made before, keep this layer intact with its style so you can hide the style later, making the system appear to be off.)

Figure 9.57 *The completed light, after dodging and burning here and there. An outer-glow style makes it appear to be "on."*

53. Create an "off" state for the light—this is simply another layer just below the light itself, but filled with a deep blue gradient. In Figure 9.58, you can see the difference between the "off" state and the "on" state.

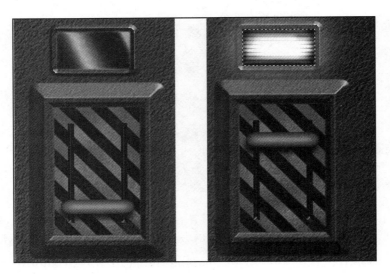

Figure 9.58 *The "off" and "on" states of the texture. A video game will call one of two different textures depending on the player's actions.*

54. Now it's all a matter of creating two textures—one for when the glows are on, and one for when they're off. For the furnace's "off" state, simply hide the original red texture, create another layer, and fill it with a very small glow, indicating that the furnace is hot but not at full power (see Figure 9.59).

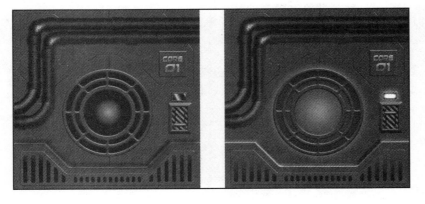

Figure 9.59 *Create two textures for the final output: one with all glows turned down or off and the red handle moved down, and one with the handle up and everything lit.*

Time Counts

No artist will be allowed to spend an entire work day on a single texture, unless it's for a main character, manual, cover art, or something similarly major. Table 9.1 is designed to help you estimate how much time you should spend on various textures.

Table 9.1 General Texturing Work-to-Time Ratio

Texture Type	Time Spent Texturing
Small/insignificant (for example, Wood Crate texture)	< 1 hour
Medium/moderate (for example, Medieval Door texture)	2 hours
Large/complex (for example, High-Tech texture)	3–5 hours
Ground texture (set of eight)	2–3 hours
Weapon skin	3–5 hours
Character skin (primary)	1–2 days
Cover art	As long as it takes! (< 1 week)

Of course, the values in Table 9.1 are meant as guidelines; your ability to adhere to them depends entirely on your artistic ability and knowledge of the software you're using. Some people are so talented that they can create the most outstanding character skins in mere hours, when it would take me days or even a week! Just keep these numbers in mind when working, because your boss at a game company will expect constant and efficient results from you.

Summary

Many advanced textures are possible using the default filters, styles, and tools encapsulated within Photoshop. Much can be accomplished—with very little free-hand artistic ability—using careful combinations of these techniques. The use of photographic images is always an advantage as well, as it makes your texturing job easier and your work more realistic. I hope you've enjoyed these textures, and that you noticed that I employed a repeating set of texturing functions. Nothing is too difficult or requires much artistic skill—just some patience and perhaps a wild imagination! Happy texturing!

CHAPTER 10

ORGANIC TEXTURE TUTORIALS WITH PHOTOSHOP

When a texture is called "organic," it means that the texture would most likely be applied to some animate, carbon-based life form or the terrain from whence it came. In this chapter, you will learn how to create textures for

- Organic entities, such as animal skins and plant leaves
- Displacement mapping for use in 3D texture development
- Planetary entities, such as ground and water

Skin and Bones

What monster would be complete without crackled, smelly, scaly skin, with areas gouged out by medieval weaponry? There are a million ways to create all the textures discussed in this section, but yours truly invented these basics, just for you. They are designed to whet your appetite and get your wheels spinning.

> **NOTE**
>
> Compared to Chapters 8, "Inorganic Texture Tutorials with Photoshop," and 9, "Advanced Texturing Examples," this chapter is relatively short; that's because many of the techniques I described in those chapters—especially in Chapter 8—apply here.

> **TIP**
>
> If you've skipped to this chapter before reading Chapter 8, and/or are new to Photoshop, you might be a little lost when I demonstrate the use of many of the filters and other Photoshop operations. If so, refer to Chapter 8, where I show you how to apply many of these techniques in detail.

> **NOTE**
>
> For more detailed skinning applications, see Chapter 12, "Skinning the Slogre with Deep Paint 3D and Photoshop."

Lizard/Dinosaur Skin

I came up with this texture by accident; I was trying to create a good rock texture, but out popped a perfect texture for a creepy Basilisk or Maiasaur instead.

1. In Photoshop, start a new 512×512-pixel RGB image.

2. Set your foreground color to a slimy-green, like hex#D5E043, and your background to a reddish-brown, like hex#783522.

3. Choose Filter, Render, Clouds (see Figure 10.1).

Figure 10.1 *Apply the Clouds filter using bright green and reddish-brown colors.*

Filter:	Render, Clouds
Foreground:	hex#D5E043
Background:	hex#783522

4. In the Channels palette, create a new alpha channel.

5. Apply the Filter, Render, Clouds filter to the new alpha channel.

6. Choose Filter, Render, Difference Clouds; press Ctrl+F to apply the filter several times until you get a nice blend of black and white (see Figure 10.2).

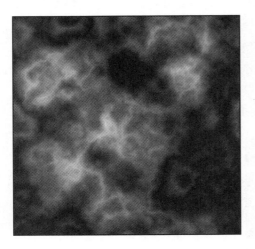

Figure 10.2 *Create a new channel, and apply both the Clouds and Difference Clouds filters.*

7. Choose Filter, Noise, Add Noise, about 5%. (Be sure Gaussian and Monochromatic are checked off within the filter.)

8. Click the background layer in the Layers palette.

9. Choose Filter, Render, Lighting Effects, using the Alpha 1 channel as a displacement map (see Figure 10.3).

Figure 10.3 *Render the background layer using the Alpha 1 channel as a displacement map.*

Filter: Render, Lighting Effects
Light Type: Spotlight (from above)

Intensity:	24
Focus:	63
Gloss:	75
Material:	96
Exposure:	0
Ambience:	8
Texture Channel:	Alpha 1
Height:	100

What do you think? You can polish this texture off using Filter, Texture, Craquelure if you're looking for a more scaly or cracked-skin appearance (see Figure 10.4).

TIP

Any time you base your textures using the Clouds filters, the pattern within your textures will be seamlessly tileable. For example, if you were to tile the texture from Figure 10.3 onto a large surface, you'd see that all the neighboring edges match up. This is due to the built-in offset the Clouds filters have. However, because you rendered the texture at the end using a spotlight with the Lighting Effects filter, the top edges will be brighter than the bottom edges, which will leave a noticeable seam. Sometimes using an omni light instead of a spotlight with this filter will help fade these seams. See the "Grass" section later in this chapter for more on this technique.

Figure 10.4 *Apply the Craquelure filter for an added touch.*

Rhinoceros Skin

This texture can be applied to just about anything requiring thick, tough skin, especially if it needs scales. Of course, rhinos don't have scales, but their skin, like that of other behemoths like elephants, is well defined and cracked in sort of a geometrical pattern.

1. Start a new 512×512-pixel RGB color image.

2. Set your foreground color to black and your background color to medium gray (try hex#808080).

3. Choose Filter, Render, Clouds.

4. Choose Filter, Noise, Add Noise, about 5%.

5. Make a copy of this layer.

6. With the copy open, choose Filter, Texture, Stained Glass (see Figure 10.5). This will create the cell pattern that you'll use for the scaly look.

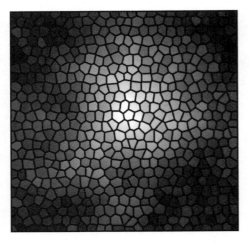

Figure 10.5 *Apply the Stained Glass filter to a copy of the background layer.*

Filter:	Texture, Stained Glass
Cell Size:	10
Border Thickness:	5
Light Intensity:	5

7. You want to make a selection based on only the cell pattern in this layer. To begin, click on the Magic Wand tool. In its Options bar, set the Tolerance to 0 and select Contiguous.

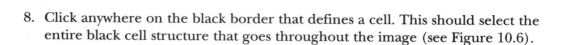

8. Click anywhere on the black border that defines a cell. This should select the entire black cell structure that goes throughout the image (see Figure 10.6).

Figure 10.6 *Use the Magic Wand tool to select the cell pattern in the top layer.*

9. With the selection loaded, delete the top layer—the selection will remain active on the background layer.

10. Add a new, blank layer.

11. Choose Edit, Stroke. Stroke the selection with black, 1 pixel wide, and centered (see Figure 10.7). You should now have the cell pattern outlined on a separate layer.

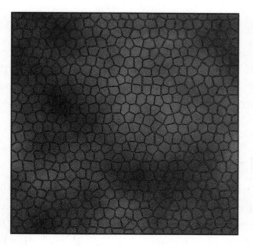

Figure 10.7 *Stroke the selection with black on a new, blank layer.*

12. To the top layer, which has the cell pattern, apply a downward outer bevel (see Figure 10.8). Be sure to check the settings I have listed in Figure 10.8.

Figure 10.8 *Apply an outer bevel to the layer with the cell pattern.*

Style:	Bevel and Emboss
Style:	Outer Bevel
Technique:	Smooth
Depth:	300%
Direction:	Down
Size:	6
Soften:	0
Shading Angle:	90 degrees

Adjust the levels on the background layer to lighten it up a bit. You can also choose Image, Adjust, Variations to change the color scheme to suit other animals. Finally, try decreasing the Size setting for the outer bevel to get a more snake-like appearance.

Bone (Using Displacement Maps)

This texture can be applied to so many things that require a nice, smooth, 3D look, especially metallic surfaces. You might, however, be able to use this texture—in conjunction with the one discussed in the next tutorial—to make a gruesome texture that could be applied to a zombie or other creature whose epidermis has been hacked away, exposing bone and flesh.

1. Start a new 512×512-pixel RGB color image.

2. Fill the image's background layer with pure black (hex#000000).

3. Create a new channel in the Channels palette.

4. Using the Lasso tool, draw a bone-shaped outline that you want to eventually fill with the bone texture. As shown in Figure 10.9, I made mine resemble a cartoon-like bone, so you can see things more clearly.

5. Fill the selection with pure white (hex# FFFFFF).

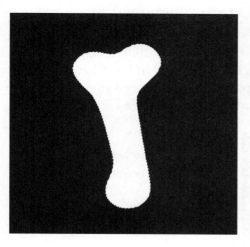

Figure 10.9 *Create a new channel and make an outline of a bone with the Lasso tool, then fill it with white.*

6. With the selection still loaded, choose Filter, Blur, Gaussian Blur, about 15 pixels (see Figure 10.10).

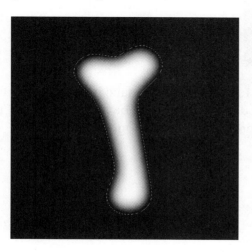

Figure 10.10 *Apply the Gaussian Blur filter to the selection, and adjust the levels to darken the edges.*

7. Choose Image, Adjust, Levels, and drag the Shadows slider to the right until it's about midway across so the edges become even more defined. You're generating the displacement map for the bone here, so when you render it, it'll look nice and 3D.

   Filter: Blur, Gaussian Blur
   Radius: 15 pixels

8. Choose Filter, Noise, Add Noise, about 5%.

9. Choose Filter, Noise, Median, with a radian of 1 pixel. This will add pock marks to the bone for some nice texture.

10. Your selection is still loaded in the Channels palette, but does not properly surround the bone object. Ctrl+click the channel in the Channels palette to reload the selection—notice that your selection moved inward a bit, indicating that the selection contains a feathered image (see Figure 10.11).

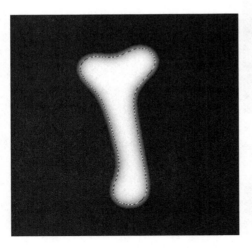

Figure 10.11
Ctrl+click the channel to reload the selection properly.

11. Click the background layer in the Layers palette to make it active. The channel's selection should have followed suit, and should be active as well (if not, go back to the Channels palette and Ctrl+click the bone channel).

12. Fill this selection with a light cream color (or white, if you want). I used hex# E7E6D3 (see Figure 10.12). This is the base image for your bone, but you're not finished yet!

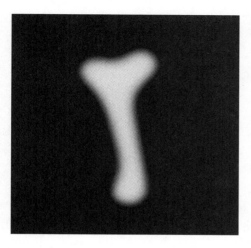

Figure 10.12 *Fill the selection with an off-white color in the background layer.*

13. Press Ctrl+D to deselect the outline.

14. Choose Filter, Render, Lighting Effects, and render the layer using the Alpha 1 channel as a displacement map (see Figure 10.13).

15. Adjust the levels to polish it off. This looks great for bone, but could be used for other surfaces that require a 3D look.

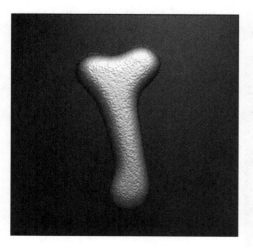

Figure 10.13
Render the layer with the Lighting Effects filter, using the Alpha 1 channel as a displacement map.

Filter:	Render, Lighting Effects
Light Type:	Spotlight (from above and right)
Intensity:	25
Focus:	25
Gloss:	0
Material:	0
Exposure:	0
Ambience:	6
Texture Channel:	Alpha 1
Height:	100

Torn Flesh

As I mentioned, this texture can be used in conjunction with the bone texture discussed earlier. It's rudimentary, but requires a little finesse and effort. In this tutorial, I'll use the image from the previous example as a base. Either use your own, or open the file **bone.psd**, located in the Chapter 10 Data section on the CD-ROM.

1. Because this image still has the alpha channel associated with the previous example, begin by Ctrl+clicking the Alpha 1 channel in the Channels palette to load the bone selection.

2. Click the background layer in the Layers palette.

3. Expand the selection to encompass the entire bone by choosing Select, Modify, Expand, with a value of 10 pixels (see Figure 10.14).

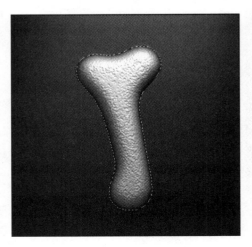

Figure 10.14 *Load a selection around the entire bone and cut it to its own layer*

4. Right-click on this selection and choose Layer Via Cut. This will place the bone on its own layer.

5. Select the background layer. You want to fill it, as well as a layer above the bone, with an exposed muscle texture.

6. Set your foreground color to a medium-dark red, like hex# 9D0F0F, and your background color a medium-dark purple, like hex# 6D0620.

7. Choose Filter, Render, Clouds. This is a nice base mixture for general flesh and blood.

8. Choose Filter, Noise, Add Noise, about 15%.

9. Choose Filter, Noise, Median, 1 pixel.

10. Choose Filter, Sketch, Graphic Pen (see Figure 10.15).

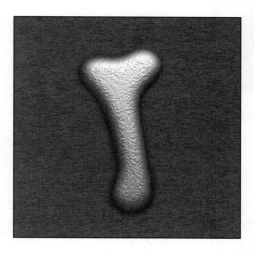

Figure 10.15 *Fill the background layer with a bloody mix using the Clouds, Noise, and Graphic Pen filters.*

Filter:	Render, Clouds
Foreground:	hex#9D0F0F
Background:	hex#6D0620
Filter:	Sketch, Graphic Pen
Stroke Length:	15
Light/Dark Balance:	59
Stroke Direction:	Horizontal

11. Press Ctrl+A to select the entire background layer, then Ctrl+C to copy the selection's contents. Then go to the Channels palette and create a new channel.

12. Press Ctrl+V to paste a copy of the contents of the background into this channel (see Figure 10.16). This will serve as a displacement map to give the meat a 3D look.

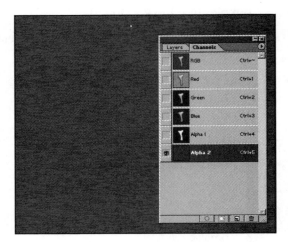

Figure 10.16 *Copy the contents of the background layer and paste it into a new channel.*

13. Click on the background layer in the Layers palette to make it active.

14. Choose Filter, Render, Lighting Effects, and use the new Alpha 2 channel as a texture channel (see Figure 10.17). I made my light source in this filter point in the same direction as the previous bone example, from top-right to bottom-left.

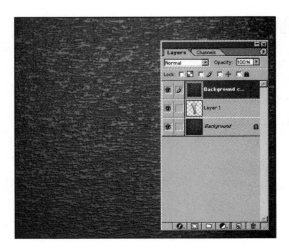

Figure 10.17 *Render the background layer with the Lighting Effects filter, using the new Alpha 2 channel as a displacement map. Duplicate this layer and place the copy above the bone layer.*

15. Make a copy of this background layer, and move the copy above the bone layer.

Filter:	Render, Lighting Effects
Light Type:	Spotlight (from above and right)
Intensity:	25
Focus:	25
Gloss:	0
Material:	0
Exposure:	0
Ambience:	6
Texture Channel:	Alpha 2
Height:	100

16. You should now have three layers in the image: a bone layer surrounded by two flesh layers. Create another new layer above all other layers; this will be the skin layer.

17. For the sake of example, I'm going to use a typical Caucasian flesh mixture for the skin in this tutorial. I recommend you use two similar colors as the base mix. For my example, I applied the Filter, Render, Clouds filter using hex# AC883B and hex# CA8C4A.

TIP

Getting skin tones correct is a trial-and-error process, but the best way to do it is to search the Web for images of people whose skin matches the color you want, and sample it in Photoshop.

18. Choose Filter, Noise, Add Noise, about 5%.

19. Choose Filter, Noise, Median, with 1 pixel. The results are shown in Figure 10.18; I also adjusted the skin with the Levels command, and desaturated it a bit using Image, Adjust, Hue/Saturation.

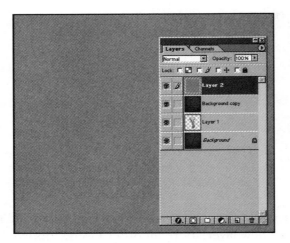

Figure 10.18 *Create a new layer and fill it with the Clouds filter, using skin colors of your choice. Also add noise, and adjust the levels and saturation to suit.*

20. Now it's time to tear the skin and expose the muscle and bone. To the top skin layer, use the Lasso tool to make a large gouge surrounding the underlying bone (see Figure 10.19).

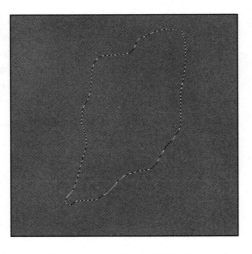

Figure 10.19 *Create a selection on the skin layer that will represent a gouge in the flesh.*

21. Press Q to enter Quick Mask mode.

22. To tear up the skin a bit more, as if a monster or something swiped at it, choose Filter, Brush Strokes, Sprayed Strokes (see Figure 10.20).

Figure 10.20 *Enter Quick Mask mode and apply the Sprayed Strokes filter.*

Filter:	Brush Strokes, Sprayed Strokes
Stroke Length:	20
Spray Radius:	22
Stroke Direction:	Right Diagonal

23. Press Q to exit Quick Mask mode.

24. Press Delete to remove the skin and expose the muscle layer beneath it.

25. To expose bone, click on the muscle layer itself, and contract the selection by choosing Select, Modify, Contract with a value of about 20 pixels.

26. Press Delete. You should end up with something like Figure 10.21.

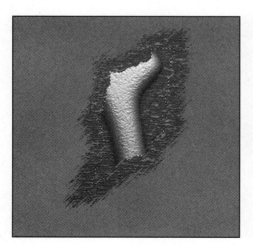

Figure 10.21 *Delete the skin contents of the selection. Select the muscle layer below the skin layer, contract the selection, and delete the muscle tissue as well.*

27. Apply a Bevel and Emboss style of your choice to both the top skin layer and the muscle layer below it. I played around, and found that the Pillow Emboss style looks great.

TIP

I cover using styles in more detail in Chapter 8, and in the Photoshop tutorials located on this book's CD-ROM.

28. Change the colors of the Highlight and Shadow modes of these styles to a reddish color. Overall, you should end up with a nice 3D look to the skin and muscle (see Figure 10.22).

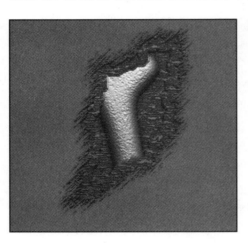

Figure 10.22 *Apply a Bevel and Emboss style to both the skin and muscle layers.*

29. Use the Burn tool with a very low setting (less than 5% exposure) to char the edges of the skin, the muscle, and areas of the bone (see Figure 10.23).

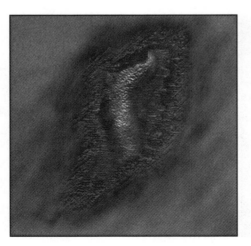

Figure 10.23 *Use the Burn tool to dirty up the image, particularly at the edges.*

Clothing

I'm tossing in a quick section on rendering clothing here because, well, it usually goes on something organic! First I'll show you how to create camouflage clothing, then move on to demonstrating the use of a displacement channel to aid in making its appearance look more 3D. The displacement channel helps you falsify folds in cloth and thereby avoid the inefficient process of modeling wrinkles in shirts and pants.

Camouflage

There must be dozens of different schemes for this type of material, from jungle to desert to what appears to be camouflage meant for the Arctic tundra. None of those are difficult to make; it's just a matter of getting the four to ten colors recorded and applying them to foliage-like patterns. In this tutorial, you'll do regular Army camos; then I'll show you samples of other types. The trick to doing camouflage is alternating the layering properly.

1. Start a new 512×512-pixel RGB color image.

2. Fill the image using the Clouds filter, with your foreground set to a dark green, like hex# 081406, and the background set to a more grayish dark-green, like hex# 192517.

3. Using the Channels palette, start a new channel.

4. Using the Lasso tool, create a goofy, foliage-like pattern that appears very random—like an amoeba or something, as I have done in Figure 10.24. Fill this selection with pure white.

Figure 10.24 *In a new channel, draw a foliage-like shape using one of the Lasso tools.*

NOTE

You don't have to create a perfect pattern; in fact, you could even use the Polygonal Lasso tool, because you'll smooth it out in the next step. Just don't be too square with your design.

5. Press Ctrl+D to deselect.

6. Choose Filter, Blur, Gaussian Blur, with a radius of about 5.0 pixels.

7. Choose Image, Adjust, Levels, and slide the Shadows and Highlights markers toward each other until the shape in the channel becomes crisp and sharp (see Figure 10.25). Don't bring the markers completely together, or you'll get aliased edges.

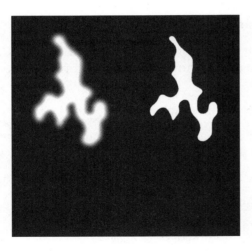

Figure 10.25 *Apply the Gaussian Blur filter to the shape, then re-sharpen it using the Levels command.*

8. Repeat steps 3–7 to make about nine more of these shapes, some very small, and others larger but not too big. *Make sure each shape is on its own channel!* That way, you can call up the individual shapes and overlap them later. Also make sure each of the shapes is unique compared to the rest.

9. Ctrl+click one of the shape's channels to load its selection.

10. In the Layers palette, start a new layer.

11. Fill the selection with a medium tan (hex# 737244), a dark orange-brown (hex# 3F250E), or pure black (hex# 000000).

12. Repeat steps 9–11 for each of the remaining shapes you created, fill them with one of the three colors mentioned. Try to make things very random, overlapping, but not too cluttered, as I have done in Figure 10.26. The trick to a nice camo is to even out the color scheme, and to have the colored shapes interlayered nicely.

TIP
Store your color selections in the Swatches palette for quick retrieval.

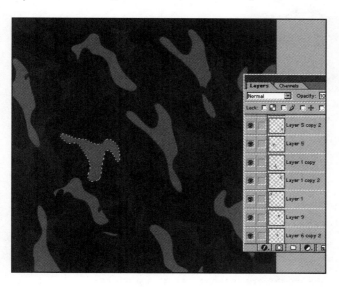

Figure 10.26 *Fill the selections of the different shapes you created with dark tan, dark orange-brown, and black, in different arrangements and on separate layers.*

13. When you're satisfied with your camo, choose Layer, Flatten Image.

14. Choose Filter, Texture, Texturizer, and select the Canvas option—this will give the camo a perfect, rough style.

15. Adjust the levels to suit.

16. Choose Image, Adjust, Hue/Saturation, and desaturate the colors a tad to wash them out appropriately (see Figure 10.27).

Figure 10.27 *Flatten the image, and apply the Canvas filter. Adjust the levels and saturation to suit.*

Filter:	Texture, Texturizer
Texture:	Canvas
Scaling:	50%
Relief:	2
Light Direction:	Top

TIP

By the way, this texture works great when set as a pattern; just be sure not to make the individual shapes in the texture go beyond the edges of the image. That way, the texture will tile, somewhat seamlessly, around the pants or jacket of your favorite Hamburger Hill action model.

Wrinkles (Using Displacement Maps)

When you make a texture meant to be clothing for a character model, the cloth itself should almost never hang straight down like it's made of cardboard. The au natural look of clothing always has some sort of fold, crease, or seam somewhere. It's somewhat difficult to modify the character's mesh so it physically wrinkles your texture map, aside from being a waste of polygons. The logical thing is to put the wrinkles in the texture map, creating the illusion of the clothing hanging naturally (see Figure 10.28).

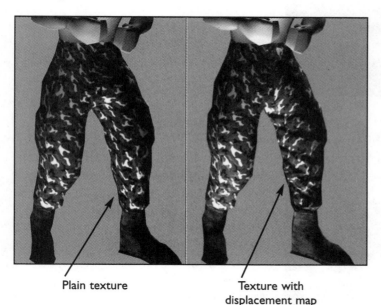

Plain texture

Texture with displacement map

Figure 10.28 *The pants leg of a soldier mesh with the camouflage texture from the previous example. It's much more efficient to fake some wrinkles in the texture map than to model the mesh to do so.*

Creating the illusion of wrinkles can seem like a pain if you haven't much traditional artistic ability, but all it is, is a matter of dodging, burning, and cutting/pasting the texture in just the right places to get a good fold effect. Alternatively, you can use a displacement channel, like so:

1. With the camouflage texture you created in the previous section open (if you don't have it, load the camo1.png file on the CD-ROM), start a new channel.

2. Click on the Airbrush tool, and select a large feathered brush like Soft Round 65 pixels, with about 30% pressure. (You don't want to spray anything heavy or too white or the folds in the texture will look too sharp and artificial.)

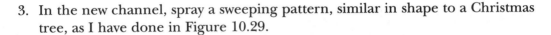

3. In the new channel, spray a sweeping pattern, similar in shape to a Christmas tree, as I have done in Figure 10.29.

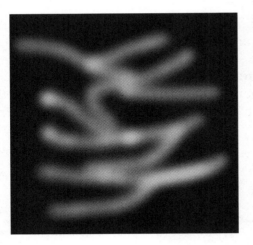

Figure 10.29 *To create a displacement map for the cloth, lightly spray a sweeping pattern in a new channel.*

4. To generate the wrinkles in the camo, select the camo layer itself and apply the Lighting Effects filter using the newly created Alpha channel as a displacement map. In that filter I have the Texture Channel set to Mountainous (100) to bring out the bumps in the cloth to their fullest (see Figure 10.30).

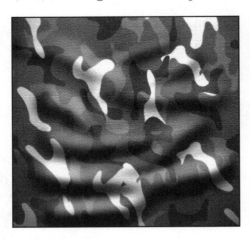

Figure 10.30 *Render the wrinkles in the camouflage with the Lighting Effects filter, using the new Alpha channel as a displacement map.*

5. Augment the wrinkles in the final rendering by using the Dodge and Burn tools. With each tool's setting cranked all the way down, and using the Soft Round 65 Pixels brush, darken the valleys and lighten the peaks of the texture. Seeing this in action can give you a feel for how traditional artists create these illusions by hand.

This is a fairly effective technique to create folds and wrinkles in fabric. There is, however, another technique I use for creating similar displacements in skin, without using the Lighting Effects filter—see Chapter 12, "Skinning the Slogre with Deep Paint 3D and Photoshop."

Planetary Textures

This section is dedicated to a handful of textures that pertain primarily to any geometry belonging to a planet, be it Earth or another large oblate spheroid. Some of these textures are meant to be tiled uniquely upon a single mesh or plane, while others can (and should) be grouped in a texture set of similarity, since the same image tiled dozens of times can be quite monotonous.

Earth

This is a quick but effective tile that's useful for stretching itself over medium-sized distances. That is, if your level contains a ground mesh of around 50 meters square, you might be able to get away with tiling this texture just a few times in each direction.

1. Start a new 512×512-pixel RGB color image.

2. To create the dirt layer, set your foreground to a medium tan color, like hex# 978F36, and your background to a dark orange-brown, like hex# 7D5810.

3. Choose Filter, Render Clouds.

4. Apply the Noise filter, about 10%.

5. Apply the Median filter, 1 pixel.

6. Create a new layer; this will be the grass layer above the dirt.

7. Fill the new layer with the Clouds filter, using medium and dark green colors such as hex# 1F871A and hex# 144A0A.

8. Apply the Noise and Median filters.

9. Using the Channels palette, create a new channel.

10. To the new alpha channel, apply the Clouds filter, and then apply the Difference Clouds filter.

11. Adjust the levels until you significantly sharpen the white areas in the channel, but keeping a good bit of fuzziness to it (see Figure 10.31).

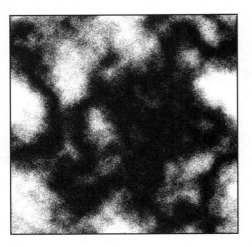

Figure 10.31
Apply the Clouds and Difference Clouds filter, and adjust the levels.

12. Add Noise to this channel, about 10%, and reapply the Difference Clouds filter.

13. Adjust the levels again until the white areas are sharpened somewhat but still fuzzy, as I have done in Figure 10.32.

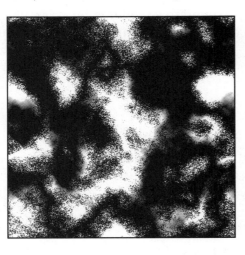

Figure 10.32 *Add noise and reapply the Difference Clouds filter. Sharpen the image again with levels.*

14. Ctrl+click this channel to load a great, scatter-like selection, and go back to the Layers palette.

15. Click on the top layer, which should be the grass layer.

16. With the selection on the grass layer active, press Delete to get the dirt layer to show through (see Figure 10.33); if you like, continue pressing Delete to make the dirt show through more and more.

17. Adjust the levels for both layers to your liking.

Figure 10.33 *Load the channel's selection and use it to delete the colors from the grass layer.*

The great thing about this texture is, because you used the Clouds filters, the texture will be inherently seamlessly tileable. Try clicking Filter, Other, Offset, and entering a value of 256 pixels for both width and height to see what I mean. In Figure 10.34, I shrank the texture to 256×256 pixels, and applied it by itself to a rocky terrain in the *Torque* editor. Not too shabby, eh? In addition, you can use this texturing technique to create base textures for other landscapes—just change the colors!

Figure 10.34 *The grassy texture in action in the* Torque *editor.*

Dry Lake Bed

This texture makes use of the Stained Glass filter that I presented earlier in the section "Rhinoceros Skin." Essentially this is a feeble attempt to mimic the dry lake beds in the Utah/Nevada area—you know, where they test those highly practical supersonic cars. Anyway, there's not much to this procedure, but it makes good use of an Alpha channel to get the job done:

1. Start a new 512×512-pixel RGB color image.

2. Fill the background layer with the Clouds filter, using sandy colors like hex# AC9059 and hex# BEB85C.

3. Apply the Noise filter, about 10%.

4. Create a new channel.

5. To the new channel, apply the Clouds filter.

6. Choose Filter, Texture, Stained Glass.

7. Choose Filter, Stylize, Find Edges. This will nix everything fuzzy and augment the cell definition of the pattern (see Figure 10.35).

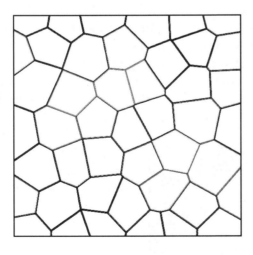

Figure 10.35 *The Stained Glass and Find Edges filter combination makes for a good dry, cracked lake bed pattern.*

Filter:	Texture, Stained Glass
Cell Size:	40
Border Thickness:	1
Light Intensity:	0

8. Choose Filter, Brush Strokes, Spatter. This will chop up the edges of the cell pattern.

9. Ctrl+click the channel to load its selection.

10. Using the Layers palette, create a new layer.

11. With the selection active in the new layer, choose Select, Inverse. This will invert the selection so the cell pattern itself—not its contents—is what is selected.

12. Press Alt+Backspace to fill this selection with the foreground color (see Figure 10.36).

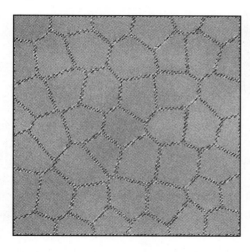

Figure 10.36
Spatter the cell pattern, and use it to create the same pattern on a new layer.

Filter: Brush Strokes, Spatter
Spray Radius: 4
Smoothness: 5

13. To the top layer that contains the cell pattern, apply a downward inner bevel. The bevel should have full depth to enhance the dark features of the cracks (see Figure 10.37).

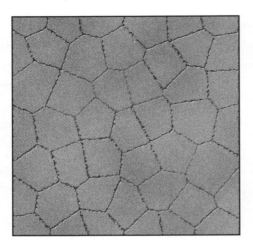

Figure 10.37 *Add a downward inner bevel to finish the texture.*

That's it! You can adjust the levels to suit your needs from here—just remember to flatten the image. The only down side to this texture is that it's not quite seamlessly tileable—you need to manually offset it with Filter, Other, Offset, and take your time getting rid of the obnoxious seams with the Clone Stamp tool. Figure 10.38 shows this texture in action. Also, you might try using the Alpha channel you created as a displacement map in conjunction with the Lighting Effects filter to raise (or lower) the individual cells of the texture.

Figure 10.38 *Not an attractive scenario. Sun block 200, anyone?*

Water

Here's a quickie with guaranteed results using a filter I've yet to demonstrate in this book. The uniqueness of this texture is not just in the filtering, but in the mesh onto which it is placed. In almost every 3D game on the market, there exists the level-design capability to activate some type of vertex displacement mesh. That is, you should be able to dictate certain areas of your terrain to be in constant, random, wave-like motion within a fixed range. In the case of this example—which could easily apply to lava, boiling acid, and the like—a water texture is applied to an area of geometry within a level whose vertices slowly shift back and forth, slightly expanding and contracting the texture to make the area appear liquid. *Torque*, *Unreal*, and *Quake*, to mention a few, are engines quite capable of this physics technique. Pretty much any organic-looking texture will work on these objects.

1. Start a new 512×512-pixel, RGB color image.

2. Fill the background layer with the Clouds filter, using medium and light sky blue colors, like hex# 476378 and hex# 547890.

3. Choose Filter, Texture, Stained Glass (see Figure 10.39).

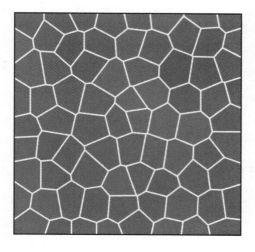

Figure 10.39 *With a bluish background, apply the Stained Glass filter.*

Filter:	Texture, Stained Glass
Cell Size:	30
Border Thickness:	5
Light Intensity:	0

4. Choose Filter, Distort, Wave. (This is a complex filter, and I had to play around a bit to get it right; see the Settings alongside the figure for my adjustments.)

5. Choose Filter, Distort, Ocean Ripple. This will add that signature water look to the texture (see Figure 10.40).

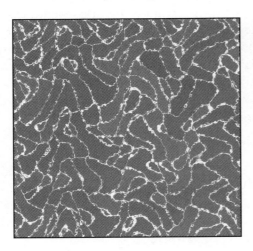

Figure 10.40 *Apply both the Wave and Ocean Ripple textures to get the water in motion.*

Filter:	Distort, Wave
# Generators:	15
Wavelength:	30/87
Amplitude:	39/97
Scale:	21/21
Type:	Sine
Filter:	Distort, Ocean Ripple
Ripple Size:	3
Ripple Magnitude:	3

You're set! Figure 10.41 shows the *Torque* engine with the water slowly moving back and forth—giving the illusion that it is washing up on the shore. Keep experimenting with different-size cell patterns and whatnot for more blatant effects.

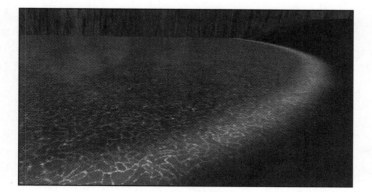

Figure 10.41
The water texture in action. Literally.

Summary

Organic textures are those that I consider representative of living things or other worldly objects not man-made. This chapter covered the redirection of many of the texturing techniques described in the previous chapters so that you can create textures suitable for skin, clothing, land, sea—all of which can be used in nearly every 3D game engine on the market.

CHAPTER 11

Skinning the RF-9 Plasma Gun with Deep Paint 3D and Photoshop

This chapter picks up where Chapter 5, "U-V Mapping the RF-9 Plasma Gun with DeepUV," left off. Here, you'll use your newly developed U-V texture map to texture the RF-9 in both Deep Paint 3D and Photoshop. Figure 11.1 illustrates your current location in the compound-asset creation process.

In this chapter you will

- Dissect the RF-9 sketch and consider texturing possibilities.
- Receive an overview of what texturing techniques you'll be employing.
- Link 3D Studio Max, DeepUV, Deep Paint 3D, and Photoshop to create a fluent texturing operation.
- Use Deep Paint 3D to assist your 3D texturing in conjunction with Photoshop.
- Texture the RF-9 using advanced texturing techniques.

In this chapter, you'll use Lars' sketch of the slogre's weapon, the RF-9 Plasma Gun, in combination with the 3D mesh you created in Chapter 3, "Modeling the RF-9 Plasma Gun with trueSpace 6," to develop a nice, futuristic skin texture for the weapon. Figure 11.2 shows the completed texture applied to the weapon.

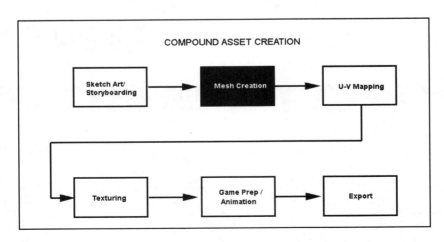

Figure 11.1

This stage in the compound asset–creation process.

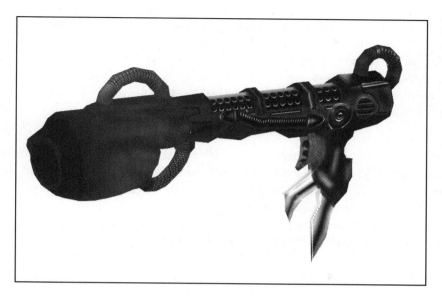

Figure 11.2 *The texture you'll be making in this chapter, applied to the RF-9.*

Identifying the RF-9

In Chapter 3, you created the RF-9 using trueSpace 6. As you went along, I briefly explained what certain sections of the gun were and gave a quick explanation of the function of that particular part of the weapon. I'm going to re-list them here, but go into further detail to give you an idea where my thinking goes for texturing that part. Figure 11.3 shows Lars's sketch again, labeled numerically.

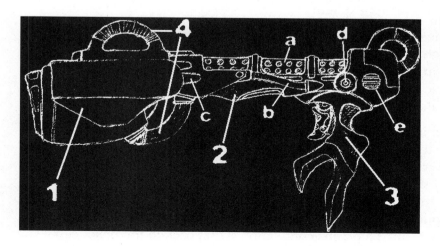

Figure 11.3 *The RF-9 sketch and its various parts.*

The overall theme is that of a futuristic, other-world weapon that the huge slogre character will be wielding against his enemies. I want the weapon to look purposeful and weathered, but made from materials that are familiar to our own planet. The shape alone is enough to sell anyone on the fact that it's from some sort of sci-fi saga, but the texture will authenticate it even further. By knowing a bit more about the portions of the weapon, you'll be able to envision your own texturing process more easily.

1. **Muzzle.** This is the resonating chamber, where the charged energy pellet enters a plasma-injection chamber and gets superheated in a fraction of a millisecond, before it gets on its way to removing a nearby targeted object from existence. This is a large, smooth area but has a metal support plate welded to the lower half to support the upper cylinders. Because you didn't model that, you'll add that detail in as a faux finish. Notice that the front of the muzzle steps down and ends up with a flashing with vent holes. You'll put in shaded/beveled areas to represent them nicely. Overall, the muzzle obtains the highest concentration of energy compared to the rest of the weapon, and therefore should exhibit more signs of heat exhaustion and wear and tear.

2. **Barrel.** The barrel is the acceleration chamber for the charged energy pellet. See the circular device at the back of the chamber, just above the grip and trigger? That's the removable pellet clip, holding up to 100 rounds of static energy pulse modules that, when activated by the trigger, bolt forward and begin expanding along the length of the barrel. Once it hits the resonating chamber (muzzle), it gets superheated with plasma, after which all hell breaks loose, literally, from the end. There are several key points about the barrel I want to further explain:

   a. This is the cooling jacket of the inner barrel. That is, essentially there are two barrels, one inside the other, which you'll simulate in Photoshop (see the sections on rendering pipes, wires, rivets, and screws in Chapter 8, "Inorganic Texture Tutorials with Photoshop"). By knocking out an array of holes along the outer barrel, you can achieve that cool style.

   b. This is an insulating cable jacket that guides processing and timing wires from the trigger to the resonating chamber. Essentially, when the slogre pulls the trigger, the charged energy pellet is released, and instantaneously a signal is sent from the trigger through the wires in this cable jacket to the area just behind the resonating chamber to release a plasma concentration. There is a cable jacket for each side of the RF-9—the other side returns a plasma-completion signal back to the pellet clip, indicating that the cycle is complete and that the clip is allowed to turn, electronically, to prepare the next pellet.

Because you didn't make any mesh modifications to make way for these cable jackets, you'll have to fake them. Making that flexible hose-like pattern in Photoshop, however, is a pain, so I'm going to create a hose model in trueSpace, render it, and apply the rendering as a 2D image within the texture space.

c.   These are metal braces that further fasten the muzzle to the barrel. You didn't model these either, so some clever beveling will give it a 3D look.

d.   This is the pellet clip—it sticks out on only one side, so when the slogre expends the clip, it ejects and he slaps in a new one. No big texturing deal here. You'll use some Photoshop bevels to make it look raised.

e.   This is the vent hole for the energy cell located directly behind it that powers the entire weapon. The cell is very heavy, in the ballpark of 20 pounds, but the slogre's overpowering arm is quite capable of hoisting the RF-9 upward. There is an identical vent on the other side.

3.   **Grip.** The slogre's hand is huge, and has 10-inch long nails for slashing enemies. Such bulk, however, hinders his dexterity, which is why the grip and trigger are simplified and oversized. The end of the grip is a twin blade that our lovely behemoth can use to impale the heads of unfortunate saps that get too close. Notice that the back curve is designed to fit snugly in the recess of the slogre's hand, between his thumb and index finger. There is a slightly organic pattern to this area too, with knurled hash marks that act as anti-slip areas. The blades at the bottom are very sharp and beveled, and have that familiar shiny, polished steel look. You'll use bevels and gradients to simulate them.

4.   **Hoops and hose.** These donut-like appendages give the RF-9 its futuristic, *Mad Max* look. The top two hoops are meant for big, thick leather straps or a harness, while the hose beneath the gun vents power toward the muzzle's resonating chamber at the exact moment the energy pellet enters it. The top hoops are wrapped in dark leather, but are otherwise a dull, flat-colored metal. The hose attaching the barrel to the muzzle is a dull steel mesh (I have a picture in my mind of that braided metal hose used in high-tech machinery).

You might say that I'm going a little overboard with detailing the weapon. This is a good idea, however, if you want to make your models look believable. If you can provide a logical explanation of feature parts of an object, then envisioning their textures will come much more easily. Besides, making up all this nonsense is a blast—and you might have to, eventually, for cover art or game manuals!

Thoughts on Texturing

Some of my other texture ideas for the RF-9 come from the world of movies. Of course, you can't go wrong with any of the *Mad Max* movies; they contain nothing *but* post-holocaustic weapons and machinery pieced together in an awkward yet futuristic fashion. The materials were rusty, dusty, and generally roadster-like. More favorites for great texture ideas are all the *Alien* movies, particularly the third one, in which Ripley winds up on a penal colony. The set for that movie must've been wonderful but exhausting to create, because the entire atmosphere was dungy, corroded, dismal, and generally not pleasant. I could easily imagine finding the RF-9 neglected in a pile of rubbish in the scrap-metal heaps near the incinerators. The great thing about the *Alien* series was the concept art—extraordinarily eerie, organic shapes that made much of the non-living materials look alive. The RF-9 has some of those organic curves to it, particularly with the muzzle and grip.

Texturing Techniques You'll Use

There's a bit of freehand work that needs to be done here and there to make the texture look more believable. I'm assuming, however, that you don't have much traditional artistic ability (as I don't), and will therefore try to employ techniques that are somewhat automated. Most of the techniques I'll be using to complete the RF-9's texture will consist of

- Filters, for generating base textures
- Styles, for occasional beveling and drop shadowing
- Compositing a 3D trueSpace rendering, for the insulating cable jackets on the sides
- Reference painting, using Deep Paint 3D to help with texture alignments
- Airbrushing, dodging, and burning, for finalizing and touch-up

As you can see, much of what you'll do will require only a modest amount of hand-eye coordination, so there's no need to panic if you stink at painting!

TIP

This chapter consists of images created with lots of color, but this book is printed primarily in black and white. To ensure you get a good feel for the colors I'm using, make sure you refer to the color figures I've saved for you in the Chaper 11 Data section on the CD-ROM.

Texturing the RF-9

As in the tutorials where you built the RF-9's mesh and unwrapped the U-Vs, I'll break the texturing process into sections dictated by the weapon's parts. By all means, texture this thing however you want; I just want you to have the option of being able to look over someone else's shoulder and get other ideas!

Step 1: Linking the U-V Map to Deep Paint 3D and Photoshop

The U-V and texturing portions of this project are closely related and, in this case, rely on four separate programs all inter-linked with one another, as shown in Figure 11.4. With enough system memory, you can efficiently work with all these programs open, and bounce back and forth between them as you model, U-V, and texture.

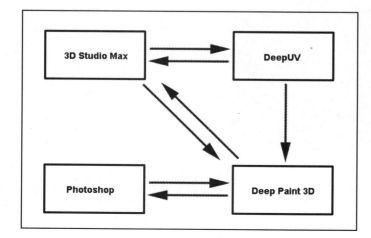

Figure 11.4 *The dynamic link and work structure between the U-V and texturing programs you'll be using.*

In Chapter 5, you installed the demo version of DeepUV (if you didn't already have that program) as well as the necessary Max plug-ins. For the remainder of this chapter, you'll also use Deep Paint 3D, also from Right Hemisphere, the demo of which is located on the CD-ROM. Install that now (if you don't already have it), as well as the necessary plug-ins for both Max and Photoshop. If you need additional help with the installation of the Deep Paint 3D demo, visit http://www.righthemisphere.com/support.

Once everything's installed, the first thing you need to do is bounce your U-V map from Max (or DeepUV) over to Deep Paint 3D. (Mind you, this is only one way to do this kind of work; you could just as easily work between 3D Studio Max and Photoshop. I simply want to expose you to a great work structure that many other game artists employ.) Start by opening up your U-V-mapped RF-9 in 3D Studio Max. This should be the file you saved in Chapter 5 (if you don't have it, open the file **RF9_mapped.max**, located in the Chapter 11 Data section on the CD-ROM). Then do the following:

1. With the U-V mapped version of the RF-9 loaded in 3D Studio, click on the Utilities tab at the top-right of the screen.

2. Click on the Right Hemisphere button to expand the list. This should include two sections, one for DeepUV and one for Deep Paint 3D.

3. Make sure your RF-9 model is selected, and click the Paint Selection button in the Right Hemisphere utility panel (see Figure 11.5). This will fire up Deep Paint 3D and begin the U-V-importing procedure.

> **NOTE**
>
> Even though DeepUV is a linked part of the scheme in Figure 11.8, you'll be skipping it for now. You can always bring your model into DeepUV and click File, Export, Paint with Deep Paint 3D; that way, you can make U-V adjustments, if necessary, while you work.

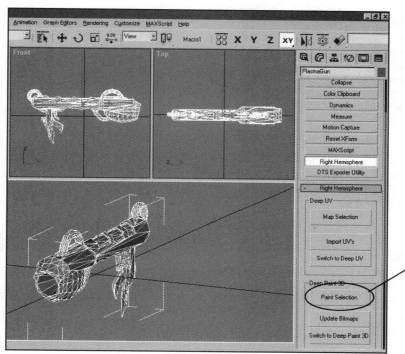

Figure 11.5 *Click on the Paint Selection button in the Right Hemisphere section of the Utilities panel.*

The Paint Selection button

> **NOTE**
>
> You may have to manually start Deep Paint 3D (and/or DeepUV if you want that open as well) if you get a Couldn't Connect error when trying to paint the selection. If you still can't link Max with Deep Paint, consult Right Hemisphere's technical support at http://www.righthemisphere.com/support.

4. A Material Import screen pops up (see Figure 11.6); in it, Deep Paint 3D asks you what material size you want your texture to be and what channel to assign it to. The panel is broken into two sections: The top is the mesh object with U-V mapping coordinates, and the bottom is the untextured material that Max automatically assigned when you did your U-V'ing. Click the material name itself (mine is Material #2), then click the Edit/Resize button.

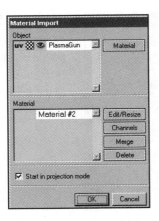

Figure 11.6 *The Material Import screen pops up, asking you about the properties of your new texture map.*

5. Change the X and Y dimensions of the texture map to 1024 each. This will make a huge texture map so you can do detailed work (you'll shrink it down later on).

6. Click OK, and then give the map a name (I called mine PlasmaGun). Click OK again.

7. Click on the Channels button.

8. The material must be placed in a shader channel so the program knows how to display it. The first item in the list is the letter "C" for "Color"; click it.

9. A small menu pops up; choose Nothing. This adds a New Blank Map entry in the list.

10. Click OK once, and then again in the Material Import screen, and your RF-9 model will load in a 3D painting screen (see Figure 11.7).

11. Your RF-9 model is loaded into Deep Paint 3D; you can now manipulate and paint it with the tools in the floating toolbox. The tools are very similar to the ones in both DeepUV and Photoshop, and are very easy to use. The great thing about Deep Paint 3D is you can actually paint directly on a model, going across U-V seams and everything! However, you need to do your detailed artwork within Photoshop. To do so, click the Export Materials to Photoshop button at the top of the screen (see Figure 11.8). This sends the current U-V map and material over to Photoshop 6 or higher (that is, if you've properly installed the plug-ins that came with the Deep Paint 3D demo). Once imported to Photoshop, you should end up with a U-V layered image, as seen in Figure 11.9.

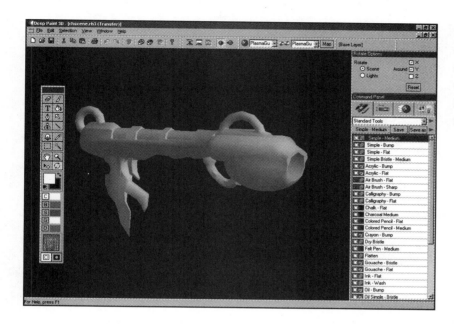

Figure 11.7 *The Deep Paint 3D painting interface. You can dynamically manipulate and paint the RF-9 here.*

Export to Photoshop

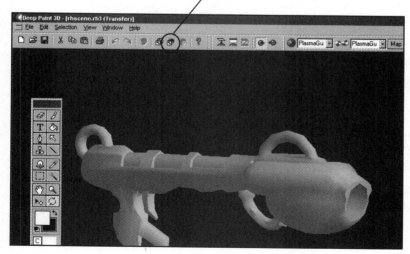

Figure 11.8 *Click the Export Materials to Photoshop button to transfer the U-V map.*

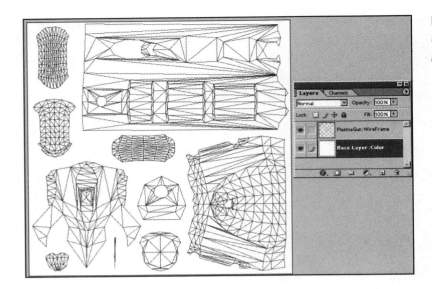

Figure 11.9 *The U-V map, imported into Photoshop.*

Now you're ready to rock-and-roll! With Photoshop linked and fired up, you'll get a new 1024×1024 canvas with two layers. (Open the Layers palette and you'll see.) The top layer represents the U-V mesh that you made in DeepUV; this is just a guide for you to paint with, and can (and will) be deleted when you're finished. Because this map is so big, you'll have to zoom into it to see the fine details. I changed the color from that default blue to black so it's easier to see.

The bottom layer of the image is the actual painting layer you'll be working on. *Make sure you don't change the name of or delete this layer!* You'll need to send this texture back over to Deep Paint 3D, and it uses this base layer (called Base Layer: Color) when sending and fetching the texture. If this layer is renamed or deleted, you'll have to start all over in Deep Paint 3D.

TIP

If you need help with Photoshop, or are otherwise new to the program, see the Photoshop tutorials on this book's CD-ROM.

Fixing U-Vs: Add a Checkerboard Map

Even though you did a careful job of unwrapping and organizing the U-Vs in DeepUV, there's still a chance that the isolated U-V portions of the texture map may be inverted (like looking in a mirror); or that texture coordinates are crossed (resulting in smearing), overlapped (causing a duplication of texture), or not properly relaxed (causing bloating or shrinking of the texture). I can almost guarantee that at least one of the aforementioned scenarios exists in your setup, but it's not a huge ordeal; it just means you have to go back to DeepUV and fix them.

One outstanding way of detecting problems before you begin the skinning process is to set up a checkerboard map. By simply filling your texture map with a small checkerboard pattern, and then applying the texture to the model, you will have a much easier time checking for errors. I like to fill the individual areas of my texture map with differently colored patterns to make a clear definition of what each of the U-V sections are. I also like to add some text to the area, which not only helps me to identify that area but will display an inverted map area as well; if one exists, the text comes out backwards.

To see what I mean, first fill the individual U-V sections of the Base Layer: Color layer on the texture map. I've saved eight checkerboard patterns for you—just load the **checkerboard.pat** file (located on the CD-ROM) in Photoshop. Then use the Lasso tool to create selections around the U-V areas, and fill the selections with the different-colored patterns using either Edit, Fill or the Paintbucket tool (Figure 11.10 shows my map). Finally, use the Type tool to position text on the separate U-V areas, or put any non-symmetrical symbol on them, so that if any particular area happens to be inverted you'll be able to tell instantly.

Next, you need to transfer the material back to Deep Paint 3D. Do this either by clicking Filter, Right Hemisphere, Material to Deep Paint 3D, or by going back to

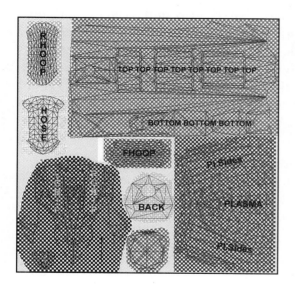

Figure 11.10 *Fill the separate U-V areas with different-colored patterns.*

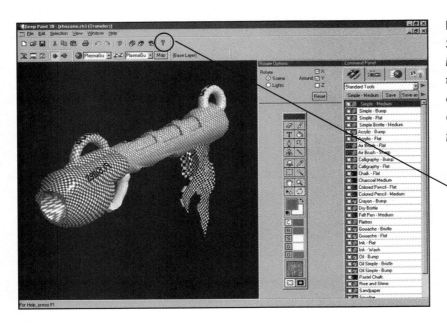

Figure 11.11

Send the checker-board material back to Deep Paint 3D, and check for signs of smearing, overlapping, or inverting.

The Fetch Material from Photoshop button

Deep Paint 3D and clicking on the Fetch the Material from Photoshop icon at the top. You might get a warning in Deep Paint saying that the operation is undoable; just click OK. Figure 11.11 shows the initial material on the model.

The checkerboard map that is applied to the model already shows that certain portions are inverted—in my case, the muzzle, barrel, grip, and trigger. That's no big deal; it just means I need to go back to DeepUV and flip them. Also, check for any signs of smearing; the most noticeable one on mine is inside of the muzzle's chamber, where you can see the checkerboard is stretched and non-uniform. This is fine for this area, because it will be filled with a cloudy dark texture, but if it were a portion of the barrel or something, the texture would smear. Because I relaxed nearly all portions of the U-V map in DeepUV, I don't see any other problems with smearing.

Notice that the text on the muzzle is inverted; this means you need to go back to DeepUV and flip them. From the beginning, I've kept DeepUV open, so it's just a matter of selecting the texture coordinates of the section that needs inverting, and clicking Edit, Transform, Flip (either Horizontal or Vertical). Figure 11.12 shows my corrected texture map.

Figure 11.12
After inverting the muzzle's texture points in DeepUV, the texture map is corrected.

If you find any areas where a different-colored checkerboard crept illegally into another section, that means the texture coordinates are overlapped or crossed. Again, go back to DeepUV, select those points, and either move them away from the area they're overlapping/crossing or relax them.

CAUTION

If you close Deep Paint 3D while it is linked to Photoshop, it will remove the texture map from Photoshop, thereby destroying your work! If you need to shut down Deep Paint 3D and continue texturing, first save the texture map in Photoshop, *then* close down Deep Paint 3D.

Step 2: Texturing the Hoops

Once you've fixed your U-V map and your material is re-imported back to Deep Paint 3D and Photoshop, you can close DeepUV. You'll be doing the texturing in Photoshop, and occasionally sending it back to Deep Paint to see how it looks, so those are the only two programs you really need to have active. The easiest part to texture on this model will be the top hoops, so you'll start there.

NOTE

If you don't have anything set up to this point and want to start fresh here, open the **plasmagun.dp3** file, located in the Chapter 11 Data section on the CD-ROM, in Deep Paint.

NOTE

I'm going to be rather general about the texturing steps in this tutorial, because nearly everything is repetitious. (Besides, I'm assuming you've already read Chapter 8, which covers the various techniques in detail.)

1. With the U-V map imported from Deep Paint 3D, open the Layers palette and click on the Base Layer: Color layer to make it active. (From now on, I'll refer to this as the *background layer.*

CAUTION

Don't delete or rename the background layer (Base Layer: Color)! Deep Paint 3D uses this layer, referring to it by name, when sending and fetching the texture map back and forth with Photoshop. You can merge layers down to it (press Ctrl+E), but if the layers are linked to it and *then* you Ctrl+E, the name will disappear.

CAUTION

If you close Deep Paint 3D while it is linked to Photoshop, it will remove the texture map from Photoshop, thereby destroying your work! If you need to shut down Deep Paint 3D in order to continue texturing, first save the texture map in Photoshop, and *then* close Deep Paint 3D.

2. Choose Image, Image Size and change the Resolution field from 72 to 1024. This will make your artwork very detailed, as well as affecting the print resolution.

3. Now let's fill the background layer with a decent base texture. First, apply the Clouds filter.

4. Apply the Difference Clouds filter.

5. Apply the Noise filter, about 10% Monochromatic.

6. Choose Filter, Stylize, Emboss.

7. Alter the color of the new texture to a dark green by choosing Image, Adjust, Variations.

8. The U-V layer on top is difficult to see; just Ctrl+click that layer to load its selection, and fill it with white (Alt+Backspace). Figure 11.13 shows my base texture.

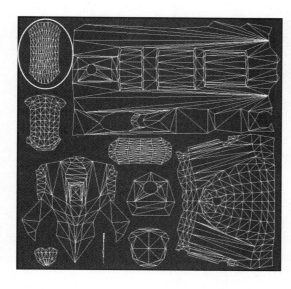

Figure 11.13
The dark-green base texture for the plasma gun.

9. In Figure 11.13, I've circled the rear hoop, where you'll start. If you look back to Lars' sketch of the RF-9 (or open **RF-9 Plasma Gun.jpg** on the CD-ROM), you'll see that a sort of leather or twine has been wrapped around the hoops. To render this detail, start a new layer, then create a single strip of the twine using the Rectangular Marquee tool (see Figure 11.14).

10. Press Q to enter Quick Mask Mode.

11. Fray the edges of the rectangle by choosing Filter, Brush Strokes, Sprayed Strokes (see Figure 11.15).

12. Press Q again to exit Quick Mask mode.

13. Fill the selection with the Clouds filter, using tan and brown colors, like hex#594909 and hex# 8C6807.

14. Apply the Noise filter, about 10% (see Figure 11.16).

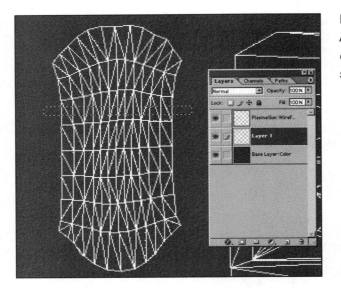

Figure 11.14
Arranging the orthogonal views on the screen.

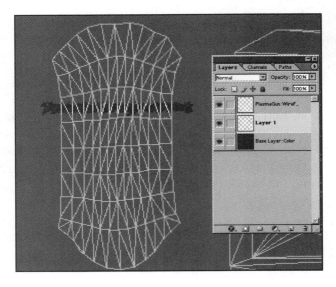

Figure 11.15
Enter Quick Mask Mode and apply the Sprayed Strokes filter.

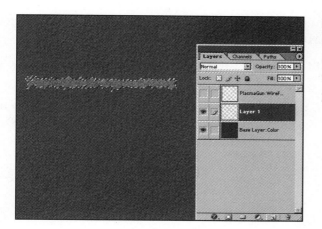

Figure 11.16 *Fill the selection with a dark tan mix using the Clouds and Noise filters.*

15. Press Ctrl+D to deselect the selection.

16. Apply an inner bevel to the active layer, with a shading angle of roughly 90 degrees. (I also played around with the different light contours to get more lines going through my little rectangular, frayed strip.)

17. Duplicate the strip's layer and position the copy beneath the first. Repeat this until you've covered two-thirds of the hoop, as I have done in Figure 11.17.

TIP

With all of the styles you'll apply throughout this tutorial, make sure you understand the orientation of the object in question on the U-V map, and how the style's lighting direction should be. In this case, the hoop is vertical, so the Shading Angle setting in the style dialog box should point to around 90 degrees.

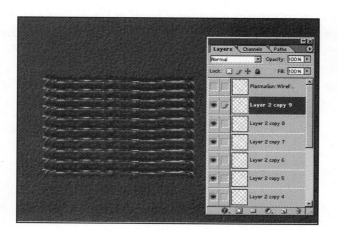

Figure 11.17 *Bevel the strip, and duplicate it over and over to create the twine-like wrapping.*

18. Merge each layer (except the background layer) until only two layers remain: the background layer and the layer resulting from the merged layers.

19. Make a selection around the hoop's background texture, then adjust the levels to darken it.

20. Use the Dodge and Burn tools to highlight the center of the hoop (which represents the top) and darken the edges, respectively (see Figure 11.18).

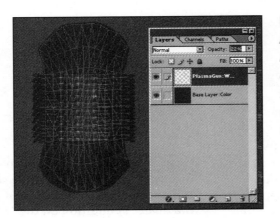

Figure 11.18
Merge all the strips into a single layer, darken the hoop's background texture, and adjust highlights and shadows.

21. Merge the frayed-strip layer to the background layer—just make sure the background layer's name doesn't change (it should still be Base Layer: Color).

22. Repeat steps 9–20 for the other hoop on the map, or copy and paste the work you did for the first hoop.

23. When satisfied with your hoops, and when all of your new work is merged onto the background layer, transfer the material back to Deep Paint 3D so you can see what it looks like. To do so, switch to Deep Paint and click the Fetch Material from Photoshop button at the top of the screen (click OK when it warns you that the operation is not undo-able). You should end up with something like the image shown in Figure 11.19.

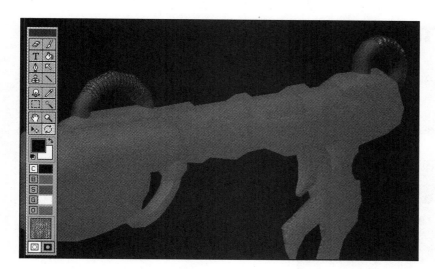

Figure 11.19

Complete the same procedure for the second hoop, then transfer your material over to Deep Paint 3D.

Once your material is properly imported back to Deep Paint, you might want to do a bit of housekeeping. For one, you'll notice that the model is very shiny—this is due to the default lighting and material channel setup. To resolve this problem, click the Settings (F8) tab in the Command Panel; the Lighting section enables you to adjust the Ambience and Spot lights so you can see your material a bit more naturally. (I reduced the Spot light and increased the Ambience, which tones things down significantly.)

NOTE

Don't freak out if your material doesn't look perfect in Deep Paint. This program is not meant for keen rendering; its purpose is to allow you to dynamically paint right onto your model. In general, you work on your material in Photoshop, and occasionally update it to Deep Paint to get an idea of how it is starting to look. If you have problems with a certain area, Deep Paint can help out by allowing you to do the work directly on the model.

Step 3: Texturing the Bottom Hose

Next on the hit list is the hose located underneath the RF-9. I think of this as a loose length of tubing with a metal mesh jacket surrounding it; similar hoses can be found in scientific equipment and even in air-conditioning units. To generate the effect I want, I'm simply going to create a hatch-like pattern and apply a bevel to it. Figure 11.20 shows the U-Vs for the hose on the texture map.

Figure 11.20 *The U-V location of the hose object.*

1. Start a new layer above the background layer.

2. To create a quick but effective mesh, use the Line tool with a weight of about 4 pixels. In Figure 11.21, I drew a number of gray parallel lines (with Photoshop's Snap and Grid features enabled), holding down the Shift key while drawing. (You don't have to be too precise because these will all be a jumble of lines in a moment.)

TIP

Set the Opacity of the U-V layer down to 20% so you can see the background layer clearly, as well as a ghosted image of the U-V map.

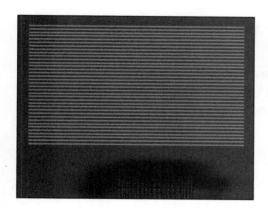

Figure 11.21
Draw a few dozen gray parallel lines using the Line tool.

3. Copy the layer you just made and rotate the copy 90 degrees to form a mesh.

4. Make a third copy, rotate it 45 degrees, and merge the three layers to complete the dense mesh.

5. When all three layers are aligned, scale and crop the mesh to cover the area of the hose U-V (see Figure 11.22).

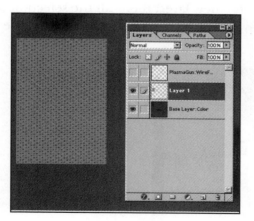

Figure 11.22
Make two copies of the line's layer, and rotate and position them so a mesh is formed.

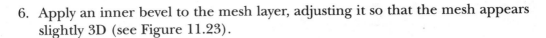

6. Apply an inner bevel to the mesh layer, adjusting it so that the mesh appears slightly 3D (see Figure 11.23).

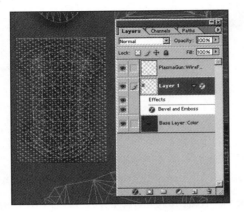

Figure 11.23

Apply an inner bevel to the mesh layer.

7. The top and bottom of the hose U-V represents the areas where the hose bolts onto the weapon. Because the model is detailed in this area, you don't have to do too much to simulate the nuts that fasten it. Simply make a Lasso selection around the ends and begin a new layer; then, fill the selection with a Clouds filter (black and dark gray), and apply another inner bevel (see Figure 11.24).

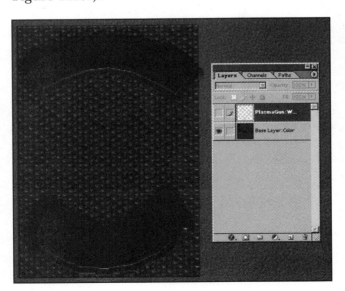

Figure 11.24

Create and fill selections at the two ends, and apply another inner bevel.

8. Merge the hose components (but not the background layer) into a single layer, and adjust the levels so that the layer is darkened. (This area is attached to the muzzle of the gun, so it should look a bit charred.

9. Merge the mesh to the background layer, and transfer your work back to Deep Paint. Figure 11.25 shows my results.

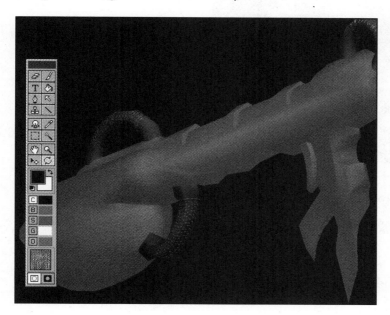

Figure 11.25

The completed hose mesh in action

Step 4: Texturing the Grip and Trigger

Now for the grip portion of your weapon. This should be cool, because there will be a sharp transition (no pun intended) where the grip becomes a twin blade. I'll employ the Gradient tool for the blades, and polish them off with an inner bevel to give them that sharp-edged look.

Figure 11.26 shows the location of the U-Vs for this object. Looking at the U-V map for the grip, you can see that the left and right sides have been joined at the back edges; that is, you're essentially looking at the weapon from behind. The very front portions of the blades are located just below and to the right of the U-V assembly (there's just a small sliver). The trigger itself is unfolded at the bottom left.

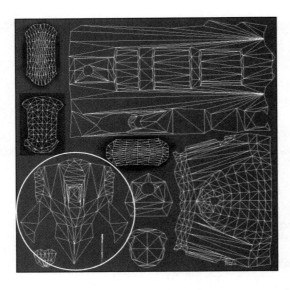

Figure 11.26 *The U-V location of the hose object.*

1. Start a new layer.

2. Create a Polygonal Lasso selection around the top-half of one side of the blade.

3. Use the Gradient tool to fill this selection, with the tool's Options set to Reflected Gradient (See Figure 11.27). I used black and light gray as my colors for this operation.

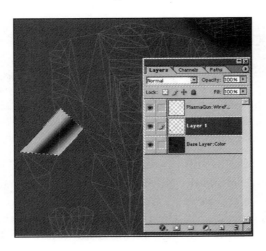

Figure 11.27
Create a polygonal selection around the top-half of one blade and fill it with a gradient.

4. Repeat steps 2–3 for the bottom-half of the blade.

5. The completed gradient for the blade should be on its own layer. Apply an inner-bevel style to it, with the Chisel Hard option set, just enough so the edges bevel and make the blade look sharp (see Figure 11.28).

NOTE

The gradient is applied to the blade in two separate sections because the blade is angled, and a single gradient wouldn't look quite right.

Figure 11.28
Apply a hard-chiseled inner bevel to the gradient layer.

6. Repeat steps 1–5 for the other portions of the U-V that represent the blade.

7. Merge the blade layers with the background layer (see Figure 11.29).

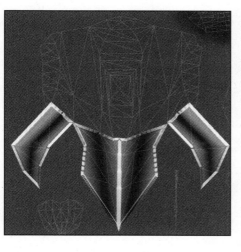

Figure 11.29
Repeat the gradient-beveling procedure for the rest of the blades, and merge them with the background layer.

8. Use the Polygonal Lasso tool to select the rest of the grip area, and adjust the levels to darken it, as shown in Figure 11.30. (Most of the U-V map will be selectively darkened this way as you go.)

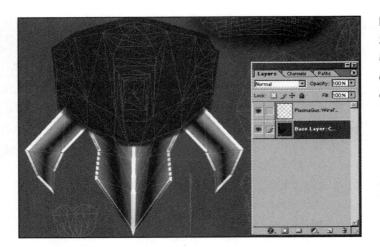

Figure 11.30

Select the rest of the U-Vs for the grip and adjust the levels to darken it.

9. If you look at Lars' drawing of the plasma gun (see the RF-9 Plasma Gun.jpg file), you'll notice that the rear and front of the grip are knurled, as if an anti-slip feature has been installed (typical of many real weapons). To mimic this, first create a selection around the area

10. Adjust the levels so the area is very dark.

11. Choose Filter, Brush Strokes, Crosshatch.

12. Copy the selection to a new layer.

13. Apply a downward inner bevel, and adjust the lighting contour so it glosses uniquely (see Figure 11.31).

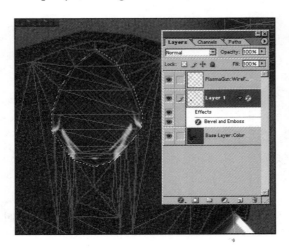

Figure 11.31

Create a knurled area at the back of the grip with the Crosshatch filter.

14. Repeat steps 9–13 for the outer U-V areas that represent the knurled front portion of the grip, but omit the inner bevel (because the area is somewhat obstructed by the trigger). Figure 11.32 shows my results.

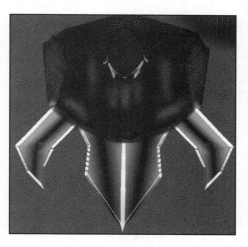

Figure 11.32 *Knurl the front portion of the grip, and adjust the image with the Dodge and Burn tools.*

15. Merge the grip layers with the background layer.

16. Use the Burn and Dodge tool to darken much of the grip's area and to highlight the back spine a bit.

17. Now for the front of the blade. Select it, and fill it with a light-gray Clouds mix (I sampled the colors for this mix from the edge of the gradient in the blade area).

18. Select the trigger, fill it with another gray Clouds mix, and add some noise (see Figure 11.33).

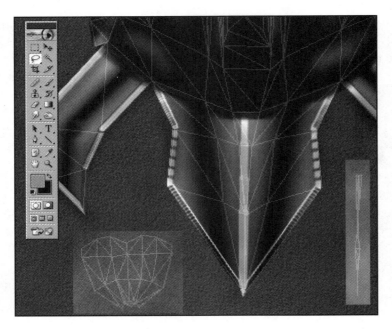

Figure 11.33
Select the front blade and trigger U-V's, and apply a light gray Clouds mix.

19. To finish off the trigger, create three circular selections.

20. Fill each selection with a very dark gray.

21. Apply an inner bevel to each selection. This will make the trigger look like it has finger indentations, or possibly punched holes (see Figure 11.34).

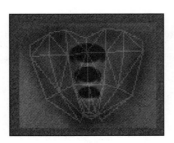

Figure 11.34 *Add several small circular patterns and apply an Inner Bevel style to them.*

You're finished with the grip area! Transfer your work back to Deep Paint to see how things look (see Figure 11.35). (This stuff will look even better when it's imported back to 3D Studio Max.)

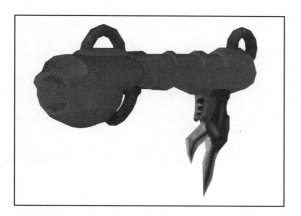

Figure 11.35 *The completed grip and trigger texture.*

Step 5: Texturing the Barrel

The area circled in Figure 11.36 is what you'll tackle now. (This is the most complex texturing portion of the weapon, but ironically is the easiest to model.) This area shows the sides and top of the barrel as one continuous piece, with the top in the center, and the sides on, er, each side. It'll make your life much easier to create one half of the texture, then copy and flip it to the other side.

NOTE

Low-mesh detail generally indicates an area that needs a lot of attention when texturing, while high-mesh detail means that the mesh itself will take care of the intricate details.

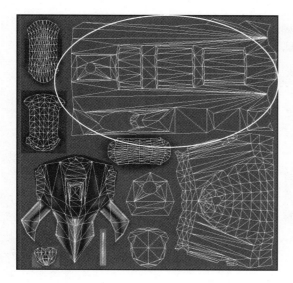

Figure 11.36 *Time to texture the barrel's U-Vs.*

1. Create a new layer above the background layer.

2. Using the Polygonal Lasso tool, create three selections around the area on the U-V map that represents the cooling-jacket portion of the barrel.

3. Fill the selection with a reflected gradient composed of black and light gray (see Figure 11.37). This will give

> **NOTE**
>
> Upon close inspection of the U-V map, you'll notice a small border encompassing each section. Be sure not to include those areas, because they represent the walls around the jacket.

the jacket a realistic pipe look. (See the section "Pipes, Wires, Rivets, and Screws" in Chapter 8 for more information on creating pipes of this nature.)

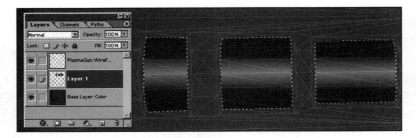

Figure 11.37
Select and fill the cooling jacket of the barrel with a reflected gradient.

4. To create the cooling holes in the jacket, begin by creating a circular selection.

5. Copy the selection to a new layer.

6. Apply an inner bevel to the selection, making sure the style's lighting direction comes from above (90 degrees). Figure 11.38 shows my results.

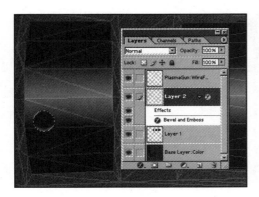

Figure 11.38
Create cooling holes by copying circular selections and beveling them.

7. Copy the hole over and over across the bottom half of the U-V map.

8. When satisfied, merge them all into one layer.

9. Copy the newly merged layer, and choose Edit, Transform, Flip Vertical.

10. Move the copied layer into place (see Figure 11.39). This process reverses the bevel directions for the holes so that both sides contain the proper perspective. If you don't flip it this way, the bevels on the other side will appear inverted, as though there are raised cylinders sticking out of the jacket. Figure 11.40 shows the results on the model itself.

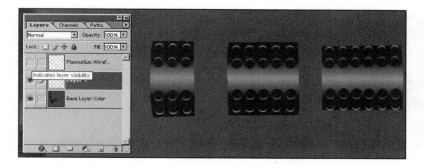

Figure 11.39
Copy the hole pattern across the entire jacket, and then flip a copy of the bottom half to the top half.

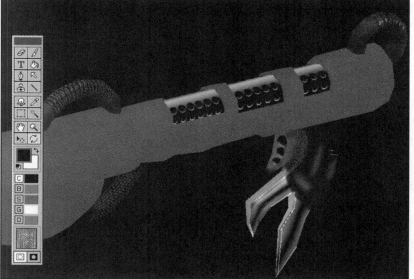

Figure 11.40 *The results of the finished cooling jacket.*

11. Moving to the back of the barrel where the rear hoop meets, make a rectangular selection.

12. Copy the selection to a new layer.

13. Apply an inner-bevel style. The light source should come from the front now, about zero degrees.

14. Use the Levels command to darken the area (see Figure 11.41).

Figure 11.41
Select, bevel, and darken the area where the hoop meets the barrel.

15. In the RF-9 Plasma Gun.jpg sketch, the rear of the weapon has a round vent hole, which you'll create next. To begin, create a circular selection.

16. Use the Rectangular Marquee tool, while holding down the Alt key, to subtract sections to make that slotted-vent look (see Figure 11.42).

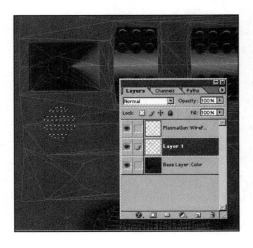

Figure 11.42
Create the vent pattern using both the Elliptical and Rectangular marquee tools.

17. Make a copy of the background within this selection, and apply an outer bevel to the vent's layer.

18. Adjust the levels to darken it. Then, copy the vent and flip the copy over to the other side (see Figure 11.43).

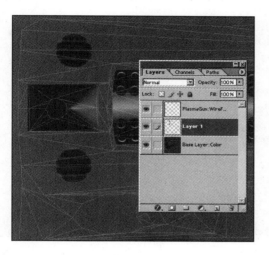

Figure 11.43
Finish off the vent with an outer bevel. Make a copy of the vent and flip it over to the other side.

19. The sketch of the weapon indicates a beveled detail in the rear that curves around the vent hole. To create this effect, make that type of selection using one of the Lasso tools.

20. Copy the background area in this selection, and apply an outer bevel to it.

21. Adjust the levels to darken the selection.

22. Flip the pattern to the other side (see Figure 11.44).

NOTE

With each of these beveling operations, make sure the lighting direction is correct, or your bevels will look awkward.

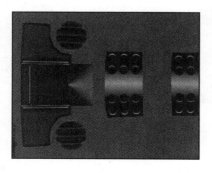

Figure 11.44
Create a beveled pattern in the rear that matches the sketch.

23. In the sketch, along the axis are two rounded indentations that exist just below the lip of the barrel, beneath the cooling jacket. To generate this effect, create selections on the background layer, and then round them using an Alpha channel (this technique is demonstrated in Chapters 8, 9, "Advanced Texturing Examples," and 10, "Organic Texture Tutorials with Photoshop").

24. Fill the selections with a dark Clouds mix, and apply an inner bevel (see Figure 11.45).

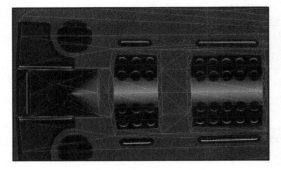

Figure 11.45
Create the rounded indentations along the barrel near the top edges.

25. Now for the ammunition clip—that circular thing near the rear of the gun, just in front of the vent. As in Figure 11.46, start with a circular copy of the background layer and bevel it.

Figure 11.46
Start the ammunition clip with a beveled circle.

26. Apply two more bevels to smaller circular selections on top of the ones you just created, and adjust the levels to darken them. (The bevels are a combination of both inner and outer styles, and a contour thrown in for fun.) Figure 11.47 shows the results.

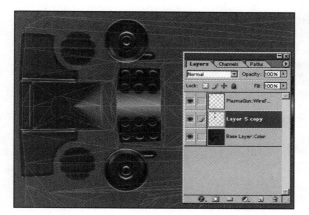

Figure 11.47

Finish the clip using a few more bevels applied to smaller selections.

You're nearly finished with the barrel portion of the weapon, but I want to isolate the cable-jacket portion because you'll be using a flattened 3D image of the jacket I created in trueSpace. (The cable jacket is that hose-like structure stemming from the side of the barrel, just in front of the ammunition clip, and running up to the front.)

1. Using whatever selection technique you prefer, create the exit protrusion. (I used the Polygonal Lasso tool.)

2. Round the edges using the blur-levels technique in an Alpha channel (see Figure 11.48).

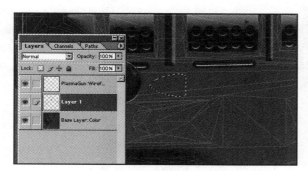

Figure 11.48

Create a selection for the area where the cable jacket begins.

3. With the selection in place, make a copy of the background layer within it.

4. Apply an inner bevel to this new layer to raise the object and make the top look rounded. (You can further enhance this rounded feature by burning the sides and dodging the top.)

5. Chop off the front of it and burn a bit just ahead of the object to give it more depth (see Figure 11.49).

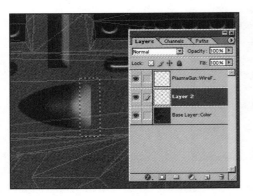

Figure 11.49
Bevel the selection to raise the surface, and use the Dodge and Burn tools to further augment the effect.

6. Lars' sketch shows that the front portion of the barrel is connected to the muzzle with a large, angled plate. Use the Polygonal Lasso tool to create and bevel a selection in this shape.

7. Copy the cable jacket's end object, which you created in the previous steps.

8. Flip the end object horizontally, and move it into position as I have in Figure 11.50. The cable jacket itself will now run between these two points.

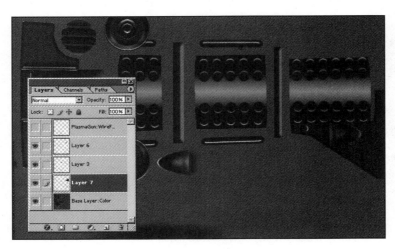

Figure 11.50
Create a polygonal shape for the front portion of the barrel, and place a copy of the cable jacket's end object there.

9. Now for the jacket itself. Open the file **hose.tif** (Figure 11.51), found on the CD-ROM.

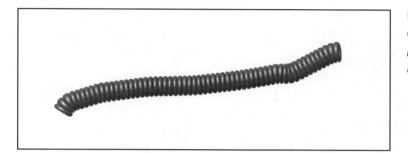

Figure 11.51
*Open the **hose.tif** image on the CD-ROM.*

> **NOTE**
>
> The file hose.tif contains a hose-shaped object that I created in trueSpace, whose SCN file is also on the CD-ROM. All I did was glue a bunch of torus primitives together and apply a bones structure through it so I could deform it as one piece. Then it was just a matter of rendering the object in a top orthogonal view.

10. Using the Magic Wand tool, with a Tolerance setting of 0 and the Contiguous option checked, click once in the white area of the hose.tif image. This will select all white that is placed contiguously in the image.

11. Choose Select, Inverse. Your hose object will be selected at this point.

12. Click Edit, Copy, and paste the selected area into your texture map.

13. Using the Free Transform tool (Ctrl+T), resize and move the hose into position. Figure 11.52 shows this operation in action.

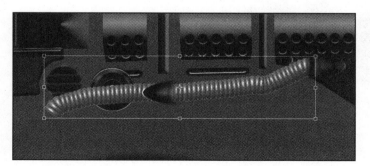

Figure 11.52
Make a copy of the hose object, paste it, and resize it in the texture map.

14. Choose Image, Adjust, Variations to change the color of the hose, and adjust the levels to suit. In Figure 11.53, I also added a drop shadow to give it some depth before copying the entire structure to the other side of the weapon.

Figure 11.53
Adjust the color and levels of the hose, and apply a drop shadow.

That's about it for this portion of the image—just merge everything with the background layer, and transfer it to Deep Paint, as shown in Figure 11.54. (The light green that sticks out like a sore thumb will be adjusted at the end.)

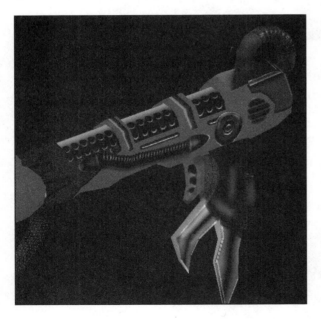

Figure 11.54
A preview of the completed barrel portion of the plasma gun.

Step 6: Texturing the Muzzle

This area is fairly easy to texture, especially since it's supposed to be very charred, which makes hand-painted details difficult to see. Therefore, a simple gradient overlay will suffice. The highlight of this part will be the gradient inside of the muzzle, which will give it an eerie heat glow. Figure 11.55 shows the front end of the muzzle, which you'll work on first.

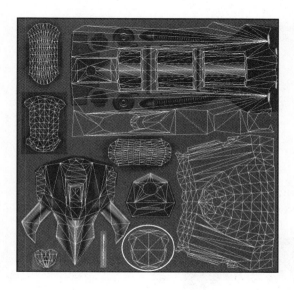

Figure 11.55
The front portion of the muzzle's U-V map.

1. Create a selection around the entire muzzle's end.

2. Adjust the levels to darken the selection.

3. Use the Polygonal Lasso tool to follow the hexagonal shape indicated by the U-V lines; this represents the *inside* of the muzzle.

4. Using a black foreground color and a deep red background color, fill the selection with a radial gradient (see Figure 11.56).

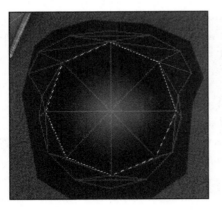

Figure 11.56
Fill the inside of the front portion of the muzzle's U-V with a black-to-red Radial Gradient.

5. For the muzzle itself, create a polygonal selection around it and fill it with a black-to-gray linear gradient. (Make sure this is done on a new layer.)

6. When the gradient is in place, change the layer's mode from Normal to Overlay (see Figure 11.57). This gives the weapon a nice charred look.

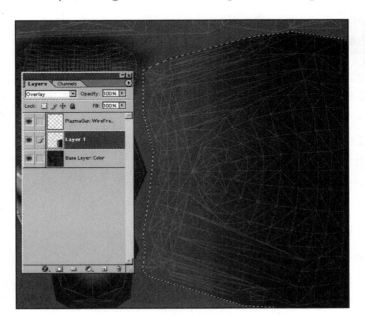

Figure 11.57
Create and fill a selection around the muzzle with a dark linear gradient. Set this layer to Overlay so the background texture seeps through.

That's about it for the muzzle; now you can go over the entire texture map and darken those nasty green areas that are burning a hole in my eye. I also made several polygonal selections and adjusted the levels, and used the Burn and Dodge tools to lightly adjust areas that needed more depth and height, respectively. The rear of the barrel was done, as usual, with a couple of bevels. Figure 11.58 shows the entire, somewhat-completed texture map.

NOTE

When you get really good at texturing, you'll all but eliminate bevels and drop shadows, and instead stick to freehand texturing. With the aid of Photoshop's styles and filters, however, you'll quickly get used to what certain areas of the texture should look like; you'll start doing it all by hand in no time!

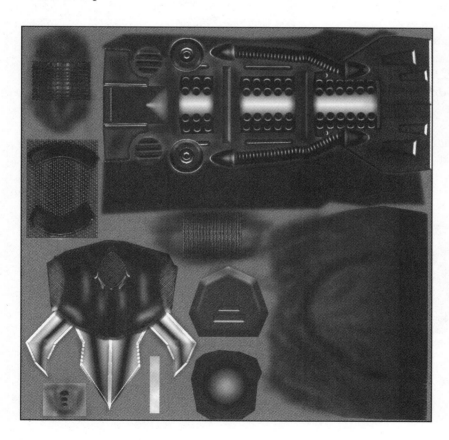

Figure 11.58 *The somewhat-completed texture map. This texture could use more finesse, but I don't want to write an entire book on it!*

Preparing the Map for 3D Studio Max

When you finish your texture, you need to resize it so the game engine can handle it. For *Torque*, it needs to be 512×512 pixels or smaller, and saved as a PNG file. After the file is saved, you can close Deep Paint and load the texture in Max; see Chapter 13, "Making the RF-9 Plasma Gun Game-Ready with 3D Studio Max," for details on adding the skin and preparing the RF-9 for use in the *Torque* (as well as *Half-Life* and *Unreal*) engine.

To save the texture properly, do the following:

> **NOTE**
>
> Other game engines, such as *HL* and *Unreal*, require the maps to be saved as palettized **BMP** and **PCX** files.

1. Save the entire image file in Photoshop as is, with the U-V layer on top and a single, merged background layer on the bottom, as a PSD file. That way, you can modify it later if need be.

2. Delete the U-V layer entirely.

3. Choose Image, Image Size, and set the dimensions to 512×512 pixels, with a resolution of 512. (Also, set the Resampling to Bilinear to avoid creating a border around the image.)

> **NOTE**
>
> Most games these days use 256×256 bitmaps, but I hate that. We're at the end of those days, and I demand higher resolutions!

4. With the texture map properly resized, choose File, Save As, and save the image as a PNG file. (The PNG file format is one of the best formats you can use for games.) Figure 11.59 shows the completed texture on the model in 3D Studio.

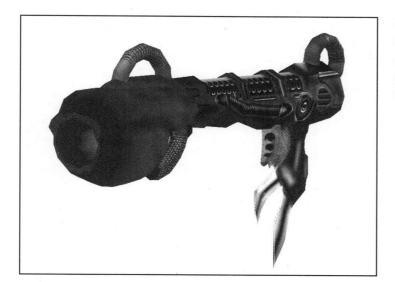

Figure 11.59 *The completed texture map applied to the plasma gun in 3D Studio Max.*

Summary

Texturing a 3D model is accomplished using the U-V map for the model as a painting guide. In this chapter you took the modified U-V map from DeepUV, sent it over to Deep Paint 3D and Photoshop, and checked the weapon's U-V structure using checkerboard map to reflect tell-tale signs of smearing, inverting, and/or overlapping. The clever use of filters and beveling techniques made for a great futuristic weapon texture; all the while you had Deep Paint 3D as an aid in seeing the texture come to life on your model.

CHAPTER 12

Skinning the Slogre with Deep Paint 3D and Photoshop

ontinuing with the compound asset–design path, this chapter picks up where
you left off in Chapter 6, "U-V Mapping the Slogre with DeepUV" (see Figure
12.1). Here, you'll use your newly developed U-V texture map to texture the slogre
in both Deep Paint 3D and Photoshop.

In this chapter, you'll use Lars' sketch of the slogre in combination with the 3D
mesh you created in Chapter 4, "Modeling the Slogre Character with trueSpace 6,"
to develop an eerie, otherworld-style skin texture for the character. Figure 12.2
shows the completed texture applied to the slogre.

In this chapter, you will

- Dissect the slogre sketch and consider texturing possibilities.
- Receive an overview of what texturing techniques you'll be employing.
- Link 3D Studio Max, DeepUV, Deep Paint 3D, and Photoshop to create a
  fluid texturing operation.
- Use Deep Paint 3D to assist your 3D texturing in conjunction with
  Photoshop.
- Texture the slogre using advanced texturing techniques.

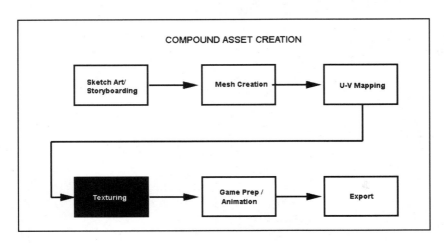

Figure 12.1
This stage in the compound asset–creation process.

Figure 12.2
The texture you'll be making in this chapter, applied to the slogre.

Identifying the Slogre's Body

Before you start tossing paint onto your texture canvas, let me point out highlight areas of the slogre's body, just as I did with his RF-9, so that you have a somewhat logical plan. Figure 12.3 maps out the areas I'm about to discuss.

1. **Face/tusks.** The sketch in Figure 12.3 shows the slogre as having large, pursed lips that cover jagged teeth; I was thinking that the lips themselves should be more reptilian, instead of big Mick Jagger–style ones. Other sketches Lars drew also included a pair of uncomfortable-looking tusks or fangs—nearly a half meter long—protruding from the sides of his mouth. These will be easy; just apply an off-white, powdery texture like that of elephant tusks. Two other areas in the front of the face of interest to me are the nose, which I envision to be two small vertical slits (like a sea lion's), and a wrinkly forehead that seemingly has way too much fat present beneath it. Notice, too, that the underside of the neck area appears much different from the rest of the body—very reptilian, almost like the underbelly of a snake. You can use some dodging and burning for the forehead to enhance the fatty bulges, and apply shadowed bevels for the neck.

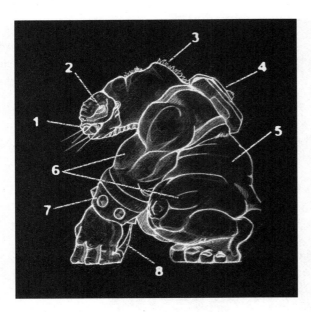

Figure 12.3 *The areas that are most critical to the slogre.*

2. **Eyes.** The location of the eyes in this sketch are a bit higher than I imagined; I'd like to see them down on the side of the face, like the eyes on a fish or a bird, making this character appear much more alien. The eyes themselves should be a glossy, menacingly deep red, and slightly recessed into the head. The ridge that's underneath the eye in the sketch should be on top for shading from the intense heat generated by the twin-sun solar system from which the slogre originates.

3. **Mane.** The hairs on the back of the slogre could have been done nicely on a separate, perpendicular plane with a transparency channel, but I think I'm going to opt for no hair at all. I'd rather see this creature look more reptilian. The hump in this area might be a little more weathered since the suns in his world beat down on it constantly, so you'll make use of the Dodge tool here.

4. **Backpack.** During my initial discussions with Lars about the look of this character, I envisioned him (the slogre, not Lars) carrying a pack of ammo wherever he went. Now, however, I'm wondering how the hell he's going to reach around and nimbly remove a small pellet clip with half-meter-long claws! For this reason, I neglected to model a backpack onto this character; besides, the pack can always be modeled separately and attached by the game engine if needed. (All you have to do is add an appropriate mounting dummy; see

Chapter 14, "Making The Slogre Game-Ready with 3D Studio Max and Character Studio," for more information.)

5. **Body.** I'm going to cover the entire body with a scaly green/red/orange base texture, very much like the full-color image Lars provided (see the color-plate section in the middle of the book). This is easily done with the Stained Glass filter. I'll also bevel the individual cells of this texture to raise it upward and give it a nice rough feel. Some areas around the tail, gut, and middle are folded with a fat/muscle composition; careful dodging and burning should do the trick.

6. **Arms and legs.** The arms and legs will be textured in the same way as the body, only you'll deepen the shadows that define the edges of the muscles to make them bulge more. The geometry of the slogre's mesh will take care of the rest.

7. **Cuffs.** These are the only inorganic objects on the slogre. You'll apply a base metal texture to them, and scratch them up a bit as needed. The metal should be a nice, worn, tarnished steel. (At first I pictured shiny brass, but would he really have that?)

8. **Claws/nails.** These will have a texture similar to that of the tusks. You'll define the toenails by drawing them with a lasso selection and filling them with the off-white texture, then possibly applying inner bevels to raise them a bit.

> **NOTE**
>
> Feel free to try texturing this model (or your own) however you want. In fact, I'd really like to see your own texturing attempts at this model put mine to shame! If you like, you can e-mail your attempts to me at g_lok434@hotmail.com.

Thoughts on Texturing

As I mentioned in Chapter 2, "Getting Ready to Model: Concept Art," I get lots of my ideas from animals that live on Earth; you probably remember that much of the slogre's appearance derives from the extinct sloth. I also get lots of ideas for texturing from watching movies and reading books (more so from movies). Some movies I considered while creating the sloth include

- **The *Alien* series.** The aliens' oblong heads gave me insight for the slogre's head.

- The *Predator* series. These movies helped me envision the slogre's skin texture, size and strength, and claws.
- *Relic.* The massive fangs the beast in this movie used to grip its victims before yanking out their hypothalamuses was what I envisioned for the slogre's tusks. Also, the size and structure of the beast's body is very similar to the slogre's.
- *Dreamscape.* At the end of this movie, the antagonist transformed himself into a hideous, huge snake monster; the underside of the slogre's neck is patterned after the underside of this monster's neck.
- The *Jurassic Park* series. The dinosaurs' skin in these movies is of particular interest to me; mottled green/red/brown, and rough like that of a rhinoceros, it looks much like the skin of a reptile—even though dinosaurs were warm blooded. The claws and fangs of the larger Rexes interest me too—off-white, dulled and pitted from use, and stained near the skin and gum lines.
- *Return of the Jedi.* Remember the part where Luke is dumped into the pit at Jabba's lair? The pit contained a Rancor—a five-meter tall beast with similar qualities to your slogre model, particularly in the face.

Texturing the Slogre

I like to make great use of many of Photoshop's filters and styles to lay the ground work for my textures. The organic stuff, however, needs a bit more traditional artwork applied—mostly through dodging and burning the base texture to enhance the muscular and fatty features of the animal. Other than that, most of what I've covered in previous texturing chapters should suffice.

Let's kick this into gear just like you did in Chapter 11, "Skinning the RF-9 Plasma Gun with Deep Paint 3D and Photoshop," by linking the model to your painting programs and applying a test U-V map. The linking steps presented here are nearly identical to the ones in the previous chapter.

Step 1: Linking the U-V Map to Deep Paint 3D and Photoshop

The U-V map and texturing portions of this project are closely related and, in your case, rely on four separate programs all inter-linked with one another, as shown in Figure 12.4. With enough system memory, you can efficiently work with all these programs open, and bounce back and forth between them as you model, U-V, and texture.

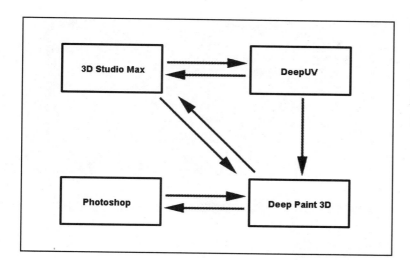

Figure 12.4
The dynamic link and work structure between the U-V and texturing programs you'll be using.

In Chapter 5, "U-V Mapping the RF-9 Plasma Gun with DeepUV," you installed the demo version of DeepUV (if you didn't already have that program) as well as the necessary Max plug-ins. For the remainder of this chapter, you'll also use Deep Paint 3D, also from Right Hemisphere, the demo of which is located in the Programs section on the CD-ROM. Install that now (if you don't already have it), as well as the necessary plug-ins for both Max and Photoshop. If you need help with the installation of the Deep Paint 3D demo, visit http://www.righthemisphere.com/support.

Once everything's installed, the first thing you need to do is bounce your U-V map from Max (or DeepUV) over to Deep Paint 3D. (Mind you, this is only one way to do this kind of work; you could just as easily work between 3D Studio Max and Photoshop. I simply want to expose you to a great work structure that many other game artists employ.) Start by opening up your U-V-mapped slogre in 3D Studio Max. This should be the file you saved in Chapter 6 (if you don't have it, open the file **slogre_mapped.max**, located in the Chapter 12 Data section on the CD-ROM). Then do the following:

1. With the U-V mapped version of the slogre loaded in 3D Studio, click on the Utilities tab at the top-right of the screen.

2. Click on the Right Hemisphere button to expand the list. This should include two sections, one for DeepUV and one for Deep Paint 3D.

3. Make sure your slogre model is selected and click the Paint Selection button in the Right Hemisphere utility panel (see Figure 12.5). This will fire up Deep Paint 3D and begin the U-V–importing procedure.

NOTE

Even though DeepUV is a linked part of the scheme in Figure 12.4, you'll be skipping it for now. You can always bring your model into DeepUV and click File, Export, Paint with Deep Paint 3D; that way, you can make U-V adjustments, if necessary, while you work.

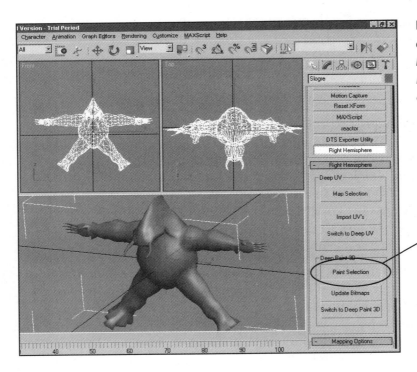

Figure 12.5 *Click on the Paint Selection button in the Right Hemisphere section of the Utilities panel.*

The Paint Selection button

NOTE

You may have to manually start Deep Paint 3D (and/or DeepUV if you want that open as well) if you get a Couldn't Connect error when trying to paint the selection. If you still can't link Max with Deep Paint, consult Right Hemisphere's technical support at http://www.righthemisphere.com/support.

4. A Material Import screen pops up (see Figure 12.6); in it, Deep Paint 3D asks you what material size you want your texture to be and what channel to assign it to. The panel is broken into two sections: The top is the mesh object with U-V–mapping coordinates, and the bottom is the untextured material that Max automatically assigned when you did your U-Ving. Click the material name itself (mine is New Material), then click the Edit/Resize button.

Figure 12.6

The Material Import screen pops up, asking you about the properties of your new texture map.

5. Change the X and Y dimensions of the texture map to 1024 each. This will make a huge texture map so you can do detailed work (you'll shrink it down later on).

6. Uncheck the Start in Projection Mode option. Projection mode enables you to paint directly on a model, regardless of distortions or other arrangements of the U-V map, as though the U-V are 1:1 with the mesh vertices. (This is very useful for painting along seams!)

7. Click OK, and give the map a name (I called mine slogreSkin). Click OK again.

8. Click on the Channels button.

9. The material must be placed in a shader channel so the program knows how to display it. The first item on the list is the letter "C" for "Color." Click it.

10. A small menu pops up; choose Nothing. This adds a New Blank Map entry in the list.

11. Click OK once, and then again in the Material Import screen, and your slogre model will load in a 3D painting screen (see Figure 12.7).

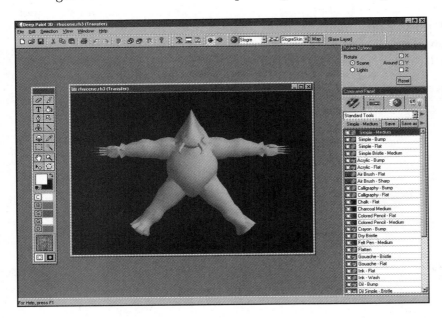

Figure 12.7
The Deep Paint 3D painting interface. You can dynamically manipulate and paint the slogre here.

12. your slogre model is loaded into Deep Paint 3D; you can now manipulate
and paint it with the tools in the toolbox as shown in Figure 12.7. The tools
are very similar to the ones in both DeepUV and Photoshop, and are very
easy to use. The great thing about Deep Paint 3D is you can actually paint
directly on a model, going across U-V seams and everything! However, you
need to do your detailed artwork within Photoshop. To do so, click the
Export Materials to Photoshop button at
the top of the screen (see Figure
12.8). This sends the current U-V map
and material over to Photoshop 6 or
higher (that is, if you've properly
installed the plug-ins that came with
the Deep Paint 3D demo).

NOTE
Notice that there is a Send Materials to 3D Application button at top as well; click this to update your texturing back to 3D Studio Max while you work.

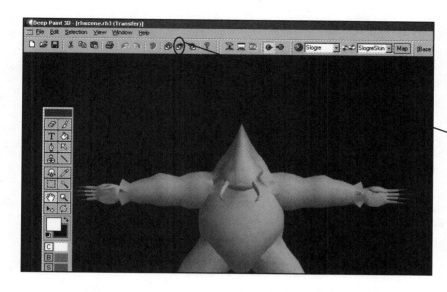

Figure 12.8
*Export the U-V map
and material to
Photoshop.*

Export to
Photoshop

NOTE

Photoshop 7 users: I've found that if you haven't had Photoshop 6 installed on your system, the Deep Paint 3D plug-in might not work. To resolve this problem, you need to set a registry key in the Registry Editor (Start, Run, Regedit). The plug-in key directory is listed under \HKEY_CURRENT_USER\Software\Right Hemisphere\Deep Paint 3D\Directories\. In this area, you should make sure the keys are set to point to the proper plug-in folder where Photoshop 7 is installed. I've also saved a deeppaint.reg file on the CD-ROM that you can double-click to install, but my software installation folders listed in this key may be different from yours. It might be best to manually browse the Registry Editor and adjust the keys yourself, or contact Right Hemisphere's technical support for help (see http://www.righthemisphere.com/support).

With Photoshop linked and fired up, you'll get a new 1024×1024 canvas with two layers. (Open up the Layers palette and you'll see.) The top layer represents the U-V mesh that you made in DeepUV; this is just a guide for you to paint with, and can (and will) be deleted when you're finished. Because this map is so big, you'll have to zoom into it to see the fine details. I changed the color from that default blue to black so it's easier to see (see Figure 12.9).

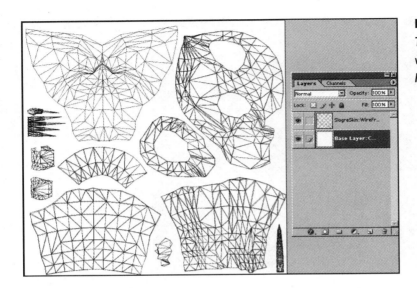

Figure 12.9
The new texture canvas courtesy of Deep Paint 3D.

The bottom layer of the image is the actual painting layer you'll be working on. *Make sure you don't change the name of or delete this layer!* You'll need to send this texture back over to Deep Paint 3D, and it uses this base layer (called Base Layer: Color) when sending and fetching the texture. If this layer is renamed or deleted, you'll have to start all over in Deep Paint 3D.

TIP

If you need help with Photoshop, or are otherwise new to the program, see the Photoshop tutorials located on this book's CD-ROM.

Fixing U-Vs: Add a Checkerboard Map

Even though you did a careful job of unwrapping and organizing the U-Vs in DeepUV, there's still a chance that the isolated U-V portions of the texture map may be inverted (like looking in a mirror—not a big deal for the slogre character); or that texture coordinates crossed (resulting in smearing), overlapped (causing a duplication of texture), or not properly relaxed (causing bloating or shrinking of the texture). I can almost guarantee that at least one of the aforementioned scenarios exists in your setup, but it's not a huge ordeal; it just means you have to go back to DeepUV and fix them.

One outstanding way of detecting problems before you begin the skinning process is to set up a checkerboard map. By simply filling your texture map with a small checkerboard pattern, and then applying the texture to the model, you will have a much easier time checking for errors. I like to fill the individual areas of my texture map with differently colored patterns to make each of the U-V sections clear. I also like to add some text to the area, which not only helps me to identify that area but will display an inverted map area as well—if one exists, the text comes out backwards.

To see what I mean, first fill the individual U-V sections of the Base Layer: Color layer on the texture map. I've saved eight checkerboard patterns for you—just load the **checkerboard.pat** file (located on the CD-ROM) in Photoshop. Then use the Lasso tool to create selections around the U-V areas, and fill the selections with the different-colored patterns using either Edit, Fill, or the Paintbucket tool (Figure 12.10 shows my map). Finally, use the Type tool to position text on the separate U-V areas, or put any non-symmetrical symbol on them, so that if any particular area happens to be inverted you'll be able to tell instantly.

Next, you need to transfer the material back to Deep Paint 3D. Do this either by clicking Filter, Right Hemisphere, Material to Deep Paint 3D, or by going back to Deep Paint 3D and clicking on the Fetch the Material from Photoshop icon at top. You might get a warning in Deep Paint saying that the operation is undoable; just click OK.

Now, check for any signs of smearing, overlapping, and/or unevenness. The most noticeable one is the very front of the face, where the density of the checkerboard map is less than its surroundings. This indicates that you should go back to

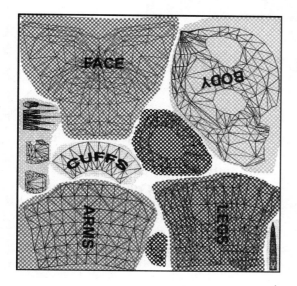

Figure 12.10
Fill the separate U-V areas with different-colored patterns.

DeepUV and select the points in that area and relax them, or scale them up a bit so the *greed* for the material map is even in that section (greed is just the way DeepUV gives relaxing preference to certain texture points over others). Because I relaxed nearly all portions of the U-V map in DeepUV, I don't see any other problems with smearing (see Figure 12.11).

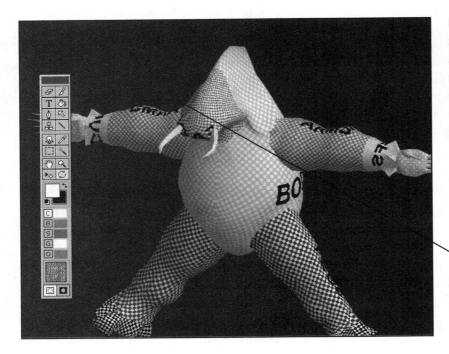

Figure 12.11

Send the checker-board material back to Deep Paint 3D, and check for signs of smearing, overlapping, or unevenness.

Face area not even with rest of head

Step 2: Texturing the Head

Once you've fixed your U-V map and your material is re-imported back to Deep Paint 3D and Photoshop, you can close DeepUV. You'll be doing the texturing in Photoshop, and occasionally sending it back to Deep Paint to see how it looks, so those are the only two programs you really need to have active.

CAUTION

If you close Deep Paint 3D while it is linked to Photoshop, it will remove the texture map from Photoshop, thereby destroying your work! If you need to shut down Deep Paint 3D and continue texturing, first save the texture map in Photoshop, *then* close down Deep Paint 3D.

NOTE

If you don't have anything set up to this point and want to start fresh here, open the **slogre.dp3** file, located in the Chapter 12 Data section on the CD-ROM, in Deep Paint.

CAUTION

Don't delete the bottom base layer! Deep Paint 3D uses this layer when sending and fetching the texture map back and forth with Photoshop.

Create a Base Texture

Before you proceed with creating a base texture in Photoshop, adjust the resolution of the image by choosing Image, Image Size, and changing the Resolution parameter from 72 to 1024. Make sure the dimensions of the image are 1024×1024 as well, because the resolution is linked to those settings. I'd like to create a basic, scaly skin texture first; one that resembles sort of a dinosaur skin by doing the following:

1. Fill the Base Layer: Color layer (from now on, I'll refer to this as the *background layer*) with the Clouds filter, using a mix of dark yellow-green (try hex# 415C07) and dark brown (say, hex# 4F3105).

2. Apply the Noise filter, about 5% monochromatic.

3. Choose Filter, Texture, Stained Glass. Crank the settings for this filter all the way down so you get a nice scaly texture for your slogre (this filter at this resolution will take a while to work—mine took over two minutes).

TIP

If you're having trouble using the filters or other tools and operations native to Photoshop, read Chapter 8, "Inorganic Texture Tutorials with Photoshop." Also, there's a Photoshop tutorial on the CD-ROM that accompanies this book.

4. Choose Image, Adjust, Variations, and change the color scheme to a darker, redder mix. Figure 12.12 shows the result of this operation, after I had switched back to Deep Paint 3D and clicked on the Fetch Material from Photoshop button to apply the new texture to the model.

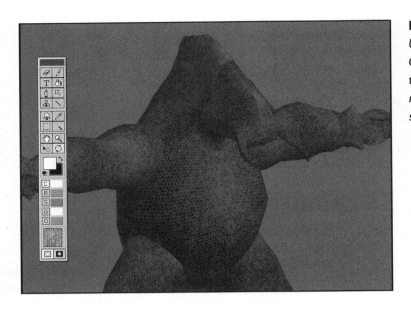

Figure 12.12

Using the Stained Glass filter on a mottled green/red/brown mix makes for great scales.

Filter: Texture, Stained Glass
Cell Size: 2
Border Thickness: 1
Light Intensity: 0

5. Create a displacement map so you can selectively bump the surface of the individual sections of the slogre's body. To do so, press Ctrl+A to select the entire background layer—which should contain the cell pattern you just made—and then press Ctrl+C to copy it. Use the Channels palette to create a new channel, and paste the copy of the entire background layer into the new channel with Ctrl+V. Adjust the levels to make the pattern a bit brighter and crisper.

6. According to the U-V layout, nearly all the body parts are oriented normally (up and down), but the body portion at the top right is upside down. You'll have to render that one separately. To begin, switch to the background layer, and use the Lasso tool to select the upside-down body portion.

7. Choose Select, Inverse; your selection should now encompass the entire background layer minus the body.

8. With the selection active, choose Filter, Render, Lighting Effects, using the new Alpha 1 channel you created as a displacement map (see Figure 12.13).

I used a Directional light type, pointing at a slight angle from top-right to bottom-left. Play around with this filter to get the results you want; you're trying to achieve a pitted, scaly look.

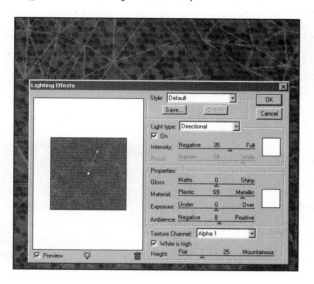

Figure 12.13
Render the background layer using its copy as a displacement map.

9. With the selection still active, choose Select, Inverse to reselect only the upside-down body portion. Apply the Lighting Effects filter a second time, but invert the direction of the light source. This will make the bump map render properly (see Figure 12.14).

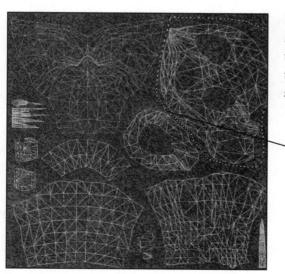

Figure 12.14
Render the body portion of the U-V map, this time with the light source inverted.

Render this selection upside-down

Make a few adjustments to this base texture, such as clicking Image, Adjust, Hue/Saturation, and desaturating it so the colors don't burn a hole in your eyes. A slight levels adjustment would be good too, just to sharpen it up and tone it down. (You'll almost always make last-minute adjustments like these to get your textures looking good!)

Make the Eyes

The slogre character's eyes really make this creature look evil. To bestow shiny, red snake eyes upon your own beast, do the following:

1. Create a new layer.

2. Using the Elliptical Marquee tool, create an elliptical shape.

3. Fill the shape you just created with the Clouds filter, using two reddish colors of your choice (see Figure 12.15).

> **NOTE**
>
> The eye you're making now should be huge. When you're finished, you'll scale it down and position it as needed.

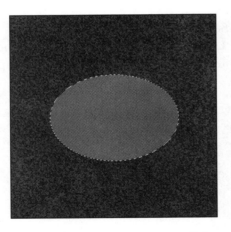

Figure 12.15 *Start making the eyes by filling an elliptical selection with a Clouds mix of red.*

4. Create a new layer on top of the red-eye layer.

5. Make another elliptical selection, but this time in the shape of a snake's pupil.

6. Fill the new selection with black, and apply an inner-bevel style to the layer (see Figure 12.16).

Figure 12.16
Create a snake-eye pupil on another layer and apply an inner bevel to it.

7. Press Ctrl+E to merge the pupil layer with the eye's layer.

8. Ctrl+click the newly merged layer to reload the eye selection, and start a new layer.

9. With the eye-shaped selection on a new layer, apply a white-to-black radial gradient (see Figure 12.17) to simulate the curvature of the 3D eyeball.

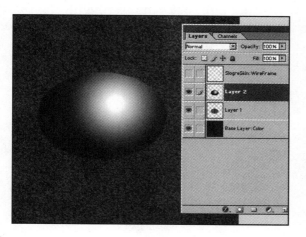

Figure 12.17 *Fill the eye shape with a white-to-black radial gradient on another layer.*

10. In the Layers palette, change the gradient layer's blending mode from Normal to Color Dodge (dodging will turn the gradient into more of a lighting source that fades from the darker to the lighter areas). Notice in Figure 12.18 how the gradient makes a cool lighting effect on the eyeball layer below it; the eyeball looks shiny and 3D.

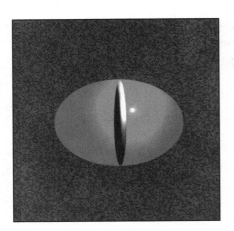

Figure 12.18
Change the gradient layer's blending mode to Color Dodge.

11. Merge this layer with the eyeball layer so it's complete. You should now have three layers: the background, the eyeball, and the U-V guide.

12. Inset the eyeball into the texture map by applying a slight outer-bevel style.

13. Scale and position your eye according to the U-V map (this may be a best-guess thing at first).

14. When the eye is in approximately the right place and is roughly the right size, temporarily merge it with the background layer and send your material back to Deep Paint to see how it looks. After a few tries, I got my eyeball in just the right spot (see Figure 12.19).

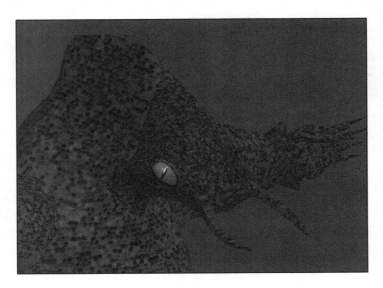

Figure 12.19
Scale and position the eye on the U-V map. Use Deep Paint to adjust its location.

15. When you're satisfied with the location of the one eyeball, go back to Photoshop and copy it to the other side. (Remember to choose Edit, Transform, Flip Horizontal with the second eyeball so the lighting effects on it are mirrored.)

16. When you're satisfied with the position and scale of the eyes, merge them permanently with the background layer.

Create the Brows

I don't recall mentioning the technique I'll discuss here thus far in this book; it provides a fantastic way to create realistic bump maps in skin and cloth, and will enable you to fake the brows that shield the slogre's eyes (you'll also use this technique throughout the map to create muscular folds in the skin). If you're like me and are not big on freehand art, you'll appreciate this technique to its fullest.

1. Create a new layer above the background layer.

2. Apply an inner bevel to the new layer, copying the bevel settings I have in Figure 12.20. You should now have a blank layer with an inner-bevel style applied to it, located on top of the background layer.

> **NOTE**
>
> The most important part of this bevel is the Highlight Mode's color; change it from that hideous pure white to a dark green-brown. The highlights and shadows should be very dull and subtle, or your bumps will look like silly streaks of paint.

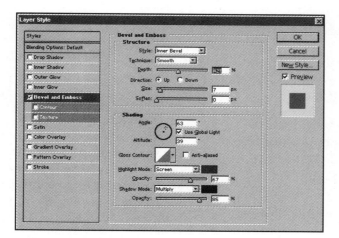

Figure 12.20
Create this inner-bevel style and store it in the Styles palette for quick retrieval. You'll use this for bumping the surface.

3. You'll be using this style to bump the texture map for the remainder of this tutorial, so save it in the Styles palette for quick retrieval.

4. Click on the Clone Stamp tool, change that tool's flow rate to about 10%, and pick out a brush size like Soft Round 21 pixels.

5. Select the background layer, and Alt+click on an area of skin, away from the eyes to sample that area.

6. Select the blank layer with the style on it, and use gentle strokes to shape the brow as I have done in Figure 12.21. The surface seems to raise magically! You can adjust the effect simply by going back into the style for that layer and adding more depth, a larger size, and so on. And of course, if you totally screw it up, just press Ctrl+A to select the layer, and delete the pixel contents to start anew.

Figure 12.21 *Use the Clone Stamp tool to brush in a brow on the effects layer.*

7. When you're finished with the brow, merge it down and transfer it to Deep Paint to see how it looks.

8. When you're satisfied with the brow's appearance, return to Photoshop and copy it to the other side of the face, mirroring it as usual. Figure 12.22 shows the bump results of this operation. The slogre looks a little meaner now, doesn't he?

CAUTION

As I mentioned, you can use this technique to create muscle peaks and valleys on the legs, arms, and body. The only thing is, you need to be subtle about it or your character will look like he got the snot beat out of him.

Figure 12.22 *The bumping technique applied to the slogre's brows.*

Texture the Tusks and Create Some Fangs

The problem with the face of this ugly guy is he looks too docile to do any harm. In fact, his snout is perfect for sniffing daisies. To make him appear a bit more ferocious, you can add some vicious, gnarled fangs protruding from his lip area (the texture for the teeth can also be used on the tusks). The technique I'm about to show you makes such realistic fangs, you'll think you got them from a photo!

1. Start a new 512×512-pixel image, with a resolution of 512.

2. Set the background layer to transparent. You'll be making a single tooth here, and copying it over to the slogre texture.

3. Use the Lasso tool to create a tall, slender, tooth shape on the background layer.

TIP

When performing just about any texturing operation like dodging, burning, or even painting, remember to turn the settings for those tools way, way down—like less than 10%. That way, there won't be any dramatic changes that look totally goofy!

4. Fill the tooth with a light beige mix of the Clouds filter, as shown in Figure 12.23. (I used hex# BEB4A0 and hex# ABA18D for the foreground and background colors for this filter).

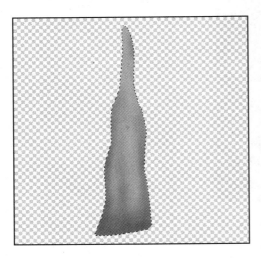

Figure 12.23
Create a tooth-shaped selection and use the Clouds filter to fill it with beige. Burn the edges and add some red to the base.

5. Keeping the selection active, use the Burn tool to burn some darkness into the base and edges of the tooth.

6. Lightly spray a bit of red to the base, simulating the gum line or perhaps blood stains.

7. With the selection still active, apply an inner bevel to the tooth to give it a nice, 3D curve (see Figure 12.23).

8. Make a copy of the tooth layer.

9. With the tooth selection still active, press Ctrl+C to copy it.

10. Using the Channels palette, create a new channel.

11. In the new channel, press Ctrl+V to paste the tooth.

12. With the new channel still active, choose Filter, Noise, Add Noise, about 10%; then apply Filter, Noise, Median, 1 pixel (see Figure 12.24). You'll use this channel as a bump map for the second tooth layer.

Figure 12.24

Create a copy of the tooth layer, and place a copy of the tooth layer in a new channel for a bump map. Add noise to the channel as well.

13. You should have two tooth layers in the Layers palette. With the top one active, choose Filter, Render, Lighting Effects, and use the Alpha 1 channel as a displacement map.

14. Change this layer's blending mode from Normal to Overlay (see Figure 12.25).

15. Merge the two layers together, copy the tooth, and paste it back over to the slogre's texture map.

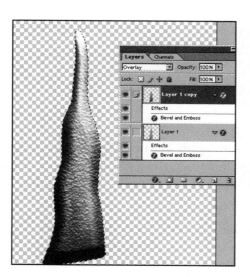

Figure 12.25

Render the top tooth layer with the Lighting Effects filter, using the alpha channel as a displacement map. Changing this layer to Overlay finishes the effect.

To finish off the mouth, scale, rotate, and duplicate multiple copies of the tooth you just created and form something like I have done in Figure 12.26. When all is said and done, merge all the teeth to one layer and apply a drop shadow to make the teeth appear like they've got some depth on the face. I also used the Airbrush tool to add some red around the mouth, making the slogre look like he's just eaten some enemy. I also placed a large copy of a single tooth over the U-Vs that represented the tusks.

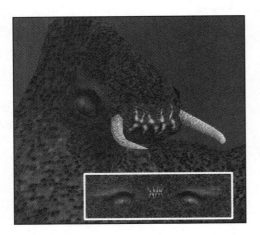

Figure 12.26

Multiple copies of the tooth staggered to create a fanged mouth. The inset shows the portion of the texture map being applied to the model.

Texture the Neck

The sketch of the slogre demonstrates that the underside of the slogre's neck is very much like the belly of a snake. You can render this effect by doing the following:

1. Create a thin rectangular selection across the U-Vs of the neck area.

2. Select the background layer.

3. Right-click the selection and choose Layer Via Copy.

4. To the sliver of the skin you just copied, apply an inner bevel to round out the surface (see Figure 12.27). Copy and paste this layer over and over; when finished, trim the pattern at an angle so it sweeps underneath the slogre's neck area.

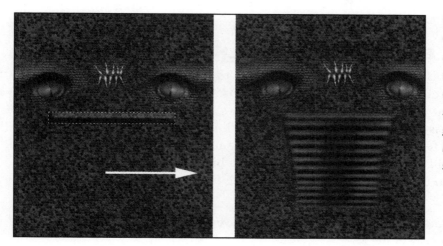

Figure 12.27
Complete the neck area of the slogre with multiple copies of a thin rectangular selection of the background layer. An inner bevel will raise the surface.

5. Use the Dodge and Burn tools to touch up the edges and center of the neck area. Figure 12.28 shows the completed neck on the model.

TIP

If you notice that I explain something but my results seem much better than yours, that's because I took a few extra minutes to polish it off, adjust the levels, and so forth. Always take your time putting finishing touches on your work.

Figure 12.28 *The finished neck texture applied to the model.*

Step 3: Texturing the Arms, Legs, and Body

When I showed you how to do use an effects layer to create the slogre's brow, you saw how easy and effective it was to dynamically raise the surface in a few brush strokes; that's what you'll do here. Fortunately, however, because your slogre mesh is as detailed as it is, you don't have to do too much in the way of muscle definition. Some of the features that could use some augmenting are the pectorals, calves, thighs, and back. As an example, let's add a big fat bicep muscle using an effects layer as you did before; after that, I'm going to cut you loose to create your own effects.

1. Make sure that every layer except the U-V layer is merged with the background layer.

2. Create a new layer.

3. Apply the same inner-bevel style to the new layer as you did when you created the slogre's brow.

4. Using the Clone Stamp tool, sample the background layer.

5. Switch to the effects layer, and lightly brush in an oval-shaped bicep muscle using the U-V map as a guide. Figure 12.29 shows my bicep; you can see how nice a job it does with the arm on the model.

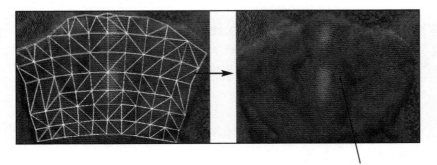

Bicep created

Figure 12.29 *The muscles of the arms, legs, and body can all be created using the effects-layer technique in conjunction with the Clone Stamp tool.*

> **TIP**
>
> These things typically don't come out looking just right at first because the highlights and/or shadows are too intense, leaving a more painted-on appearance; try toning those colors and opacities down to make the effect look a bit more real. Also, gentle, organic muscles will look much better than a bunch of random bumps all over the place.

Figure 12.30 shows the results of my texture map after I applied this technique to the appendages and body. Much of what I was doing was guesswork, since the U-V maps really only display the boundaries of the body parts. My advice to you is to start small, and keep going back and forth between your texture and Deep Paint to see if you like it or not. After all, the great thing about effects layers is, you can always erase your work without disturbing the base texture underneath.

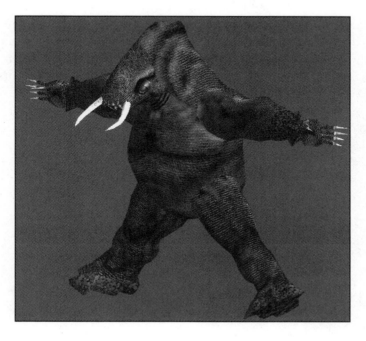

Figure 12.30 *Apply the effects-layer technique all over the body parts to simulate the bulging of muscle and fat, and the wrinkling of the skin.*

> **NOTE**
>
> You may have noticed that my texture map is starting to have a much more realistic feel to it than the base layer originally did. That's because when I used the Clone Stamp tool to create all the muscles and whatnot, I had that tool's Align option *unchecked*. That way, as I went over the map, the texture I was cloning from the background layer was becoming completely uneven, almost massaging it into what it looks like now. Had I had the Align option checked, the original base texture would probably look the same, and would have made it very difficult to use the Clone Stamp tool without constantly running into areas I didn't want cloned to the effects layer.

Step 4: Texturing the Feet and Hands

Texturing the feet and hands is a snap. For the feet U-V area, I used exactly the same techniques I described for making teeth, only this time I made small, square shapes with rounded edges for the toe nails. Then, I used the effects-layer technique to create muscles in the feet and to make indentations around the nails (see Figure 12.31).

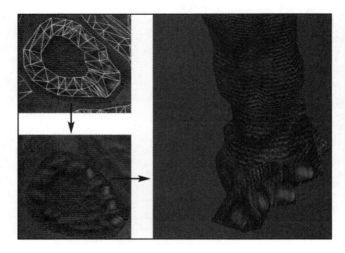

Figure 12.31 *The foot's nails are created using the same technique as the teeth, only using a square shape. Here, I used the Burn tool more liberally to dirty up the nails.*

The hands aren't much to talk about either—there's so much mesh definition, the base texture nearly suffices. The only thing I did (aside from applying a simple beige Clouds filter to color the nails) was lightly apply the effects-layer technique to make an indentation in the palm of the hand (see Figure 12.32).

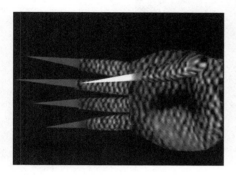

Figure 12.32 *The hand is done the same way as the foot, but an indentation was added to the palm for more depth.*

Step 5: Texturing the Cuffs

The cuff area on the U-V map represents the only inorganic object present, since the cuffs are made from metal. You'll need to use a dull gray metal for this area, but you'd be surprised at what another effects layer can do for dents and scratches.

1. On a new layer, create a lasso selection around the U-Vs that represent the cuffs.

2. Use the Clouds filter to fill the lasso selection with a mix of medium and dark gray.

3. Add Noise to the selection.

4. Using the U-V map as a guide, lasso an edge selection for the top of the cuff.

5. Copy this selection to a new layer, and apply an inner bevel to it. This will raise the edge of the cuff (see Figure 12.33).

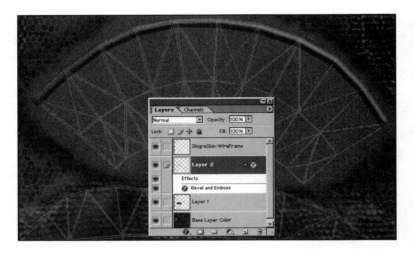

Figure 12.33
Bevel the edge selection of the cuff.

6. Repeat steps 4 and 5 for the bottom edge of the cuff, as well as for the middle.

7. Merge everything with the background layer.

8. Start a new layer, and apply the same effects style as you've been doing, only make the style a downward outer bevel. The Highlight mode should be off-white.

9. Create dents and scratches in the new, blank layer by using the Clone Stamp tool to clone the gray from the layer below it. Use the smallest brush possible—such as 1 pixel wide—to make nice shaded scratches, and make dents by scribing the area over and over (see Figure 12.34).

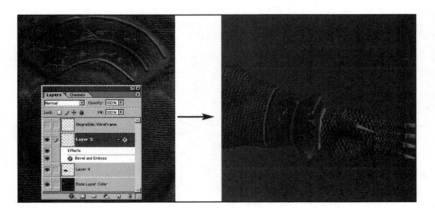

Figure 12.34
Create scratches and dents in the metal with an effects layer that utilizes a downward outer bevel.

Clean Up

Once all is said and done, you'll probably need to make some final adjustments to the map. For example, I find that almost every time I texture, my skins have way too much color definition; you can take care of this by choosing Image, Adjust, Hue/Saturation, and desaturating the entire image until it looks a little washed. Adjusting the levels and color balance are also good last-minute operations to perform. Figure 12.35 shows my final texture map, ready to be placed on the model in 3D Studio Max.

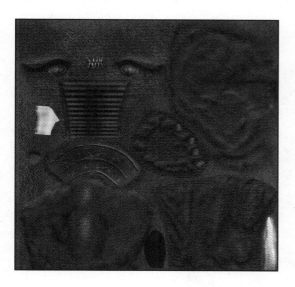

Figure 12.35

Finish the texture with a bit of desaturation and level adjustments.

Preparing the Map for 3D Studio Max

When you are finished with your texture, you need to resize it properly so the game engine can handle it. For *Torque*, it needs to be 512×512 pixels or smaller, and saved as a PNG file. (Other game engines, such as *Half-Life* and *Unreal*, require the maps to be saved as palletized BMP and PCX files.) Here's how it's done:

1. Save the entire image file as is—with the U-V layer on top and a single, merged background layer on the bottom—as a PSD file. That way, you can come back to it and make modifications as needed.

2. Delete the U-V layer.

3. Choose Image, Image Size, and set the dimensions to 512×512 pixels with a resolution of 512. (Most games these days use 256×256 bitmaps, but I hate that. We're at the end of those days, and I demand higher resolutions!)

4. Set the Resampling option to Bilinear to avoid creating a border around the image.

5. Choose File, Save As, and save the image as a PNG file. (The PNG file format is one of the best formats you can use for games, and is used by the *Torque* game engine.)

6. After the file is saved, you can close Deep Paint and load the texture in Max. Figure 12.36 shows the completed texture on the model in 3D Studio.

Figure 12.36 *The completed texture map applied to the slogre in 3D Studio Max.*

When you're ready to move on to placing the new texture on the model in Max and preparing it for use in the *Torque* game engine, skip to Chapter 14.

Summary

In this chapter you performed texturing operations, similar to those with the plasma gun in the previous chapter, by exporting the slogre's U-V map from DeepUV over to Deep Paint 3D and Photoshop. Using a checkerboard map, you were able to identify any areas on the slogre's U-V map that may have been skewed, distorted, overlapped, and/or inverted. In this chapter you made great use of some of Photoshop's filters to create a scaly, organic skin texture. You also used clever bevel effects layers to simulate wrinkles and muscles in the slogre's skin, all the while using Deep Paint 3D as a reference and texturing guide.

PART FOUR

Preparing Assets for Games with 3D Studio Max

CHAPTER 13

Making the RF-9 Plasma Gun Game-Ready with 3D Studio Max

With respect to the logical structure of compound-asset creation, you're at the last stage with one of the two models you're developing for a video game, as represented in Figure 13.1.

More specifically, in this chapter, you'll take your newly modeled and U-Ved RF-9, slap on the tasty skin you made in Chapter 11, and get it ready for use in the *Torque* game engine. You will

- Apply your newly developed texture skin to the RF-9.
- Adjust the model's pivot point.
- Learn about resetting transforms.
- Create the weapon's bounding box.
- Add dummy nodes for critical mount and firing points.
- Export the RF-9 to the *Torque* engine.
- Add level of detail (LOD) to the model.

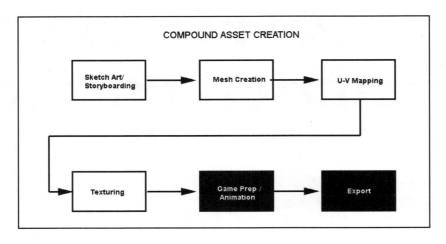

Figure 13.1

The last stage of compound-asset creation.

Applying the Skin to the RF-9

Let's start by skinning your model with the texture you created in Part III, "Texturing with Photoshop and Deep Paint 3D." You should have in your possession the 3D Studio Max MAX file you created in Chapter 5, "U-V Mapping the RF-9 Plasma Gun with DeepUV," that contains the RF-9 mesh that's been checked for errors and then U-Ved with DeepUV. If not, open the **RF9_mapped.max** file located in the Chapter 13 Data section on the CD-ROM. Nothing else has been done to this file since then (see Figure 13.2).

Open your U-V mapped model in 3D Studio Max. You'll need to be able to see your weapon's texture applied dynamically, so make sure you have at least one viewport's Rendering Level set to Smooth + Highlights. Do this by clicking Customize, Viewport Configuration, and, under the Rendering Method tab, choosing Smooth + Highlights. Below that you'll see Apply To; I have it set for Active Viewport Only, which will apply these settings only to the viewport I was last using (User).

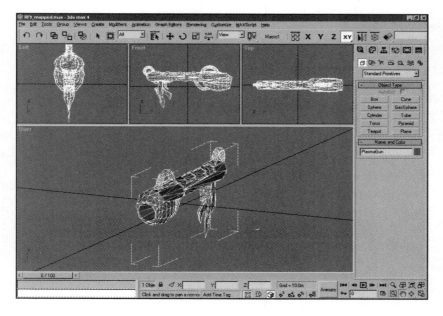

Figure 13.2 *The RF9_mapped.max file*

Next, select the model with the Select Object tool (black arrow icon at top) to make it active. Enter the Material Editor by pressing M or click Rendering, Material Editor (at the top-right of the screen). The very first cell at the top-left should be blank; that's the one you'll fill with the bitmap. You saved your texture from Chapter 11, "Skinning the RF-9 Plasma Gun with Deep Paint 3D and Photoshop," in different file formats, meant for different game engines. For now, let's get this model ready for *Torque* because that's what you'll be using primarily. The file you want to load is **RF9.png**, also located on the CD-ROM.

Click on the first cell to make sure it's active. (It should be "1—Default"). Now click on the Show Map in Viewport icon, which looks like a Rubik's Cube. This will let the material display itself automatically on the weapon. Just below that is the currently named material, which you can change by clicking in its window and deleting the text (I named it "RF-9 Skin"). Next, under the Blinn Basic Parameters section, click on the small blank gray button next to Diffuse. This will load a Material/Map Browser screen (see Figure 13.3). In shader terms, *diffuse* is simply the absolute color or material that is reflected when general lighting is applied to the object. Because you're not really interested in other rendering-specific values (for now), that's the only material parameter you need to fill.

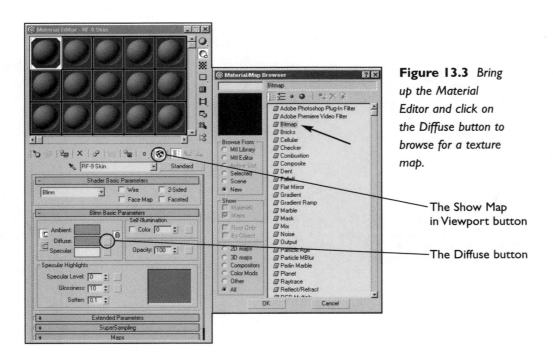

Figure 13.3 *Bring up the Material Editor and click on the Diffuse button to browse for a texture map.*

The Show Map in Viewport button

The Diffuse button

Figure 13.4 *Select Bitmap from the Material/Map Browser screen and add the* **RF9.png** *texture. Apply it by clicking Assign Material to Selection.*

In the list on the Material/Map Browser screen, double-click Bitmap. You'll get a bitmap-file browser screen; search for your RF-9 skin texture or use the **RF9.png** file in the Chapter 13 Data section on the CD-ROM. Finally, click the Assign Material to Selection button (see Figure 13.4). You should now see your texture applied to the weapon.

Now would be a good time to save your work. It is imperative, by the way, to store your MAX, PNG, and other texture files, as well as configuration files (which you'll see shortly), in the same directory, because the export plug-ins need to reference everything at once in the same location.

Aligning the Pivot Point

All weapon and character models in games must have a pivot point (or axis) that is aligned according to the game engine for which they are being designed. This ensures that the model faces the proper direction when manipulated, or mounted, onto the player's hand, body, or other appendage. In the case of the *Torque* engine, the programming code requires that the weapon's axes align

NOTE

When you built the RF-9 in trueSpace, I didn't bother mentioning anything about the weapon's axes because I knew you'd take care of it here. You could just as well have made that modification in trueSpace, but I consider Max the end-all-be-all of getting things ready for games.

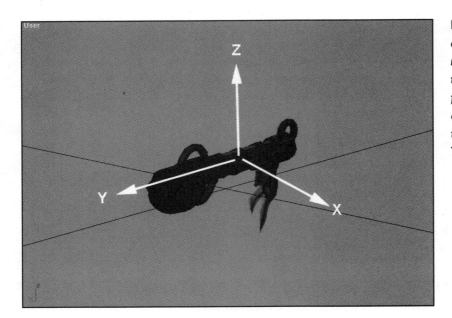

Figure 13.5 *The axes of the RF-9 must be aligned so that the weapon faces in the proper direction. Note that this applies to the Torque engine.*

so that the y axis points directly forward, the z axis points straight up, and the x axis points to the object's right side (see Figure 13.5).

If you look at the Perspective view of the model, notice that the axes floating around the middle of the object match up with the World axes, shown at the bottom-left corner of the view screen. When you imported the STL file, Max took whatever axes were set and aligned the World axes with it. Notice that the z axis is pointing up, just like you want it to, but that the x axis points forward (see Figure 13.6). This you need to fix.

Before you begin, note that it's easiest to do all your pivot-point (axes) alignments using a User view. Select a viewport arrangement that allows this, as I have in Figure 13.6, by clicking Customize, Viewport Configuration, Layout. Then, click the Angle Snap Toggle button at the top of the Max interface to make things snap to default five-degree increments. That way, you won't have to eyeball anything when rotating your pivot points. (You could just as well use the Transform Type-In dialog box, but it's nice to see things happen dynamically.)

Finally, note that at the top of the screen, the Reference Coordinate System list is set to View. This displays the coordinate system's axes in relation to the rest of the world while you move things around. (If you pull down the list and set it to Local,

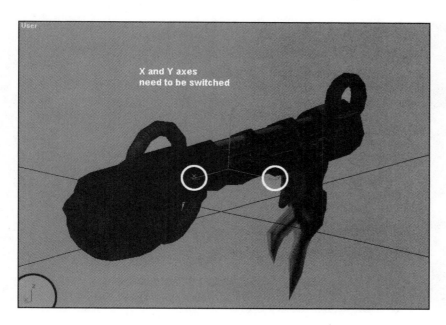

Figure 13.6 *The axes of the RF-9 need to be adjusted so the y axis points forward.*

the object's axes will move with the RF-9 as you swing it about any axis.) Then do the following:

1. Click on the Rotate tool.

2. You'll need to rotate the object so that the muzzle is parallel to the y axis. To do so, position the tool over the z axis, and click and drag. (Remember, the y axis rotates itself around the z axis.) Rotate the RF-9 so that the muzzle points along the y axis as shown in Figure 13.7.

> **NOTE**
>
> As an alternative, you could also right-click the Rotate tool to open the Transform Type-In dialog box, and enter 90 for the z-axis value.

3. With the object rotated 90 degrees, you need to permanently lock it down. (Max likes to keep track of all object transformations, so until you reset the transformations, the pivot point won't be set.) Do this by clicking on the Hierarchy panel next to the Modifier panel; in this list, click the Reset: Transform button toward the bottom. (If you had the Transform Type-In dialog box open, the 90-degree value you entered for the z axis would be reset to 0.) See Figure 13.8.

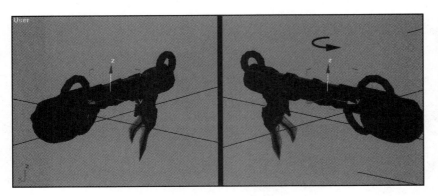

Figure 13.7 *Use the Rotate tool with Angle Snap enabled to rotate the RF-9 so it is aligned with the y axis.*

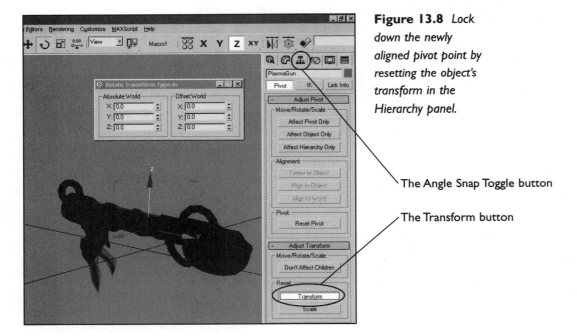

Figure 13.8 *Lock down the newly aligned pivot point by resetting the object's transform in the Hierarchy panel.*

The Angle Snap Toggle button

The Transform button

4. Verify that the model's muzzle is pointing along the y axis by clicking the Affect Pivot Only button at the top of the Hierarchy panel. All axes should be aligned on top of one another.

5. With the Affect Pivot Only button depressed, click Center to Object. This will place the pivot point at the object's center.

6. Toggle off the Affect Pivot Only button. (You can use that option to quickly move the pivot to any location or orientation you like, but make sure to reset the transform if you want that change to stick.)

NOTE

Remember to use the Arc Rotate tool (bottom-right) to look around the weapon if you want to change your eye view of the model.

Creating the Bounding Box

Every model in a game must be surrounded by an invisible square box, called a *bounding box*, which tells the game engine the extent of the model's dimensions. That way, objects (including characters) can collide with other objects using their bounding boxes as determinant points of the actual collision. The collision determination is done within the game code; it's your job, however, to properly set these bounds.

Basically, all you do is create a box or cube primitive that completely surrounds the model (in this case, the RF-9) in all directions, and set the bounding box's pivot point in the same fashion as before—with the y axis pointing forward. Finally, the box needs to be named Bounds. (This is for the *Torque* engine; check your engine's specifications for information about what the bounding box should be named.)

1. In the Create panel (next to the Modifier panel), click the Geometry button.

2. In the Geometry section, click on the Box button.

3. In the User perspective view, which shows the RF-9 in full textured 3D, click and drag to create a box. The first pass of clicking and dragging creates the base of the box, and when you release the mouse and drag again, it will create the height of the box. By creating the box in this User view, the box will inherit the correct x, y, and z axes it needs for the Torque engine.

4. Scale and move the box to completely encompass the RF-9 (see Figure 13.9). Try to get the box as close to the dimensions of the RF-9 as possible while ensuring sure the RF-9 is completely enclosed.

TIP

When working on a single object while using multiple view windows, it helps to have the Selection Lock Toggle (the one found on the bottom of your screen that looks like a padlock) button toggled on. This will keep your operations confined to just that object. When you're finished, just click the button again to toggle it off.

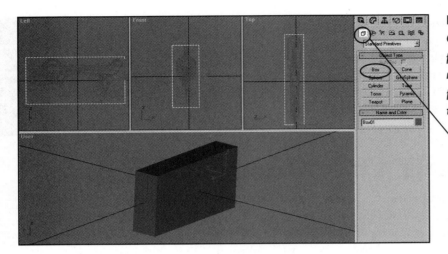

Figure 13.9
Create a box primitive, scale it, and move it so it completely encompasses the RF-9.

The Geometry button

5. In a solid rendered viewport, the box will hide the gun. To rectify this, right-click the bounding box and choose Properties from the shortcut menu that appears.

6. In the Display Properties section, check the Display as Box check box. That way, all you'll see is an outline of the box.

7. Still in the Object Properties dialog box, at the very top in the Name field, change the object's name to Bounds, as shown in Figure 13.10. (It doesn't have to be capitalized, but I like to do that for labeling reasons.) Click OK.

8. In the Hierarchy panel, click the Affect Pivot Only button.

9. Notice that the bounding box's axes are correct, but are located at the base of the box. Just click the Center to Object button in the Hierarchy panel to move the pivot point to the center of the bounding box (Figure 13.11). Some game engines use this pivot point as the center of gravity of the model, which is used for actions like rotation when the weapon is ready for pickup on the floor of a game.

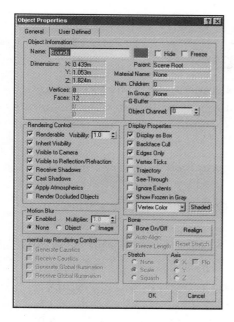

Figure 13.10
Change the properties of the bounding box to Display as Box, and rename the object Bounds.

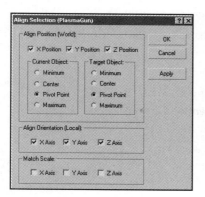

Figure 13.11 *Center the Bounding Box's pivot point in the Hierarchy panel. Make sure the axes of the pivot point are pointing the same way as the weapon, with the y axis forward.*

Now you have a bounding box in your scene that can be effectively used with your weapon in a game. But the RF-9 needs some special features so that a character can actually pick it up and fire it; that's covered next.

Adding and Manipulating Nodes

Along with the hidden treasure of bounding boxes come node points, which are essentially dummy objects that play a specific labeling role within an object's hierarchy to allow players to mount and fire the weapons. Dummies are quite featureless primitive boxes in Max that

- Act as target markers on a model for preprogrammed game functions to hook or attach to
- Have a pivot point that will dictate the direction of the attaching function, such as a muzzle flash, grip, or camera
- Are linked directly to the object's hierarchy at particular locations according to function

To start with, click on the Open Schematic View icon located in the top-right portion of the screen. A window opens containing tags that represent objects in your scene; these tags are structured in an expandable/collapsible tree hierarchy, as shown in Figure 13.12. You might have to zoom in to see the labels, especially when the hierarchy gets big. Also, click on the red arrows to expand the branches, if they exist.

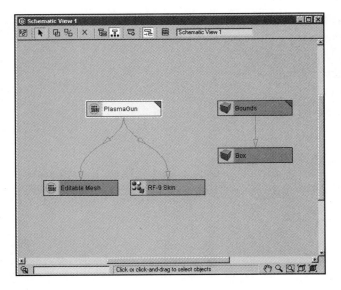

Figure 13.12

Open the Schematic view to see the scene's node hierarchy.

For now, you have two main branches in your hierarchy here: PlasmaGun and Bounds. As shown in Figure 13.12, when the branches are expanded, the modifiers you added earlier are part of the underlying structure of the model. You don't need them isolated anymore, so it's okay to collapse the stack; to do so, momentarily minimize the Schematic view and click on the Modifier panel. Then, select the RF-9 model so it is selected, and then right-click on the items in the stack and choose Collapse All from the menu that appears. You might get a warning; just accept it. You should end up with just an Editable Mesh item in the stack. Open the Schematic view again, and you should have just the RF-9 with its material and mesh below it. (Some game engines require you to link the Bounds object directly to the model, but *Torque* needs it to be a separate entity.)

Now for the interesting stuff. You need to create several dummy objects to represent those critical game hooks I mentioned previously (a *hook* is just terminology for the way a game engine seeks out and attaches something to a particular game function). Some common dummy objects for *Torque* are

- A mounting location called **MountPoint**. This is where a player's hand (or other appendage) grabs the weapon. Required on all weapon models.

- A muzzle flash location called **MuzzlePoint**. This is where a weapon's projectile will originate. Required on all weapon models.

- An ejection location called **EjectPoint**. This is where spent ammunition casings might originate and project outward.

- A detail object, called **Detail#**, where **#** defines the level of detail. Required for all models.

Similar points are possibly required for other game engines (see the last section for more details). In addition to these nodes, all *Torque* models are required to have **Base01** and **Start01** dummy nodes to indicate the base and start of the object's node hierarchy, respectively. Those get installed automatically with the DTS Exporter utility (more on that in a moment). Also, some games and their engines might require additional mount and sprite locations—perhaps a **FizzlePoint** location for the programmers to hook a smokey sprite onto. It's up to you to communicate with the programmers as to what will be attaching to where, and what it will be called.

NOTE

Your RF-9 really only needs the **MountPoint** and **MuzzlePoint** dummy objects for now. The **Detail#**, **Base01**, and **Start01** objects will be taken care of with the DTS Exporter utility.

Embedding the Shape (for *Torque* Users)

Before you continue, remember to save your MAX file, and be sure to have the texture file located in the same directory. In this section you'll tell the *Torque* plug-in to get your model ready for export as a .DTS file format.

Located in the Chapter 13 Data section on the CD-ROM is a DTS Export plug-in utility called **max2dtsExporter.dle**; if you haven't done so already, copy it to the \PLUGINS\ folder in your 3DSMAX5 program directory (you'll have to restart Max). Once Max has been restarted, load up your RF-9 scene file and do the following:

NOTE

The plug-ins listed in this chapter work for 3D Studio Max version 4 and higher.

1. Click once on the PlasmaGun mesh in your scene to select it.

2. In the Utilities panel, click the DTS Exporter Utility button. (If this button isn't listed, click the More button and search the list. If it's still not listed, the plug-in might not have been loaded properly.) DTS, by the way, is *Torque's* object format.

3. In the Exporter section, choose Renumber Selection.

4. A blank dialog box opens; type **2** and click OK. This will affect the level of detail (LOD) of the gun, enabling the mesh to have the highest detail in the game (more on LOD later in this chapter).

5. Click Embed Shape. In a flash, the exporter places the RF-9 into a nice DTS-required hierarchy. You can see this by opening the Schematic view and expanding the tree, as shown in Figure 13.13.

The RF-9 is now placed in a structured hierarchy pertinent to creating DTS shapes for the *Torque* engine.

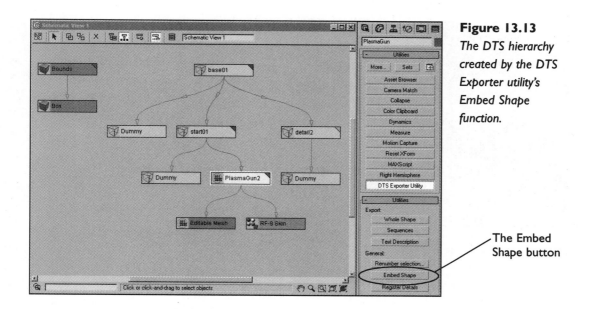

Figure 13.13
The DTS hierarchy created by the DTS Exporter utility's Embed Shape function.

The Embed Shape button

Adding the Dummies

With the required DTS hiearchy now in place, let's add some dummy objects so that a player can mount and use the RF-9.

1. Minimize the Schematic view.

2. In the Create panel at top-right, click on the Helpers icon (it looks like a tape measure).

3. Within the Helpers section, click on the Dummy button, and click and drag to create a small box in the User view of your scene. (The size of the dummies is negligible; they're just there for your reference. I keep mine small, like in Figure 13.14.)

4. Name this first dummy object MountPoint, and position it on the middle of the grip as shown (make sure it's in the middle, as seen from all views).

5. Align the pivot point as you did the other objects before (this isn't critical, but it helps to stay consistent).

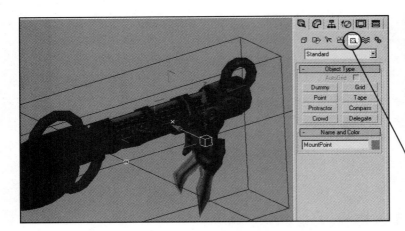

Figure 13.14
Add a dummy object to the scene in the Helpers section and call it MountPoint. *Position it on the grip area.*

The Helpers button

6. Add another dummy object to the scene and call it MuzzlePoint.

7. Position the new dummy object directly in front of the muzzle, as in Figure 13.14. This will be the origin of the plasma balls that are launched from the end. Note that the pivot point of this dummy is critical; ammunition will be directed where the y axis is pointing.

8. Now link the dummy objects to the PlasmaGun object in the hierarchy. To begin, open the Schematic view; you'll see your newly created dummy objects listed.

9. Click on one of them, then click the Link button at the top of the Schematic View screen.

> **TIP**
> A quicker technique would be to click on the MountPoint object and choose Edit, Clone, and then rename the object MuzzlePoint. This will also copy the pivot point of the MountPoint object.

10. Your cursor turns into two boxes linked together; just click and drag a line from the dummy to the PlasmaGun object, located below and linked to the Start01 object in the hierarchy (see Figure 13.15). This will make the dummy object a child to the parent weapon object.

11. Click on the black arrow at the top to deselect the Link mode, then do the same for the other dummy object as well.

Now you have all your required mounting nodes attached properly and are ready to proceed with dumping out the model.

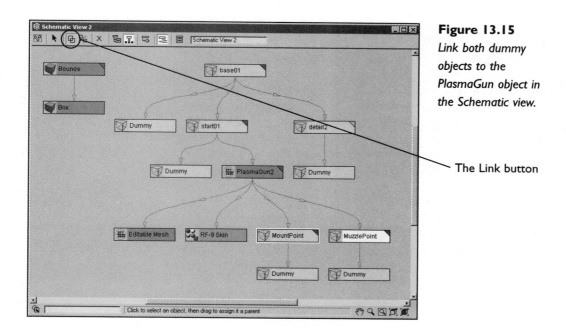

Figure 13.15
Link both dummy objects to the PlasmaGun object in the Schematic view.

The Link button

Exporting the RF-9 for the *Torque* Game Engine

The last and simplest thing to do is to dump your hard-earned game-ready model for use in *Torque*. Before dumping out the model, however, you'll need a CFG file that will tell the exporter exactly what to dump out. This is common for almost all exporters for all game engines.

Located in the Chapter 13 Data section on the CD-ROM is a file called **weapon.cfg**; Place a copy of that file in the same folder as your RF-9's MAX file and the texture file. The configuration file simply tells the exporter what to include or occlude during the exporting process. All that's listed in this text file is

```
AlwaysExport:
MountPoint
MuzzlePoint
```

NOTE

When it comes time to export the slogre model, the configuration file will be fairly complex. Just make sure to update the AlwaysExport section with whatever nodes you want included during the export, or else they won't be present in your DTS model. Also note that you can have only one CFG file present, and the name is arbitrary.

In the Utilities section, the DTS Exporter utility has an Export: Whole Shape button. Click it, give the shape a name, and make sure that the directory it is exporting to is the same as the one in which your MAX, CFG, and texture files reside. These files should all be located in a separate folder within the \RealmWars\rw\data\shapes\plasmagun\ folder.

Viewing the Model in *Torque*

You can view the model in *Torque* using the `TorqueDemo.exe -show` command. Just pick up the shape by clicking the Load Shape button and selecting the model from the list, as in Figure 13.16. Use the W and S keys to zoom in and out, and A and D to rotate.

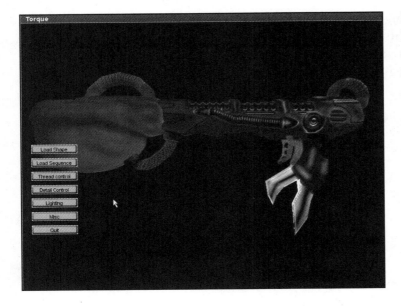

Figure 13.16

Viewing the completed RF-9 Plasma Gun in the Torque viewer.

Adding Levels of Detail (LODs)

I hinted at creating levels of detail for game objects earlier in this book, and now's the time to explore this process. The RF-9 plasma gun currently has over 1,300 polygons associated with it, which is a bit pricey for just a weapon. Most game engines will handle such a large amount just fine, but having many such weapons—along with the rest of the game's geometric detail—will certainly bog down your computer system. Ultimately, your system will slow down and seem a bit choppy at times, especially if you're playing over the Internet.

One way to resolve these high geometry issues is by assigning *levels of detail (LODs)* to your objects. Level of detail mesh objects are simply copies of the same model, but each has varying polygon counts. This way, the game engine can replace a higher mesh object with a copy whose mesh is lower in polygon count as the player's view increases with distance. After all, how much detail on another player's weapon can you possibly discern from far away? Try to picture an opponent standing far away on a hill, holding the RF-9—it would only appear that he's holding a tiny dark item—an unnecessary detail for a game engine to have to render, to your view, of 1,300+ polygons.

If the game engine in question supports LODs—and most do (including the Torque engine)—creating them is fairly easy using a MultiRes modifier. All you need to do for the RF-9 is clone the model, apply the MultiRes modifier, make a few adjustments to the hierarchy, and register the new levels of detail for the model.

TIP

Levels of detail are not necessarily a requirement for any model. Having them is just a way to speed up game play, without noticeable loss of model quality, from the distance between the player's view and the model itself.

The RF-9 is currently embedded in the structured hierarchy as seen in Figure 13.15; it is labeled **PlasmaGun2**. Notice that there is also a dummy object called **Detail2**, linked to the **Base01** object. This is a detail marker that both the exporter and game engine use to refer the appropriate detail mesh object—that is, when the game engine needs to display the lowest resolution of your detail mesh, it looks for the **Detail2** dummy marker, which, to the exporter, is directly related to the **PlasmaGun2** object. Subsequent dummy objects and meshes with higher numbers (for instance, **Detail32:PlasmaGun32** or **Detail64:PlasmaGun64**) will be used as the object comes closer to the player's view.

Let's make for the RF-9 just one optional level of detail that has only half of the polygon count (or about 650 polygons), so that the engine can display that model when the player is far away from it:

1. Open the Schematic View again so that you can see the entire hierarchy of the RF-9. Currently, there's only one level of detail—**PlasmaGun2**, which also has a dummy reference marker called **Detail2**. The mesh right now is at the highest quality (1,350 polygons) possible, so you need to change this numbering scheme so that the number located at the end of the label will represent the highest level of detail of the model (the higher the number, the greater the polygon count of the model). Click once on the **PlasmaGun2** label to select it, then click once more, and rename it **PlasmaGun64** (see Figure 13.17). Torque needs to have detail markers in binary increments, such as 2, 4, 8, 16, 32, 64, and so on. In this case, the name "PlasmaGun64" will represent the highest level of detail.

2. Double-click the **Detail2** dummy object in the Schematic View. Press Del to delete it—new dummy markers will be recreated at the last step.

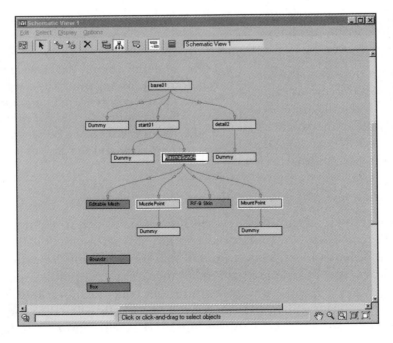

Figure 13.17 *In the Schematic View, change the name of the RF-9 from* **PlasmaGun2** *to* **PlasmaGun64**.

3. Now make a clone of the plasma gun mesh. With the RF-9 actively selected, click Edit, Clone. A Clone Options dialog will open, allowing you to chose the cloning method. Be sure the Copy option is selected, then, in the Name field, change the name to **PlasmaGun2** and click OK. You've now made an identical copy of the weapon's mesh; this will be apparent in the Schematic View (Figure 13.18).

CAUTION

You can make as many level of detail meshes as you want, but keep in mind that the greater the number of detail levels present, the larger and more cumbersome your .dts file will be to the game engine.

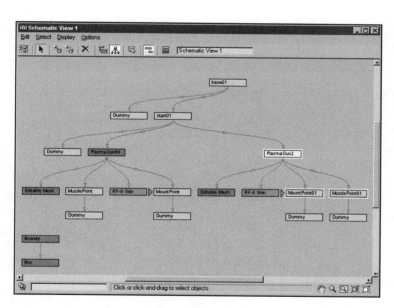

Figure 13.18
Choose Edit, Clone, and clone the RF-9. Change the name to **PlasmaGun2**.

4. The new clone you've just created will represent the lowest level of detail, but since it is in fact a clone, it still has the same polygon count—1,358 in this case. To cut this count in half, go to the Modifier panel and apply the MultiRes modifier. In the MultiRes panel, click the Generate button to apply the modifier to the **PlasmaGun2** object. Not much happened. Now look to the top of the MultiRes panel in the Resolution section—change the Vert Percent from 100 to 50 (Figure 13.19). You'll see the mesh reduce its polygon count in half, to about 682 polygons.

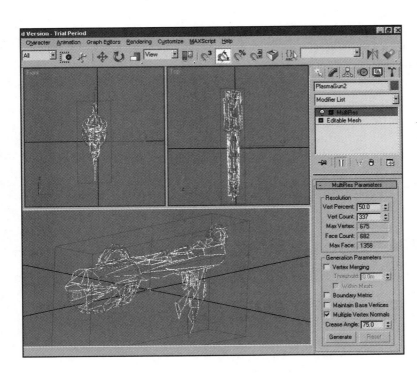

Figure 13.19
*Apply a MultiRes modifier to the **PlasmaGun2** clone, and set the Vert Percent to 50.*

5. You should now have two detail meshes in your scene—one RF-9 with 100 percent detail, and one with 50%. You'll see the difference in the two when viewed in the Torque engine. Lastly, you'll need to register these new detail meshes for the Torque engine. Open up the Schematic View again; you will see both detail meshes linked to the **Start01** dummy. Double-click the **Base01** dummy to select it, then open the Utilities panel. In the DTS Exporter Utility section, click Embed Shape. The utility will now create two dummy objects, **Detail64** and **Detail2**, linked to the **Base01** object (Figure 13.20).

And that's it; you've now created two different levels of detail that the Torque engine can use to swap in the game—one for up close, and one for far away. You can view the detail meshes in the same way you viewed the RF-9—using the Torque -show utility.

NOTE

Continuous level of detail is supported in newer game engines. This means that the engine develops a smooth mesh detail transformation from the highest to lowest mesh quality in relation to distance. This is fairly taxing, due to the intensive mathematical calculations required; that's why it's not available in many other engines.

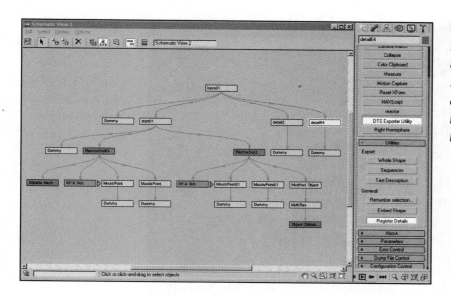

Figure 13.20
*Select the **Base01** dummy object in the Schematic View, and click the Register Details button in the DTS Exporter Utility.*

Just click the Export:Whole Shape button in the DTS Exporter Utility and replace the existing **plasmagun.dts** file, which should be located in the \RealmWars\rw\data\shapes\plasmagun\ folder.

Viewing the New Level of Detail in *Torque*

Once you've saved your .dts object with new levels of detail, view it in Torque using the TorqueDemo.exe -show command. Select the plasma gun model and zoom in close to see it. No changes to the mesh will be apparent. To see the two separate levels of detail, click the Detail Control button. In the Detail Control panel, adjust the slider left and right to see the two detail models dynamically swap in front of your eyes! (See Figure 13.21). Not bad detail, considering one mesh contains half as many polygons as the other!

Tips for Exporting to Other Game Engines

What I've covered in this chapter, as far as preparing your model for the Torque game engine, is very similar when using most other game engines. It's just a matter of reviewing the specifications that the game engine calls for. Plug-ins are usually

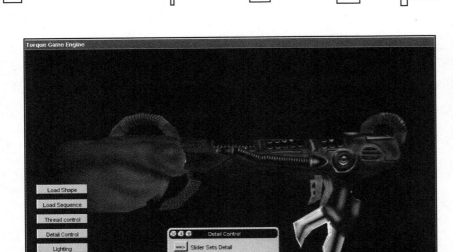

Figure 13.21

Once you open and zoom in on the RF-9 in the Torque -view utility, use the Detail Control panel to view the two new levels of detail.

available for most popular game engines; for instance, the Half-Life exporter for 3D Studio Max is called **smdexp.dlo** and is available free in the Half-Life SDK, downloadable at the Valve resource site (http://hlsdk.valve-erc.com). Just consult the game engine's SDK (software development kit) documentation for further details.

Summary

In this chapter you imported the RF-9 plasma gun model into 3D Studio Max, and used this program to prepare and finalize the weapon for use in the *Torque* game engine. In 3D Studio, you applied the skin texture you developed in Chapter 11. You also created a bounding box, which tells the engine the extents of your model, and attached key game objects called dummies, which dictate to the game engine certain areas of your model where a player can pick up and use the weapon. All of these components are linked in a structured hierarchy that is understood and read by the game engine's Max exporter. The entire preparation of a game model in this way is very common for most engines.

CHAPTER 14

Making the Slogre Game-Ready with 3D Studio Max and Character Studio

A s shown in Figure 14.1, you're now at the last stage of compound-asset creation with one of the two models you're developing for a video game. In
English, that means this is the chapter in which you'll take your newly modeled and
U-Ved slogre, slap on the eerie skin you made in Chapter 12, "Skinning the Slogre
with Deep Paint 3D and Photoshop," and get it ready for use in the *Torque* game
engine.

In this chapter you will

- Apply your newly developed texture skin to the slogre character.
- Adjust the model's alignment and scale.
- Learn about resetting transforms.
- Create the character's bounding box.
- Change the character's shape with modifiers.
- Add a Character Studio Biped bones structure to the mesh.
- Learn about and adjust envelopes for the skin.
- Add dummy nodes for critical mounting and camera points.
- Add level of detail (LOD) to the model.
- Export the slogre to the *Torque* engine.

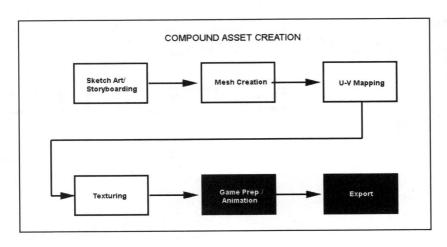

Figure 14.1
The last stage of compound-asset creation.

Applying the Skin to the Slogre

Let's start by skinning your model with the texture you created in Part III, "Texturing with Photoshop and Deep Paint 3D." You should have in your possession the MAX file you created in Chapter 6, "U-V Mapping the Slogre with DeepUV," which simply contains the slogre mesh that's been checked for errors and U-Ved with DeepUV. If not, extract the **slogre_mapped.max** file located in the Chapter 14 Data section on the CD-ROM. Then, extract the file **SlogreSkin.png** (also found on the CD-ROM); this contains your texture. Place these two files in the same folder on your hard drive. Then, in 3D Studio Max 5, open the **slogre_mapped.max** file (Figure 14.2).

> ## NOTE
>
> Although you saved your texture from Chapter 12 in different file formats, meant for different game engines, you'll use the **SlogreSkin.png** file here to get this model ready for *Torque*, which is the engine you'll most likely be using for this book.

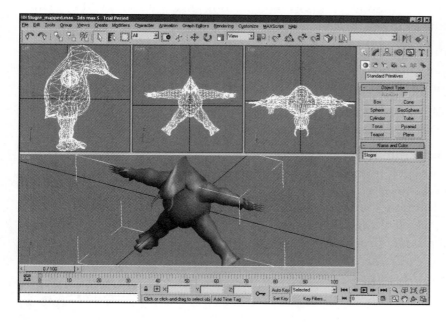

Figure 14.2 *Open your U-V–mapped model in 3D Studio Max.*

> **NOTE**
>
> This file has the User viewport at the bottom set to a smooth, dynamic rendering, which is what you'll need for viewing your texture. If for some reason none of your views are set to rendering (that is, all views display a wireframe mesh of the slogre), press F3, or click Customize, Viewport Configuration; then, under the Rendering Method tab, choose Smooth + Highlights.

Once the MAX file is open on your desktop, do the following:

1. Using the Select Object tool (the button at top with a white arrow on it), select the model to make it active.

2. Enter the Material Editor by pressing M or choosing Rendering, Material Editor.

3. The very first cell at the top-left should be blank; that's the one you'll fill with the texture bitmap. Click on the cell (it should be named "1—Default") to make sure it's active.

4. Click on the Show Map in Viewport icon (it looks like a Rubik's Cube). This will display the material, once it is loaded, on the character.

5. Just below the Show Map in Viewport icon is the currently named material, which you can change by clicking in its window and replacing the text with the name you prefer (I typed SlogreSkin).

6. Under the Blinn Basic Parameters section, click on the small blank gray button next to Diffuse to load a Material/Map Browser screen (see Figure 14.3).

7. In the Material/Map Browser screen, double-click Bitmap. A bitmap file browser screen opens; search for your slogre skin texture, which should be located in the same directory as the slogre's MAX file. If you can't find the .png file, use the **SlogreSkin.png** file on the CD-ROM.

> **NOTE**
>
> In shader terms, *diffuse* simply refers to the absolute color or material that is reflected when general lighting is applied to the object. Because you're not really interested in other rendering-specific values (for now), that's the only material parameter you need to fill.

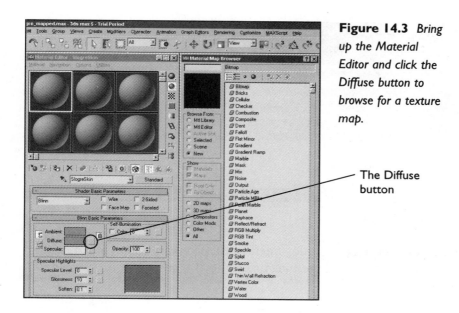

Figure 14.3 *Bring up the Material Editor and click the Diffuse button to browse for a texture map.*

The Diffuse button

8. Click the Assign Material to Selection button (see Figure 14.4). You should now see your texture applied to the slogre mesh.

9. Save your work.

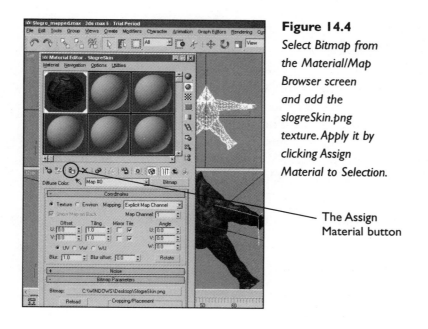

Figure 14.4
Select Bitmap from the Material/Map Browser screen and add the slogreSkin.png texture. Apply it by clicking Assign Material to Selection.

The Assign Material button

> **NOTE**
>
> It is imperative that you store your MAX, PNG, other texture files, and configuration files (which you'll see shortly) in the same directory, because the export plug-ins need to reference everything at once in the same location.

Scaling and Aligning the Pivot Point

All weapon and character models in games need to be properly scaled and must have a pivot point (or axis) that is aligned according to the game engine for which they are being designed.

- Generally speaking, the scale of the model is measured in meters; the game engine will render models according to this measurement. That means if the coffee mug you just exported is set to 10 meters, you'll have enough java to keep an entire country awake all night!

- The pivot point makes the model face the proper direction when placed in the game environment.

Scale the Mesh

When Lars (my artist friend and colleague) and I were conceptualizing the slogre model in Chapter 2, I envisioned a beast that would lumber around at approximately four meters tall. To scale the slogre accordingly, select the slogre object, right-click it, and choose Properties in the Transform menu that appears; you should end up with an Object Properties panel that shows critical information such as polygon count, user-defined properties, and size (see Figure 14.5). As shown, the slogre model currently stands at a z-axis height of over five meters, a bit taller than necessary.

To scale this big guy down to around four meters, do the following:

1. Exit the Object Properties panel.

2. Click the Select and Uniform Scale tool located at the top of the screen.

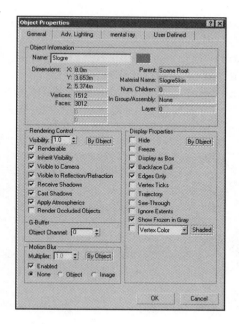

Figure 14.5 *Right-click the slogre model to bring up its Object Properties panel.*

3. Right-click this tool to open the Scale Transform Type-In dialog box, where you can manually enter a new scale percentage.

4. After doing a little math, I've determined that to reduce the slogre's z-axis height from 5.374 meters to 4.000 meters, you'll have to scale him down about 74.4 percent. Type 74.4 in the X, Y, and Z fields, as shown in Figure 14.6 to shrink the slogre down to size.

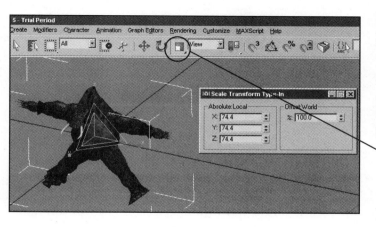

Figure 14.6 *Use the Scale Transform Type-In dialog to scale the slogre down about 75%, which makes him just about four meters tall.*

The Select and Uniform Scale tool

Notice that if you right-click the slogre and view his properties, the height is still the same. That's because 3D Studio keeps tab on every single move you make, including when you physically move, rotate, and scale your objects. These types of operations are commonly known as *transforms,* and can be utilized in hundreds of applications. When you perform an operation such as scaling the slogre, the slogre's size on the screen will change, but the new measurements won't be locked down until you reset the transforms on the model; the quickest and easiest way to do so is to add a Reset XForm modifier onto the modifier stack. To make the transform permanent, click the Reset XForm button in the Utilities tab of the Command Panel, and then click the Reset Selected button below it to add the modifier to the modifier stack (see Figure 14.7). Then, return to the slogre's Object Properties screen to confirm that the slogre has, indeed, been scaled down in size.

> **NOTE**
>
> If you're fiddling around with your model, and aren't ready to commit to the changes you've made, don't reset your transforms. That way, 3D Studio maintains a history of the model, enabling you to quickly and easily undo any transform you've performed.

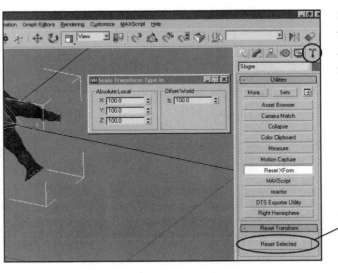

Figure 14.7 *Apply the Reset XForm modifier to lock down the scale changes.*

The Reset XForm button

If you're sure you want to retain the changes you've made, feel free to collapse the item in the modifier stack; in the Modifier panel, just right-click the item in the stack and choose Collapse To (or Collapse All, which will collapse the entire stack). Figure 14.8 shows the Reset XForm on top of the character mesh in the stack.

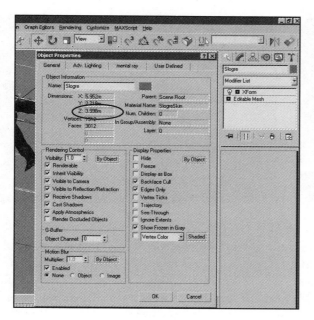

Figure 14.8 *The Reset XForm added to the modifier stack. Collapse this to retain your changes forever.*

Set the Pivot Point

In the case of the *Torque* engine, the programming code requires that the character mesh (and all other meshes, for that matter) have its axes aligned so that the y axis points directly forward (through the front of the model), the z axis points straight up, and the x axis points to the object's sides. In Figure 14.9, the x and z axes are correct, but the y axis is backwards.

Figure 14.9 *The axes of the slogre must be aligned so that the he faces in the proper direction in the game. Here, his y axis is pointing 180 degrees in the wrong direction.*

To correct the orientation of the model, you can use the Select and Rotate tool to manually rotate the model 180 degrees so his y axis faces the front, or you can right-click the tool and enter a value of 180 in the Rotate Transform Type-In dialog box's Z field (see Figure 14.10). When the axes are correct, use the Reset XForm modifier to lock down the transform as you did in the previous section. (You'll have to use the Arc Rotate tool, located in the bottom-right portion of the screen, to swing the scene around to see the slogre's face again.)

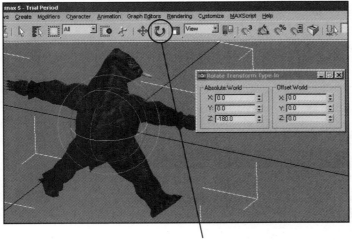

Figure 14.10 *Use the Select and Rotate tool to swing the slogre around so he faces along the positive y axis. Reset the XForm to lock the transform down.*

The Select and Rotate tool

Some Final Mesh Adjustments

With your slogre character properly aligned and scaled, now is your last chance to fix any other irritations or abnormalities with the model. (Of course, the longer you stare at your work, the more you think it stinks—no matter how much work you put in to perfecting it, it'll never be quite satisfactory!) I, for one, think he needs to be more menacing and less portly. And maybe his head should be elongated a bit, and his legs and arms made a bit thicker. After all, you want this thing to look so ferocious it startles other players, not to look like Barney.

With the modifier stack collapsed, you can expand the Editable Mesh element that remains by default and choose Face. Then, using the Select Object tool while holding down the Ctrl (to add) or Alt (to subtract) key, make selections of the character mesh that you want to modify (these are the same selection techniques you used with trueSpace and DeepUV). In Figure 14.11, I'm carefully selecting the torso of the slogre using a combination of Left, Front, and Top views. Try pressing F3 to switch to a shaded wireframe to easily see your selections about the mesh.

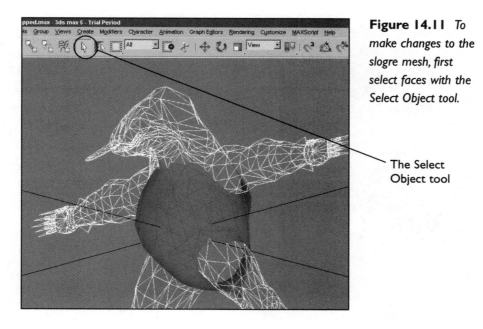

Figure 14.11 *To make changes to the slogre mesh, first select faces with the Select Object tool.*

The Select Object tool

> **TIP**
>
> **Uncheck the Ignore Backfaces option in the Selection section of the Editable Mesh modifier's panel if you want to select all faces in front and back of your mesh at once, or check it to grab only those faces nearest your view.**

When the area of the character you'd like to change has been selected, you can apply one of many different parametric modifiers listed in the Modifier List. For instance, in Figure 14.12, I've applied the Taper modifier to give the slogre a dose of Body by Jake. (These modifiers are called *parametric* because their options, once activated, allow you to dial in the parameters and see the effects dynamically.)

You can add other modifiers on top of the existing ones; for example, if you're satisfied with the top-to-bottom taper, add a front-to-back taper to finish the job. Just be careful when making these changes. If you go nuts, you can end up distorting the U-Vs, which means you'll have to go back to DeepUV and/or modify the texture map accordingly. Subtle changes are the key if you want to avoid lots of work.

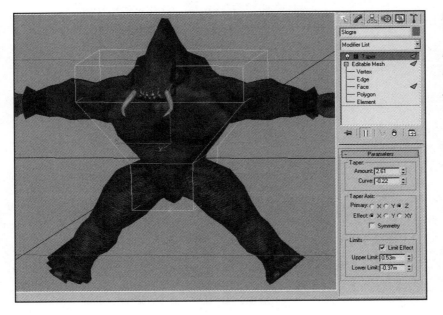

Figure 14.12

Trimming out the model with the Taper modifier makes this guy look a bit more menacing.

TIP

Place an Edit Mesh modifier on the existing modifiers in the stack to continue making changes to other body parts. That way, you can keep all modifiers on the stack without having to collapse it.

In any case, finish up your mesh and texture changes here, because the next step is to add bones to deform the slogre for animations. This is a fairly complex process that affects the mesh directly; additional mesh changes will result in you having to alter the bones, redo the skin-weighting process, and so on. Figure 14.13 shows my final results, after I enhanced a few other areas of the slogre.

Lastly, once you've finished making the changes by applying different modifiers, be sure to save your work, then right-click the modifier stack and choose Collapse All. The Torque engine won't be able to read all mesh modifier items in this stack; in fact, it must see only an Editable Mesh object with a Skin modifier during exportation.

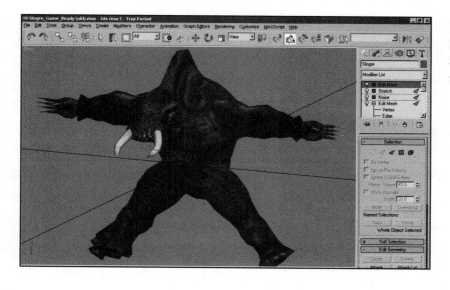

Figure 14.13 My final (but I'm still not satisfied!) changes to the slogre mesh.

Creating the Bounding Box

Every model in a game must be surrounded by an invisible square box, called a *bounding box*, to communicate to the game engine the extent of the model's dimensions. These bounding boxes are used to determine when one object, such as a character, collides with another object, such as the ground or a bullet. Collision determination happens within the game code; it's your job, however, to properly set these bounds.

If you're using the *Torque* engine, all you have to do is create a box or cube primitive that completely surrounds the model (in this case, the slogre) in all directions, and set the bounding box's pivot point in the same fashion as before, with the y-axis pointing forward. Finally, the box needs to be named Bounds. Here's how:

> **NOTE**
>
> If you're not using the *Torque* engine, check your engine's specifications as to what the bounding box might need to be named (as well as for other required objects in the scene).

1. In the Create panel (next to the Modifier panel), select the Geometry section.

2. Click on the Box button and, in the User perspective view, which shows the slogre in full textured 3D, click and drag to create a box. The first pass of clicking and dragging creates the base of the box, and when you release the mouse and drag again, it will create the height of the box. By creating the box in this User view, the box will inherit the correct x, y, and z axes of the slogre, that it needs for the Torque engine.

3. Scale and move the box to encompass the slogre, as shown in Figure 14.14. The box doesn't have to surround it precisely; make sure it's close, but definitely completely around the slogre.

3. In a solid-rendered viewport, the box will hide the slogre. To prevent this, right-click the bounding box and choose Properties from the menu that appears.

4. In the Display Properties section, check Display as Box. That way, all you'll see is an outline of the box.

> **TIP**
>
> When manipulating the same object using multiple view windows, it helps to have the Selection Lock Toggle button (the one with a padlock on it, located at the bottom of your screen) toggled on. This keeps your operations confined to the selected object. When you're finished, click the button to toggle it off.

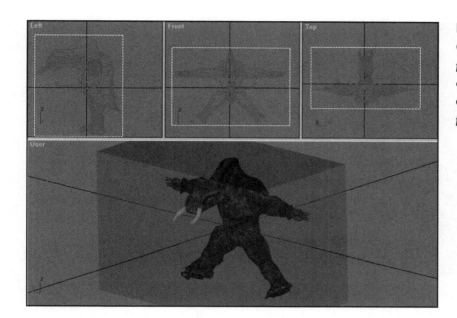

Figure 14.14
Create a box primitive, scale it, and move it so it completely encompasses the slogre.

NOTE

The bounding box must also completely surround any animations the character goes through. That is, if a single animation has the character jumping, the overall size of the bounding box must encompass this jump.

5. While you're in this screen, type Bounds in the field at the very top to rename this object. (It doesn't have to be capitalized, but I like to do that for labeling reasons.) Click OK.

6. In the Hierarchy panel, click the Affect Pivot Only button.

7. Notice that the bounding box's axes are correct, but are located at the base of the box. Just click the Center to Object button in the Hierarchy panel to move the pivot point to the center of the bounding box (Figure 14.15). Some game engines use this pivot point as the center of gravity of the model, which is used for actions like rotation when the weapon is ready for pickup on the floor of a game. The *Torque* engine defines the floor of the slogre using the slogre's pivot point.

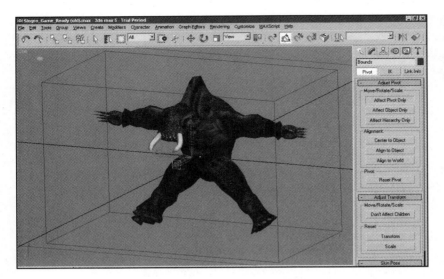

Figure 14.15

Center the pivot point of the slogre's bounding box

8. Lastly, in the Hierarchy panel, click on the Link Info button. In this area, in the Move section, uncheck the Z axis. This will allow the slogre's bounds to remain static with him, but when he jumps in the game, the z portion of the bounds won't move.

Preview in Torque

Before proceeding any further with this character, let's dump him into the *Torque* engine and view the results in the *Torque* demo, *Realm Wars*. (This demo and the required plug-ins are located on the CD-ROM.) First, make sure you're able to see the model in *Torque*'s model viewer:

1. Click the DTS Exporter Utility button to view a number of options that allow you to export your object and animations.

2. In the Utilities panel, click the Renumber Selection button in the General section.

> **NOTE**
>
> If you haven't done so already, place the **max2dtsExporter.dle** file, located in the Chapter 14 Data section on the CD-ROM, in 3D Studio Max's \plugins\ folder and restart the program. You should then have a DTS Exporter utility listed in the Utilities section of the Command Panel. Add a button for it by clicking on the **Configure Button Sets** button.

3. A dialog box opens; type 2 and click OK to renumber the slogre model to slogre2, representing the current detail level of the model that will be displayed in the game engine (see the LOD section later in this chapter).

4. Click the Embed Shape button in the Utilities panel's General section to place the mesh in a *Torque* engine required hierarchy, viewable in the schematic view. You'll refer to this view as you manually link other required dummy objects to the slogre. For more detailed information on torque's hierarchy and dummy objects, see Chapter 13 where I explained all about them when setting up the RF-9 plasma gun.

5. By clicking the Embed Shape button, you added some required dummy nodes to the scene and linked them along with the slogre mesh into one organized hierarchy. Click the Schematic View button to see the hierarchy (see Figure 14.16).

When you export the mesh as a DTS file, the exporter looks for this hierarchy in the scene and uses it to logically create the character. If the slogre mesh is not present in this exact scheme, the exporter won't know what it is trying to export. Note that the bounding box is still on its own; the exporter simply checks the scene for any object named "Bounds" and uses that as the bounding box.

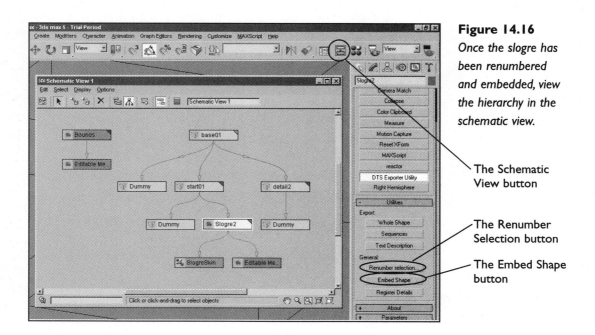

Figure 14.16

Once the slogre has been renumbered and embedded, view the hierarchy in the schematic view.

The Schematic View button

The Renumber Selection button

The Embed Shape button

Exporting the Model

Now that everything is in place, it's time to export the model. To properly export anything for *Torque*, you must place the MAX scene file, a single CFG file, and the model's skin file in the same export folder. The CFG file can have any name with a .cfg file extension, but only one may exist; the contents of this file vary depending on what you want to do. The default configuration file that comes with the *Torque* engine looks like this:

```
AlwaysExport:
eye
cam
mount0
//mount1
//jetnozzle0

NeverExport:
Bip01
Bip01 L Finger*
Bip01 R Finger*
Dummy*
Bip01 L Toe*
Bip01 R Toe*
start01
mountpoint
DELETE*
//Ski0
//Ski1
Light0
Light1
//Mount1
//Mount2

+Error::AllowEmptySubtrees
+Error::AllowCrossedDetails
+Error::AllowUnusedMeshes
-Error::AllowOldSequences
-Error::RequireViconNode
-Param::CollapseTransforms

-Param::findMergeIndices
-Param::computeScreenError
=Params::T2AutoDetail 0
```

This configuration file is commonly used for character models, because it includes a few critical dummy nodes required for proper game play (mounting weapons, player view dummy, and so on). The most important section is AlwaysExport, which is where you enter the labels of all items you want the exporter to include in the creation of the *Torque* engine's game shape object, a DTS file.

I've named this file **player.cfg** and placed it in the Chapter 14 Data section on the CD-ROM; you can use it, or you can type the code you see here in a text file and name it **player.cfg**. Either way, place the file in the same folder as the MAX and PNG files. When your MAX scene file, **player.cfg** file, and PNG skin file are all in the same folder, do the following:

1. Click the Whole Shape button in the DTS Exporter panel.

2. You are prompted for a name. You can enter any name you wish, but for now, type **player.dts** and click OK.

3. The exporter will take a few seconds to process the mesh. If all went well, the exporter will also create a **dump.dmp** file; read this file if any of your objects weren't exported properly.

> **NOTE**
>
> When it comes time to export the model with a bones structure, it's a good idea to retain the same naming convention because all *Realm Wars'* default animation sequences refer to the model name "player.dts."

Viewing the Model

To view the model, do the following:

1. Place the **player.dts** file and the slogre's skin file (in my case, **SlogreSkin.png**) in a separate folder in the \RealmWars\rw\data\shapes\ directory. (The *Torque* viewer looks to the root of the \shapes\ folder for all models in the game.)

2. Create an icon for the *Realm Wars* demo that uses the -show parameter. The *Torque* viewer is essentially the *Realm Wars* game, but activated by the -show switch. For example, the command line parameter for the *Torque* viewer would be

   ```
   RealmWars.exe -show
   ```

3. When you run the viewer, you should end up in a simple GUI screen; click the Load Shape button and choose the slogre model from the list. If you set the axes properly and all's well, you'll see the back of the beast.

4. Press the W, S, A, and D keys to zoom in and out and rotate around the slogre (see Figure 14.17).

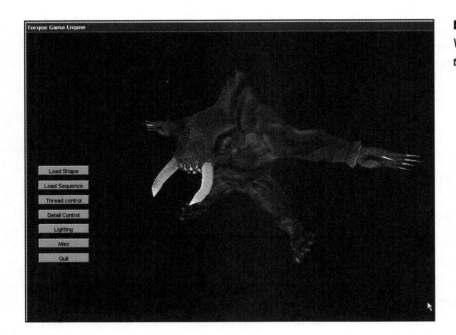

Figure 14.17
Viewing the slogre in the Torque viewer.

If you're not able to view the model, then something went wrong during the export process. Most likely, your bitmap was too large, the mesh wasn't linked in the hierarchy properly, or some other minor problem foiled the process. Just check the **dump.dmp** file and look for signs of trouble. If you are having problems, be sure to resolve them now; things just get more complex from here!

Bones, Skeletal Weighting, and Animating with Character Studio

By installing a bones and skeletal weighting system, you ensure that the mesh will deform properly during animations. Any 3D video game's character that is capable of performing any type of movement contains a bones structure—invisible to the game world—that resides inside of and is attached to the mesh itself. The bones can consist of anything from a set of inverse kinematically linked primitive objects, like boxes, to a special Biped object that comes with a modifiable joint system. Once a skeletal system is designed and placed properly, the bones themselves can be animated. Then, once an animation sequence is created, the *Torque* exporter may export the sequence, and in the game the sequence will drive the bones system, which in turn animates the character mesh.

When you're finished with your mesh, the animated bones take care of the rest. It's up to you, however, to design animation sequences that the game engine can call during game play. For instance, if the user presses the Run Forward key, the *Torque* engine calls the **player_forward.dsq** animation, and the mesh deforms accordingly (that is, the left and right leg bones move in a running motion). For every action that is required of your character in a game, you must develop a sequence that drives it. Thankfully, however, the *Torque* engine (as well as many other engines) comes with default character animations that you can use to drive the skeleton you create (see the Adding and Attaching a Biped section below).

NOTE

In many games, animation sequences can be blended, as is the case when a character is running and firing a weapon at the same time.

How Character Studio Works

Character Studio is simply a nicely written plug-in that features a predefined bipedal skeleton system that you can modify to your character's shape, attach to your character, vertex weigh, and animate. (Of course, you could set up your own skeletal system from scratch, but why bother when someone else has already done it for you?) In fact, this plug-in also contains many pre-defined basic animations that you can apply to your characters. Here's a short list of the main steps you'll take to get the slogre running, so to speak:

1. **Install the biped.** This involves adding and modifying a bipedal bones system, which starts off as a template of sorts. The biped is positioned and scaled to the inside of the limbs of the mesh, and finally attached using the Skin modifier. Once the biped is attached, you can deform the mesh around the bones by grabbing them and moving them around.

2. **Weight the skin.** This is the process of defining the envelopes of influence the bones have over the neighboring vertices. Put simply, there is a 1:1 bone-to-mesh ratio for deformation. The bones apply themselves directly to the vertices of the mesh. In some cases, however, you must further define preferences that the bones themselves have for moving vertices over others. This is called *weighting*, and is fun but somewhat tedious. If you don't weight certain

areas correctly, like where the upper arm meets the forearm, the movements will look weird, such as seeing the forearm bulge instead of the bicep.

3. **Animate the bones.** Once the skeletal weighting is satisfactory, the next step is to generate individual animation sequences for the bones to follow. You can use presets in Character Studio, and you can define your own. Animation of bones is subject for an entire book, literally, so for now we'll use the default *Torque* sequences.

4. **Export the mesh/animation.** The last steps are to export the mesh (as well as the individual animations that drive the skeletal system) to the game engine of your choice using that engine's proprietary Max exporter plug-in. In this case, you'll dump out just the mesh with a biped object installed to the *Torque* engine, without any animations (the game engine's default animations will do the trick and drive the bones of the slogre character). Generally speaking, the game needs a reference mesh—which is just the static, unanimated model—and a series of animation sequences without the mesh that drive the static model. Typically, the static mesh model is referred to as a *reference.*

Adding and Attaching a Biped

The first thing you should do before you begin adding a Character Studio biped is hide all of the objects you created earlier, except for the slogre mesh itself. Doing so will help unclutter your workspace so as to avoid confusion. To hide all your objects, click on the Display panel, then choose Hide by Name within the panel's rollout. In the Hide Objects dialog box that pops up, select everything except the slogre2 item and then click Hide (Figure 14.18). Use the Display panel for hiding and unhiding objects, as well as for freezing and unfreezing them (freezing will lock down any objects so they can't be manipulated).

It would be difficult to install the biped in the slogre while it's in solid render mode, but it would be helpful to have a visible, see-through shape of him. Click on the slogre to select it, then, at the bottom of the Display panel, check See-Through in the Display Properties section. The solid rendered mesh should turn into a see-through object (see Figure 14.19). Finally, to prevent the slogre from being affected while you're adjusting the biped, freeze him in place by choosing Freeze Selected in the Freeze section of the Display panel rollout.

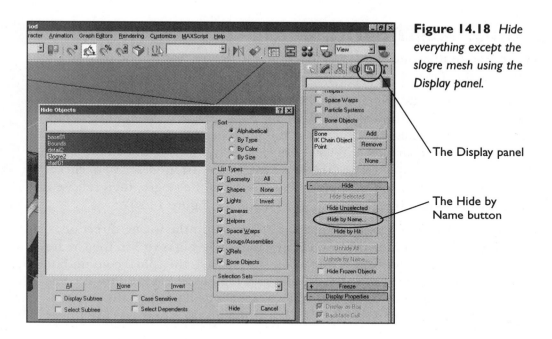

Figure 14.18 *Hide everything except the slogre mesh using the Display panel.*

The Display panel

The Hide by Name button

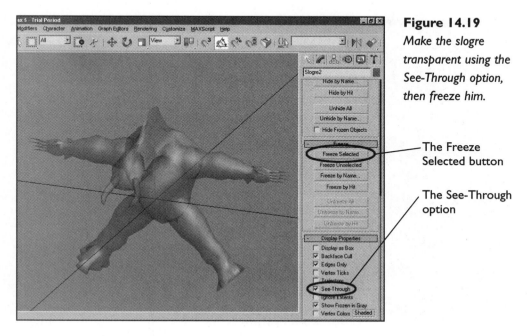

Figure 14.19 *Make the slogre transparent using the See-Through option, then freeze him.*

The Freeze Selected button

The See-Through option

Adding, Adjusting, and Aligning a Biped

Follow these steps to install and position a biped structure that will be used by the animations in the *Torque* engine to move the slogre mesh:

1. Click on the Create panel, then click the Systems button. Under the Systems section, click the Biped button. A default parameterized panel will roll out, allowing you to make adjustments to the number of limbs, fingers, toes, and so on that your character will have. For now, leave that section alone, as you can adjust those settings once the biped is created. In the User view, click and drag the cursor to the approximate height of the slogre, then release it. In a flash, the new biped skeleton is created (see Figure 14.20).

2. Notice that the biped itself is rotated 180 degrees in the wrong direction; you'll fix that in a moment. Now change the Spine Links to 3 in the Create panel's Biped rollout. Notice that when you do that, the spinal-column bone count of the biped drops automatically, and the entire biped shifts to compensate (see Figure 14.21). Next, change the Fingers to 1 and the Finger Links to 1. Do the same for the toes. Even though the slogre has five fingers,

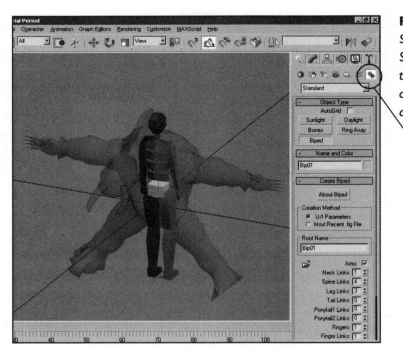

Figure 14.20

Select Biped from the Systems section of the Create panel, and click and drag to create a biped.

The Systems button

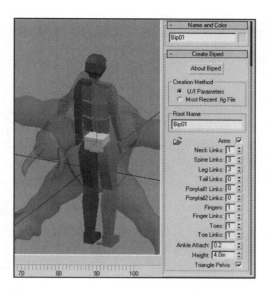

Figure 14.21

Adjust the parameters of the biped to change the bone structure.

and you could just as well install all five, his hand will be the only thing animating that portion of the general appendage, according to the default animations of the *Torque* engine (for other game engines, you might need to utilize these finger bones to articulate the fingers in the mesh). Finally, change the Height parameter to 4.0m; this will be the approximate height of the slogre.

NOTE

The parameters in the Biped rollout can be changed to create a nearly infinite amount of skeletal structures that would fit and work with almost any shape mesh. There are a couple of interesting features of the possible bipedal arrangements—for instance, the Ponytail links can be used to drive the lower jaw of a character, to which you can then animate it to simulate speech.

3. Now the biped must be moved and rotated into position. The goal here is to place the biped in the exact center of the slogre mesh; then you can adjust the individual limbs to coincide with the slogre's joints. To do this, click on the Motion panel, then click on the Figure Mode button (see Figure 14.22). The Figure Mode button will allow you to fine-tune the biped's shape to match the slogre's. The Motion panel is also where you can make and modify animations for the biped.

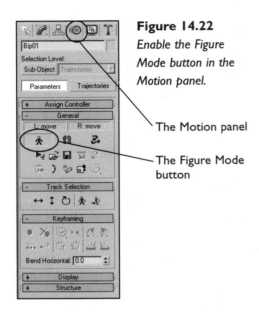

Figure 14.22
Enable the Figure Mode button in the Motion panel.

The Motion panel

The Figure Mode button

4. In Figure Mode, click on the Select and Rotate tool and enable the Angle Snap Toggle button. In the User view, rotate the biped 180 degrees so it is facing in the same direction as the slogre. Use the Select and Move tool, along with the Left, Top, and User views, to position the biped so the pelvis (the box where the thighs meet) is in the approximate location of the slogre's pelvis (see Figure 14.23). The pelvis area houses the biped's Center of Mass (COM), which helps determine the overall balance possessed by the character when in motion. Be sure to align the biped so that it is as centered as possible within the mesh.

> **NOTE**
>
> The *Center of Mass* (COM) is a separate element of the biped structure, and not really a bone object. It can be positioned during animations to change the way a character moves. For instance, when a character transitions from a walk to a sprint, it would be more natural for the COM to shift forward, causing the character to lean forward. If the COM stayed exactly in the center of the pelvis, the character would remain unnaturally erect when going from walking to sprinting.

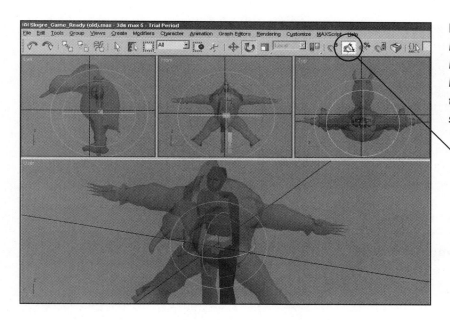

Figure 14.23

Rotate and move the Bip01 object so the biped pelvis is centered to match the slogre's pelvis.

The Angle Snap Toggle button

Matching the Biped Skeleton to the Slogre

Now for the fun part (note sarcasm). This next part, where you have to scale, transform, and align all of the bones of the biped so they take on roughly the same shape as the character mesh, is probably one of the most time-consuming and tedious of things to do in the modeling industry. The point of this careful aligning is to make the skin-weighting job (discussed in the next section) much easier. Character Studio does a fantastic job of making biped alignment a fairly smooth process, but let me warn you now—you must take your time, and have patience. This process will become easier and easier with experience.

The bones in the biped have special properties called *envelopes*, which are mechanisms with which the animator makes adjustments so that the bones properly control their nearby vertices. The size of each bone itself directly corresponds, generally speaking, to the size of the control envelopes once the Skin modifier is applied to the mesh. Therefore, the more precise you are about matching the biped bones to the mesh, the easier the overall weighting process will be.

Following are the general steps you need to take in order to align the biped skeleton to the slogre mesh:

1. Switch to a Back view (this will display the front of the model) and press the Min/Max toggle button at the bottom-right corner of the screen. This will make your character take up the entire screen space.

2. Start by swinging the biped's arms up so that they generally match the slogre's. Do this by clicking once on the Select and Rotate tool, then once on the left upper arm, which should then become highlighted. Next, click on the Symmetrical button in the Motion panel; the right upper arm of the biped will be selected. It's best to work symmetrically; that way, everything stays even. Now click and drag on the first yellow concentric circle of the Rotate gizmo, which represents the z axis of the bone. As you drag, notice that both arms swing upwards (see Figure 14.24)! You may have to turn off the Angle Snap Toggle button to position the arms more precisely. The arms should now be somewhat in the same position and shape as the slogre's.

> **NOTE**
> The biped object's bone structure works in almost the same way that a human's does. That is, if you try to rotate the forearm back and forth, it will only go towards the body, and will not bend backwards at the elbow. Also, as you pull forward on the forearm, the upper arm naturally (and not rigidly) follows with it. This process is called *inverse kinematics*, and is a characteristic feature of Character Studio Bipeds.

3. Now you need to scale the upper bones of the biped to match the slogre's mesh. First click on the Select and Non-Uniform scale button, then click on one of the clavicle bones. Then, select the Symmetrical button in the Motion panel and scale the bones so that they spread the arms away from the body a bit. This will push the upper arm bones out so that they're in better position (see Figure 14.25).

4. Continue scaling the other spine, neck, and head components to fit the mesh. The spine doesn't need to precisely fit the belly of the slogre; simply adjust the spine so that the arms drop down and center themselves within the mesh. The head can be scaled fairly big and elongated, in order to cover the entire neck, face, and tusks of the slogre.

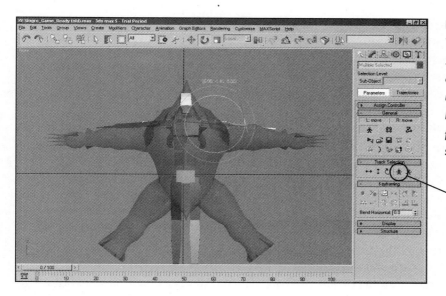

Figure 14.24
With the Symmetrical button enabled, rotate the upper arms so that both are in the same position as the slogre's.

The Symmetrical button

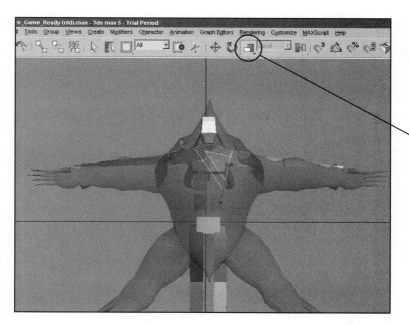

Figure 14.25
Symmetrically scale the clavicles so that they spread the arms away from the body.

The Select and Non-Uniform Scale button

5. Next, the arms can be stretched and scaled outward. A cool feature of Character Studio is the Rubber Band option, located in the Motion panel. Click on this option, then select the forearms and scale them—notice that as the forearms are scaled towards the palms, the upper arm bones follow in a stretching attitude (see Figure 14.26). The Rubber Band feature can only be used with the arm and leg bones, but it does make your job much easier. Finally, rotate the forearms 90 degrees backwards so that the entire arm, including the palms, fits the slogre mesh.

> **TIP**
>
> If you're having trouble conceptualizing the rotation of bones, or if you try to rotate one bone and, annoyingly, another bone moves, mimic the same movements yourself. For example, in Step 5, the arm needed to be rotated backwards to fit the mesh. Just place your arms straight out, palms down, then rotate your forearms backwards. Your hands have no choice (unless you're weirdly jointed!) but to rotate backwards as well.

6. Continue scaling and adjusting the biped's upper arms, forearms, and hands to completely fill the slogre. Be sure the joints generally match up to the joints of the slogre mesh—that is, the elbow is where the upper arm and the forearm meet, and the end of the forearm is the wrist, just after the slogre's metal cuff.

7. Repeat Steps 2 through 6 for the legs (see Figure 14.27).

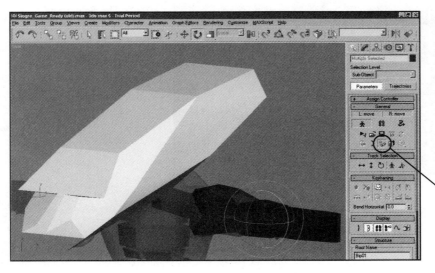

Figure 14.26

Enable the Rubber Band option and symmetrically scale the forearms to match the slogre's. Rotate them 90 degrees so that the palms match the slogre's.

The Rubber Band option

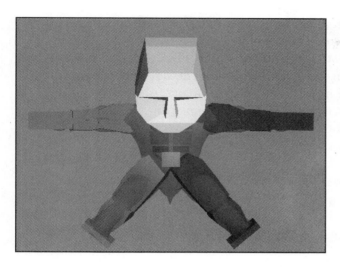

Figure 14.27
Repeat the moving, rotating, and scaling procedure for the legs. Be sure that the joints match up.

8. When the bones are scaled and they match the slogre as well as possible, press the Min/Max toggle button to go back to the orthogonal view screens. Scale and move all of the bones so that the entire biped structure fits as well as possible into the slogre mesh (see Figure 14.28). Note that the spine objects don't have to be big; in fact, scaling them to the size of the mesh will only make the weighting envelopes enormous and cause them to hog all of the vertices of the slogre.

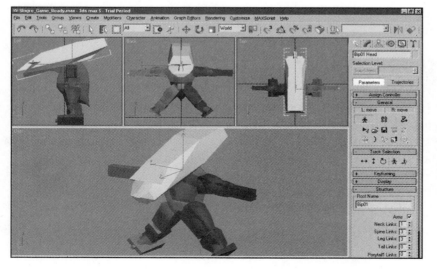

Figure 14.28 *Use the other orthogonal views to scale and rotate all of the components to match the side profile of the slogre's body. Note that the spine objects don't have to be scaled to match the slogre's body.*

You can now click on the Save Figure button, located in the Motion panel. This will save the current figure of the biped itself, which you can recall should anything go awry later on. Also, when you're satisfied with the biped, click the Figure Mode button in the Motion panel to exit this mode. Once out of the figure mode, try pressing the Save button again—it will now save the Biped object itself (that is, the bones structure itself that you created). Saving these items (.fig and .bip files) is a good idea so that you can recall them later in case you've accidentally moved any of the bones, or retrieve the biped for another character (see Figure 14.29).

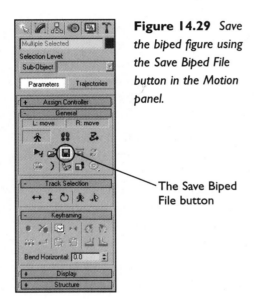

Figure 14.29 *Save the biped figure using the Save Biped File button in the Motion panel.*

The Save Biped File button

Attaching the Biped to the Slogre Using the Skin Modifier

You must apply the Skin modifier before the biped can drive the mesh of the slogre. Before you proceed, change the view of the bones to a more comfortable one by clicking on the Bones button in the Motion panel; a wireframe version of the bones will be displayed. Click on the Objects button right next to the wireframe. This turns on and off the 3D representation of the bones themselves (see Figure 14.30). The small + signs between bones represent the joints, giving you a better view of their alignment with the mesh. Hmm, doesn't look like all that work you put in was worth it now, eh?

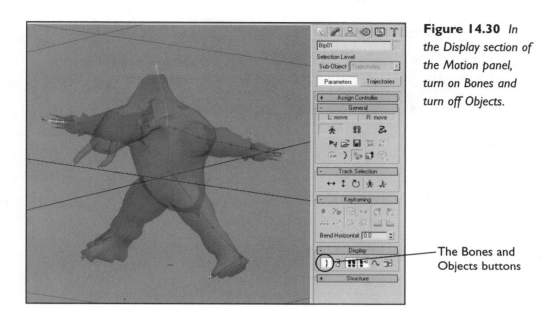

Figure 14.30 *In the Display section of the Motion panel, turn on Bones and turn off Objects.*

The Bones and Objects buttons

You'll need to unfreeze the slogre and unhide any object you hid earlier in the chapter. Go to the Display panel and choose both Unhide All and Unfreeze All. Earlier I showed you how to embed the slogre mesh into a DTS hierarchy using the DTS Exporter utility. The *Torque* engine doesn't require that structure for a bipedal arrangement; instead it uses the Bip01 object as the top level of the hierarchy. Therefore, you'll need to unlink the Slogre2 and detail2 objects. Do so by opening the Schematic View, which you saw earlier, and expanding the Start01 and Base01 dummy objects. Using the Unlink Selection tool, click on the Slogre2 and detail2 objects to unlink them (see Figure 14.31). Finally, delete the Start01 and Base01 objects by clicking on them and pressing Del. All that should be in the scene now are the Bip01 biped structure, the Slogre2 mesh, the Bounds (bounding box), and the detail2 dummy.

Now select the slogre mesh and, in the Modifier panel, apply a Skin modifier. This modifier doesn't look like much, because you haven't yet added the bones. Click on the plus sign to the left of the Skin modifier to expand the modifier, then select Envelopes. In the Envelopes rollout, click on the Add button; doing so will display a Select Bones screen (see Figure 14.32). This screen will allow you to select which bones you want to drive the mesh itself. For the *Torque* engine, you'll need everything except the Bip01 object itself, Footsteps, all toes, any fingers, and nub objects (make sure you don't select detail2 either).

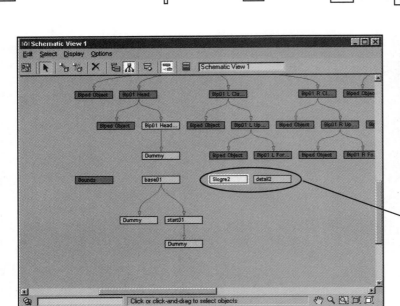

Figure 14.31 *In the Schematic View, use the Unlink Selection to unlink both the Slogre2 mesh and Detail2 dummy objects from the old DTS hierarchy.*

Unlinked objects

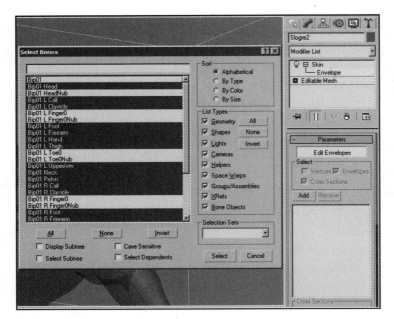

Figure 14.32 *Apply the Skin modifier to the slogre mesh. Expand the modifier, select Envelopes, then add all biped objects (except detail2, Bip01, Footsteps, toes, any fingers, and nubs) to the Envelopes section.*

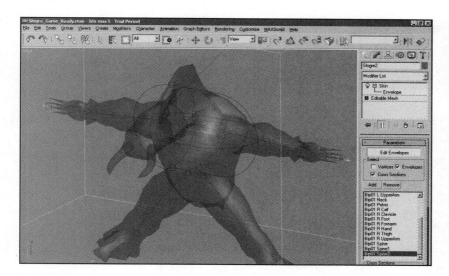

Figure 14.33
The attached biped, displaying the skin envelopes.

You're excluding the toes and fingers because you'll only really need them to help position the arms. You could have included additional fingers in the original biped object, in order to curl the fingers of the slogre mesh, but the *Torque* engine's default animations don't use them—the hand bones will move both the hands and fingers of the slogre. Once the proper selection of bones has been included in the Skin modifier, you'll see the slogre mesh surrounded by wireframe representations of the adjustable skin envelopes (see Figure 14.33).

Weighting the Model

Once the bones have been added to the Skin modifier, the bones are linked to the mesh and you're free to grab them and move them, which in turn should drive the mesh that surrounds them. However, before you move the bones, you need to be sure that the envelopes of the bones equally surround all vertices of the mesh, so that the mesh moves smoothly at each bone location of the slogre's body. Also, stray vertices not included in any envelope stick in 3D space and don't move with the bones, preventing the slogre character from working properly (or at all) in the game engine. Following are the steps for adjusting the weights (balance of bone usage) of the vertices:

1. To make viewing the weighting much easier, make the mesh solid by going to the Display panel and unchecking the See-Through option in the panel's Display Properties section. Next, in the Display Color section at the very top

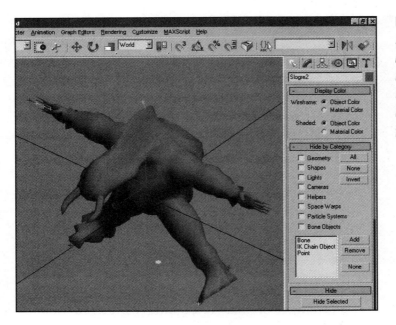

Figure 14.34

Select the slogre mesh, and in the Display panel select Shaded: Object Color. Press F3 to see the flat, shaded slogre.

of the Display panel, check the Shaded: Object Color option. This will make the slogre mesh a solid color (Figure 14.34).

2. Now go back to the Modifier panel and select Envelope in the Skin modifier. The currently selected bone should now display its envelope as varying shades of light yellow (least influenced vertices for that bone) to dark red (strongly influenced vertices) (see Figure 14.35). The various shades represent the weighting of the skin (mesh) for that particular area. Try selecting different bones from the list to see their influence on the vertices of the mesh. Also, by pressing F3, you can switch back and forth between the solid rendered mode and the wireframe mode that shows the vertices themselves.

3. Click on each bone and take a look at the weighting around that area. Check for bones that are taking up too much weight on vertices that don't really belong to them. For instance, in my situation, the head is covering vertices that belong to the slogre's back (see Figure 14.36). In a case like this, the envelope for this bone needs to be adjusted so that it covers only the head of the slogre.

> **TIP**
>
> You can turn off the grid by clicking Views: Show Home Grid in the top menu bar. This will help make your workspace even less cluttered.

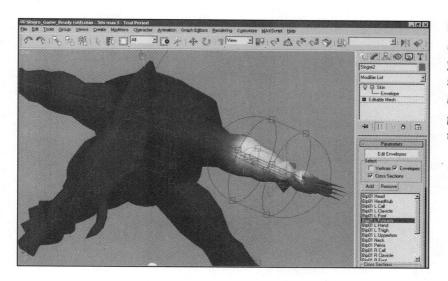

Figure 14.35
By clicking on a bone you can see various shades of color that indicate the bone's preference to the vertices nearest its area.

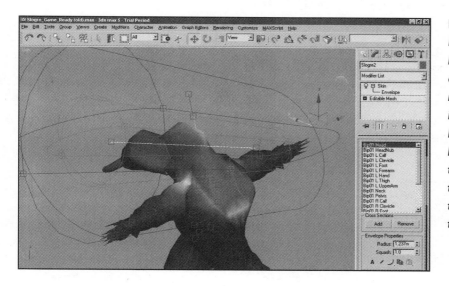

Figure 14.36
Notice that the head's envelope encompasses too many vertices, including those from the back. Adjust the head's envelope so that it uses mainly those vertices from the head portion of the mesh.

4. In the Skin modifier's rollout, just below the bone list, you'll see an Envelope Properties section. By changing the value of the Radius, you can effectively increase or decrease the size of the envelope. Or, you can click on the Move tool, then click on any one of the envelope's control points to move or scale them. In Figure 14.37, I tapered one end of the back of the head envelope, which effectively occluded the vertices of the back.

Figure 14.37
The adjusted head's envelope.

5. Sometimes it's hard to see if there are any stray vertices not enclosed by an envelope. Try this: click on the Skin portion of the Skin modifier to exit envelope mode, then click on the Select by Name button at the top of the screen, and select the hand bone. Use the Move tool to swing the slogre's arm forward. Notice in Figure 14.38 the stray vertices that need to be encompassed by the hand's envelope—they seem to stick in place.

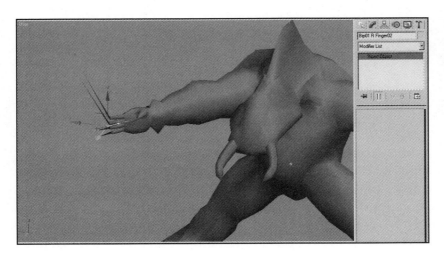

Figure 14.38
By moving certain bones around you can detect stray vertices that need to be encompassed by the bone's envelope.

6. With the arm still swung outward, I went back to the Envelope portion of the Skin modifier and adjusted the hand's envelope to extend a little further beyond the fingers. In a flash the stray vertices got sucked back in, becoming part of the hand bone's control (see Figure 14.39). The stray vertices, in this case, are due to the fact that the finger bones were not included in the envelope list.

7. Continue checking the rest of the bones for stray vertices. Pressing F3 to enter wireframe mode is another good way to do this, as the strays will not show up in colored envelopes, but will instead be a blue-colored vertex—just play around a bit with the bones, and see how the mesh behaves around them. Also, adjusting the envelopes where one bone meets another can help improve on the bulge of the mesh when the bones are flexed.

> **NOTE**
>
> The Physique modifier is much better than the Skin modifier for deforming the mesh of character models (for instance, the realistic bulging of muscles). However, Physique is not supported in this book's versionof *Torque*. If you're developing models for another game engine, be sure to check with its documentation to see if it supports Physique.

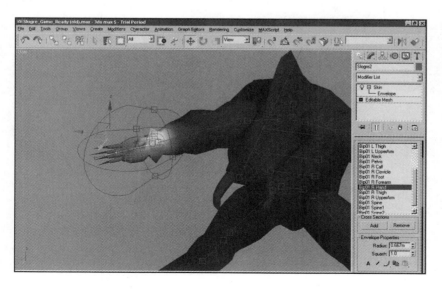

Figure 14.39 *By adjusting the hand's envelope near the end, the stray vertices are sucked in to the hand and corrected.*

8. Another way to adjust the weighting of the vertices is by using the Paint Weights option in the Skin modifier's envelope rollout. For instance, press F3 to enter wireframe mode, and look at the tail area; I'd like to have the pelvis bone take control of this area, since the tail doesn't do much else aside from following the pelvis in motion. With the Paint Weights button active, click the ellipse button to bring up the Painter Options screen. Here you can adjust the brush size and strength, along with about a billion other parameters. Change both the Max Strength and Max Size to 0.2; doing so will make the painting brush a small crosshair with not so much strength. Then, with the pelvis bone selected, just click and drag over the tail area to paint the weighting onto the vertices (Figure 14.40).

The Paint Weights option is handy if you're positioning bones and notice weird or improper bulges between bones. By painting on these affected areas, you'll dynamically see the bulges shift around accordingly. Continue adjusting weights all over your model until you're satisfied, then save your scene as a .MAX file.

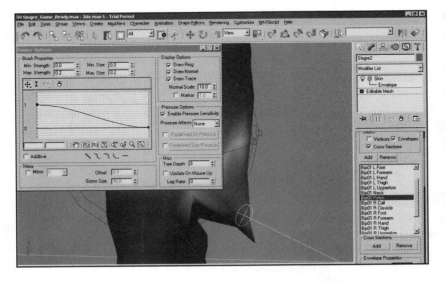

Figure 14.40
Use the Paint Weights option in the Envelope rollout to manually paint the vertices of the tail to be included with the Pelvis bone.

Adding and Manipulating Dummy Nodes

You'll need to create several dummy objects to represent those critical game hooks I mentioned in the previous chapter. *Dummies* are simply inert boxes you create, label, and link to specific parts of the character's body so that the game engine knows where to place items like weapons, backpacks, and so on. Some common ones for *Torque* are

- A mounting location called Mount0. This is the primary weapon-mounting location on all characters; for the slogre, it will be on the hand of your choice. Required on all character models.

- Secondary mounting locations, called Mount#, where # is a successive number 1, 2, and so on. These locations represent other mounting areas, so that the slogre can attach items like backpacks, other weapons, and vehicles. Mount1 and Mount2 are required dummies to be located just outside of the slogre's back.

- A dummy called Eye. This is located and oriented directly in front of the character's face. Eye represents the camera through which the player sees the game world when playing the game, using the character model as his or her own player mesh. For bots (non-player characters), this might not be required. Consult your game engine's requirements.

- A dummy called Cam. This is the camera mounting location, which can represent several things. For instance, when a player switches to a flying mode, in which he is no longer manipulating a character mesh (such as in post mortem, which is when you fly around the game world undetected until you re-spawn), the camera uses Cam to see the world. Some programmers use Cam to circle around a player who has been killed, as is the case in *Unreal*. For the *Torque* Engine, this dummy is attached to another dummy called Unlink.

- Detail objects, called Detail#, where # defines the level of detail. Required for all models, you must have at least one detail dummy to represent the base polygon count of the character's mesh. Level of detail (LOD) is critical for character meshes, because having a game full of 3,000+ characters walking around at all distances would be a complete waste of polygons. (See the LOD section ahead for details on creating, er, details.)

- Vehicle dummies, such as Ski0 and Ski1—which are located near the character's calves—enabling the character to mount or sit in a vehicle.

- The character can also have Light# dummies to allow for a lighting source for special situations like self-illumination and so on.

Some games and their engines might require additional mount and sprite locations, such as an ExplodePoint location for the programmers to hook a death explosion sequence onto. It's up to you to let the programmers know what will be attaching where, and what it will be called.

For now, your slogre really only needs the Detail2, Mount0, Mount1, Mount2, Eye, Cam, Ski0, and Ski1 dummy objects, plus another one called Unlink (for death camera purposes). Here's what to do:

1. In the Create tab of the Command Panel, click on the Helpers button (it looks like a tape measure).

2. In the Object Type section, click the Dummy button.

3. In an orthogonal view, click and drag to create a small dummy box (see Figure 14.41), and position it in one of the slogre's hands, just in front of the palm and between the thumb and first finger. This is where the slogre will hold the weapon.

4. Type Mount0 in the field in the Name and Color section.

> **NOTE**
>
> The size of the dummy is irrelevant; the *Torque* engine simply looks for a dummy object with the name Mount0 for a weapon mounting location, and references the dummy's axes for weapons location and alignment.

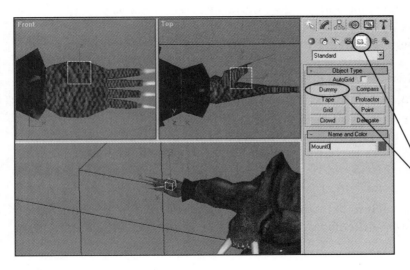

Figure 14.41 *Create a dummy object named* Mount0 *and position it in the slogre's hand. This will represent the mounting location for weapons.*

The Helpers button
The Dummy button

5. You need to align the axes of the Mount0 dummy just like you did earlier with the slogre's axes. In this case, however, the y axis must point in the direction you want the weapon to point. To begin, click on the Hierarchy tab in the Command Panel, then click the Affect Pivot Only button.

6. Use the Select and Rotate tool to rotate the axis so that the y axis points toward the slogre's fingers (see Figure 14.42). Use the Angle Snap tool, located at the bottom of the screen, to constrain this rotation in degree increments. With the y axis pointing forward, the weapon's grip will mount to it and face in the same direction.

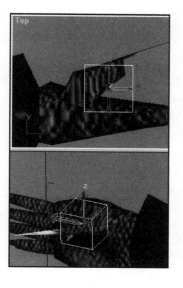

Figure 14.42 *Align the pivot point (axes) of the dummy object so the y axis points in the direction that the weapon should point.*

7. Create and position two more dummies, Eye and Cam; these should be placed right between the slogre's eyes and a few inches ahead of them, respectively.

8. Align the pivot point so the y axes for both are pointing forward, with the z axes pointing up.

9. Create and position two dummies, Mount1 and Mount2. Both of these should be located at the slogre's back, between the shoulders.

10. Create and position another two dummies, Ski0 and Ski1. The first should be located behind the left calf bone, and the second in the same location behind the right calf. Position the y axes so that they face forward.

11. Create a final dummy called Unlink. Just position it on the floor between the slogre's feet.

Linking the Nodes

Now that you've created all of the basic nodes required to make the slogre work in *Torque*, you need to link them to the proper locations in the Schematic View. Open the Schematic View and link each node as follows:

- The detail2 dummy must be linked to the Bip01 node (at the very top of the hierarchy).
- The Mount0 dummy must be linked to the Bip01 Right Hand.
- The Mount1 and Mount2 dummies must be linked to Bip01 Spine2.
- The Eye dummy must be linked to the Bip01 Head.
- The Unlink dummy must be linked to the Bip01 node. Then, the Cam dummy must be linked to the Unlink dummy.
- The Ski0 and Ski1 dummies must be linked to the Bip01 Left Calf and Right Calf, respectively.

Finally, the Bounds (bounding box) must be linked to the Bip01 node (at the top of the hierarchy). Figure 14.43 shows the exploded schematic view you should have.

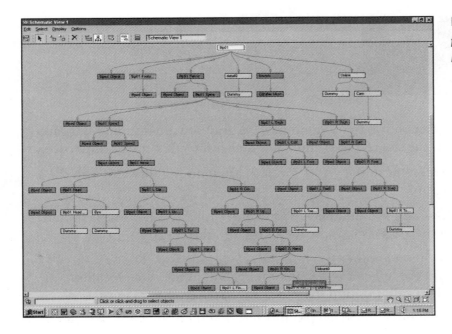

Figure 14.43 *The properly attached nodes to the biped.*

Create a Root Pose

When you export the slogre to the *Torque* engine, he'll need a default pose (unless you want him standing with his arms spread wide!). Create a root pose simply by manipulating and moving his arms and legs so he's in a position of your liking. In Figure 14.44, I modified the biped in the slogre's mesh so he looks ready to hold and fire the RF-9 plasma gun.

Figure 14.44
Create a root pose by moving the bones of the slogre.

Exporting and Viewing the Slogre in Torque

Exporting with the DTS Exporter utility in the Utilities panel is a bit different this time than it was earlier in this chapter. Go to the exporter and select Whole Shape. Make the name **player.dts**, and save the file to the \RealmWars\rw\data\shapes\player\ area instead. Be sure to have your **player.cfg** file in the same directory, along with the 3D Studio Max .MAX file and the **SlogreSkin.png** skin file. The difference in exporting this time is that you need to create the .DTS object in the existing \player\ folder. Navigate over to that folder and you'll see over 30 different .DSQ files, which are Torque's animation sequence files. These were also generated using the DTS Exporter utility. These files will animate the slogre's bones structure during game play.

The exporter might take a bit longer than it did the last time, as there is a lot to process. Remember to look at the **dump.dmp** file if anything goes wrong, or if an animation sequence does not work properly. Sometimes when a certain animation sequence won't work, you need to adjust the .CFG file and include or exclude node or bone labels.

Once the model is loaded using the realmwars.exe -show utility, click on the Thread Control button. This will load a Thread Control panel that you can use to view the different animation sequences being applied to the bones in the slogre (see Figure 14.45). Make sure that the animations work or you'll have problems using the slogre during the game!

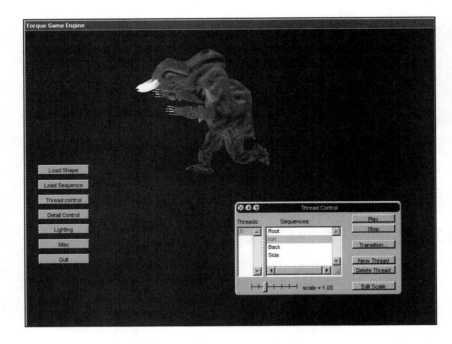

Figure 14.45

Use the Thread Control button in the Torque -Show utility to view the animation sequences driving the slogre.

Levels of Detail (LODs)

Here's the last thing you can do to optimize the mesh in the game, just as I said in the previous chapter. The levels of detail for the slogre represent the varying mesh densities the character will have in relation to the distances of the other players. It's important to have these levels of detail, as it would bog down the game engine to unnecessarily process a 3,000-polygon model that a player can't see from afar. In Chapter 13 I showed you how to make two LODs; here I'll show you how to make two as well.

1. In the Schematic View you should have the detail2 and Slogre2 objects; they currently should not be linked to anything. Just link the detail2 dummy object to the Bip01 object (the root of the biped itself). This will represent the lowest level of detail—the higher the number, the higher the detail. Of course, these are just reference markers for the game engine to use.

2. With the detail2 object still selected, you need to create another dummy object representing the highest level of detail. The easiest way to do this is by clicking Edit, Clone on the top menu bar. In the Clone Options dialog box, make sure Copy is checked. For the name, type in detail64 and click OK. The number is arbitrary, but it's good to keep the trailing number large, so you know that the larger the number, the higher will be the mesh density. Now look back to the Schematic View, and notice that the new detail marker has been added and attached to the Bip01 object, as it is a clone.

3. With the detail markers in place, you need to create a single level of detail mesh using the MultiRes modifier, just as you did for the RF-9 in Chapter 13. First select the Slogre2 object in the Schematic View, then create a clone of the mesh. Just click Edit, Clone, and name the new copy Slogre64. This will represent the highest level of detail.

4. Finally, reselect the Slogre2 object. Then, in the Modifier panel, apply a MutliRes modifier to this mesh. In the MultiRes rollout, click Generate. Change the Vert Percent parameter to 50.0; this will reduce the polygon count to 50% of the original mesh, or in this case about 1500 faces—not bad, considering there's not much loss in detail. This represents the lowest level of detail that will be seen by other players from afar. You should now have two slogre meshes in your scene (Slogre2 and Slogre64) that are referenced, by the *Torque* engine, by the detail dummy markers detail2 and detail64, respectively. Be sure that you can view these two detail meshes in the RealmWars.exe -show feature, using the Details button.

Last Note on Other Game Engines

You're probably wondering about using the RF-9 and Slogre models in other games. Most of the information about creating meshes, skinning them, and setting them up for use in the *Torque* engine apply to other games like *Half-Life, Quake,* and *Unreal.* All that's really necessary is to obtain the 3D Studio Max plug-ins for those games in order to export your models and change the naming of an object or two, add a dummy, and so on. I decided to avoid getting into any detail on those engines, as getting permissions to use plug-ins, screen shots, and so on from companies like that is *very* difficult, not to mention time-consuming. GarageGames were kind enough to allow me to use *Torque,* an excellent 3D game engine, and coupled with the fact that it's so affordable ($100), what could be better! Remember, for that small price you're not just getting a game, but an entire game engine whose code you can modify to create your own game, including your own personalized graphics. Anyway, for other game engines, just get on the Web and download their SDK (software development kit) for which you want to develop; I'm sure the kits (not the engines) will be free of charge.

See Appendix E, "Related Websites and Links," for information on popular game engine sites. The SDKs are usually free for download, and contain the plug-ins and instructions necessary to get you rockin' and rollin'.

Summary

The last stage in preparing a character mesh for a video game is usually the most time consuming—installing a skeletal system to animate the mesh itself. Applying a texture to your mesh, installing biped systems, adjusting skin envelopes, setting up dummy objects for game hooks, and adding levels of detail are just the basics of readying your character for a game engine. Most games work in such a similar manner, and it's only a matter a making a few adjustments to get your model to work in them. This chapter covered these foundations in detail.

PART FIVE

Bringing it All Together

15 Bringing Your Work into the *Torque* Game Engine

CHAPTER 15

Bringing Your Work into the Torque Game Engine

I decided to focus on developing models for the *Torque* engine because it is one of the most affordable 3D game engines around. Indeed, GarageGames.com offers this engine for a mere $100; using it, you can reprogram and develop your own publishable game. So unless you can shell out the $50,000–$300,000 required for high-end game engines like *Quake* and *Unreal*, I think *Torque* will do.

In this chapter you will

- Use the *Torque* game engine demo to see your character, weapon, and textures in live gaming action.
- Learn how to create and manipulate the terrain.
- Texture the landscape with your own images.
- Add and manipulate your own game objects.
- Have fun playing with your own game art creations!

Playing *Realm Wars* Using the Slogre and RF-9

The *Torque* demo, as I mentioned in Chapters 13, "Making the RF-9 Plasma Gun Game-Ready with 3D Studio Max," and 14, "Making the Slogre Game-Ready with 3D Studio Max and Character Studio," is aliased *Realm Wars*, the demo of which is also on the CD-ROM that came with this book. In the previous chapters, I outlined how to install this demo and use the Show feature to view your completed weapon and character models. Now it's time to see it all live!

Testing the Slogre

If you properly produced your slogre bipedal arrangement and were able to view it using the Show command, you should have the model (aptly named **player.dts**) located in the \RealmWars\rw\data\shapes\player\ directory, along with all the animation sequences. The default sequences, as I said in Chapter 14, will be at the very least sufficient to animate the bones structure embedded within the slogre model. Go ahead and fire up the demo, playing a single-player game; as soon as

Figure 15.1 *The fruits of your labor, awaiting your command in* Realm Wars.

you're in the game, start running around. If everything appears to be working, you're in business! Just press Tab to switch to third-person mode and see the big guy in action (see Figure 15.1).

Locating the RF-9 Plasma Gun

The plasma-gun model (aptly named **weapon.dts**) you created should also be in place in the \RealmWars\rw\data\shapes\crossbow\ directory; you're simply substituting the existing weapons and character models with your own. (You'll need to purchase the game engine and modify the code to make these models more unique to the game, such as telling the engine to call up and use a primary player character called **slogre.dts**, adding different sprite effects, and so on.) The ammo, clip, and sounds for the RF-9 can be substituted for the existing crossbow items; grab them from the Chapter 15 Data section on the CD-ROM and place them in the \crossbow\ and \sounds\ folders. Then, in the game, start hunting around and you'll soon find the RF-9, along with some ammo; walk over it, and you'll be ready to blast things away to your heart's content (see Figure 15.2). The default sprite action that is generated when you fire the weapon is almost perfect for the RF-9!

Figure 15.2

Search the area for the RF-9 plasma gun and pick it up!

Editing the World

When you're in _Realm Wars_, the game engine allows you to edit the terrain, sky, and water, and to place or remove objects. Just press F11 to enter the World Editor to see what I mean; by default, you'll be in World Editor Inspector mode (see Figure 15.3). Just open the Window menu up top, and choose from several modes.

Terrain Editor

If you choose Window, Terrain Editor, your tools will change and allow you to edit your game's ground; open the Action menu and select from a list of actions that you can perform. When you move your cursor over any area of the ground, you'll see a multitude of lit rectangles, the size of which is dictated in the Brush menu. For instance, to change the height of the ground, select Action, Adjust Height, and click and drag the ground up and down (see Figure 15.4). With what seems like the hand of God, you can literally move mountains! This engine is well known for its outdoor environment and infinite landscape; try wandering around for a while to see what I mean.

While in the Terrain Editor, you can also add your own diligently created textures by choosing Window, Terrain Texture Painter. A list appears on the right, displaying all

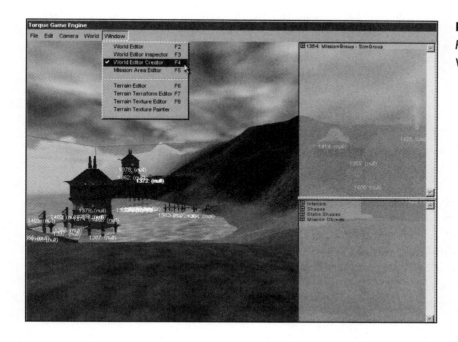

Figure 15.3 *Press F11 to enter the World Editor.*

Figure 15.4
In seconds you can carve your landscape and create mountains at will in the Terrain Editor.

the textures you've saved as .png files and stored in the \RealmWars\rw\data\ terrains\ folder. Add a useable texture to the cell by clicking the Add button in an empty cell, and then browse for the texture you want. To paint the texture, choose Action, Paint Material, and then click and drag over the terrain. In Figure 15.5, I used the lava texture developed in Chapter 8 (and saved as **lava.png**, a 256×256 pixel texture), to cover the sandy beach near the water. If your texture is properly tileable, you should have some awesome results.

Adding Other Objects

You can continue to add textured models to the world using the World Editor Creator, also located in the Window menu. While in that mode, you can expand the Shapes directory tree at the lower left and browse for any .dts shape files you've placed in the \RealmWars\rw\data\shapes\ folder. These shapes can be created in exactly the same way as the RF-9; you just don't have to include a mounting location on them (obviously). Try adding one of the trees in the Trees subfolder by single-clicking the tree2 item to place it in your scene (see Figure 15.6). The tree object may initially be right on top of you; just back away a bit, and you'll see the object's axes, which you can move, rotate, or scale.

Some of the actions require keyboard commands. For instance, holding down the Alt key while clicking on an x, y, or z axis of the tree will rotate the tree along that axis. To look around while editing in this manner, just right-click and drag. The forward, backward, and strafe keys allow you to move around as well (W, S, A, and D, by default, respectively).

Texturing Buildings

By default, buildings and other static 3D shapes in the Realm Wars game are not texture-modifiable within the Torque game engine. These objects were created and textured in a level-editing program like Valve's Hammer editor (go to http://www.valve-erc.com to download the Hammer editor), or they were created in the Milkshape 3D modeler and textured in the same way as the RF-9. GarageGames has a *Torque* plug-in for these editors that allows you to export

> **NOTE**
>
> Level editing is a subject for another book entirely! In any case, there are a number of free level editors on the Web that are compatible with creating buildings and levels for Torque (and other game engines), as well as a plethora of tutorials for them on the GarageGames.com Website.

Figure 15.5
Applying new textures to the ground in the Terrain Texture Painter.

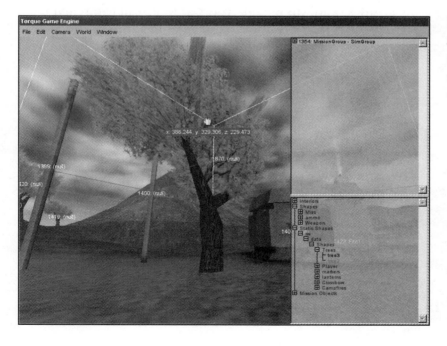

Figure 15.6
Adding and manipulating a tree object in the World Editor Creator.

building models as DIF files (located in the \RealmWars\rw\data\interiors\ folder), which are map files converted into solid objects.

Saving Your Modifications

When you're finished re-creating your world, save your changes by choosing File, Save Mission As, and entering a new name for the mission. (Mission is another word for level.) Then, press F11 to exit the World Editor mode and see your results. The next time you start the game, select your mission from the mission list, and rock and roll!

The Last Word

Here it is, the last paragraph of my book. I truly hope you've enjoyed this stuff, and are ready to tear up the gaming universe! I poured in as much as I could think of (and as much as my publisher would allow me), and hope you got something out of it. I've only scratched the surface with the basics here, but I think that after reading this book you'll see the unlimited possibilities and excellent occupational fun of game-art creation. Please feel free to e-mail me with your work; I'm developing a Web site to catalogue my artwork, and will include yours as well. You can reach me at g_lok434@hotmail.com. I truly would like to see your modifications of the models and textures in this book, as well as any original models of your own! Take care, and happy gaming!

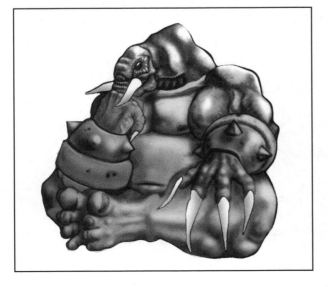

Figure 15.7 *Our hero (image courtesy Lars Ricaldi).*

Finding Work as a Game Artist

So you've decided to follow your dream, and pursue a career as a game developer. The good news is that the last several years have seen a boom in the video-game industry, meaning there are lots of companies looking for people with skills just like yours. The bad news is that most of those companies are clustered in California and neighboring states, which means that you may need to move there to get the job you want—unless, of course, the company that snatches you up agrees to let you work remotely, via the Internet.

Getting a Job with a Game Company

When you decide to take the plunge, the first thing you should do is send your resumé and portfolio to companies listed in the back of magazines like *Game Developer* (I'd stick with companies that are actively seeking artists, as opposed to trying to get into id Software, Gearbox, and the like), or post them at job search engines like **http://www.monster.com**. For best results, you'll probably want to indicate that you're willing to relocate if needed.

If a company likes what it sees on your resumé and in your portfolio, you'll probably get an interview—either in person or on the phone, depending on where you live in relation to the company's headquarters. In addition, there's a 99.99-percent chance you'll be asked to create a textured model, animation, or some other game element (depending on the position you're after), and to turn it around in 24 hours or so. By all means, spend every waking moment and use all available time to give them the most impressive thing you can devise.

If you're not interested in relocating, and none of the companies you've interviewed with will let you work remotely, fear not. There are many game-development teams out there that work with satellite

> **TIP**
> Assuming you get the job, and you don't currently live near the company's headquarters, consider asking the company to relocate you. If they agree, it means they pay to set you up in an apartment in their area until you can find your own digs, and for moving expenses.

Your Portfolio

When you apply at a game company, a simple, one-page resumé listing your job experience (if any) and software/hardware knowledge will suffice. (Don't list previous work experience that isn't related to art or the industry.) Game companies are much more interested in seeing samples of your game artwork, and determining how quickly you're able to bang them out. This is great news if you're 18 with no relevant work experience but have an ungodly way with game art! It's also why your portfolio should contain any piece of game artwork you've ever done that relates to the position you're interested in, and then some. Include as many samples as you can without going overboard.

The type of portfolio you submit—paper or digital—depends on what type of position you seek. For example, if you're looking to get hired as a texture artist, your portfolio would consist of printouts of all your best textures. (For variation, you should toss in textures suitable for all sorts of games, like *Quake*-type games, World War II games, children's games, medieval games, and so on. That way, the company can see that you're capable of just about anything.) You don't need to send them 100 pages; 20 would probably be sufficient. Just make sure that each sample is on its own page, filling the page, and NEVER double-sided. In addition, the printout of each sample should be of the highest quality; make sure you've set both the printer and the paint program you use for your samples to the highest possible resolution (300 dpi or higher), and that you use high-quality photo paper. After you print out your samples, you should place them in individual, clear-plastic inserts, and have them bound professionally at a place like Staples or Office Max.

Other positions require different sorts of portfolios. For example, if you're looking for an animator's position, you'll need to render out your best animations using very good models (most likely 10,000+ polygon types rather than game-ready animations). These models should be nicely textured as well, because chances are the company will want to see that you're capable of skinning. You should have at least a dozen short animations that demonstrate your ability to control bones and skin weighting, including a handful of interesting and common actions—not just running. For instance, demonstrating a character running, then squatting, jumping, and landing, would be one sequence. Another might show a character firing a weapon and then reloading. It puts a nice touch on things if you make them loop seamlessly, without hiccupping when it restarts at frame 0. Your sequences should also contain varied characters. Don't just send a human mesh object for all sequences; rather, demonstrate your ability to do other animals and beings, exhibiting cool and/or bizarre behavior in short cycles. Lastly, burning everything onto one CD-ROM with individual .AVIs would suffice. You might want to include the MAX files (or related formats) too, along with low-res versions ready for games, just to crown everything off.

personnel—that is, people who joined together to make a game, and live all over the world. It's usually easy to become part of one such team, and doing so will offer you the chance to work on a real game from home. The downside is, you probably won't get paid until the game gets published (if at all); the teams creating these games are typically startup companies (called "Indies," or independent developers) whose resources are limited. (Of course, on the off chance that the game you make while working with such a development team hits the big time, you may be able to reap some serious financial rewards!) In any case, you can track down these types of positions at many Web sites dedicated to the gaming community, such as **http://www.gamedev.net** and **http://www.garagegames.com**.

> **NOTE**
>
> GarageGames has created the Torque engine, a great 3D FPS engine that is expanding all of the time. It works quite well, and has an attractive license price: only $100.

Job Positions

If I cited every title that has been invented for the game art industry, I'd fill a few pages. Instead, I'll list some general positions, describe them, and show you approximately how much money a person in certain positions might expect to make in relation to years of experience. The details of these positions are by no means carved in stone; titles can be used interchangeably in some instances, and roles can be grouped or performed by others (or not at all) as each game company sees fit. I've simply defined them based on what I've read or experienced myself. The salaries for these positions vary; it seems however that beginning artists receive an approximate $30,000 to $40,000 during their first year, and upwards of $70,000 to $100,000 with five or more years of experience.

> **NOTE**
>
> Salaries vary by location, so don't expect to be paid $100,000 a year for a modeling job in Podunk, U.S.A.! (No offense, by the way, to any Podunkians.)

- **Concept artist.** A person in this position is capable of drawing/sketching anything. Typically, the position requires the ability to render conceptual art— the first step in developing game assets—in a very short period of time. This

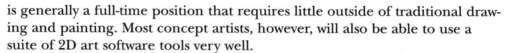

is generally a full-time position that requires little outside of traditional drawing and painting. Most concept artists, however, will also be able to use a suite of 2D art software tools very well.

- **Texture/environment artist.** A person in this position is proficient in creating all forms of texture on a 2D digital painting program. The program the person uses is not really a big issue, because most 2D software works similarly and with familiar tools. The texture/environment artist is responsible for creating textures for player and object skins, as well as for maps/levels. He or she should also be capable of U-V manipulation and setup for texture design.

- **Lead artist.** The Lead artist has a good deal of experience creating concept and texture art for games, and supervises (and participates in) the work flow of the 2D art team. Typically this person is also good with other game arts like modeling and animation.

- **3D modeler.** This individual spends much of his or her time creating 3D mesh objects for a video game. This is more of an entry-level position, but fun nonetheless. Other responsibilities include U-V manipulation and prepping models for the texture artist and animators. The 3D modeler is often the animator as well, and is usually expert with at least one high-end 3D modeling package such as Max or Maya.

- **Lead modeler.** The lead modeler is much like the 3D modeler, only with much more experience. He or she oversees the general workflow of the other modelers, and is there to assist in any modeling snags. Most modelers at this level are also expert animators, because modeling in itself can be a bore in no time. Basically, this job includes anything having to do with mesh design and manipulation at the expert level.

- **Animator.** Animation is very tricky, especially without catalyst systems like motion capture. The animator's job is not easy, and requires thorough knowledge of keyframing and bones systems. Skin weighting is also part of the job; properly assigning mesh vertices to bones objects is a key factor in making meshes deform properly. This person's job is to take mesh objects and install a bones system, weight vertices, and animate the bones in a life-like manner.

- **Lead animator.** Just like the animator, only with much more experience. After several years animating, this person leads the animation team and works closely with the creative/project directors to ensure continuity in the game.

- **Level designer.** The level designer is an architect at heart. (In fact, there are a handful of people with degrees in architecture who have been hired as level designers.) The level designer's responsibilities include creating buildings and generalized structures for maps, terrains, and everything else that involves some form of a level-editing program, be it off the shelf or proprietary. Higher-end software like 3D Studio Max is also used for level design, so proficiency with that tool is a plus.

- **Lead level designer.** This is a position typically found only within larger game companies. The lead level designer will have years of experience designing levels for games, and oversee the daily operations of the other level designers. He or she also works closely with the project director so everyone's on the same, er, level.

- **Designer.** This person is like a concept artist, but generates the overall themes for video games. The modelers, texturers, and animators then produce their assets based on his or her game plan.

- **Lead designer.** The lead designer, who has the last say in the design of the game, is just like the designer, but, should more than one exist, will brainstorm the game flow with other designers and make the final decisions. This person works closely with the project director.

- **Art director.** The art director works closely with the project director in envisioning the proper art content for the game. He or she oversees the other artists, and has usually held several art positions in past years.

- **Creative/project director.** These positions can comprise two individuals or be combined to be one in the same. In any case, the creative/project director stands atop of the game company, overseeing the production of all departments. He or she makes sure the game is going in the proper direction, and makes decisions as to what content should be created or removed.

NOTE

The location of your team will be a significant factor in your salary. When I worked in New York City, the salaries were incredible; the same position in Wyoming, however, would decrease proportionally to the cost of living there.

Working on a Game Development Team

So you're hired, and this is your first real job as an artist in a game-development environment. Don't think that this will be some easy ride, where you have fun making artwork all day long! Nine times out of ten you'll be under heavy deadline to get models, textures, levels, and whatnot finished on schedule, and many of these projects might seem monotonous or uninteresting. Working at a studio is so much different from sitting at home, making 3D models at your leisure! The work will be non-stop and then some, and if it isn't, then something's wrong. There should never be idle time—there's no such thing as finishing all your assignments and then kicking back—and everything you do should be tweaked to the best you can deliver.

At the same time, think of it this way: You're doing what you love to do and getting paid for it! How many people in America, or the rest of the world for that matter, truly love their work and get paid well? I used to work at a big law firm, and saw many of the attorneys raking in the cash ($300 per hour!), but I wondered, were they happy with their job, or only happy with their salary? I'd rather take a 75% pay cut and be ecstatic about my job than be loaded but have to deal with trademark agreements all day long.

In any case, assuming you are (or will be) an entry-level artist, you should put yourself into the mindset of pure hard work, and be serious about it, for at least the first year to prove that you're truly interested in your job and in the company, and to show that you have the desire to be part of the team. Most people who have even the slightest problem with their jobs drop out within the first six to eight months. If you really can't stand the game you're working on, and can't stand to stay at the company, then find another job, but continue to give your current one your absolute best—putting a cork in your personal opinion. Don't burn any bridges by denouncing the quality of the project you're on; if you're unhappy, keep working hard until you've been accepted elsewhere. That way, you'll always have your current company as a good reference.

Tools of the Trade

Before even setting foot on a game company's soil, you should already have a decent knowledge of a handful of popular 2D and 3D art tools. Nobody wants to hire someone who only knows 3D Studio Max, even if you're an expert at it. Your job, even if you've been hired as an animator, will always require little in-betweens like modeling or texture mapping. You should be proficient in several programs, such as trueSpace, 3D Studio Max, Maya, and Photoshop. (Besides, learning graphics programs takes only a short time; everything you need to know about nearly any program can be found at Borders or Barnes and Noble.)

Also, there's a good chance that when you start work, your company will have other software tools that you need to learn that are either proprietary or available for purchase—that is, the programmers have either developed their own tools for you to use on specific projects, or have modified or created plug-ins for off-the-shelf software you might already know. In either case, be prepared to learn even more software, and go into it with a hungry attitude.

Working with Programmers

In my view, the single most divisive force within a game-development team is the contrast between artist and programmer. Artists and programmers are just so different from each other. Programmers tend to be highly focused, intelligent, and hard working, but typically range from slightly nerdy to King of Dweebs. (No offense to anyone intended, and besides, being a sometimes-programmer myself, I should know.) The fact is, however, that a programmer's general lack of cool in the eyes of a prom queen (or king) stems from the fact that his or her mind is typically highly tuned and mathematically astute. Indeed, a programmer's job in the game-programming environment always consists of having to think hard, all day long, on issues like matrici transformations, artificial intelligence, physics simulations, and more—all of which involves intense math and problem solving. Their work is unending, they usually have the longest hours of the lot, and get paid the most because of it.

Artists, on the other hand, have a much different mindset: extraordinarily creative, visual, outgoing, and many times flat-out bizarre! This persona ports to such behavior as the way artists behave and dress, which is generally considered more acceptable to someone like Madonna than to someone like Bill Nye the Science Guy.

The point is, artists' and programmers' personalities tend to clash. The programmer will often see the artist as a pain in the ass, especially as the artist sends up red flags about how much he or she doesn't like the game engine and what it does to his or her artwork. Compounding this problem is the fact that most artists have no concept of the programming demands involved with even the most simple request. When an artist marches over to the programmer and says, "Make the code so that when my character throws the grenade, the grenade doesn't look like it sticks to the floor after a few bounces," the programmer's blood boils; a simple demand like that requires the programming of an entire physics simulation that could amount to a couple of days' work.

The artist, on the other hand, is quick and creative, and can usually bang out models, textures, or whatnot in a very short time. As a result, he or she might assume that this mode of work ports directly to the programmer's. In retaliation, a programmer might be quick to critique the artist's work, expecting the artist to put in extra effort to make his or her artwork better than the best. Programmers often forget that the creative process isn't easy; it, too, requires a lot of work, especially when making and animating outstanding characters for a game. Plus, programmers often forget that artists aren't getting paid as much as they are, which may explain why many artists feel they shouldn't have to work as hard.

As a programmer and artist, I understand both sides of these issues, and I hope that you're starting to, too. My advice for working with programmers is, truly, to take a quick course in programming. It's like Sean Connery said in *The Hunt for Red October*: "It is wise to learn the ways of one's adversary." Alternatively, pick up a simple primer on C++; that way, you can quickly gain some understanding about what's really going on under the hood of the game's engine, and you'll have some sense of what the programmers deal with day in and day out.

I'm not saying you should become a full-out programmer. Just having a fundamental knowledge of the C programming language will help you understand things from a programmer's perspective. Of course, you may quickly lose interest with programming; after all, you're used to seeing things come to life in three dimensions with spectacular color in little time, unlike coding, which might seem monotonous and unproductive. In any case, a little programming knowledge gives you a much clearer picture of the entire game-development process.

PART SIX

APPENDICES

APPENDIX A

A 3D MODELING PRIMER

If you've never used a 3D modeling program before, or if you're relatively new to 3D modeling, then this is the appendix for you. It covers the basic terminology and components of 3D modeling, including

- The principles of 3D objects in a 3D world
- Object and world axes and coordinates
- The constituent vertices, edges, and faces of objects
- Triangles and polygons that make up the mesh of a 3D object
- Modeling with splines and NURBS objects
- Properties of the normals of an object's faces

Object Geometry in 3D Space

A 3D object in a modeling program is anything that has, at the very least, exactly what its adjective describes: three dimensions. Every 3D modeling program and every 3D game is designed around a Cartesian coordinate system that is used to describe the dimensions and positions of a 3D world and the objects it contains, typically using three perpendicular (90 degrees from one another) axes, x, y, and z.

You may recall from your scholastically coerced days of high-school geometry that this system, when drawn on paper, had a y axis pointing up and down, an x axis pointing left and right, and a z axis pointing perpendicularly into and out of the paper. Figure A.1, however, seems to show a discombobulated mess of what you learned in school. Don't panic; this is simply the *world-coordinate system* as seen from a *perspective* point of view. That is, if you walked around to the right of the box in Figure A.1, then stood on top of it, you'd see the familiar XYZ system in its proper place. All that has happened in this scene is that the viewpoint has been moved 45 degrees away from the y axis, then 45 degrees from the z axis, just to give a decent perspective of everything.

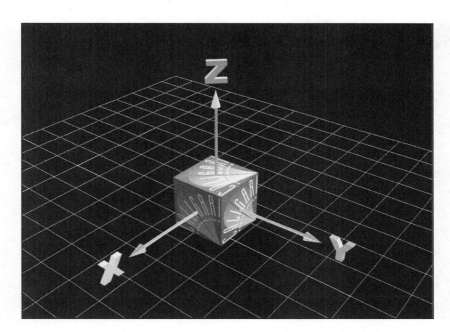

Figure A.1 *The Cartesian coordinate system for a 3D world.*

Now back to the definition of a 3D object. Any 3D object in a graphics program (including games) contains, at the very minimum, three points, or *vertices*, connected by lines, or *edges*. You may be thinking, "Hey, I've seen a single line in 3D space, just floating there, consisting of only two points connected by one line!" Well, it may seem that way, but the logical makeup of computer systems can't understand a 2D object that's supposed to exist in a 3D world. Therefore, what you perceive as a line is actually a three-point triangle that has one side with zero distance. Weird, huh?

Figure A.2 shows a series of 3D objects in a world-XYZ perspective: a line (a triangle with a base of zero distance), a triangle with three definite vertices, a pyramid with a triangular base, and a cube. Notice that each object has its own XYZ set of axes— each point (or vertex) on each object is defined, in the 3D program, by an x, y, and z coordinate distance relative to the origin of the object to which it belongs, or the *object origin*. From here, to position the 3D object in the world, each object's origin in return has its own XYZ coordinates relative to the *world origin*.

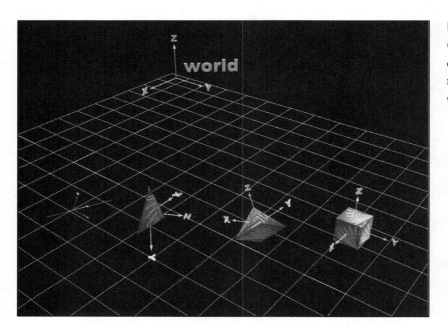

Figure A.2
Objects and their corresponding vertices related in a 3D world.

TIP

When it comes to axes, the most important thing to pay attention to is the axes of the object itself. Forget about the world axes and whatnot—the axes of the object help you to do things like elongate a cube or sphere along a single axis of choice, creating the shape you want. The axes of the object are also handy if you want to change the way an object rotates in 3D space—instead of the sphere rotating in place around its own origin, maybe you want it to rotate the way the moon rotates around the earth. Simply move the object's axes away from the center of the sphere and out somewhere else in space, then the sphere will rotate in orbital circles. See?

You might be confused, but just like a famous quote from the *Hitchhiker's Guide to the Galaxy* says, "Don't panic!" You'll get it all when you start moving and building things in trueSpace.

Polygons, Polygons, and More Polygons

Let's talk triangles here. At a minimum, a 3D object consists of three vertices connected by three edges. This is the basic form of a *polygon*. Any 3D object you create will have at least one polygon (a plane), or as many as several thousand (however many your computer can process). No matter what shape your 3D object is, it will be made up of these basic polygonal units—even a cube, which appears to have six single sides with four vertices and four edges, technically has *two triangles* (hidden from view in computer memory) that make up each side or *face* of the object. Figure A.3 shows a simple polygon, a cube, and the behind-the-scenes polygonal makeup of the cube.

It's important to know this, especially when it comes to optimizing 3D models for video games. You see, as an object grows larger in polygonal density, the computer attempting to move and render it will have to process more and more information about each individual vertex and where it's supposed to go. This mathematical computation is called a *transformation*. For instance, if you're playing a video game and you walk around a 3D object such as an oil drum, the computer gives you the illusion that you're moving around it. What's actually happening, however, is the computer is moving (transforming) the vertices of the drum (and the world surrounding it) within the world-coordinate system, and for every movement you make, the vertex locations must be recalculated to a new spot. Got me? Now imagine that you made your oil drum jam-packed full of polygons simply by increasing the detail. In that case, the computer has to crunch away full time, and things will appear slow and choppy. Figure A.4 shows two of the same model, one with a low polygon count and one with an unnecessarily high count. (Incidentally, the

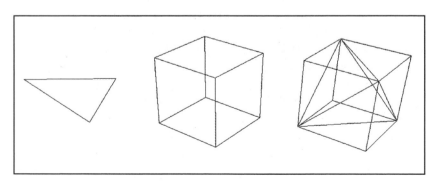

Figure A.3 *All 3D objects in a 3D world are comprised of simple triangular polygons.*

Figure A.4 *Similar mesh objects with both low and high polygon counts.*

makeup of a 3D object that includes only the vertices and edges that define the object is called a *mesh*.) To learn more about and perform 3D optimization, see Chapter 3, "Modeling the RF-9 Plasma Gun with trueSpace 6," where I show you how to model and optimize a game weapon.

Splines

Not too long ago, mechanics and drafts people used flexible wooden or metal devices called *splines* to aid in creating smooth, curved lines between two points on paper. In 3D modeling, a *spline* is simply a curved line that ends where it began, and contains varying numbers of points or vertices along its shape. You'll use splines a lot when modeling in 2D or 3D space, especially when creating a curved surface and then extruding (or sweeping) that surface outward to produce a 3D object. For instance, suppose you want to make a heart-shaped plane in 3D space. By using a spline, all you have to do is click points on a 2D view that make up the general shape of the heart. A line will be automatically created that connects each point, but the line itself will be curved, as in Figure A.5. You can also use a spline as a path that an object would follow during an animation.

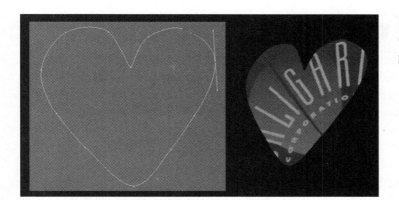

Figure A.5
Creating curved sur-faces using splines.

Revenge of the NURBS

Sorry, I just had to say that—it's one of my favorite movies. (I'm a nerd at heart.)
A *NURBS object* is a complex mesh object that has special properties enabling it to be molded and shaped like clay to produce a more organic 3D look. *NURBS* stands for Non-Uniform Rational B-Spline, the internal definition of which is a bit compli-cated—what it translates to is that portions of a NURBS object behave differently, relative to the shape of the rest of the object. When you manipulate a NURBS object, such as by stretching, twisting, or shaping a portion of it, the object will deform in an organic manner, as if you were working with clay (see Figure A.6). This is a great feature of many graphics programs, including trueSpace, particularly when making character faces and bodies. For more information on using NURBS to create 3D models, see Chapter 4, "Modeling the Slogre Character with trueSpace 6."

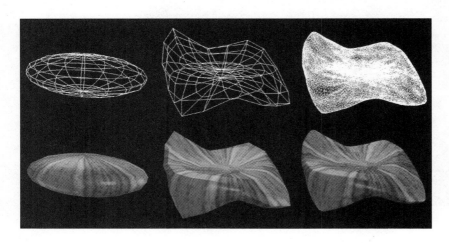

Figure A.6 *The clay-like properties of a NURBS object.*

Just Try to be Normal

When working with a 3D graphics program, you first define the faces of an object, and then define the normal of each face. The *normal* is an invisible vector (or arrow) that points straight out of and perpendicular to the middle of each face that helps the graphics program determine how the object presents itself to the user. The default normals of an object have all the vectors pointing outward, as in

Figure A.7. This means that during render time (the process where the program creates the final 3D product that includes surface textures and lighting), the object will appear solid. If you were to flip the normals so that they point inward instead, the object would take on a hollow property, as in Figure A.8—the view is actually from inside the sphere.

TIP

By flipping the normals of an object, you can quickly and easily do things like build a room out of a cube or a world atmosphere from the inside of a sphere. By the way, this type of operation is done with the click of a button.

Figure A.7
The default normals of a 3D object.

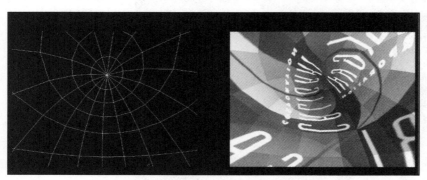

Figure A.8
Here, the normals are flipped.

Texturing and U-V Coordinates

A completed mesh model isn't much to look at without some type of texture applied to it. A *texture* is simply a 2D bitmap that's created in a paint program (like Photoshop) and applied to the surface of the model, hence the commonly used term "skin". But the question here is, how can a texture map be "wrapped" around a mesh object?

A while ago software engineers were inventing a way to apply texture maps to 3D objects. In the course of their brainstorming they came up with the idea of *U-V coordinates*, which are simply an exact copy of the vertices that make up a model's structure (only they're not visible to the user). These coordinates (dubbed U and V, which correlate to X and Y coordinates of a 2D texture map, respectively) define how texture maps should align themselves to the outside of the mesh. The cool thing about UV's is that they can be moved and rearranged so that texture maps may fit precisely onto the model. Typically artists will use special programs like Right Hemisphere's DeepUV to 'unwrap' the UV coordinates and place them flat on a texture map to ease the texture generation process (for detailed information on unwrapping texture coordinates, see Part II, "Unwrapping the U-V's with DeepUV").

A good example of unwrapping UV's is that of a globe. You may have seen from your grade school days the map of the Earth laid out as a flat 2D image. Back in the 1500s, Flemmish mapmaker Gerardus Mercator invented a technique of unfolding a globe and laying it out flat so that one could view the map of the Earth in two dimensions, thus making it possible to draw straight lines for shipping courses. A program like DeepUV can do just that with the UV coordinates of an object.

As another example, in Figure A.9 the tire's mesh is initially untextured; that is, it is simply a mesh object rendered in a default gray color. If I were to apply a 2D texture map to the object, the results will be unpredictable since the UV coordinates are not arranged in a way that makes the texture map correspond one-to-one with locations on the sphere. By flattening and arranging the UV coordinates to my liking, then reapplying the texture, everything fits nicely (Figure A.9).

See Part II of this book, "Unwrapping the UV's with DeepUV", where I demonstrate how to adjust the UV coordinates of real game objects for proper texture alignment.

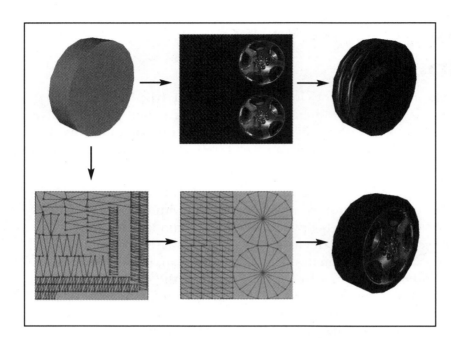

Figure A.9
Manipulating the UV texture coordinates of a mesh object so a texture map may be properly aligned.

Lights, Camera, and . . . Render!

Rendering is the final stage in the 3D world—it happens when you're finished with your model or animation and want to see the polished, realistic result. For example, suppose you've built a nice-looking army tank and applied textures all over it. As you were modeling it, the graphics program displayed a meshy draft version in real-time (see Figure A.10). In order to view the tank properly, you must tell the program to render the object—that is, perform intense mathematical lighting calculations (a form of ray tracing) that will simulate the way objects reflect light off of their material surfaces in the real world. The output would then be a fairly

> **NOTE**
>
> When you're working with a 3D modeling program, rendering is really just a way for you to review the final product of your model or animation—it's not a required step. Under normal circumstances, game engines handle rendering for you.

realistic looking tank (see Figure A.11). The Photoshop Tutorials section, located on this book's CD-ROM, goes into details about how to use trueSpace to render 3D objects. This is also a great place to start if you have no knowledge and/or experience in 3D modeling.

NOTE

Computers are becoming so powerful that soon you'll be able to work with your models and animations in real-time render mode. That is, you won't have to render the object to see what it will look like with all the textures and lighting effects applied.

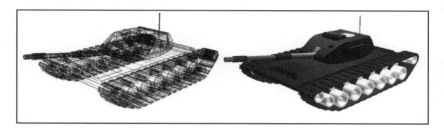

Figure A.10 *An army tank before it's been rendered.*

Figure A.11 *The same army tank, after being rendered.*

APPENDIX B

A 2D GRAPHICS PRIMER

A Few Graphics Concepts

First I want you to be familiar with some of the ways computer images are displayed on your screen. When making graphics for games, you can't just make the images any size or color you want. Graphic artists create images for games using certain guidelines so that when the artwork is imported into the game in production, the image won't change or distort much.

Let's look at the basic graphic unit of an image: the *pixel* (short for *picture element*). Windows displays images on your screen in terms of pixels—rows and columns of miniscule "dots," each square-shaped with varying color, that form an image. The higher the number of pixels per inch, the sharper the image becomes.

Assume you had an archaic monitor and video card that could show only one single pixel on the screen, in black and white (almost like my first video game in the 70s!). The resulting image on the screen would have a *resolution* of one pixel across the first row and one pixel down the first column, or 1×1, as in Figure B.1. Also, because you can display that pixel only in black or white (that is, monochrome), the *color depth* of that single pixel would be one bit.

Figure B.1

A single-pixel monochromatic image.

In Chapter 1, "The History of Game Graphics," I briefly mentioned the concept of bits and how they are used in computers. When it comes to pixels, each one on your screen has an assigned color depth in terms of bits. In computers, a single bit has 2^1, or two, different states—on and off, hence the use of the binary system (everything is a power of two). In the case of the pixel in Figure B.1, the "on" state could be white, and the "off" state could be black. All in all, you would call the video settings of this scenario 1×1, one bit (two color).

Obviously you can't do much of anything with something like this (aside from making a large dot blink annoyingly), so you'll have to increase your resolutions and color depths to make things a tad more viable. Look at Figure B.2—as you can see, each frame increases the resolution by a power of two, in attempts to make the image sharper. The color depth, however, remains one bit.

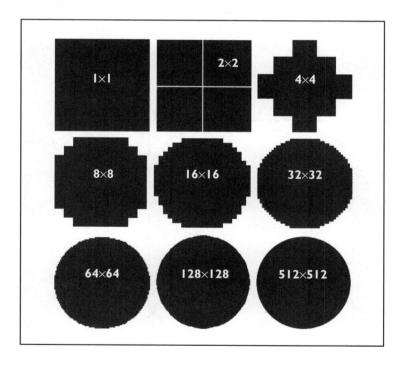

Figure B.2 *The higher the resolution, the sharper the image.*

Granularity and Aliasing

Granularity refers to the way the human eye can perceive all the minute details in an image. My brother Andy, who happens to be a superb optometrist, explained to me that the total number of photoreceptors per square millimeter in the retina determines your *acuity*. When you view an object or image, the higher your acuity, the better you can differentiate the details. When it comes to images on your computer screen, the granularity of the image is directly proportional to your acuity. In Figure B.3, for instance, as the spheres continue into the horizon, they become more and more like just a dot rather than a sphere. The granularity of the image allows your eye to perceive only so much detail at that distance. In video games, this is an important concept when you work with different *levels of detail* (LOD's) in your images and models (for tutorials on creating levels of detail for models, see Part IV, "Preparing Assets for Games with 3D Studio Max .")

Your monitor has a finite number of pixels that can be displayed per square inch (5,184, to be exact), and these pixels are generally square-shaped. If you zoom into an image, the edges and other details that you'd expect to be smooth become *staircase*—that is, choppy and step-like. This physical display limitation is known as

Figure B.3
Granularity of distant images.

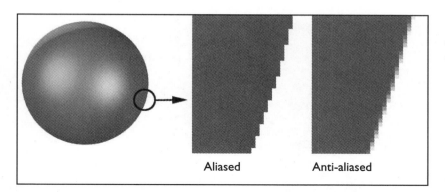

Figure B.4
An aliased and an anti-aliased image.

Aliased   Anti-aliased

aliasing. To correct this problem and make the image appear smooth, a program can anti-alias the image. *Anti-aliasing* is a technique in which the program looks at the edge detail of an image, combines the average of the colors between the two, and fills in the gaps to make it appear smooth when you zoom out (see Figure B.4). Anti-aliasing is a frequently used feature in Photoshop to help sharpen images, and also with 3D programs during render time to make them appear crisp.

RGB Color Depth

When computers were in their early stages, the video output was solely monochromatic. As time passed, however, people quickly became bored with monochromatic images and decided to produce monitors and video cards that could display color. In order to display pixels in color, they had to figure out a way to allow each pixel in an image to represent various combinations of the three primary colors: red, green, and blue.

NOTE
The primary colors are well known in the art world as being the fundamental *light* color set, in that with rays of light (in our case, from our monitors) you can produce any other color in the world using combinations of red, green, and blue. You see, the primary colors are additive in nature; as you add these colors together, you get other colors, and when you put all three together, you get white (see Figure B.5).

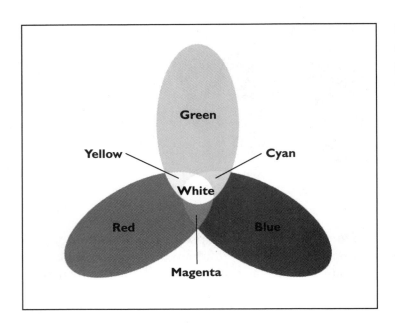

Figure B.5 *The additive nature of primary colors.*

So with your original 1×1, one-bit model, you will have to expand both the monitor and the video card in order to accept an RGB color format. You can tell the engineers to make a monitor that is capable of displaying any shade of red, green, and blue on your single pixel, but you'll have to make a critical adjustment on the video card. A one-bit video card will have only a single bit of memory to store the state of the pixel on the screen. If you want any of the three basic colors to be displayed, including white, you'll just double the memory to two-bit so you can store these colors. Two bits will have 2^2, or four, possible combinations (see Figure B.6). It's kind of like setting switches—whatever bit combination you set in the video card, the monitor will display that color to the screen.

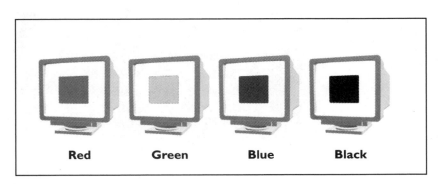

Figure B.6
A two-bit, four-color scenario.

I hope you can see where this is going—if you again increase the bit capability by another factor of two in your video card, you'll have a four-bit card capable of displaying 2^4, or 16, colors. As you increase to eight-bit, or 2^8, your card can now hold 256 different colors—which brings up a special scenario . . . the Color Palette.

The Color Palette

Depending on how they are designed, most monitors nowadays are capable of displaying an image resolution of 1024×768 pixels or higher on the screen at one time. When it comes to color depth, images that have 256 (eight-bit) colors are structured using header information that contains an index and a color look-up table (CLUT). This means that each pixel in the image can have only one of 256 different colors, and the program reading the image uses the index to determine what color each pixel will have by referencing the table (see Figure B.7). Viewing an image with only 256 colors, however, won't properly reveal its intrinsic nature (Photoshop works best at color modes higher than 256 anyway). By increasing the color depth again to 16-bit, you enable the image to use 2^{16}, or 65,536, different colors. That said, it would be cumbersome and ungainly for an image file to have a CLUT capable of containing that many colors. So, the graphics designers put their thinking caps back on . . . and came up with the concept of Color Channels.

Pixel #8,473 has this color at index 103

Figure B.7 *Eight-bit color look-up table.*

Eight-bit (256 color) image   **Image's CLUT palette**

RGB Color Channels

One solution to the problem of having an overwhelmingly large color look-up table was to separate the red, green, and blue components into eight-bit *channels*. When an image is separated into these channels, each color can contain 2^8, or 256, different brightness levels. Because RGB color properties are additive, an image can composite the three channels to form one 3×8 or 24-bit image, where each resulting pixel in the image can have one of 2^{24}, or 16,777,216, different colors—more than enough to display the true color of an image (see Figure B.8).

The highest available color depth in Windows is the ultra-true color mode, or 32-bit—nearly 4.2-billion colors. The extra eight-bit portion of the pixel that's added to the 24-bit sequence is typically used as an alpha channel. This channel represents the *transparency* of a pixel; as an example, in video games, you might have seen an object break into pieces all over the floor, then slowly vanish. The programmers use this channel to diminish the colors of the pixels in the images until they are completely transparent—then remove the image entirely from the video card to save on memory.

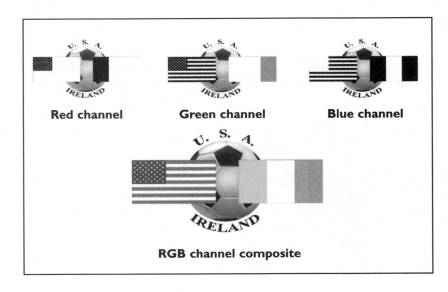

Red channel   **Green channel**   **Blue channel**

RGB channel composite

Figure B.8 *The RGB color channel composite.*

Video Memory

Modern video cards, particularly those designed for playing video games, have three main components: a GPU (*graphics processing unit*), which takes care of things like world and model transformations, lighting, clipping, and rendering; *buffers,* which are special memory areas that contain either the actual image you see on your screen (the *primary* buffer) or images waiting to be flipped to the primary buffer; and VRAM (*Video Random Access Memory*).

Your concern is more with the VRAM, which is the area where games store all the wonderful textures and video sequences that you create. For example, when you walk around in a 3D video game, all the textures, models, and animations that aren't visible but are required for the level in which you are located are stored temporarily in VRAM. As you progress to other levels, you may see the game hesitate, or receive a message that it is "loading." In this case, the game engine is queuing up the next batch of textures, sequences, and whatnot for display in VRAM.

What all this means to you is that when you create textures, models, and animations, you need to consider optimizing each for memory. After all, it'll be a while before you have video cards with 10GB! Table B.1 covers the video memory allocation needed for various image and monitor resolutions and bit color depths.

Table B.1 Video Memory Allocations

Image Resolution	Bit Color Depth	VRAM Requirement
16x16	16, 24, 32	512 bytes, 768 bytes, 1KB
32x32	16, 24, 32	2KB, 3KB, 4KB
64x64	16, 24, 32	8.2KB, 12.3KB, 16.4KB
128x128	16, 24, 32	32.8KB, 49.2KB, 65.5KB
256x256	16, 24, 32	131.1KB, 196.6KB, 266.2KB
512x512	16, 24, 32	524.3KB, 786.4KB, 1.1MB
1024x1024	16, 24, 32	2.1MB, 3.9MB, 5.2MB

Monitor Resolution	Bit Color Depth	VRAM Requirement
640x480	16, 24, 32	614.4KB, 921.6KB, 1.2MB
800x600	16, 24, 32	960KB, 1.4MB, 1.9MB
1024x768	16, 24, 32	1.6MB, 2.4MB, 3.1MB

As you can see, the higher the pixel's bit depth and the larger the dimensions of your image, the more memory it eats up in the video card. Later on you'll create your images and then optimize them to take up minimal space in memory.

You may also notice that the first seven entries in Table 2.1 are equal multiples of 16. As a game artist, you'll typically need to create textures with image sizes divisible by 16. Can you guess why? As I discussed before, computers are based on the binary system, and video resolutions and color depths are based on this as well. Game programmers design their game engines around this system, so making your images in this fashion will allow them to easily fit within the game engines' parameters.

A great example of these texture size restrictions is *Half-Life* (of course!). The developers of *Half-Life* put a ceiling on their textures so that the maximum dimensions of any image were 25×256 pixels with an eight-bit (256-color) palette. The texture is usually created at something like 512×512 at 24-bit color,

> **TIP**
>
> To quickly figure out the size of your image, multiply the width, height, and depth (in bytes). Remember, there are eight bits in a byte, so a 1024×768, 24-bit image would be 1024×768×3 bytes, or 2,400KB (2.4MB).

then reduced to this range. As technology increases, however, and better video cards and computers become available, game developers will allow higher and higher quality images. In fact, games like *Unreal Tournament* allow up to 1024×1024 texture resolutions, but are typically scaled down dynamically during game play to 256×256 due to video hardware restrictions.

Other Color Modes

You've been focusing primarily on the RGB color model, which is the most versatile for game graphics, but there are a few other modes:

- CMYK
- Grayscale
- LAB

CMYK

Often you'll see the CMYK mode (*c*yan, *m*agenta, *y*ellow, and blac*k*). If you look back to the RGB color plate in Figure B.6, you'll see that the intersections of these colors additively create the CMY colors. Printers usually use the CMYK colors due

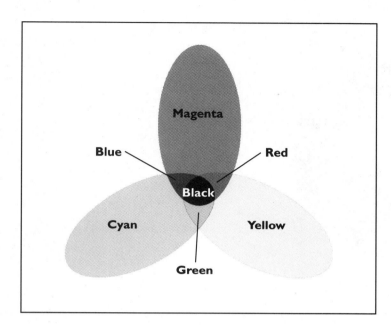

Figure B.9 *The subtractive nature of the CMYK color model.*

to their *subtractive* properties—unlike the RGB colors, which are based on light waves, CMY ink colors blend to subtractively make other colors. When all three are brought together, they make black (see Figure B.9).

It was found, however, that when bringing equal amounts of cyan, magenta, and yellow together, the resulting mix didn't really produce true black. That's why an additional black component (K) is tagged along with the other three colors whenever black is required. If you have a color printer, you can see this in action—open the lid and take a look at the ink cartridges. Your printer will probably have a CMY unit and a black unit. And when printing white? Well, just don't print anything at all!

Grayscale

Grayscale is simply an eight-bit color mode that contains 256 different shades of gray, from white to black (see Figure B.10). The uniqueness of a grayscale image is that it's not indexed like an eight-bit color image; rather, it has only one color channel of black, and the pixels in the image channel are based on 256 different intensities of black.

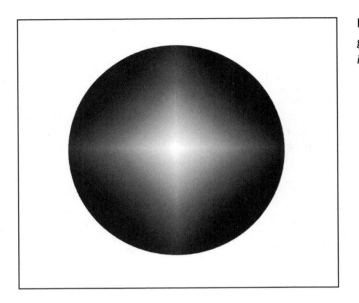

Figure B.10 *A grayscale gradient image.*

LAB

LAB images have three channels like RGB, but the first is a lightness channel and the other two are chromacity (color information) channels, A and B. The advantage of the LAB format is more for medium transportation purposes—if you view a LAB image on-screen, technically no color information will change when it goes to the print shop. Also, Photoshop uses LAB as an intermediary when converting from, say, RGB to CMYK, to suppress color loss. You don't need to be concerned about this; it's just good to know.

File Formats

I'm going to wrap up this appendix with some of the primary image formats you'll be using when saving your work. Each file format offers different techniques of saving image information, content, and compression. Your file-format options are

- PSD
- BMP
- JPEG
- PNG
- TGA
- TIFF

PSD

The default image format in Photoshop is PSD. When creating an image, all the components of the image such as layers, styles, channels, paths, and so on are stored in the PSD file. *Always* save your original work in this format first, then save to another format. If you don't save your image as a PSD, but need to go back to make a modification, you'll simply open a flattened image without the original components.

BMP

This is the Windows Bitmap file, based on an eight-bit (256) color palette. Most images you create for games in Photoshop will be saved in this format. Typically, you'll create an image in 24-bit color mode; when you save it as a BMP file, the colors in the image are palletized to eight-bit. Basically, in a game, having a 24-bit image is overkill, so having your images converted to eight-bit will display enough colors for the player not to notice—at least for now. The Half-Life engine makes use of this format.

JPEG

This is the Joint Photographic Experts Group file format, invented primarily for optimizing file sizes for things like the World Wide Web. The JPEG format is usually the least desirable nowadays, because it offers variable compression settings that will seriously degrade the quality of an image (see Figure B.11). Use this format only when you need to send pictures over the Internet.

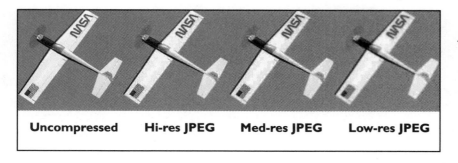

Uncompressed   **Hi-res JPEG**   **Med-res JPEG**   **Low-res JPEG**

Figure B.11
JPEG image degradation as compression increases.

PCX

This popular format was developed by ZSOFT as a proprietary format for their PC Paintbrush program back in the good 'ol DOS days. PCX has a better compression ratio than .BMP while retaining the same image quality. The Unreal and Unreal Tournament engines use this format.

PNG

The Portable Network Graphics format is one of the best ways to preserve image data and have compresson at the same time. I'm not sure why PNGs aren't used more often; this graphics format has lossless, high compression with the capability of storing alpha (transparency) information. This format was designed to replace the popular .GIF format and be seamlessly portable between computer systems. GarageGames' Torque engine makes use of the .PNG format.

TGA

The Targa format, developed originally for the Truevision video board, is used often when saving animation frames in 3D programs due to the high-quality image content–to-compression ratio. TGAs also store layers and transparency channels, and are used within the Quake engine for images requiring transparency information.

TIFF

The Tagged Image File Format is another high quality image format that allows for the storage of layers and transparency, just as with PSD files. The down side is its compression; TIF files, although containing very high quality, usually have huge file sizes.

APPENDIX C

Photoshop 6 Keyboard Shortcuts

The following tables represent many, but not all, of Photoshop's keyboard short-cuts. Unless you're weirdly obsessed with Photoshop, I wouldn't recommend trying to memorize them all—in fact, the first table contains the bulk of the short-cuts that I use most often. I recommend at least being proficient with these to make your work go quicker.

My Most Frequently Used

Action	Shortcut
Copy	Ctrl+C
Cut	Ctrl+X
Deselect	Ctrl+D
Fill with Foreground Color	Alt+Backspace
Hand Tool	Spacebar, with most other tools
Merge Layer Down	Ctrl+E
Move Tool	Ctrl, with most other tools
New Canvas	Ctrl+N
New Canvas with Previous Settings	Ctrl+Alt+N
Paste	Ctrl+V
Quick Mask	Q
Repeat Filter	Ctrl+F
Select All	Ctrl+A
Select Layer Opacity	Ctrl+Click on Layer
Step Backward	Ctrl+Alt+Z
Step Forward	Ctrl+Shift+Z
Toggle Cursor Shape	Caps Lock
Toggle Grid	Ctrl+Alt+'
Toggle Snap	Ctrl+;
Undo	Ctrl+Z

File Menu

Action	Shortcut
New	Ctrl+N
New Document with Previous Settings	Ctrl+Alt+N
Open	Ctrl+O
Open As	Ctrl+Alt+O
Close	Ctrl+W
Close All	Ctrl+Shift+W
Save	Ctrl+S
Save As	Ctrl+Shift+S
Save As Copy	Ctrl+Alt+S
Save for Web	Ctrl+Alt+Shift+S
Print Options	Ctrl+Alt+P
Page Setup	Ctrl+Shift+P
Print	Ctrl+P
Exit	Ctrl+Q
Color Settings	Ctrl+Shift+K
Preferences	Ctrl+K

Views

Action	Shortcut
Apply Zoom	Shift+Enter
Fit to Screen	Ctrl+0
Toggle Extras	Ctrl+H
Toggle Grid	Ctrl+Alt+'
Toggle Guides	Ctrl+'
Toggle Lock Guides	Ctrl+Alt+;
Toggle Menu Bar	Shift+F
Toggle Rulers	Ctrl+R
Toggle Screen Mode	F
Toggle Snap	Ctrl+;
View Actual Pixels	Ctrl+Alt+0
Zoom In	Ctrl++
Zoom Out	Ctrl+-

Toolbox

Action	Shortcut
Airbrush	J
Blur	R
Burn	O
Crop	C
Dodge	O
Eraser	E
Eyedropper	I
Gradient	G
Hand	H
History Brush	Y
Lasso	L
Magic Wand	W
Marquee	M
Move	V
Notes	N
Paintbrush	B
Path Component Selection	A
Pen	P
Quick Mask Mode	Q
Shape	U
Sharpen	R
Slice	K
Smudge	R
Sponge	O
Stamp	S
Standard Mode	Q
Type	T
Zoom	Z
Cycle Tools	Shift+Tool Letter
Decrease Brush Size	[
Increase Brush Size	]
Decrease Brush Pressure	Shift+[

Toolbox *(continued)*

Action	Shortcut
Increase Brush Pressure	Shift+]
Previous Brush	<
Next Brush	>
Tool Opacity	I through 9, 0
Default Colors	D
Switch Colors	X

My Editing

Action	Shortcut
Cut	Ctrl+X
Copy	Ctrl+C
Copy Merged	Ctrl+Shift+C
Paste	Ctrl+V
Paste Into	Ctrl+Shift+V
Paste Outside	Ctrl+Alt+Shift+V
Undo Move	Ctrl+Z
Step Backward	Ctrl+Alt+Z
Step Forward	Ctrl+Shift+Z
Fade	Ctrl+Shift+F
Transform	Ctrl+T
Transform Again	Ctrl+Shift+T
Fill with Foreground	Alt+Backspace
Fill with Background	Ctrl+Backspace
Repeat Last Filter	Ctrl+F
Liquify	Ctrl+Shift+X
Extract	Ctrl+Alt+X

Selection Modification

Action	Shortcut
Deselect	Ctrl+D
Reselect	Ctrl+Shift+D
Select All	Ctrl+A
Delete Selection	Backspace, Del
Feather	Ctrl+Alt+D
Invert	Ctrl+Shift+I
Move Selection One Pixel	Ctrl+↑, ↓, ←, →
Move Selection 10 Pixels	Shift+↑, ↓, ←, →

Palette Display

Action	Shortcut
Toggle Actions	F9
Toggle All Palettes	Shift+Tab
Toggle Color	F6
Toggle Info	F8
Toggle Layers	F7
Toggle Toolbox and Palettes	Tab

Layer Modification

Action	Shortcut
New Layer	Ctrl+Shift+N
Layer Via Copy	Ctrl+J
Layer Via Cut	Ctrl+Shift+J
Go Up a Layer	Alt+]
Go Down a Layer	Alt+[
Move Layer to Top	Ctrl+Shift+]
Move Layer Up	Ctrl+]
Move Layer Down	Ctrl+[
Merge Down	Ctrl+E
Merge Visible	Ctrl+Shift+E
Group with Previous	Ctrl+G
Change Layer Opacity	1 through 9, 0
Preserve Transparency	/

Channel Modification

Action	Shortcut
Load Mask as Selection	Ctrl+Alt+~
Select Channel	Ctrl+1 through 9
Select Layer Mask in Channel	Ctrl+\
Toggle Channel View	~

Color Modification

Action	Shortcut
Auto Contrast	Ctrl+Alt+Shift+L
Auto Levels	Ctrl+Shift+L
Color Balance	Ctrl+B
Curves	Ctrl+M
Desaturate	Ctrl+Shift+U
Gamut Warning	Ctrl+Shift+Y
Hue/Saturation	Ctrl+U
Invert	Ctrl+I
Levels	Ctrl+L

Blending Modes

Action	Shortcut
Normal	Alt+Shift+N
Dissolve	Alt+Shift+I
Behind	Alt+Shift+Q
Multiply	Alt+Shift+M
Screen	Alt+Shift+S
Overlay	Alt+Shift+O
Soft Light	Alt+Shift+F
Hard Light	Alt+Shift+H
Color Dodge	Alt+Shift+D
Color Burn	Alt+Shift+B
Darken	Alt+Shift+K
Lighten	Alt+Shift+G
Difference	Alt+Shift+E
Exclusion	Alt+Shift+X
Hue	Alt+Shift+U
Saturation	Alt+Shift+T
Color	Alt+Shift+C
Luminosity	Alt+Shift+Y
Threshold	Alt+Shift+L
Clear	Alt+Shift+R

APPENDIX D

GLOSSARY OF 2D- AND 3D-RELATED TERMINOLOGY

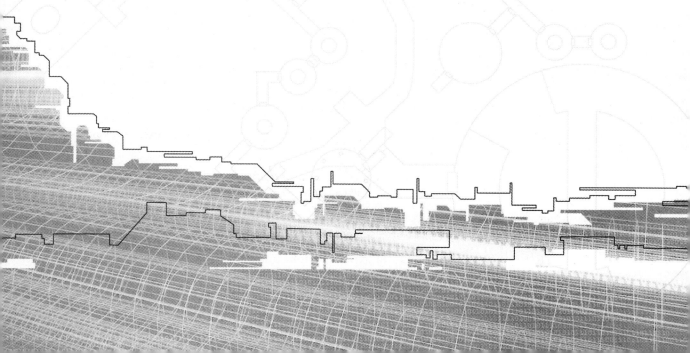

16-bit color. Also called *high color*. A color mode in which each pixel in an image is typically defined by five bits of red, six bits of green, and five bits of blue.

2D. Short for *two dimensional*. An object or image defined in two dimensions exists in a flat plane having two coordinate axes, x and y.

32-bit color. Also called *ultra true color*. A color mode where each pixel in an image is defined by eight bits each of red, green, and blue, with an extra eight-bit channel used for transparency.

3D. Short for *three dimensional*. An object or image defined in three dimensions has three coordinate axes, x, y, and z, where the z axis provides depth.

3DR. A real-time rendering mode from Intel that uses the Windows GDI to render objects dynamically. Use this mode if your video card does not support 3D acceleration.

3DS. Discreet's 3D Studio Max file format. Stores object information such as vertex coordinates, textures, and colors.

A

Aaaauuugh! The loud vocal sound emitted when your computer freezes and you forgot to regularly save your complex 3D model in progress.

Accelerated Graphics Port. See *AGP*.

Acuity. Refers to the ability to differentiate the details of an image, especially at a distance.

Adaptive. A sampling mode used when anti-aliasing an image in high quality.

Adjustment layer. A modifiable layer in Photoshop used to correct colors and tones in an image.

AGP. Short for *Accelerated Graphics Port*. A video card specification designed explicitly for 3D graphics and used in conjunction with motherboards having an AGP slot.

Alpha blend. To combine textures and/or materials with an alpha (transparency) channel to produce see-through materials and special effects.

Alpha channel. An extra color channel, typically eight bits long, to define an image's transparency.

Ambience. Light that an object can self-emit.

American National Standards Institute. See *ANSI.*

American Standard Code for Information Interchange. See *ASCII.*

Anchor point. A control point on a spline curve that can be moved or adjusted to change the shape of the curve.

Anisotropic. The simulation of the way light reflects off of real-world materials. A real-world example would be brushed metal—the surface has micro-grooves aligned in certain directions that reflect light in a characteristic texture.

ANSI. Short for *American National Standards Institute.* An organization that developed an international file standard so that files can be read and understood across multiple platforms.

Anti-alias. To remove the stair-casing or "jaggies" effect at the edge of an image by interpolating and blending the colors between edge pixels.

Artifact. An undesirable pixel or group of pixels that sometimes occurs when an object or image is viewed up close.

ASCII. Short for *American Standard Code for Information Interchange.* A text file format developed by the American National Standards Institute to define simple text that can be read across multiple platforms.

Asset. Any file, such as a texture image, model, animation, or sound clip, that is managed and organized for a video game.

Audio-Video Interleave. See *AVI.*

AVI. Short for *Audio-Video Interleave.* A video format typically read by most computer-based media players, such as Windows Media Player. Most animated textures in video games are saved in this format.

Axis. A Cartesian plane defining the dimensional coordinates of an object or world.

B

Backface culling. See *culling.*

Bevel. To raise and angle a face of an object to make it appear chiseled.

Bézier curve. Created by French mathematician Pierre Bézier, a curve that is defined by two anchor points and one or several control points between them.

Bilinear. A filtering method used to correct the appearance of textures on objects as they come closer to the user's point of view. Individual *texels*, or texture elements, are interpolated to generate a new texel so the texture appears sharp.

Binary. The mathematical system based on the power of two. In computers, bits are represented in this system by being either 0 (off) or 1 (on).

Binary space partitioning. See *BSP*.

Bit. The smallest memory element in a computer that has a binary state of either 0 (off) or 1 (on).

Bitmap. A 2D image that is represented using a palette of colors. Typically, game textures are stored as bitmaps and rendered by the game's engine.

Bone. An object that is used to define a skeletal structure in a 3D graphics program. The mesh surrounding the skeleton is deformed as the skeleton is animated or moved.

Boolean. A logical operation used to subtract, intersect, or unite two objects in a graphics program.

Bounding box. An invisible box that surrounds an object in a game or graphics program. This box is typically used for collision detection in games.

Brush. A 3D object created in a game's level using a level editor, typically constituting the geometry of the environment (for example, walls, floors, and ceilings) and usually part of a BSP tree. In Photoshop, a brush is a 2D image map used in conjunction with a painting tool to paint in the pattern of the map.

BSP. Short for *binary space partitioning*. An algorithm used to break up a 3D map into a tree hierarchy to determine the depth of objects from the camera view during rendering. This technique is performed so the renderer knows which object in the map is farthest from the camera, and can thus render successively closer objects in sequence; otherwise, the scenes wouldn't be displayed properly. *Quake* map files are compiled into a BSP format.

Buffer. A physical memory location used to temporarily cache chunks of data during program operation.

Bump map. A grayscale displacement map used to simulate raised surfaces on a 3D object. The highest bumps on a surface are indicated by white on the map, while the lowest are indicated by black.

Burn. To darken areas of a 2D image, similar to darkening photographs in a dark room.

C

Canvas. The blank workspace file used to create or place images in Photoshop.

Central processing unit. See *CPU*.

Chamfer. To smooth out the edges of a 3D object.

Clipping. In games, any part of the 3D environment not visible is clipped by a clipping plane. In Photoshop, a layer can be used to clip or mask another layer for constrained editing operations.

CMYK. Short for *cyan, magenta, yellow, black*. The subtractive primary color group used for printing.

Codec. Short for *coding/decoding*. Any program used to compress or decompress video clips.

Color channel. An inclusive range of a primary color, dictated by a brightness value. The additive primary colors red, green, and blue are separated into eight-bit channels, each channel having 256 different brightness values.

Contrast. The sharpness of an image determined by the color difference of neighboring pixels.

Coordinate. The Cartesian x-, y-, and z-axis location of a vertex in a 3D program.

CPU. Short for *central processing unit*. The core processor of a computer that carries out instructions issued by programs.

Crop. To select a portion of a 2D image and eliminate the rest.

Culling. The way in which a graphics program or engine does not attempt to draw or render polygons on an object that can't be seen by the viewer. Also called *backface culling*.

Curves. A function in Photoshop that lets you re-map the brightness values of pixels in an image to new values. Used for making precise tonal adjustments.

D

DDR Memory. Short for *Double Data Rate RAM*, a memory chip that has twice the bandwidth of standard SDRAM modules. This memory will adversely affect the speed of graphics programs on your computer.

Decal. A texture map that is applied on top of the existing materials of a 3D object or brush.

Decimation. Reducing the number of polygons a 3D object contains. Also, reducing an image's file size by reducing the resolution. Neighboring pixels in the image are averaged and combined, while others are altogether stripped.

Deformation. The transformation of vertices in a 3D mesh object to conform to a set of rules or another object.

DIMM. Short for *Dual Inline Memory Module.* This is a single memory chip that contributes to the overall amount of RAM a computer system contains.

Direct3D. Part of DirectX, a software interface that translates graphics commands from a program or game directly to the video card in a computer system.

DirectX. An application programming interface from Microsoft that allows programmers to easily create graphics programs and games that are video-hardware independent. DirectX is the standard PC game-development platform and is typically needed to run most video games or graphics programs.

Displacement map. See *bump map.*

Dissolve. In Photoshop, a mode that randomly scatters pixels along the edges of a brush stroke. Similar to the splattering of spray paint.

Dithering. The approximation of an unavailable color by selecting a mix of other colors from a reduced color palette.

Dodge. The opposite of *burn.* In Photoshop, to lighten areas of an image.

Dot pitch. In a computer monitor, the distance between the masking holes that the monitor's light rays shoot though. The smaller the dot pitch, the sharper the image. A typical monitor has a dot pitch of 0.28 millimeters.

Drawing Exchange Format. See *DXF.*

DXF. Short for *Drawing Exchange Format.* The proprietary file format of AutoCAD, a sophisticated 3D architectural and engineering design program.

E

Edge. The line that connects two vertices in a 3D mesh object.

Embossing. A graphics technique that adds highlights and shadows to the featured edges of a 2D image, making it appear 3D.

Engine. The main body of a game program that handles all graphics, artificial intelligence, actions, sequences, and player input.

Entity. An element or combination of elements that constitutes an item in a game's level. A simple example of an entity is a light object placed inside a lamp model to throw off light.

Environment map. An image used for creating rendering illusions to simulate an object's reflective surroundings.

Extrude. To pull a polygon or the face of an object out or along a defined path.

F

Face. An area of a 3D mesh object that is bounded by at least three vertices and three edges.

Faceting. The act of adding faces to a mesh object to enhance detail.

Falloff. The rate at which light decays as it moves away from its source.

Feathering. The fading of pixel brightness from the edges of an image.

Feature edge. The edges of a 3D object that make up the object's basic shape.

Field of view. See *FOV*.

Fill rate. The speed, in terms of pixels per second, at which a video card can draw on a screen.

Fillet. To smooth the corner of a shape.

Filter. A plug-in for Photoshop that performs a predetermined graphics action on an image.

FOV. Short for *field of view*. How much of a scene can be viewed from the user's or camera's perspective.

FPS. Short for *frames per second*. The rate at which a game, animation, or video takes place. Typically, games are set between 24 to 30 frames per second.

Fractal pattern. A mathematically defined graphics pattern that contains infinite iterations. Typically used to simulate organic objects.

Frag. To kill.

Frames per second. See *FPS*.

Function curve. In animation, a spline curve that represents the rate of animation between keyframes.

G

Gamma. The brightness value of a scene or game environment.

Gamut. A range of colors used in an image. Gamut Warning is used in the graphics industry to prevent unprintable colors from being used in an image.

Gourad. A shading technique that produces color gradients over a mesh object, giving an illusion of smoothness and depth.

GPU. Short for *graphics processing unit*. The core processor of a video card that handles the instructions sent by the computer to display images on the screen.

Gradient. The blending of one color or shade to another.

Granularity. The ability to perceive detail of an object at a distance.

Graphics processing unit. See *GPU*.

Grayscale. An image whose pixels consist of only 256 different shades of black and white.

H

Hierarchy. A structured relationship of glued or attached objects in a parent-child or child-child tree-like arrangement.

High color. See *16-bit color*.

Hue. Any color at its purest.

I

Indexed color. A color for a pixel that is referenced by an index that points to a color stored in a palette. Texture bitmaps store their eight-bit (256) colors this way.

Infinite light. A light object in a 3D program that emits a global light pointing in one direction.

Interlacing. Lower-end video cards sometimes cause screen flicker when set at a high resolution. Because they aren't fast enough to draw an entire screen of information at once, they skip every other line drawn horizontally on the first pass and fill in the rest on the second, known as *interlacing lines*.

Inverse kinematics. A kinetic hierarchy used to simulate the way linked objects behave in the real world. For instance, in a 3D program, if a character's hand is linked to his arm, and the arm is linked to the upper body, pulling on the hand in an inverse kinematical link will cause the arm to straighten first, followed by the upper body.

J

Joint. A 3D pivot location where two bones meet.

JPEG. Short for *Joint Photographic Experts Group*. A compressible file format meant for the World Wide Web.

K

Kerning. The spacing between characters in text. If the spacing were equal in all text, the words would contain letters that are equally spaced, making them appear very blocky.

Keyframes. The starting and ending positions of an object or objects in an animation. Keyframes are placed at every significant point where an object should change direction and/or speed. The computer fills in the rest of the frames in between the keyframes, a process known as *tweening*.

L

LAB. A color mode that consists of a Lightness channel and two chromacity channels, A and B. Typically used for color conversions between other modes or for porting work to a print shop.

Lasso. A tool used in 2D and 3D programs to make freehand pixel or polygon selections.

Lathing. The process of sweeping a polygonal shape or object around an axis to produce a 3D object that is symmetrical.

Layer. An independent sub-image that is part of an overall image in Photoshop. An image can contain many different layers, all of which constitute the final image.

Leading. The spacing between lines of text. In the old days, typesetters would place strips of lead between the lines to space them out properly. See *kerning*.

Level of detail. The varying polygon count that makes up the geometrical detail of an object in relation to the distance of the eye view of the player. Game objects usually have multiple levels of detail, so that up close the high polygon count object is displayed, while from afar it is replaced by the low polygon count object, thus speeding up the game play.

Level. A map or segment in a video game that contains rooms, objects, characters, traps, triggers, functions, and the like. A typical video game contains dozens of levels, each connected to the others in a game sequence.

Levels. In Photoshop, the levels are a combination of the adjustable highlights, midtones, and shadows the pixels of an image contain. These levels can be adjusted to change the overall contrast in an image.

Light Wave Object. See LWO.

Linear interpolation. The way a graphics program calculates the images in between keyframes of an animation. By analyzing the vertex positions of the beginning and ending keyframes, it assumes a linear path that the vertices must follow in the frames in between.

LOD. See *level of detail.*

Loft. To sweep a polygon or face along a path to create a 3D object.

LWO. Short for *Light Wave Object.* This is Newtek's proprietary object file format.

M

Map. See *level.*

Marching ants. See *marquee.*

Marquee. A boundary in Photoshop that defines a selection. The selection is displayed as a moving pattern called *marching ants.*

Mask. A graphics operation that creates a temporary overlay on an image with a specified pattern in order to isolate a particular work area.

Material. Synonymous with *texture.* An image, pattern, color, or combination of such in conjunction with displacements and transparencies to be painted onto an object.

MD3. id Software's *Quake III* character model file format.

MDL. *Valve's* (and *Quake's*) character model file format.

Mesh. A collection of connected polygons that form a three-dimensional object.

MIP map. From the Latin *multum in parvo* (many in a small area), a technique of reducing the size of a texture map for distant objects in order to improve game performance.

Mod. Short for *modification*, a game that's environment, characters, skins, or game play has been altered by means of level-editing software. Many video games are created with a set of tools for end-users to create mods if they wish.

Modifier. One of several tools used to reshape or deform the surface of a mesh object.

Monochrome. An image or device that displays a single color or shades of one color, typically white (pure RGB) to black (no color).

Morph. To transform one image to another in a smooth sequence, dictated by keyframed images.

Motion blur. A rendering effect to give objects in an animation the illusion that they are moving rapidly by blurring their images between frames.

MPEG. Short for *Moving Picture Experts Group*. A standard for compressing and streaming video without much loss in quality.

Multiply. In Photoshop, a mode that multiplies the currently selected color with the color on the image to produce a darker multiplication of the two. The effect is similar to that of repeatedly going over a piece of paper with a marker.

N

Noise. A randomly generated covering of pixels on an image to produce a grainy effect.

Normal. An invisible vector that points out of one side of the face of a polygon to tell the graphics program which side of the polygon is the outside. By flipping the normals of a 3D object, the object becomes hollow.

NURBS. Short for *non-uniform rational B-spline*. A 3D geometrical object that behaves in a complex mathematical pattern. Based on tension and bias, a NURBS object can be shaped and deformed at varying points on the mesh, while the rest of the mesh follows fluently to produce a more organic effect.

O

OBJ. trueSpace's proprietary object file format.

Offset. A filtering technique used to wrap an image around its horizontal or vertical edge. This technique is used when making textures to be tiled seamlessly.

Opacity. The amount an image or object can block light transmission through it. In Photoshop, the less the opacity of an image's layer, the more the layers beneath it can be seen.

OpenGL. Similar to Direct3D, an interface used to render 3D real-time textured objects. Originated from the Silicon Graphics corporation.

Orthogonal view. Any view in a 3D program that displays the scene perpendicular to a world axis. Typically, two or more orthogonal views are used for precisely positioning objects.

Overlay planes. In OpenGL, a layered set of materials that show through each other during render time.

Overlay. In Photoshop, a mode that preserves the highlights and shadows that exist in the texture on which you're painting. This way you can touch up a texture without interfering with the 3D edges of the texture itself.

P

Palette. A predefined color table that pixels in an image can reference for display.

Particle system. A program that generates a predefined pattern of moving objects. Particle systems are used to generate effects such as fire, smoke, explosions, and snow.

Patch. A spline-based face that is part of a 3D object. Patches can be modified like spline polygons and have a minimum of three spline segments.

Path. A spline-based segment that objects follow during a sweeping operation or animation. In Photoshop, a path is a user-defined spline selection that can be modified, saved, and recalled for other operations.

PDF. Short for *Portable Document Format*. Adobe's proprietary file format for documents, can be read across multiple platforms using the Adobe Acrobat Reader.

Per-pixel shading. A newer technique of shading objects based on shading the individual pixels of the objects rather than the vertex and faces. The result is the most realistic renderings, above that of *phong*.

Perspective. A non-orthogonal view in a 3D environment that displays the objects in the scene with depth.

Phong. A shading technique in a 3D program that calculates the colors on an object's faces based on the color at each vertex compared to the color at the normal of the face. This technique creates a more realistic rendering of an object.

Pitch. See *dot pitch*.

Pixel. Short for *picture element*. The smallest single element or "dot" of an image or object.

Plane. In Euclidean geometry, an object that has only two dimensions in a 3D world. In a 3D graphics program, a plane is composed of two triangles that make the face of the object.

Plug-in. A program developed by a third party to perform a specified action on an image, object, scene, or animation. Most graphics programs support the use of plug-ins for generating different types of special effects.

PNG. Short for *Portable Network Graphics*, this file format is commonly used as a file type in video game images, which offers one of the highest qualities, lowest file sizes, and include transparency information.

Point. Same as a *vertex*, but generally referred to when performing spline operations. The points on a spline path are adjustable, and in an animation are considered keyframe path redirection points.

Point of view. See *POV*.

Polygon. An object with three or more sides. Solid 3D objects are comprised of at least five polygons (a pyramid) connected and sharing vertices and edges.

Polyhedron. A 3D solid object comprised of at least five polygons (a pyramid).

Portable Document Format. See *PDF*.

POV. Short for *point of view*. The user's perspective view in a 3D world.

Primitive. Any basic polyhedron used in 3D modeling such as a pyramid, cube, or sphere.

Q

Quad divide. A process in which a 3D program adds an extra horizontal and vertical edge through the middle of each face of an object.

R

Radiosity. A rendering algorithm that accurately calculates the way light reflects off materials and throughout a 3D environment.

RAMDAC. Short for *random access memory digital to analog converter*. A high-speed computer chip that converts the digital images from your computer to an analog signal for your monitor. The higher the frequency of the chip, the faster the image will be displayed.

Rasterize. The drawing of images line-by-line on a computer screen. In Photoshop, *rasterization* is a process of converting vector-based graphics into ordinary pixels.

Raytrace. A mathematical rendering algorithm that calculates the reflection of rays of light bouncing off of and between 3D objects.

RDRAM. Short for *RAMBUS dynamic random access memory*. A newer memory module capable of very high speed data transfers compared to the older SDRAM and DIMM modules.

Reflection. The degree at which light bounces off an object's surface.

Refraction. The degree at which light bends as it passes through a medium such as glass, air, or water.

Refresh rate. The rate at which a computer monitor draws images on the screen in terms of Hertz (Hz), or cycles per second.

Rendering. The calculation by a graphics program of how objects in a scene should accurately reflect light from their surfaces and materials, either for a still image or animation.

Resolution. The density of pixels per inch displayed in an image. The higher the density, the sharper and more detailed the image becomes.

RGB. The additive primary colors red, green, and blue, used for accurately displaying color images on computer screens.

S

Sample. To compare neighboring edge pixels in an object and generate a blended fill in between. This will anti-alias the image, making the edges of an object appear smooth.

Saturation. The level of purity of a color.

SCN. Caligari's proprietary scene file format for trueSpace.

Screen. In Photoshop, the opposite of *multiply*. The effect will lighten an area of an image with each pass.

Script. A pre-programmed sequence that a scene, object, or character in a game will follow.

SDRAM. Short for *synchronous dynamic random access memory*. A faster memory module than the older DIMM modules, but slower than the new RDRAM modules.

Segment. An edge of a polygon connected by two vertices.

Shader. A component in trueSpace's material editor that changes the properties of the existing material.

Sharpen. A filtering or tool-based technique to enhance the highlights, shadows, and edges of an image by increasing the relative brightness and contrast of pixels.

Skeleton. A structure of connected bones that can be animated to deform an object's mesh.

Skew. To slant or shift an image's or object's structure.

Skin. An image map that is stretched over an object's mesh. The mesh itself is also part of the skin, and is deformed by a skeletal structure.

Specularity. An object's relative shininess.

Spline polygon. A 2D polygonal shape that has smoothed, adjustable corners that can be manipulated via control handles.

Spotlight. A light source that projects from a source point outwards in a cone-shaped pattern.

Sprite. A 2D image with a transparency channel typically used for game animations to simulate particle systems such as smoke, fire, and steam. Sprite images were also used in 2D games to animate characters and objects.

Stencil buffering. A way of speeding up rendering during game play. A *stencil plane* is used as a mask on the screen while the rest of the background image needs to be drawn only in areas where there is no mask. An example would be a cockpit in a flight simulator—the cockpit is the stencil mask, and the background imagery is drawn within the windows of the cockpit. Stenciling is also used when making complex shadows in games.

Stencil plane. See *stencil buffering.*

Stroke. In Photoshop, to draw pixels in a specified width and color along a marquee selection.

Subdivision surface. The faces on the surface of a 3D object that are subdivided to allow for more smooth and detailed modeling operations.

SVGA. Short for *Super Video Graphics Array*. A video card capable of 800×600 resolution.

Swatch. A user-specified collection of colors created for the convenience of color selection.

Sweep. Same as *extrude*. Pulling the face or polygon in a specified direction or along a path.

SXGA. Short for *Super Extended Graphics Array*. A video card capable of 1280×1024 resolution.

T

Tag. A pivot point on 3D character models that connects one body part to another. Commonly used with *Quake* models.

Tearing. An anomaly that occurs when a video card is sending signals out of sync with the monitor's refresh rate, resulting in the generation of artifacts.

Tessellate. A way of subdividing the faces of a 3D object to produce more detail.

Texel. Short for *texture element*, a single pixel belonging to a texture.

Texture. A 2D bitmap image that is applied to a 3D object.

TGA. The Targa file format, developed originally for the TrueVision video board. This is used often when saving animation frames in 3D programs due to the high-quality image content–to-compression ratio. Also contains transparency information.

Three dimensional. See *3D*.

TIFF. Short for *Tagged Image File Format*. A graphics file format that is highly portable across platforms and contains detailed image information.

Tile. To arrange seamless (or not so seamless) copies of a texture map either horizontally, vertically, or both on a 3D object.

Tolerance. In Photoshop, a tool's selection parameter. The tool will include pixel selections that are more or less homogenous than the currently selected pixel color depending on the tolerance setting.

Torus. A doughnut-shaped primitive 3D object.

Trajectory. The mathematically calculated path that a moving object with gravitational characteristics will follow.

Transformation. In games and 3D programs, the calculation on the vertices of an object in order to move, rotate, or scale it. In Photoshop, the act of rotating, scaling, skewing, stretching, or distorting an image or selection.

Trap. In a game's level, an invisible trigger that is activated when a character passes over it, typically snaring or killing the character.

Triangulate. Dividing in half the four-sided faces of a 3D object by connecting the diagonal vertices with an edge.

Trigger. An invisible object in a game's level that performs a specified action when activated. Activation can occur when a button on a wall is pressed, a character walks over a trigger, a door is opened, and so on.

Trilinear. A filtering technique that combines bilinear filtering with LOD and MIP mapping to produce high-quality real-time rendering in games.

Tweening. When a program fills in the successive frames between keyframes in an animation.

Two dimensional. See *2D*.

U

U-v coordinates. The coordinates of an object that a texture map uses for alignment.

Ultra true color. See *32-bit color*.

V

Vector graphics. Graphics that are drawn as mathematical lines that form an object or image. If the object is scaled or rotated, the lines will be recalculated and appear smooth.

Vertex smoothing. A process of applying smoothing techniques to polygons by analyzing the vertex angles in the mesh.

Vertex. A point in 3D space that defines the structure of a polygon and has the dimensional coordinates x, y, and z.

VGA. Short for *Video Graphics Array*. One of the first video-card technologies from IBM that was capable of displaying a 640×480 resolution at 16 colors.

Video post. A post-production operation on an image or animation that allows for adding compositing and effects.

Volumetrics. The simulation of the scattering of light within a medium such as fog, using raycasting and sampling techniques at render time.

Voxel. Short for volumetric pixel, a pixel that is defined as a point in three dimensional space.

VRAM. Short for *video random access memory*. The high-speed memory located on video cards used for storing information that will be written to the screen.

VRML. Short for *Virtual Reality Modeling Language*. A Web-based language, similar to HTML, that allows for browsing Web sites in a 3D, virtual environment.

W

Wireframe. The unrendered mesh of a 3D object.

X

X. Microsoft's DirectX file format, used for storing model and animation information for use in 3D applications and games.

XGA. Short for *Extended Graphics Array*, a video-card technology from IBM capable of displaying 1024×768 resolution at 65,000 colors.

Z

Z aliasing. A rendering anomaly that occurs when a portion of a 3D object is exposed when it should be hidden or vice versa.

Z buffer. A memory portion of a video card that is used to store pixel depth information. The Z buffer determines whether a pixel is to be drawn on screen if it is not hidden by another object.

APPENDIX E

RELATED WEB SITES AND LINKS

There are so many great graphics sites on the Web nowadays that I don't know where to start! Over the years I've amassed a number of links that currently reside on my Favorites menu, so I decided that they might be useful to you as well. Look here to find tons of free demos, plug-ins, models, textures, animations, and all around gaming stuff.

Models, Textures, and Tutorials

So much of what I've learned over the years comes from the Web. People are kind enough to post their files and tutorials for free; hopefully you'll appreciate these as much as I have!

Avalon

http://avalon.viewpoint.com

This site boasts an excellent collection of downloadable textures and 3D Studio MAX mesh objects, as well as loads of utilities, modeling and painting software, and plug-ins for MAX, Photoshop, trueSpace, Lightwave, and SoftImage. You'll also find tutorials for MAX and links to various other 3D graphics sites.

3D Cafe

http://www.3dcafe.com

3D Cafe is *the* hangout for 3D artists and animators. This site has more collections of high-resolution models, textures, tutorials, plug-ins, and fonts than you can hurl a telephone pole at. You must pay a small membership fee to get access to everything, but if you're serious about being a game artist it's well worth the cost.

3D Fuel

http://www.3dfuel.com

3D Fuel is a good site for shaders, objects, tutorials, and scripting for trueSpace.

3D Links

http://www.3dlinks.com

Looking for the ultimate resource for 3D modeling and animation programs? Check out 3D Links for information, links, plug-ins, objects, textures—oh my—to all of the most popular graphics software. It's quite awesome.

Black Knight Productions

http://www.blackknightproductions.com

Black Knight Productions is a source for purchasable high-quality models and plug-ins for trueSpace and 3D Studio MAX.

DigitalFlux Entertainment

http://www.digitalflux.com

DigitalFlux Entertainment is another good resource for plug-ins and tutorials for trueSpace.

Eyeball Design

http://www.eyeball-design.com

This site features top-quality tutorials for creating cool interfaces, textures, and Web graphics with Photoshop. It's very nicely done.

GR Site's Absolute Archive

http://www.grsites.com/textures

Lessee, how do I explain GR Site's Absolute Archive? Oh, I know: thousands upon thousands of free downloadable textures, Web graphics, and fonts. Believe it, man.

Studio LOGICBit

http://www.logicbit.com

Studio LOGICBit is Frank Rivera's excellent Web site dedicated to modeling and animation with trueSpace. Frank is one of the best 3D modelers I've seen and probably knows more about trueSpace than Caligari! He's published a book entitled *Inside trueSpace 4,* in which he divulges nearly everything you need to know about trueSpace 4.

Maxforums

http://www.maxforums.org

This site features an absolute truckload of tutorials and plug-ins for 3D Studio MAX. You must see this site—it also contains forums, resources, and plenty of links to other graphics-related sites.

Texture World

http://www.textureworld.com

If you weren't happy creating your own textures and want to get your hands on some top-quality ones, this site has them for sale at low cost. (But my tutorials were so fun and easy. . . .)

Trinity 3D

http://www.trinity3d.com

The Trinity 3D site is a great source for plug-ins and whatnot for 3D Studio MAX, trueSpace, and other graphics software. You can also purchase books and videos, and download trial software.

Map/Mod/Level Design

Beyond the scope of this book (and subject for another book entirely!) are the areas of modifying existing games on the market to create your own. Here you'll find a bunch of sites dedicated to mods and level designing in general, geared more towards *Quake*, *Half-Life*, and *Unreal*. But, you won't have to look far to find the same info for other games.

3D Map Realm

http://3dmr.gamedesign.net

3D Map Realm contains an extensive collection of *Quake*, *Half-Life*, and *Unreal* maps. There are loads of map-creation articles and discussion forums here, too.

Modpages

http://www.modpages.com

Modpages is packed with mods, mod reviews, discussions, game reviews, and the like.

Planet Half-Life, Planet Quake, and Planet Unreal

http://www.planethalflife.com

http://www.planetquake.com

http://www.planetunreal.com

By GameSpy Industries, these sites, are probably your number-one source for files, utilities, maps, mods, skins, and other resources for these games. You'll probably go blind just trying to get through all of their juicy details.

UnrealFiles

http://www.unrealfiles.com

UnrealFiles features a good selection of utilities and skins, and an excellent link list to other sites related to *Unreal*, *Quake*, and *Half-Life*.

Unrealized

http://www.unrealized.com

Dude, you have to see this site. It's packed with great tutorials, expert advice, level-design articles, scripting tutorials, you name it. In fact, I recommend you start with this site to absorb level-editing techniques (after you've finished with this book, that is). It has a very cool layout, as well.

Valve ERC

http://www.valve-erc.com

If you're hooked on *Half-Life* like I am and want all the goodies for making mods for this game, do yourself a favor and inhale the Valve ERC site. It's got it all and then some, with lots of tutorials and resources.

Graphics Software

These sites listed below are the sources of all of the software used in this book, plus additional vendors of well known 2D and 3D graphics programs.

Adobe Systems Incorporated

http://www.adobe.com

This is the site for Adobe, creators of Photoshop, the best texture-creation and image-editing program in the world. Incidentally, Adobe is also the creator of Illustrator, Acrobat, Premiere, AfterEffects—jeez, it never stops! You can download trial versions of their software from this site, along with plug-ins and documentation. You can also buy Adobe software directly from this site; Photoshop 6 runs $600.

Caligari Corporation

http://www.caligari.com

This is the site for Caligari, the creator of trueSpace, which, in my opinion, is the best and fastest. The site features a monthly image competition, 3D galleries, downloadable plug-ins, and more. You can buy trueSpace versions 4 and 6 directly from this site for $199 and $595, respectively.

Corel Corporation

http://www.corel.com

Corel's Web site sells Bryce 5, one of the best terrain-modeling programs on the market, for $299. You can also purchase Kai's Power Tools, an excellent set of filters for Photoshop, for $149.

Discreet

http://www.discreet.com

Discreet is the creator of 3D Studio MAX, the world's leading modeling and game-development graphics package; GMAX, a new game-development platform for game and level designers; and Character Studio, a character-modeling and animation program. All three are available from the Discreet Web site. Although 3D Studio MAX and Character Studio will take a bit out of your wallet, costing $3,500 and $1,495 respectively; GMAX is free.

Jasc Software

http://www.jasc.com

Jasc Software is the creator of Paint Shop Pro, a leading yet inexpensive (just $100) 2D texture and image-editing program. Visit Jasc's site, to learn more.

Microsoft Corporation DirectX Home

http://www.microsoft.com/directx

Need I explain? Well, maybe a little. Microsoft is the creator of DirectX, the world standard game development API for personal computers. You can download the latest version of DirectX at Microsoft's DirectX home page, as well as the DirectX Software Development Kit.

Newtek

http://www.newtek.com

Newtek is the creator of Lightwave 3D. This program, which sells for $2,495, is another of the most powerful and widely used 3D graphics programs on the market, much on the same level as 3D Studio MAX.

Right Hemisphere

http://www.us.righthemisphere.com

The folks at Right Hemisphere makes 3D Exploration, a totally awesome 2D and 3D viewing utility. It can view dozens of different file formats, including Photoshop images, trueSpace objects and scenes, MAX files, Lightwave files . . . the list goes on. The program, priced at just $49, also enables you to preview DirectX files in 3D real time before you dump them into a game. Just look at the demo and compare it to the cost; you'll flip. Right Hemisphere also makes Deep Paint 3D ($795) and DeepUV ($495), excellent painting and texturing applications that integrate into Photoshop, MAX, or Lightwave.

Graphics Hardware

Can't run your software without the proper computer hardware, right? Here are some key vendors of graphics hardware that usually put out the hottest video cards on the market for gaming and other hardware for graphics applications.

ATI Technologies

http://www.ati.com

ATI Technologies is the creator of the Radeon 9700 3D graphics video board ($399), featuring 128MB of video memory, with SmartShader and SmoothVision technologies that allow for advanced full scene anti-aliasing and anisotropic filtering.

Elsa Inc.

http://www.elsa.com

Elsa Inc. makes the Elsa Gloria DDC video card ($999), developed with 3D Studio MAX in mind. It features the nFinite graphics engine and the Quadro DCC graphics processor by NVIDIA, with 64MB of DDR RAM and a memory range of 7.3 GB per second. It processes more than 3.2-billion texture-mapping pixels per second.

Hewlett-Packard

http://www.hp.com

Hewlett-Packard makes the highest-quality printers and scanners on the market.

nVidia

http://www.nvidia.com

nVidia makes the GeForce4 4200 chip, which features the nFiniteFX II engine with a 256-bit graphics core. Dual Vertex Shaders process more than 100 million vertices per second, and is 50% faster than the previous GeForce3.

Tweak 3D

http://www.tweak3d.net

Tweak 3D's Web site, is a great source for tweakin' computer hardware, including getting the right drivers, settings, and resources for your system.

Wacom

http://www.wacom.com

One of the leading graphics-tablet manufacturers in the world, Wacom makes tablets that range from 4×5-inches at $200 to 12×18-inches at $700. These tablets can greatly increase the speed and quality of your 2D artwork by allowing you to draw naturally on a digitizing surface.

General Gaming and Information

These links will guide you to some very popular gaming forums where you can meet other developers, download gaming files, and feel generally right at gaming home.

Blue's News

http://www.bluesnews.com

Demos, patches, articles . . . this site keeps you current on the news in the gaming world.

ClassicGaming

http://www.classicgaming.com

Ever wanted to relive those awesome stand-up arcade video games from the 1980s? (Wait a minute . . . how old are you?) Anyway, for those of you (and me) who lost your weekly allowance on those digital enigmas, this site offers downloadable arcade emulators and the binary game files you need to play every game you enjoyed way back when.

Gamasutra

http://www.gamasutra.com

Gamasutra is the absolute fulcrum where game designers and developers meet to share their wisdom and resources. Membership is free—need I say more?

GameDev.Net

http://www.gamedev.net

The best place on the Internet to learn about game development! This site pulls together thousands of game programming and design articles, forums, and files, and is frequented by well over 250,000 game developers each year.

Game Development Search Engine

http://www.game-developer.com

The Game Development Search Engine has compiled links to every game-related hardware and software manufacturer. This site will point you in every gaming direction imaginable—graphic design, programming, forums, you name it.

Game Developers Conference

http://www.gdconf.com

This site is the online home of the Game Developers Conference, held every year—usually in March—in downtown San Jose, California. Use this site to register and to get information about airfare and hotels. (Warning: Every single hotel room will be snapped up, so make your reservations early!) The conference kicks off with a few days of interactive workshops in every area of game development, followed by presentations by leading game-related companies of their latest and greatest stuff. If you can get yourself out there, I guarantee you'll love it. (Here's a tip: Take a drive north up First Street through Silicon Valley when you get a chance; for us computer geeks who don't live out there, it's love at first site.)

Game Developer Magazine

http://www.gdmag.com

I started buying this magazine back in 1994. Now, I can't imagine not having a regular subscription. Each issue covers every aspect of the game-development world, keeping you up to date with professional tips, tricks, insights, innovations, and resources—and lots of pretty pictures, too.

GarageGames

http://www.garagegames.com

Home of independent games and game makers, this site has developed the Torque engine, one of the most popular and affordable 3D game engines on the market. This is a great site for finding work with independent game developers, as well as being able to contribute to the overall development of the Torque engine. The tutorials in this book are geared towards the Torque engine.

Premier Press Books

http://www.premierpressbooks.com

What can I say? I've never known a publisher to release such an extensive and impressive collection of game-development books. Premier Press, coupled with game guru and leading game-programming author André Lamothe, have produced the most complete game-development university in paperback, thoroughly covering game programming and design. You can buy all sorts of Premier Press titles on their Web site.

Xtreme Games, LLC

http://www.xgames3d.com

Created by leading game programming author and Premier Press Books' Series Editor André Lamothe, this site is dedicated to channeling the expertise of talented game developers, who share their products, knowledge, and ideas here. Additionally, Xtreme has founded the XGDC (Xtreme Game Developers Conference), a next-generation game-developers conference held each year at the Santa Clara, CA, Convention Center. The XGDC is a grass roots game developer conference with an affordable price, and tutorials for all skill levels.

APPENDIX F

WHAT'S ON THE CD-ROM?

The software and other files used to create graphics for games are serious disc hogs. The MAX demo alone is 300 MB! CD-ROMs, however, can store only about 700 MB. That means the CD for this book contains only the juicy essentials. That said, I really tried to include some great content in the hopes that you'll find it useful. In this appendix, you'll find a breakdown of the contents of each directory on the CD-ROM.

> **TIP**
> Although space on this book's CD-ROM was limited, space on the Web is not. Review Appendix E, "Related Web Sites and Links," for information about accessing other goodies. Also, be sure to check out www.premierpressbooks.com, the Web site of this book's publisher.

Chapter Data

I've placed the required tutorial files for each chapter in their own zip here. You'll need to access these in almost every chapter, because they contain critical textures, models, and other program-specific files.

Chapter Figures

Since most of this book is black and white, and being that it is a graphics book, I've saved nearly every figure displayed in each chapter for your full-color perusal. Just click a chapter file to download the entire set of figures for that chapter.

Programs

Adobe Photoshop 6

Caligari trueSpace 6

Discreet 3D Studio Max 5

Right Hemisphere Deep Paint 3D and DeepUV

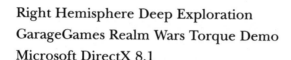

Right Hemisphere Deep Exploration

GarageGames Realm Wars Torque Demo

Microsoft DirectX 8.1

trueSpace, Photoshop, and 3D Studio Max are the focus of most of the modeling, texturing, and game preparation tutorials in this book. DeepUV is used in several chapters for the unwrapping and manipulating of texture coordinates on 3D models.

One of the best 2D/3D viewers I've ever seen is Right Hemisphere's 3D Exploration. You can use this program to view just about every texture, model, and animation on the planet, as well as proprietary formats from popular graphics programs like Photoshop, trueSpace, 3D Studio MAX, Lightwave, and so on. It can view *Quake* and *Half-Life* models as well!

The Torque demo is used to view your hard-earned textures, models, and animations in a real game engine. Aliased *Realm Wars*, it is a fully interactive 3D FPS game that you can modify to your heart's desire.

Because most of the files on the CD-ROM are stored in zip files, you'll need WinZip installed on your machine in order to uncompress everything. In addition, you'll need DirectX installed to run most of the 3D programs and games. Finally, install Adobe Acrobat so you can read the many pertinent program documentations and tutorials that are in Adobe's native PDF format.

Textures

This section alone should make you tattoo my name on your arm! I spent many hours collecting textures for your personal, license-free use, including pictures of rock, brick, and hundreds of other unique textures.

Tutorials

This section contains two tutorials that cover the basic operations (and then some) of trueSpace 4 and Photoshop 6. Use these to prime yourself for the rest of the tutorials in this book if you don't have much experience with them.

Index

License Agreement/Notice of Limited Warranty

By opening the sealed disc container in this book, you agree to the following terms and conditions. If, upon reading the following license agreement and notice of limited warranty, you cannot agree to the terms and conditions set forth, return the unused book with unopened disc to the place where you purchased it for a refund.

License:
The enclosed software is copyrighted by the copyright holder(s) indicated on the software disc. You are licensed to copy the software onto a single computer for use by a single user and to a backup disc. You may not reproduce, make copies, or distribute copies or rent or lease the software in whole or in part, except with written permission of the copyright holder(s). You may transfer the enclosed disc only together with this license, and only if you destroy all other copies of the software and the transferee agrees to the terms of the license. You may not decompile, reverse assemble, or reverse engineer the software.

Notice of Limited Warranty:
The enclosed disc is warranted by Premier Press, Inc. to be free of physical defects in materials and workmanship for a period of sixty (60) days from end user's purchase of the book/disc combination. During the sixty-day term of the limited warranty, Premier Press will provide a replacement disc upon the return of a defective disc.

Limited Liability:
THE SOLE REMEDY FOR BREACH OF THIS LIMITED WARRANTY SHALL CONSIST ENTIRELY OF REPLACEMENT OF THE DEFECTIVE DISC. IN NO EVENT SHALL PREMIER PRESS OR THE AUTHORS BE LIABLE FOR ANY OTHER DAMAGES, INCLUDING LOSS OR CORRUPTION OF DATA, CHANGES IN THE FUNCTIONAL CHARACTERISTICS OF THE HARDWARE OR OPERATING SYSTEM, DELETERIOUS INTERACTION WITH OTHER SOFTWARE, OR ANY OTHER SPECIAL, INCIDENTAL, OR CONSEQUENTIAL DAMAGES THAT MAY ARISE, EVEN IF PREMIER AND/OR THE AUTHORS HAVE PREVIOUSLY BEEN NOTIFIED THAT THE POSSIBILITY OF SUCH DAMAGES EXISTS.

Disclaimer of Warranties:
PREMIER AND THE AUTHORS SPECIFICALLY DISCLAIM ANY AND ALL OTHER WARRANTIES, EITHER EXPRESS OR IMPLIED, INCLUDING WARRANTIES OF MERCHANTABILITY, SUITABIL- ITY TO A PARTICULAR TASK OR PURPOSE, OR FREEDOM FROM ERRORS. SOME STATES DO NOT ALLOW FOR EXCLUSION OF IMPLIED WARRANTIES OR LIMITATION OF INCIDENTAL OR CONSEQUENTIAL DAMAGES, SO THESE LIMITATIONS MIGHT NOT APPLY TO YOU.

Other:
This Agreement is governed by the laws of the State of Indiana without regard to choice of law principles. The United Convention of Contracts for the International Sale of Goods is specifically disclaimed. This Agreement constitutes the entire agreement between you and Premier Press regarding use of the software.